EUCHARIST

Theology and Spirituality of the Eucharistic Prayer

EUCHARIST

THEOLOGY AND SPIRITUALITY OF THE EUCHARISTIC PRAYER

LOUIS BOUYER

Translated by
CHARLES UNDERHILL QUINN

UNIVERSITY OF NOTRE DAME PRESS
Notre Dame   London

Nihil obstat: Joseph Hoffman, C.S.C.
                  Censor Deputatus
Imprimatur: ✠ Leo A. Pursley, D.D.
                  Bishop of Fort Wayne-South Bend
                  July 8, 1968

PUBLISHER'S NOTE:
All translations of liturgical texts in this book are literal translations made for use by scholars and not necessarily the translations officially sanctioned for liturgical use.

ORIGINAL FRENCH TITLE:
Eucharistie: théologie et spiritualité de la prière eucharistique
First published by Desclée, Paris, 1966

Library of Congress Catalog Card Number: 68-17064
Printed in the United States of America

Acknowledgment is made to the following works for quotations used:

For the Jewish meal prayers:
    David Hedegard, *Seder R. Amram Gaon,* Pt. I (Lund, 1951).

For the Andrieu-Collomp papyrus:
    P. F. Palmer, S.J., *Sacraments and Worship* (Westminster, Md., 1955).

For the Didache:
    Henry Bettinson, *Documents of the Christian Church* (London, 1959).

For the liturgy of Our Lord and the liturgy of Our Lady:
    John M. Harden, *The Anaphoras of the Ethiopic Liturgy* (London and New York, 1928).

For the new translation of the Roman canon in English:
    International Committee for English in the Liturgy (ICEL).

For the liturgy of Taizé:
    Max Thurian, *The Eucharistic Liturgy of Taizé* (London, 1959).

For the later Anglican liturgies:
    Jardine Grisbrooke; *Anglican Liturgies of the Seventeenth and Eighteenth Centuries* (London, 1958).

For the Calvinish liturgy and Cranmer's *Book of Common Prayer,* as well as John Knox's liturgy:
    Bard Thompson, *Liturgies of the Western Church* (Cleveland and New York, 1961).

For the Lutheran liturgy (new):
    Luther D. Reed, *The Lutheran Liturgy,* 2nd ed. (Philadelphia, 1960).

For the Church of South India:
    The Book of Common Worship of the CSU (Oxford, 1962).

For the Swedish Lutheran liturgies:
    Eric E. Yelverton, *The Mass in Sweden* (Henry Bradshaw Society, Vol. 57, London, 1920).

For the Liturgy of Addai and Mari:
    F. E. Brightman, *Liturgies Eastern and Western* (Oxford, 1896).

For the Roman preface for Easter (plus Christmas and Epiphany inserts:
    Confraternity of Christian Doctrine.

For guidance in translating and for some passages reprinted from the Roman canon:
    The New St. Andrew Bible Missal (Bruges).

Contents

Foreword

This book is the result of more than twenty years of research.

It is appearing at a moment when the understanding of the traditional eucharistic prayer, and especially the canon of the Roman mass, is more timely than ever. On one hand it has been a very long time since we have seen such a lively and widespread desire in the Catholic Church to rediscover a "eucharist" that is fully living and real. Yet, unfortunately, there has also never been a time when we have been so confidently presented with such fantastic theories that, once put into practice, would make us lose practically everything of authentic tradition that we have still preserved. May this volume contribute its part toward promoting this renewal and discouraging an ignorant and pretentious anarchy that could mean its downfall.

We are exceedingly grateful to all who have helped us in this work. Among more recent researchers, we are particularly indebted to E. Bishop and A. Baumstark. No contemporary scholar has more enlightened or stimulated us than this so upright and perceptive a master with whom we have had the honor of being associated as one of his more modest first-hour collaborators in founding the *Institut d'études liturgiques* of Paris, Dom Bernard Botte. The best homage that we could render to his critical knowledge is to say that even when we came to part company on a few secondary points we were able to do so only by attempting to apply his own principles in the spirit that he himself had inculcated in us.

At this point may we also express our gratitude to all who have facilitated our research, particularly the Benedictines of Downside Abbey who put the treasures of the library of the late E. Bishop at our disposal. Professor Cyrille Vogel who did the same for the University of Strasbourg libraries, Canon A. Gabriel whose warm hospitality, equalled only by his impeccable scholarship turned the Medieval Institute in the Library of the University of Notre Dame into a kind of seventh heaven for scholars and researchers. Also the many Jewish friends who showed so much sympathy for our studies, especially Rabbi Marc H. Tannenbaum of New York for his heartwarming encouragement and Cantor Brown of Temple Bethel, South Bend, Indiana, who was not merely content with generously lending us the most precious books of his own library, but also helped us with his experience with the Synagogue ritual. If this book could make even a slight contribution toward friendship between Jews and Christians, it would be the realization of one of our most heartfelt wishes.

A last tribute of our gratitude must go to our young confrere Jean Lesaulnier who untiringly devoted himself to procuring or photocopying for us the documents which we needed.

Since the first edition in French of this work, a renewal of authentic Roman formularies has been effected through the work of the *Consilium ad exsequendam Constitutionem de Sacra Liturgia*. For this edition we have therefore added a supplementary chapter analyzing the reform of the Roman canon and the three new texts that have been added to it. It is useless to underline the fact that this reform has fulfilled some of the most important *desiderata* of this book, a fulfilment which could have never been hoped for at the time that I undertook to write it.

Louis Bouyer
Corpus Christi, 1966
Abbaye de la Lucerne
Feast of the Epiphany, 1968
Brown University, Providence, R.I.

Theologies on the Eucharist
and Theology of the Eucharist

THIS BOOK IS WRITTEN TO TAKE ITS READERS ON A VOYAGE
of discovery. We believe that such a long journey is one of the
most exciting that can be offered to those who have some inkling about the rarely or not at all quarried riches of Christian
tradition. We embarked on it ourselves some thirty years ago,
and if we have frequently gone back to it, we make no claim to
have brought to light all the treasures we foresaw from our first
excursion.

Our intention here is to try step by step to follow the progressive unfolding of the Christian eucharist. Our understanding of
"eucharist" here is exactly what the word originally meant: the
celebration of God revealed and communicated, of the mystery
of Christ, in a prayer of a special type, where the prayer itself
links up the proclamation of the *mirabilia Dei* with their *re*-pre-
sentation in a sacred action that is the core of the whole Christian ritual.

We will be told that many others before us, have undertaken
this exploration. Yet our aim is not quite the same. In the first

1

place it is not the whole of the eucharistic liturgy which will concern us, but once again, its core: what in the East is called the
anaphora, inseparably uniting the equivalents of our Roman
preface and canon. But as mindful as we should wish to be of
it, the description of this eucharist is not our ultimate objective.
What we shall be attempting is an understanding of what is common and basic in its different forms, and also the more or less successful, more or less full-blown development of this kernel or
rather this matrix of Christian worship.

We may perhaps be forgiven if we mention here the emotion,
which has still not cooled, that we experienced the first time we
thumbed through these great texts in an old copy of Hammond[1]. It
was the sense of unity that shone through in so many facets with
the dazzling sight produced by the discovery of the most spar-
kling jewels of liturgical tradition. We would discover the eucharist as a being overflowing with life, but a life of incomparable innerness, depth and unity, even though this life could be
shown only in a multiplicity of expressions, as through a harmony or rather a symphony of concerted themes that are gradually orchestrated. Before our eyes we had this iridescent robe,
this sacred vestment in which the whole universe is reflected
around the Church and her heavenly Bridegroom. In no poem,
in no work of art, and even more emphatically in no system of
abstract thought does this νοῦς Χριστοῦ, which is at the same
time the *Mens Ecclesiae*, seem to us to be so well expressed.

People may think us rash (what does it matter?) if we add
that it is doubtless necessary to have had such an experience
before we can engage in liturgical studies. The liturgical movement is something quite different from a game of antiquarians,
a merely esthetic experiment, a questionable "mass mysticism"
or a deadly and childish popular teaching method. This is a test
which allows us to look at the liturgists of the past or the present
and distinguish with certitude between those who are true "friends
of the Bridegroom" and those who are merely scholars, not to
say common pedants or commonplace hobbyists. There are people
who have gone through all the texts but who have most assured-

---

[1] *Liturgies Eastern and Western*, 1878.

ly never had such an experience. And there are others, mono-
maniac rubricists or eager "game masters," who, as far removed
from the first as they may be, still share their same callousness.
Some, as learned as they are, are nothing more than liturgical
archeologists and others, even if they have convinced themselves
that they are wardens or restorers of the liturgy, will never be
anything other than its morticians or its underminers. Only God
can probe the heart, but we are not prohibited from having our
own impressions. For my part, I am convinced that Cyril of Jerusalem (or the author of the catecheses that bear his name),
Gregory Nazianzene, St. Maximus or St. Leo are not among those
to whom grace was lacking, nor, on the threshold of the modern
era, was Cardinal Bona, nor Edmund Bishop or Anton Baumstark who are close to our own age. I admit that I am much less
sure of the liturgical salvation of other men from the past who
because of their position had great influence in this field, not
to mention some people of the more recent past or even of our
own day, all of whom I should never be pardoned for relegating
in petto and by name to my own private little hell. If I should
be asked how I can justify such audacity, I should answer that
it is enough to have eaten a few little morsels of ambrosia to spot
with ease the *sobria ebrietas* of some and not to be taken in by
others who leave crumbs everywhere behind them; they may
soil the whole tablecloth with their grimy hands, but since they
undoubtedly came to the Lamb's banquet without much of an
appetite, they have not even noticed that the food before them
had a special savor.

Not so long ago a Benedictine abbot who honors me with his
friendship was telling me how he thought he had discovered what
the liturgy was. When he was a novice he courageously undertook to read the whole of Migne, beginning with the first volume.
Practically at the start he stumbled upon the eucharistic liturgy
of the 8th book of the *Apostolic Constitutions*. All at once his
eyes were opened. In this confidence I found an echo of my own
long-standing impressions, for undoubtedly the text which most
moved me in Hammond's collection was also this same one: the
anaphora which seemed aimed at literally realizing the famous
formula of Justin on the celebrant who "gives thanks insofar

as he can."[2] Everything, absolutely everything that can summon
up what the ancient eucharist implied, is brought together in
this text, even if it is true that more sober texts like the wonderful anaphora of St. James give more appreciable expression
to its progression and momentum.

I hasten to add that both of us were merely echoing the pa-
trologists of the Christian Renaissance, not to mention many
most distinguished Anglican liturgists, who thought they had
found in this text the apostolic anaphora itself, and as it were
the original and permanent model of every ideal eucharist.[3] Yet
how many contemporary liturgical scholars will turn up their
noses at my displaying such naïve enthusiasm at the outset of
this book (which I admit is still far from being quelled!). A be-
lated compilation by a heretic (or half-heretic), and an impostor
to boot, a paper liturgy which never became (and morover never
could become) in any sense a reality... All of this, as the most
respectable manuals show us so well, is what we should have
learned! Be assured, all of this we shall discuss at our ease, and
if we do not retain all of these equally peremptory but unequally
secure judgments, it will appear that we also have good reasons
for rejecting the apostolicity of the pseudo-Clementine liturgy
(to say nothing of the liturgy of St. James). But at the very least
we believe that these texts as a *terminus ad quem* if not as a *terminus a quo* of a very ancient evolutionary process have something to justify the rather juvenile fancy of the 17th- and 18th-
century liturgists and of some others after that period, more
than the negligence with which they are now treated by critics
who are a bit too smug about their preliminary findings.

Whatever the case, it is no hazy romanticism, based on inade-
quate knowledge, that explains the interest, even the fascination
to which the *Apostolic Constitutions'* anaphora has for so long
given rise. It is a particularly informative witness of what on
the contrary is most theological in liturgical tradition. It un-

---

[2] Justin, *First Apology*, 67, 5.

[3] Cf. W. Jardine-A. Grisbrooke, *Anglican Liturgies of the seventeenth and
eighteenth Centuries* (London, 1958), and our eleventh chapter.

doubtedly constitutes the greatest effort ever made to explicate in depth the theology which was latent in the ancient eucharist.

Obviously what we have here is a theology with which our modern manuals have not familiarized us—and this is surely why its discovery can be so delightful! This theology, as exacting as it may be (and it is in its own way), remains very close to the first meaning of the Greek θεολογία, which designates a hymn, a glorification of God by the λόγος, man's expressed thought. This thought is obviously rational in the highest degree, but rational in the way harmony is; it is an intellectual music whose spontaneous expression is therefore a liturgical chant and not some sort of hair-splitting or tedious labeling.

What the study we are about to undertake should give us is precisely a theology of this type, which alone lends itself to a eucharistic theology worthy of the name. Let us go further and say that this *is* the theology of the eucharist. This terminological accuracy is not irrelevant. There is actually a great gulf between the eucharistic theologies that have abounded in the Catholic Church and outside, beginning with the end of the Middle Ages and going through modern times, and what alone deserves to be called the theology of the eucharist. At a time when such a statement by anyone other than the pope would have appeared not only scandalous but absurd, Pius XI was not afraid to say that "the liturgy is the chief organ of the ordinary magisterium of the Church." And if this is so for the proclamation of the Christian mystery in general, we may think that this has to be pre-eminently true in proclaiming what is its very essence: the eucharistic mystery, and especially the celebration of this mystery. But it is a fact that current theologies on the eucharist in general do not pay attention to the "eucharist" in the primary sense of the word, to the great traditional eucharistic prayer. There are many theologies *on* the eucharist. They are practically never *the* theology *of* the eucharist, a theology proceeding from it, but rather something applied to it externally, for better or worse or reduced to skimming over it without ever deigning to come to grips with it.

We have to admit that this is true, even of the best works that in recent generations have given us a healthier vision of the eucharist than the one given to us by previous centuries. We must be grateful to Lepin[4], de la Taille,[5] Vonier,[6] and Masure[7] who rejected the views of Lessius and Lugo on the eucharistic sacrifice, and restored to us a much more satisfactory notion particularly of its relationship with the sacrifice of the Cross although we may perhaps be too quickly led without verification to endorse the grievances they have against their predecessors. But it is hard to admit that their own syntheses can be any more definitive when we observe that the place they give to the testimony of the eucharist on its own significance and its own content is just as sparse as that of their predecessors. Their works rely on a few words from Scripture: practically only the words of institution, and possibly something from the sixth chapter of St. John and the first Epistle to the Corinthians. Moreover they interpret them only in the context of medieval or modern controversies, without even a hint of the shift in perspective that is made inevitable by a primarily philological and historical exegetical study, like the one recently undertaken by Jeremias[8] on the eucharistic words of Jesus. But above all their constructs proceed much more from *a priori* notions of sign or sacrifice than from these texts. And if in the course of their study they encounter or run across a few liturgical formulas it is merely as a confirmation of their own notions that they use them. More often they cite them, at the expense of more or less belabored reasoning, to show how they can agree with theories of sacrament or sacrifice that have been worked out without their help.

That such a fact has to be pointed out even in regard to recent authors so careful in trying to take stock of, and understand, all the riches of patristic and medieval theological tradition like

[4] M. Lepin, *L'Idée du sacrifice de la Messe d'après les théologiens depuis l'origine jusqu'à nos jours* (Paris, 1926).

[5] M. de la Taille, *Mystery of Faith* (New York, 1940-1950) 2 vols.

[6] A. Vonier, *The Key to the Doctrine of the Eucharist* (New York, 1925).

[7] E. Masure, *The Christian Sacrifice* (London, 1944).

[8] J. Jeremias, *The Eucharistic Words of Jesus* (London, 1966), English translation of the new German edition, published in 1960, at Göttingen, of *Die Abendmahlsworte Jesu*, but taking into account modifications made by the author in his text in 1964.

those we have just mentioned, stresses the pure and simple ignorance about the eucharist (in the sense that we always use the word here, which is still its basic sense) manifested in so many other prior speculations with which our manuals are still encumbered. The consequences of this state of affairs are grave primarily, but not solely, on the doctrinal plane. If they remain within the bounds of orthodoxy, at least in the sense that they do not contradict it, eucharistic theologies so constructed create and multiply false problems. They cannot resolve them (which is not surprising since they are badly posited), nor can they ignore them since these theologies themselves are what created them in the first place. The theology of the eucharist is thus found to be swamped by interminable controversies which have the disappointing and futile result of diverting attention from the eucharistic mystery which ought to be its whole concern.

One primary example of these bootless and fruitless quarrels is furnished in the High Middle Ages by the argument between the Byzantines and the Latins on the moment and especially the "how" of the eucharistic consecration. Does it come about through the words of institution or through a special prayer which will be called the epiclesis? When one reads the authors of the patristic era in both camps (a time when anaphoras were still in the process of formulation and men were able to have a connatural grasp of them) one has the impression that decisive arguments could be found in favor of one theory to the exclusion of the other. But, and we shall return to this point, this is because these texts are read in a light and with concerns that are foreign to them. If, on the other hand, we immerse ourselves again in the context of the ancient eucharistic celebration, the need for making a choice seems to vanish. The essential that either side wishes to retain and affirm can be equally upheld once a particular faction stops opposing it artificially to something on which it is in fact interdependent.

Just as is the case for the old controversy that gradually became set and hardened in the theologies of both East and West, for an even stronger reason we may expect this to happen in later controversies arising at times when no one was any longer able to reread the ancient formularies in accordance with their co-ordinates. This is the case particularly with the Protestant-Catholic controversy that bogged down and came to a standstill during the baroque era. Is the eucharistic celebration an actual sacrifice or the memorial of a past sacrifice? Formulated in this way as it has been and still is repeatedly, the question raised only defies any satisfactory answer, because strictly speaking it makes no sense. Beneath the words "sacrifice" and "memorial", it supposes realities that are quite different from what the same words stand for in the ancient eucharistic formularies.

What may then be said about modern controversies which continue to trouble men's minds within Catholicism itself on the problem of the eucharistic presence: not only Christ's presence in the elements, but also and especially the presence of his redemptive action in the liturgical celebration?

If we look at the eucharistic mystery either from the light of a philosophy that we might call prefabricated or from the point of view of a history of comparative religions which compares it with a thing to which it was not originally related, we get into an impasse whose only value is to warn us that we have been on the wrong track from the beginning. How can the same body be locally present in several places at once? How can a unique action from the past become present again every day? To get out of this trap it may be enough (and this is surely necessary!) to return to the ancient texts for a start. Provided we allow these texts to speak for themselves, the puzzles vanish, and the truth of the mystery, without losing its mysteriousness, becomes intelligible again, and therefore believable and worshipable.

But the theologies on the eucharist which are not concerned with what we have called *the* theology of the eucharist, and do not even seem to suspect its existence, not only give rise to absurd questions and sterile controversies. They inevitably react on the eucharist by more or less seriously altering and corrupting its practice. If the liturgy experiences deterioration through wear and tear, routine, and sclerosis, it buckles even more radically under theories which owe it nothing, when people are trying wrongly to remake it in accordance with them. For here we are dealing not with those errors that are mere negligences or more or less profound oversights. They are errors that are committed solemnly and on principle, and on the pretext of enrichment or reform they cripple and mutilate irreparably.

Actually it is an established phenomenon that a liturgical theology which does not proceed from the liturgy, and finds nothing really satisfying in it, soon comes up with pseudo-rites or aberrant formulas. Riddled with these, the liturgy soon becomes disguised if not even disfigured. Sooner or later the feeling of incongruity in such a situation awakens a wish for reform. But if, as is too often the case, the reform then simply starts from a theology that is in vogue at the time and not from a genuine return to the sources, it cuts without rhyme or reason into what is still left of the original, and completes the incipient process of camouflaging the essential beneath the secondary.

We have only to think of the 16th century Protestant reform of the eucharistic liturgy. Under the guise of a return to the Gospel eucharist, it merely achieved an artificial isolation of the words of institution into which medieval theology had already placed them in theory. From the tradition in which they had come to us, it kept only the late medieval tendency to substitute a psychological and sentimental recall of the Gospel events for the profoundly mysterious *and* real sacramental action of the New Testament and the Fathers. And it crowned everything by flooding the celebration with the penitential elements which in latter centuries had tended to overburden it. The end result is a eucharist in which there is no longer any eucharist at all properly speaking. If there is still in it some mention of a "thanksgiving" (which is not always the case), this now has merely the sense of an expression of gratitude for the gifts of grace received individually by the communicants: a late medieval sense, degraded beyond the point of recognition, given to a New Testament expression which has almost nothing left of its original sense.

These false theologies which weigh down the eucharist under a pretext of developing it, and then destroy it in claiming to reform it, obviously foster debased forms of eucharistic piety, which they in turn feed upon. Does it not say a great deal that in modern times the expression "eucharistic devotion" came preferentially and even exclusively to designate practices of piety connected with the eucharistic elements *outside* the liturgical action,

the eucharistic celebration? We should therefore not be surprised if in fact this devotion too frequently did not content itself
with ignoring the celebration and developed to its detriment, or
reacted on it only to blur its meaning and misrepresent it. The
mass becomes merely a means for refilling the tabernacle. Or
else it is interpreted as if it culminated in the "adoration of the
Blessed Sacrament" which the consecration emphasizes through
the elevation, added to it at a late date.

We shall see that far from reacting succesfully against this sub-
version of the original perspectives, the Lutheran liturgy on the
contrary merely brought it to its logical term, by cutting out
of the Roman canon everything that followed the consecratibn
and the elevation, and by transferring the *Sanctus* and *Benedictus* to this point. It is so very true that the "reforms" that
do not proceed from a better understanding of the traditional
liturgy always do nothing more than put the finishing touches
on its falsification.

Without even going this far, what are we to think of a eucharistic piety that multiplied "Benedictions" at the same rate that
it made communion rarer and rarer? One that delighted in increasingly elaborate "Expositions" and in the most *private* "low
masses" possible? One that made devout visits to "the prisoner
of the tabernacle," but had not the least thought for the glorious
Christ even though the eucharist sings (or sang) only of his victory?

Here again it is easy for us to see the mote in the eye of our
predecessors, but we run the risk of not perceiving the beam that
is imbedded in our own. Certainly we may congratulate ourselves on our rediscovery of the collective sense of the eucharistic
celebration through a return to notions of the eucharistic sacrifice that imply our own participation. But it is already a very
bad sign that the values of adoration and contemplation, which
yesterday focused on a eucharistic devotion that was in fact foreign to the eucharist, seem hardly to have come back to our celebration of it, but have rather simply vanished into thin air along
with the progressive disappearance of the practices in which they
were expressed "Benediction of the Blessed Sacrament," "visits
to the Blessed Sacrament," "thanksgiving after communion,"

etc. In this situation, the collective celebration, animated neither by contemplation nor even less by adoration of Christ present in his mystery, runs the great risk of deteriorating into one of those "mass demonstrations" so cherished by contemporary paganism, with a superficial aura of Christian sentiments. Is it not inevitable then that our union through the mass with the Savior's sacrifice comes to be identified there, as we see only too often, with a simple addition of our own quite human works not to say a pure and simple substitution for the *opus redemptionis*?

Since people cannot find satisfaction for such tendencies in a liturgy that certainly did not inspire them, we shall not be surprised that they wish to profit from the present liturgical reform to obtain or impose what would be its ultimate deformation. Mixing superficial ecumenism with "conversion to the world," they propose remodelings of the mass which, as always, claim to bring it back to its evangelical beginnings, though retaining (and if necessary introducing) only what, as we are told, suits the "man of today," a man who is said to be completely "desacralized!" Having failed in his proposal of such a project to the Council, a bishop held a press conference to assure the widest publicity for this secularized "ecumenical mass," that today's man could comprehend without having anything to learn. Not daring to venture quite so far a conciliar theologian suggested that at the very least the canon should be shelved and replaced by the liturgy of Hippolytus, accomodated to the times. Others by-pass words for acts. People are already preparing for the liturgy of tomorrow by "brotherly agapes" (which of course are also ecumenical) where unconsecrated bread and wine are distributed as objects of a simple "thanksgiving"; obviously any suspicion of "sacramental magic" is absent from them. Undoubtedly all of this is in the realm of fantasy and appears so threadbare and ridiculous that we hesitated for quite some time before deciding to mention it here. But let us be wary, for this is the way through which "pressure groups" in a short time could indeed bring considerable weight to bear on eventual reforms, and if they never did succeed in actually supervising them, they might at least curb or pervert their realization.

Dom Lambert Beauduin said that the relative fossilization of
the liturgy in modern times may perhaps have been its salvation.
Had this not been the case, he explained, what still would have
remained for us today of the great tradition of the Church? The
time of mummification has passed, and that is good. But it is
not enough to change again in order to come alive. We must not
permit a Lazarus who has just emeiged from the grave to be
submitted to such a decomposition which this time would bring
him back to it for good.   Already we only too often observe how
individual aberrations or collective day-dreams succeed in spinning
a web around the best orientations of conciliar authority. For
all the defects in the liturgy, whether of the past or the present,
and for everything that accompanies, sustains or produces them
in piety as well as religious thought, there can be but one remedy.
And this is a return to the sources, as long as it is authentic and
not one that is pretended or miscarried.

What a singular encouragement it is for the Catholic theologian
to see what positive things this return has already produced even
outside the Catholic Church! Our spur-of-the-moment ecumenists
who think they can go to meet Protestants by scuttling Catholic
tradition don't have the slightest hint that the Protestants themselves have often rediscovered things which they themselves are
still incapable of appreciating. For all the Protestants who are
not resigned to living with what is most dead in their own past,
there is no longer any attraction in a eucharist without mystery,
without the real presence, which is nothing but a joyful brotherly meeting in a common grateful remembrance of a Jesus who
would appear as man only in so far as it could be forgotten that
he is God. And, as a Protestant ecumenist recently told me "the
greatest obstacle today to our coming together could be in those
Catholics who think that for them ecumenism must consist in
giving up everything which we are in the process of recovering,
and in adopting everything that we are in the process of getting
rid of." And what can be said about attempts at making Christianity acceptable to modern man by secularizing it to the hilt,
at a time when psychologists and anthropologists agree in acknowledging that the sacred, the "myth" (in the sense the term
is used by modern historians of religion, which has nothing in

common with the incredibly backward terminology or problem-
atic of Bultmann) cannot simply be taken away from a human
being without causing him to suffer a fatal devitalization?

More than any argument, the best cure for these various illusions of Catholics who wish desperately to be modern, but who
have not yet had the time to inform themselves about what is
most interesting in the evolution of their contemporaries, will
be found in a rediscovery of this pre-eminent source that is the
newly formed eucharist. However, in order to do so, it is necessary to re-read and reinterpret the texts in taking pains patiently
to discern the movement of the living faith of the Church which
caused *her* eucharist to take shape, a eucharist which was the
most pure and at the same time most full expression of that faith.
This is what we at least wish to sketch out in the following pages.

We shall not be concerned with rediscovering the formula of
the apostolic anaphora, that was thought first to have been found
in the 8th book of the so called *"Apostolic" Constitutions*, precisely, and then in many other texts. Even very close to our
own day, the good Dom Cagin thought he had discovered it in
the equally *"Apostolic" Tradition* as many admirers of Hippolytus still do, who still appear not to be entirely disabused of
this illusion. We shall not be dealing with this question quite simply
because such a formula certainly never existed. If it had, everyone would know it, for no one would ever have dared to fashion
another one!

But this is far from meaning that there was not a type, a schema,
a living *anima*, as it were, of every eucharist that was faithful
to its original purport, an *anima* which revealed itself and is pro-
jected in the most ancient eucharistic formularies. We can grasp
it there again in its innate unity, as in its inexhaustible richness,
somewhat as the Gospel, which eludes any simple formula and
could not be contained in all the books that could fill the earth,
is still authentically given to us in the four canonical Gospels.
Undoubtedly for the eucharist there is no inspired, and to that
extent definitive, formula. But this is because the eucharist of
the Church, being by nature a human response to the Word of
God in Jesus Christ, cannot be fully accomplished as long as the
Church is not consummated in her perfect union with her Bride-

groom, the whole Christ reaching his adulthood only then in the definitive multitude and the perfect union of all his members. It is this movement, this spiritual burst of energy of the eucharist, which from the first is oriented toward the "sign of the Son of Man," that the documents of the Christian liturgy's creative period must allow us to recapture, and then to rediscover in the great prayers which have remained classic and which still today continue to consecrate our eucharists. In rediscovering their inner core, and in encountering, so to speak, the breath of life which penetrated them to form them from the inside, we shall at last be able to perceive the sense of what the Church does when she confects the eucharist, without which sense the Church herself could not become a reality in us and through us.

Jewish Liturgy and Christian Liturgy

IN ORDER TO RECOUNT THE GENESIS OF THE CHRISTIAN LIT-
urgy, and even more importantly to understand it within its
own context, we must get a proper start. In a work of this kind,
the first steps determine all that follows. To imagine that the
Christian liturgy sprang up from a sort of spontaneous generation,
motherless and fatherless like Melchizedek, or trustingly to give
it a sort of putative paternity which would definitively erase any
perception of its authentic genealogy, is from the start to reduce
all reconstructions to a more or less scholarly, more or less ingenious mass of misconceptions.

It is true that the Christian liturgy, and the eucharist especially,
is one of the most original creations of Christianity. But however
original it is, it is still not a sort of *ex nihilo* creation. To think
so is to condemn ourselves to a minimal understanding of it. For
it would mean that we should be mistaken about the materials
that went into its construction, but, what is much more serious,
we should already be misled about the movement that hatched
them in order to build this spiritual temple, or rather this great
tree of life that the anaphora is. The materials from which the
Christian eucharist was formed are something quite different

15

from mere prime matter. They are stones that have already been polished and skillfully worked. And they do not come from some demolition yard where they would have then been refashioned without concern for their original form. Quite the contrary. It is in a studio which has consciously inherited both a long tradition of experience and its finished products that these will be prepared for their new function. And this will not be to do away with the first results but to complete them, through some refinishing in which not a jot of the original engraving will be effaced.

With the first eucharistic formulas we can no more start from zero than we can with the Gospel. In both cases, by providential design, there is an Old Testament which cannot be overlooked. For if providence evidently did judge this stage necessary, we have neither the right nor the ability to push it aside.

Stating this already gives the direction in which we shall have to look for providence's preparatory work. It would be at least surprising if the Old Testament of the liturgy were not the same as that of the Gospel. It is nevertheless just what many scholars seem to admit as an axiom which needs neither proof nor discussion. It is a foregone conclusion, they would like to tell us, that either there is no prehistory to the eucharist or else, if there is, it can be found only outside of Judaism.

We must admit that the continued persistence of this state of mind, even with scholars who are as deeply intuitive as they are well informed, is somewhat disconcerting.

When we see Dom Odo Casel's immense effort to find the antecedents of the mystery of Christian worship in the most incongruous pagan rites, and the small concern he brought to the least contestable Jewish antecedents of this same mystery, we wonder how such an open mind could have remained so little open to certain obvious matters of fact. What is most surprising is that he was in no way ignorant of the Jewish texts whose comparison with Christian texts is indispensible before any other comparison can be made. He cites them.[1] He observed their

---

[1] Cf. O. Casel, *Le Mémorial du Seigneur dans la liturgie de l'antiquité chretienne*, Fr. trans. (Paris, 1945), pp. 23 ff.

most striking parallels. But for him they are just noteworthy
parallels. It seems he cannot see that the origin, and also the
explanation of what is most *sui generis* in the Christian eucharist
is to be found here. He looks for neither origin, nor explanation
anywhere except in the pagan mysteries.

Another liturgist, still more scholarly and perhaps more ingenious than Casel, Baumstark, cannot resist the obvious.[2] For
him there can be no doubt that there are borrowings from the
Jewish liturgy in the Christian liturgy, as well as affiliations with
it. But he did not arrive without difficulty at accepting this dependence as an original fact. In this area of the eucharistic prayer
in particular there is a reluctance to assume that the thematic
correlations (i.e. in the wording) can be original. For the most
part, people seem to believe it is merely a question of a secondary
fact, of a later contamination that came about at the time of the
final working out of the eucharistic texts which were to become
classic. This is an hypothesis with nothing positive to back it
up and its unlikelihood will be weighed when we observe the fre-
netic antisemitism that unfortunately afflicted Christians from
the end of the patristic period onward. Let us point out that
it is the Syrian authors who generally evidence the most pointed
antisemitism. We have only to think of the shocking texts of
St. John Chrysostom that Lukyn Williams has assembled on this
theme.[3] Now it is they also who would have been responsible
in this case for this overlaying of Synagogue forms upon those
of the Church! How could we seriously believe that?

The question which then arises is unavoidable. Why have
people wished with all their might to search so far and wide, and
with such unlikely detours, in order to avoid finding the true
sources of the Christian liturgy close at hand? It seems that
we must give a series of answers to this question, answers which

[2] A. Baumstark, still reticent in *Trisagion und Qedušâ*, in *Jahrbuch für
Liturgiewissenschaft*, III (1923), pp. 18-32, in the third chapter of *Comparative
Liturgy* (Westminster, 1958), reaches an opinion that is very close to every-
thing that the present book will uphold.

[3] Cf. A. Lukyn Williams, *Adversus Judaeos. A Bird's Eye View of Christian Apologiae until the Renaissance* (Cambridge, 1935). See texts like: Chrysostom, *Adversus Judaeos*, P. G. 48, col. 843 ff.

are furthermore interconnected and interlocked. Our critical
knowledge of the origins of Christianity first of all remains too
dependent upon the work of Protestants and consequently reflects a basic Protestant prejudice: far from completing Scripture, tradition could only be a degradation and a corruption
of it. Furthermore, the same knowledge remains overladen with
conceptual contradistinctions of a Hegelian dialectic that sees
no other explanation possible for the Catholic synthesis than a
conflict between a "pagan-Christian" antithesis and the "Judeo-
Christian" thesis. Finally, all of this becomes clogged in one of
those erroneous critical "obvious facts" that the latter part of
the 19th century accepted as intangible facts, but which are
merely a sophistic development of tentative findings. What appears to be solid rock actually flakes off under the pressure of
genuine criticism.

Let us take these points one by one. Catholic scholars do admit that in Christianity, starting with the New Testament, the
inspired texts may not be isolated from that body where the Spirit
who inspired them dwells. They admit it because they are Catholics and, without this, would no longer be so. Having admitted
this they have no difficulty in establishing the well-foundedness
of this *a priori* on the most irrefutable facts to the extent that
Protestant scholars themselves, willingly or not but more and
more decisively, are coming to agree with them. However, once
we are no longer dealing with Christianity but with Judaism,
the Catholic reflex no longer works. The old Protestant *a priori*
then regains the upper hand. In the case of Christianity there
was no difficulty in admitting and proving the reality of the statement that the inspired texts cannot be opposed to tradition nor
isolated from it. To the contrary, it is in it and from it that they
were derived. Since this truth, for the Old Testament, seems no
longer necessary as of faith, it is forgotten that it is first of all
a matter of a truth of good sense. And although one is Catholic
for the New Testament, one becomes Protestant for the Old Testament. Here tradition can be synonymous merely with a "su-
perfetation" that is foreign to the sacred texts and ends up as
the degradation and ultimately the radical adulteration of their
content. This was admitted once and for all by the old Protestant

school. The more modern Catholic school, seeing no obligation
to doubt it, accepts it and idly endorses it.

Still it ought to seem peculiar that what is the condition of
the truth of life in the New Testament is not the same in the Old,
—that the sacred texts in one case cannot be separated from living
tradition, whereas in the other they must be. Strange that the
Word of God from Christ's time onward lives in the People of God
in which the Spirit who is believed to have inspired that Word
dwells, while before Christ this Word would have fallen from
heaven, as if the Spirit had directly produced its letter without
having to go through men's hearts, and therefore without having
left any evidence there of his passing through.

In fact progress in biblical studies, among Protestants first
of all, has shown the artificiality of this dichotomy.[4] Revealed
truth both in the Old and New Testaments, lives in men's hearts
before being written down. And even though it becomes once
fixed with the greatest authority, it is still living and susceptible
of being developed in these hearts and this is even truer of the
Old than of the New Testament. For, before Christ, we do not
yet have the unique and ultimate authority of a transcendent
personality, dominating every other expression of truth and imposing itself as *the* ultimate Truth. To isolate or separate the
holy Word and tradition, the Word of God expressed once and
for all and the life in the People of God of the Spirit who inspired
this expression, is therefore still more contrary, if that is possible,
to the nature of things in the Old Testament than in the New.
Consequently it is impossible to imagine the relationship of the
New Testament with the Old as a relationship that would be
connected here only with the inspired texts in the strict sense
alone and could or should ignore its contextual surroundings.

Nevertheless, on first sight, Jesus' objection that he voiced
against the tradition of the scribes and Pharisees as a corrup-

---

[4] See, as one of the first among these, Oscar Cullmann's article inspired
by the problems raised by the *Formgeschichte* and published in the *Revue
d'histoire et de philosophie religieuses* (Strasbourg, 1925), pp. 459-477, 564-
579. The Scandinavian school of exegesis deserves the credit for having
shown the capital importance of Jewish tradition, and particularly the liturgical tradition, for an exact understanding of the Old Testament.

tion of the Word of the Old Testament, which was the prime obstacle to the transition from this Word to his own word, makes
a very strong impression. Yet its power is very closely connected
with its ambiguity. What Jesus denounced is not the tradition
as such, but its aberrant or withered forms. Such a denunciation
is just as valid in regard to the deterioration and decay in Christianity as in Judaism. These are the deviations or the petrifac-
tions which produce heresies today as they did yesterday. But
it is not by those who have failed it that one should judge a tradition, whatever it may be. Our better acquaintance with the
Pharisees,[5] and more generally with these inspiratory movements
in ancient Judaism that are too easily called sectarian, and which
ought better be compared with our own religious orders, has convinced us of their positive value.[6] Even though certain minds
could become involved by them in their denial of the creative
newness of the Gospel, those who found in them an incitation to
make greater progress were no less numerous. And it is perhaps
in St Paul, the Christian apostle who was most steadfast in his
will for universalism and in his refusal to enclose Christianity
within the ready-made categories of Judaism, that we find the
best evidences of the close connection between these old categories and the newest formulations of the Gospel.[7]

Limiting ourselves merely to this unique example from St. Paul,
the manifold studies on the relationship between his thought
and rabbinical thought preclude our believing that the latter
could be of some use to understand him merely in settling the
grammatical sense of a formula or the literary type of a pericope.
Still more grievous would be the error in believing that what is
related in his thought to Jewish thought is merely dead-weight
—a sort of straight-jacket which he is not quite able to undo completely. It is to the very flesh of Pauline thought and to what

[5] Cf. the work, already old, of R. Travers Herford, which is still worth reading: *The Pharisees* (London 1924).

[6] It is impossible here to give even an elementary bibliography on everything that has been written about the problem of the Jewish "sects" since
the Qumrân discoveries. For a first glimpse, cf. A. Dupont-Sommer, *Les Écrits
esséniens découverts près de la Mer Morte* (Paris, 1959).

[7] Cf. W. D. Davies, *Paul and Rabbinic Judaism* (London, 1948).

is most personal in it that this Jewish thought is related, and not merely to its external clothing. We cannot comprehend his Christianity if we separate it from his Jewishness which antecedes it. It evolves through a process of change that lays greater emphasis on the flowering of that tradition than on its being cast off.

It will undoubtedly be said that in Christianity we have a simple criterion for distinguishing certainly authentic traditions from those that are questionable, or clearly heterogeneous: the former go back to Christ or at least to the apostles. Obviously this criterion no longer holds when we are speaking of traditions that are anterior to Christianity. But from the Christian viewpoint there is a reciprocal criterion for the latter, and its application is even easier. It is what apostolic Christianity in fact retained from Jewish tradition.

The more contemporary evidence multiplies, as has been the case since the Qumrân discoveries, the more obvious it becomes that the extent of this recreative preservation surpasses by far anything that could have previously been imagined. The supposition of the exegetes influenced by post-Hegelian views that what is original in Christianity would at the very least be defined in and by a substitution of essentially universalist themes of hellenistic thought for properly Jewish and therefore particularistic themes, seems groundless and even bereft of substance. This is merely an *a priori* mental fiction that could be imposed on the facts only to the extent that they were little or poorly known.

In the first place the knowledge we have today of hellenistic Judaism is enough to convince us that the fact that the Christians used the materials and even the instruments of Greek thought as a medium of expression, or of reflection, has nothing specifically Christian about it, and especially nothing that would permit us to oppose Christianity to Judaism. Nothing is clearer than that the Jews did this long before the Christians, and if there ever was any effective hellenization of early, if not primitive, Christianity, it was first of all a product of the school of the Jews and not a reaction against them.[8]

[8] Cf. E. R. Goodenough, *By Light Light. The Mystic Gospel of Hellenistic*

Moreover, the best contemporary studies on Philo give even better proof of the fact that for the Jews of this time already, it was much more a question of a judaization of the elements and themes of Greek thought than of a conversion to it or submersion into it.[9] For a stronger reason the same must be said of the Christian authors whose originality, it was thought, could be boiled down to a hellenization process. It is the author of the fourth gospel who was especially thought to betray an evident transference of intellectual milieu and this religious metamorphosis. However, after a more thorough study and with the help of much broader comparisons, he has been discovered to be much more dependent upon Judaism and much more faithful to its spirit than we should ever have imagined one or two generations ago.[10]

But if there is one element in the whole of Christian tradition that in all of the forms in which it is known shows the continuity with and the dependence on Judaism, it is the eucharistic prayer. There is surely no more creative creation in Christianity than this, and we believe that the whole of the following study will show it. In spite of this, however, whether we are dealing with the basic themes, their reciprocal relations, or the structure and the development of the prayer, the continuity with the Jewish prayer that is called "berakah" is so unbreakable that it is impossible to see how we can avoid speaking of its dependence.

It is at this point that the last argument against the examination of such a hypothesis is raised. Its very statement, we will not deny, has such a decisive immediate effect that we might be tempted to abandon all discussion. But this would be to say that the argument either proves too much or else proves nothing at all.

Some people pose the prejudicial objection that we have not even one Jewish text that antedates the middle ages, which

---

Judaism (New Haven, 1935), and H. A. Wolfson, *Philo*, (Cambridge, Mass., 1948).

[9] Cf. J. Daniélou, *Philon d'Alexandrie* (Paris, 1958).

[10] Cf. C. H. Dodd, *The Interpretation of the Fourth Gospel* (Cambridge, 1953).

therefore would seem to preclude any comparison between the Christian eucharists and the corresponding texts of the Jewish liturgy. How, they say, would it be possible to make a valid comparison between such late texts and the eucharist, either in its primitive state or as it has evolved in those forms which are still in use, and which became fixed for the most part in the patristic age? As striking as it may be, the argument is merely a paralogism. It relies completely on an implicit confusion between a text's date and the known date of the oldest manuscript or of the oldest collection that has preserved it for us. In this regard it is perfectly correct that the most ancient manuscripts of the Synagogue liturgy that we have are more or less recent medieval copies of the *Seder Amram Gaon*,[11] a collection which itself was composed only in the ninth century. But before coming to too hasty a conclusion, it would be good to remember that before the Qumrân discoveries we also had no copy of a Hebrew text of the Bible prior to this date.

More generally, before the more or less recent discoveries of Egyptian papyri, very few manuscripts of the authors of antiquity came down to us from before the Carolingian renaissance or the first Byzantine renaissance which is approximately contemporary with it. If there is any validity in the reasoning that concludes that the Jewish liturgy as we know it could hardly go back before this period, who would be ready to uphold a parallel thesis that should be equally valid for the literature of Greco-Roman antiquity? In fact, we might mention that as a matter of fact in the beginning of the 18th century it did find an erudite partisan to uphold it. It was Père Hardouin-Mansart, who with fearless logic did not hesitate to denounce Vergil, Horace, Cicero as well as Plato and Homer as mere pseudonyms assumed by unemployed monks of Byzantium or Gaul to cover up their own elaborate literary endeavors[12]. It is true that the author of

---

[11] Cf. David Hedegard, *Seder R. Amram Gaon, Part I, Hebrew Text with critical Apparatus, translation with Notes and Introduction* (Lund, 1951). We shall have constantly to refer to this volume, which we shall designate by the abbreviation D. H.

[12] This unbelievable story was retraced by Owen Chadwick, *From Bossuet to Newman* (Cambridge, 1957), pp. 49 ff.

this astonishing theory, as erudite as he was ingenious, was to end his days in an insane asylum...

The same external cross-checking and internal criticism that destroy his specious argumentation in the case of the classical authors are equally valid in regard to the Jewish liturgy. Even though we do not have any complete copy of the texts going back further than Amram Gaon, we have too many precise and undeniably anterior allusions and citations for us to be able seriously to doubt that these texts, in their entirety, are much more ancient than their oldest copies surviving today. And this is corroborated by their content, their style, their language which cannot seriously be looked upon as medieval. The texts of Jewish prayers that may be put on a parallel with the most ancient texts of the Christian eucharist do not reflect the Jewish theology of the High Middle Ages, but that of the Judaism that was contemporary with the origins of Christianity. And both their style and their language are related to the prayers and the hymns discovered at Qumrân much more than to the Hebrew of the later *piyutim*, not to mention medieval Hebrew. But above all, the rabbinical sayings, the prescriptions or the citations of the *Mishnah* or the *Toseftah*, which are undeniably very early and which in one way or another make reference to them, are far too numerous to permit any serious doubt at least in regard to the general tenor of the prayers.

To this a counter-proof must be added. The astonishing closeness of the texts in the Seder Amram Gaon and texts still in use in the Synagogue of our own day[13] attests to the liturgical conservatism of the Jews, which is even more noticeable than with the Christians; this assures us that here less than elsewhere we cannot deduce the date of a text from that of a manuscript or a collection. Furthermore we know on good authority that, if the Jews did in fact modify their liturgy after the beginning of the Christian era, when these modifications were not the simple

---

[13] Cf. S. Singer, *The Authorized Daily Prayer Book of the United Congregations of the British Empire, with a new translation*, 15th ed. (London, 1944) and I. Abrahams, *A Companion to the Authorised Daily Prayer Book*, rev. ed. (London, 1922, reprinted, New York, 1966).

addition of new factors, they were generally motivated by a concern for removing from Jewish worship what might have been reused and reinterpreted by the Christians. This is especially the case for the calendar of biblical readings.[14] Hence it follows that those parts of the Jewish liturgy that are undeniably parallel to the most characteristic Christian texts enjoy a special safety. If they are still there it is so because the Jews themselves judged them to be too essential and basic for the polemical concern behind the reform of their own liturgy not to have been held in check at the very point where it would have had the best opportunity to manifest itself.

Finally, we must add (and this is a capital point) that it is not only in the prayer texts that the Church's dependence on the Synagogue seems to be noticeable. It is also in all aspects of worship; architecture, sacred music, and even in an area which up until recent discoveries was never even considered, iconography.

Archeology has shown what might be called an obvious kinship between the arrangement of the synagogues contemporary with the origin of Christianity and that of the primitive places of worship like those that still exist, particularly in Syria. We have treated this point in another study, and we have just returned to it more in detail in a later volume.[15] Let it suffice here to recall a few salient points.

Like Christian churches the old synagogues are, *domus ecclesiae*, the house where the faithful assembly comes together. They remain closely connected with the Temple of Jerusalem (or the memory of it). They are oriented toward the Temple for prayer. The direction of the *debir*, the "holy of holies" where the divine presence, the *Shekinah* was thought to reside, is marked out by a porch, behind an "ark" where the Holy Scriptures are kept, which in turn is furnished in imitation of the Temple with a veil and the seven-branched candlestick, the *Menorah*. Later, the

---

[14] Cf. R. G. Finch, *The Synagogue Lectionary and the New Testament* (London, 1939).

[15] See the chapter on Sacred Space in our work, *Rite and Man: Natural Sacredness and Christian Liturgy* (Notre Dame, 1963), and our book *Liturgy and Architecture* (Notre Dame, 1967).

porch which in fact had not been used for a long time, was to be replaced by an apse where the ark was finally placed. The assembly itself is centered around the "chair of Moses" where the presiding rabbi sits, in the midst of the benches of the "elders." The congregation is grouped around the *bema*, a platform supplied with a lectern, which the lector ascends to read, as we see in the Gospel, the texts that the *hazan*, the "minister" (ancestor of our deacon) has taken from the ark. Then all turn toward Jerusalem for prayer.[16]

In the ancient Syrian churches the chair of Moses has become the episcopal seat, and the semi-circular bench that surrounds it the seat of the Christian "presbyters." But as in the synagogue they remain in the midst of the congregation. The *bema* is also there, not far from the ark of the Scriptures which is still in its ancient place, not at the far end, but some distance from the apse. It is still veiled with its curtain and the candlestick is still beside it. The apse, however, is no longer turned toward Jerusalem but to the East, a symbol of the expectation of Christ's coming in his parousia. While it was empty in the old synagogues (later the ark was installed there), in the Syrian church this eastward apse now contains the altar before which hangs a second curtain, as if to signify that from now it is the only "holy of holies" in the expectation of the parousia.[17]

Along with the Jewish origin of Christian worship a comparison of these two arrangements illustrates better than any commentary, the newness of Christianity. The eucharist has replaced the Temple sacrifices and henceforth the *Shekinah* resides in the humanity of the risen Christ, who has no earthly dwelling place, but will return on the last day as the definitive East that each eucharist anticipates.

Iconographical comparison corroborates this genealogy of Christian worship. When the Dura-Europos synagogue was discovered and its frescos could be admired, it seemed to be an exception, in contradiction to Jewish iconoclasm. Actually, as Sukenik in

---

[16] Cf. E. L. Sukenik, *Ancient Synagogues in Palestine and Greece* (London, 1934).

[17] Cf. the previously cited chapter in *Rite and Man*.

his study on the ancient synagogues shows, the Dura-Europos synagogue is an exception only because of the unique preservation of its decor.[18] But in practically all of the ancient synagogues there are vestiges of a very similar decoration. We must conclude, he emphasizes, that it was only at a late date and out of an undoubted reaction against Christianity that the synagogues came to forbid any figurative ornamentation.

Moreover, the similarity between the selection of biblical themes in the synagogues and that which is found in paleo-Christian frescos or mosaics is striking. The same episodes are kept by both. Their treatment attests that in the Synagogue and the Church they were interpreted in the sense of an actual application to the People of God celebrating their "memorial" in its liturgy. We shall return to this point later, but we must emphasize that the analogies, indeed the identities, are so striking, for example at Dura-Europos itself between the synagogue which has just been mentioned and the church which was also discovered in the same locality, that some have come to ask whether what had been taken to be a synagogue was not rather a Judeo-Christian church.[19] This supposition seemed to find support in the fact that among the manuscript fragments discovered in the supposed synagogue one was found which gives us one of the eucharistic prayers from the *Didache*, but in Hebrew! Actually too many signs indicate that we are indeed dealing with a synagogue, although it is still true that the continuity from the synagogue to the church is proved to be so strict that there is some excuse for being mistaken about it.

This discovery of a Hebrew original of a eucharistic prayer from the *Didache* emphasizes one final fact that leaves no longer any room for doubting the genesis of the Christian eucharistic prayer from Jewish prayers. We have a series of particularly valuable texts which form the connecting link between the Jewish and Christian liturgies. First there are texts, like those in the *Didache*, that are Jewish texts which the Christians were

[18] *Op. cit.*, pp. 82 ff.

[19] This viewpoint was upheld in a paper given at the *Patristic Conference* of Oxford in 1963.

able to use for a certain time with hardly any revision. They simply gave a renewed meaning to certain essential themes, like *qahal-ecclesia, berakah-eucharist,* and others.

But we soon observe other texts succeeding these, like those whose Jewish origin Bousset pointed out in the 7th book of the *Apostolic Constitutions,*[20] and which Goodenough studied more in detail.[21] Here, the essence and the body of the text remain Jewish, and only a few words were added to specify the Christian interpretation and transposition.

Go one step further and we find, as in the 8th book of the same collection, prayers that are undeniably of Christian composition, but which are still dominated by Jewish models, and even continue to incorporate fragments of Jewish prayers.

When all of these facts are taken into account, it becomes very hard still to reject textual comparisons. Therefore, in examining these texts point by point and following their evolution step by step, we believe that it will become obvious that the eucharistic prayer, like all the "novelties" introduced by Christianity, is something new that is rooted not only in the Old Testament in general, but immediately in the prehistory of the Gospel that is the prayer of those who "were awaiting the consolation of Israel."

[20] W. Bousset, "Eine Jüdische Gebetsammlung im siebten Buch der apostolischen Konstitutionen", in *Nachrichten von der Königlichen Gesellschaft der Wissenschaften zu Göttingen, Philologische-Historische Klasse,* 1915 (1916), pp. 435-485.

[21] Goodenough, *op. cit.,* pp. 306 ff.

3

The Word of God and the *Berakah*

WHEN INVESTIGATING THE ORIGINS OF THE CHRISTIAN EU-charist, the element of the synagogal liturgy that immediately attracts our attention is the type of prayers called *berakoth* in Hebrew, a term for which the Greek word εὐχαριστία was the first translation. In English, εὐχαριστία is generally translated "thanksgiving," as is *berakah*, although the Jewish usage would be to call the *berakoth*, "blessings." Fr. J.-P. Audet, O.P., in some very thought-provoking studies, has been somewhat hard on this translation.[1] He rightly emphasized that "thanksgiving," in our current use of the term, has come merely to signify gratitude. We give thanks in the sense that we express to God our gratitude for a particular favor that he has done for us. On the other hand, he emphasizes, the primitive *eucharistia*, like the Jewish *berakah* before it, is basically a proclamation, a confession of the *mirabilia Dei*. Its object is in no way limited to a gift received and to the more or less egocentric gratitude that it may awaken.

---

[1] J.-P. Audet, "*Esquisse historique du genre littéraire de la 'Bénédiction' juive de l' 'Eucharistie' chrétienne*," in *Revue Biblique*, 1958, pp. 371 ff. See also his annotated edition of *La Didache* (Paris, 1958).

29

THE WORD OF GOD AND THE KNOWLEDGE OF GOD

However justified this remark may be, it should not be made as hard and fast as he does or tends to do. Neither the Jewish *berakah* nor the Christian *eucharistia* could be in any way likened to disinterested praise, at least in appearance, as is found for example in the hymns of worship in classical antiquity, in the already more literary Homeric hymns, or in the philosophical hymns of the hellenistic era like the famous hymn of Cleanthes. Actually the *berakah*, and especially the liturgical *berakoth* which are the immediate antecedents of the Christian eucharist, is always the prayer proper to the Jew as a member of the chosen people, who does not bless God in general, in the manner of a neo-Platonist philosopher, for *mirabilia Dei* that would not concern himself. On the contrary, his is the "blessing" of the God who revealed himself to Israel, who has communicated himself to him in a unique way, who "knew" him, and consequently made himself "known" to him. This means that God created between himself and his people a *sui generis* relationship, which always remains at the very least subjacent to the praise, whatever its precise object may be.

If we wish to keep from straying too far afield, either by restricting or wrongly overextending the precise sense of an expression that designates a prayer of a very special type, we must begin by putting it back in its literary and historical context. Actually the *berakah* is a distinctive element of the specific character of all of Jewish piety. This piety is one which never considers God in general, in the abstract, but always in correlation with a basic fact: God's covenant with his people. Still more precisely, the *berakah* is a prayer whose essential characteristic is to be a response: the response which finally emerges as the pre-eminent response to the Word of God.

The indispensable preliminary to every study of the Jewish *berakoth* is therefore a study of what the Word of God came to mean for the Jews who composed and used them. And what first should be pointed out, is that for the Jews contemporary with the origins of Christianity, "Word of God" meant something much more and something quite different from the way it is understood by the majority of modern Christians. Most of the time our theological manuals prefer to speak of "revelation" rather than "Word of God." The Word of God seems to interest them only to the extent that it reveals certain truths inaccessible to human reason. These "truths" themselves are conceived as separate doctrinal statements, and the Word of God finally is reduced to a collection of formulas. They are detached from it, moreover, so that they can be reorganized into a more logically satisfactory sequence, even to the point of retouching them or remodeling them to make them clearer and more precise. After that the only thing that remains of the divine Word seems to be a sort of residuum, a kind of conjunctive material that of itself has no interest. Whether we realize it or not, the result is that the Word of God appears as a sort of nondescript hodgepodge from which the professional theologian extracts, like a mineral out of its matrix, small but precious bits of knowledge which it is his job to clarify and systematize. In this view the Word of God is no longer anything but an elementary, rough and confused presentation of more or less shrouded truth; the theologians' task is to bring them out and to put them in order.[2]

But even for those who are not at all affected directly by this professional bias, the fruit of a theology conceived as an abstract science, the Word of God, considered at the very first as "Holy Scripture," remains all too frequently a mere communication of ideas. For us today, the word, and especially the written word, tends to be little else. A scholastic bias which is practically universal persuades us that people listen and above all read only to learn something that was not known before. The rest, if there is a "rest," passes for entertainment or superfluous flights of imagination.

For the pious Jew, and to the utmost for those Jews who meditated the divine Word at the end of all that we call the Old Testament, the divine Word signified an intensely living reality. From the outset it is not merely basic ideas that are to be shaped,

---

[2] A reaction on this point is finally setting in and one particularly encouraging sign in France is the series of works by Fr. Pierre Grelot, particularly *La Bible, Parole de Dieu* (Paris, 1965) and *Bible et théologie* (Paris, 1966).

but a fact, an event, a personal intervention in their existence. For them the temptation to identify the religion of the Word with an intellectualistic religion was non-existent. The mere mention of such an identification would have seemed absurd to them, and even bereft of meaning.

In the first place, when they used the term "Word of God" they stayed very close to the primitive sense of the human word. But in addition they were submissive to what this Word said of itself, in the manner in which it is still presented to us in the Bible.[3]

Men did not begin to speak in order to give courses or conferences. And God, in speaking to us, does not make himself a theology professor. The first experience of the human word is that of someone else entering into our life. And the still fresh and in a certain sense already complete experience of the divine Word at the end of the old covenant, was that of an analogous intervention, but one that was still infinitely more gripping and more vital: the intervention of Almighty God in the life of men.

"Hear, O Israel: the Lord is our God, the Lord alone."[4] For the Jew this is not only the summary of the whole Word of God, but the most typical Word of God. God here bursts into our world to impress us by his presence which has become a tangible one. But on every page of the Bible the divine Word defines itself or better manifests itself in this way. It is not a discourse, but an action: the action whereby God intervenes as the master in our existence, "The lion has roared," says Amos, "who will not fear? The Lord God has spoken, who can but prophesy?"[5] This means that the Word, once it has made itself heard, takes possession of man to accomplish its plan. For his part, Isaiah says:

"For as the rain and the snow come down from
    heaven, and return not thither
    but water the earth,

---

[3] See M. Buber's studies on the Word. H. Urs von Balthasar has shown all that a Christian theology ought to draw from them: *Einsame Zwiesprache: Martin Buber und das Christentum* (Cologne-Olten, 1958).

[4] Deuteronomy, 6:4.

[5] Amos, 3:8.

> making it bring forth and sprout, giving seed to
>   the sower and bread to the eater,
> so shall my word be that goes forth from my mouth;
>   it shall not return to me empty,
> but it shall accomplish that which I purpose,
>   and prosper in the thing for which I sent it."[6]

For Israel, not only is the divine Word, like every word worthy of the name, an action, a personal intervention, a presence which asserts and imposes itself, but since it is the Word of the Almighty, it produces what it proclaims by its own power. God is "true" not only in the sense that he never lies, but in the sense that what he says is the source of all reality.[7] It is enough that he says it for it to be done.

This conviction is so strong that even the ungodly in Israel could not escape from it. The unfaithful kings torment the prophets to prophesy what pleases them or at least to keep silent because they are persuaded that the moment the divine Word makes itself heard, even through the mouth of a simple shepherd like Amos, it goes straight toward its fulfilment.[8]

For their part, the prophets illustrate their conviction about this power of the Word which surpasses them. Ezekiel does not hesitate to act out in advance the events that he is announcing, in symbolic actions that recall the machinations of the magicians, in order to point up their ineluctable accomplishment.[9] Yet this is magic no longer, since there is no question of an attempt by man to force events to follow his own wishes. Quite the contrary. As in a sacramental sign, it is the concrete assertion of the power of God who speaks of doing what he says by his expressed Word alone.

The end of all of this will be the certitude conveyed in the priestly account of the creation: the Word of God does not intervene simply in the course of pre-existing things in order to modify it. All things in a radical way exist only through a Word of God

---

[6] Isaiah, 55: 19 ff.

[7] See the article $\dot{\alpha}\lambda\eta\theta\epsilon\iota\alpha$, G. Kittel's *Theologisches Wörterbuch*.

[8] Cf. Amos, 7: 10 ff.; Jeremiah, 26, etc...

[9] Cf. Ezekiel, 5: 1-3, and the commentary of Adolphe Lods, *Les prophètes d'Israël et les débuts du judaïsme* (Paris, 1935), pp. 58-59.

which has caused them to be. And they are good only to the extent that they remain what the divine Word planned them to be.[10]

As long as this is not understood, or as long as we refuse to accept it, the Bible has no meaning. Or else if we find one for it, it is not its own; it is not the one which the People of God recognized in the Word of God. But to say this does not mean that the Word of God is bereft of intellectual content, or that it appeared so to the Jews. To come to that conclusion would make an absurdity of the necessary reaction against the preceding error. In fact, it is merely giving in to the permanent temptation to agnosticism which too often paralyzes modern religious thought (especially, but not exclusively, in Protestant circles), but which was as unknown to ancient Judaism just as our own anemic intellectualism was foreign to it.

The Word of God in Israel has as its correlative the knowledge of God. It is quite true that this knowledge has nothing to do with abstractions. But it is still no less a knowledge, in the richest sense that the word is capable of having.[11] The knowledge of God which results from the Word, which is its pre-eminent fruit, a knowledge of which God is the object, itself proceeds from a knowledge that is anterior to the Word and which is expressed there: the knowledge of which God is the subject.[12] The first can proceed and be understood only from the second. "I shall know, even as I have been known,"[13] this sentence of St. Paul expresses the compass and the efficacy of the divine Word, mentioned by Isaiah.

The "knowledge of God," in the radical sense of the knowledge that God has of us, is something quite different from a simple impassible or merely contemplative omniscience. In the Bible, for God to "know" a being, means that he is concerned with that

[10] Genesis, 1.

[11] On this notion, see the remarks of A. Neher in *L'Essence du prophétisme* (Paris, 1955), esp. pp. 101 ff.

[12] Cf. the excellent remarks on the importance of this consideration by Dom J. Dupont, *Gnosis, la connaissance religieuse dans les épîtres de saint Paul* (Louvain-Paris, 1949), pp. 51 ff.

[13] 1 Corinthians, 13: 12.

being, attaches himself to it, loves it and showers his gifts upon it. "You only have I known of all the families of the earth," God tells the Israelites through Amos, "therefore I will punish you for all your iniquities."[14] In other words: I have done for you what I have done for no one else; I will require of you therefore what I could not demand of any one.

The knowledge of God (let us always understand the knowledge that he has of us) will therefore go hand in hand with his preferential election: the choice that he has made of some men in order that his plan might have its fulfillment in or through them.[15] It implies his compassion, his sympathy for our misfortunes, even our weaknesses, and this results not only from the fact that he made us, but that he remains for us a father full of understanding:

"As a father pities his children,
    so the Lord pities those who fear him.
For he *knows* our weakness;
    he remembers that we are dust."[16]

Ultimately, this knowledge is love: a merciful love which condescends to unite itself, and in order to do so, to lower itself to the level of one who is farthest from it, as much and more by his unworthiness as by his weakness. This is what is expressed in the marriage image applied to the Lord and his people. More precisely, according to Hosea, God behaves towards Israel as a man who falls in love with an unworthy woman, a harlot; yet she is made worthy by the boundlessness of the love bestowed on her.[17] For Ezekiel, it is to a child of adultery, abandoned from birth, a true waif, that the unmerited love of God goes out, in order to set her on her feet, bring her up, and finally make her into a queen.[18] The royal epithalamion of Psalm 45 gives a figured description of this union under the guise of a marriage be-

---

[14] Amos, 3: 2.
[15] Cf. H. H. Rowley, *The Biblical Doctrine of Election* (London, 1950).
[16] Psalm 103: 13-14.
[17] Hosea, 3.
[18] Ezekiel, 16.

tween an Israelite king and a foreign princess.[19] And the Song
of Solomon was received in turn into the canon of inspired books
only as a result of an interpretation that sees in the Shulammite
woman the daughter of Zion called to a union with a king who
is the King of heaven.[20]

This nuptial imagery is the counterpart of a typically Hebrew
expression which we encounter from the first pages of Genesis.[21]
The union of the spouses, in their bodily oneness where the union
of two lives in one is expressed and accomplished, is "knowledge"
par excellence. Reciprocally, because of this, sexuality will receive a supreme consecration. The union of a man and a woman
will find its meaning in discovering its mystery, which is that
of the reciprocal "knowledge" in which the love dialogue between
the God who speaks and the man who responds to him is to reach
its full flower in faith in his Word.

As a consequence of the knowledge God has of us, the knowledge that we are called to have of him through the Word will
will be modeled upon its source. First of all it will be an obedient faith as Isaiah in particular will explain.[22] We *know* God
only by believing in him with the result that everything that
is not God, everything that does not proceed from his Word, will
fade away. But such a faith is not possible unless we effectively
commit ourselves to obedience to this Word.

Yet this obedience is not just *any* obedience to *any* word. As
Amos and Hosea have shown, if God requires righteousness from
us, it is because he is the pre-eminent righteous person. And we
could not benefit from his boundless mercy, or even recognize
it, without becoming merciful ourselves. This is why in God's
eyes "mercy is worth more than sacrifice."[23] Obedient faith, in-
herent in the knowledge of God to which man is called, is in fact
a conforming of our own selves to him.

---

[19] The reference is probably to a poem composed for the marriage of Ahab
with Jezebel.

[20] Cf. A. Robert, "La description de l'Époux et de l'Épouse dans Cant. V,
11-15 et VII, 2-6," in *Mélanges E. Podechard* (Lyon, 1945), pp. 211 ff.

[21] Genesis, 4: 1.

[22] Cf. Isaiah, 1: 19-20; 30: 15, etc...

[23] Hosea, 7: 6, which will be quoted by Jesus in Matthew, 9: 13.

But this conforming of ourselves is possible only because God (and this is the ultimate secret of his Word) willed to condescend to unite himself with us in order to unite us to him. It is in following this path that to know God will come down to loving him, loving him as he loved us, responding to his love by the very force of this communicated love.

It is here that the intellectual content of this "knowledge" takes shape and here that we see what is unique about it. To know God as we have been known is ultimately to acknowledge the love with which he loves us and pursues us to the ends of the earth. And precisely because we acknowledge it, it is also, in our acknowledgement of it, to consent to it, to surrender to it and to abandon ourselves to it.

We can therefore unmistakably understand how the Word of God in Jewish piety, as expressed in Psalm 119, came to be identified with the Law, the *Torah*. Of itself this identification in no way signifies mere legalism. For the *Torah* as Israel has understood it is something quite different from a law in the narrow sense of the Latin *lex*, or even in the broader sense of the Greek νόμος.[24] Nor is the *Torah* primarily a series of formal prescriptions, enjoining a certain form of behavior. And it is even much more than an interior rule, corresponding to some eternal nature of things. The *Torah* is a revelation of what God himself is in what he wills to do with his own people, those whom he has chosen, whom he has "known" in the sense that he has loved them to the point of uniting himself with them as in the indissoluble union of a man and a woman. How revealing is this *Leitmotiv* from Leviticus: "Be holy as I am holy," to which Jesus will return and explicate: "Be perfect as your heavenly Father is perfect!"[25]

The faithful observance of the *Torah* is to mark the people of God with its seal, a seal whose impression reproduces the very image of the One who communicates it. In Exodus the revelation of the *Torah* on Sinai has its prelude in the revelation of the divine

---

[24] See E. Jacob, *Théologie de l'Ancien Testament* (Neuchatel-Paris, 1955), pp. 219 ff., as well as the article νόμος in G. Kittel's *Theologisches Wörterbuch*.

[25] Matthew, 5, 48. Cf. Leviticus, 19, 2.

Name to Moses on the same Horeb mountain group.[26] This revelation of the Name of God, which signifies the revelation, the
communication of himself, remains the basis of the covenant
between him and his people.[27] Reciprocally, they will be his witnesses through the practice of the Law, because for other peoples
they will thereby constitute the living witness of what he does,
and, through what he has made out of man, of what he *is*.

In this sense, the *Torah*, in its moral prescriptions but also down
to the detail of its ceremonial ordinances, becomes like the very
expression of a common life between God and his people, a presence
which is a union. Therefore, we may already say of the *Torah*
what Jesus was to say of the law of the Gospel: it is an easy yoke
and a light burden.[28] For it is a yoke of love. It is God who through
it is placed in the life of those whom he has known and who know
him in return.

The meditation developed by the Wisdom writers will show
all the implications of the Word thus understood and accepted.[29]
In all of the ancient East, Wisdom was a practical knowledge,
nourished by meditated experience, and focusing on the supreme
art: the art of living. Kingly Wisdom in particular was nothing
but the art of sustaining not a single individual but a whole people.
Received in Israel along with the kingship, this Wisdom, like
the kingship, became impregnated with the teachings of the Word.
Just as the king is merely an epiphany of the only true King,
God known in his *Torah*, so Wisdom appears as the gift of God
to the king representing him, the gift that will make him reign
in accordance with the divine directions. The principle of true
Wisdom will therefore be the meditation of the divine Word under
the inspiration of the Spirit, the breath of divine life, which inspired that Word. Wisdom will therefore project the light of
heaven onto the experience and rational reflection of man.

[26] See E. Jacob, *op. cit.*, pp. 38 ff.

[27] *Ibid.*

[28] Cf. *Mishnah*, the tractate *Berakoth*, II, 2 and 10 b. The *Berakoth* tractates of both the Mishnah and the Toseftah have been translated into English
with a commentary by A. Lukyn Williams, *Tractate Berakoth* (London, 1921).

[29] See H. Duesberg, *Les scribes inspirés* (Paris, 1939).

[30] Cf. Ecclesiasticus, 24: 23.

Over the course of the historical experience of Israel, conducted and enlightened by the Word, it will become quickly evident that since God is the only true King, he remains the only "Sage" worthy of the name. Wisdom, identified with the essential content of the Word, the *Torah*, thus comes to signify the divine plan after which man's history is to take shape, in order to realize a people, a mankind after the heart of God. Just as the revealed *Torah* appeared as inseparable from a special presence of God with his people, the *Shekinah* through which he himself dwells under the tent with them during their pilgrimage, so Wisdom comes to be identified with this *Shekinah*.[31] But from now on the *Shekinah* no longer simply dwells in a sanctuary in the midst of its people: it makes their reconciled hearts its sanctuary.

This interiorization and humanization of the divine Word in Wisdom, a preparation for its universalization, will be found in the last visions and supreme promises of the prophets. For Ezekiel as for Jeremiah, the new and eternal covenant that the exiles are to await, carrying with them and in them the presence of the *Shekinah*, is a law engraved upon their hearts and no longer on tablets of stone. This is how "the knowledge of the Lord will cover the earth as the waters cover the depth of the seas."[32]

At this moment the mysterious character of the divine Wisdom will assert itself. It surpasses the thought of the wisest of men as the thoughts of God surpass man's thoughts. God alone knows it. For God it is like another self, to such an extent that to know it is to know God in the strongest sense. Man can achieve it only through the preeminent revelation. And so, from the Wisdom that seemed to come from the earth, fashioned by man's applying his reason to earthly experiences, although it did rise to heaven, we pass over to the apocalypse; to the revelation of God's impenetrable ultimate plans in which he will reveal himself to his people, so that he might soon be revealed to the whole world in a final way.[33]

[31] Cf. all of ch. 24 of Ecclesiasticus, where Wisdom is said to dwell in the pillar of fire, the cloud and in the tabernacle.

[32] Cf. Ezekiel 36: 26 ff. and Jeremiah, 31: 31 ff.

[33] See D. Deden, *Le "mystère" paulinien*, in *Ephemerides Theologicae Lovanienses*, t. XIII, 1936.

Hence, at the end of the old covenant we have this expectation of a supreme revelation of the Word in an unprecedented
outpouring of the Spirit.[34] With the Messiah, the heavenly Anointed coming to save his people, it is God in person who is to come
openly so that the people will recognize him and receive him,
in a world which the unveiled Presence will consume in its temporal and temporary aspects, in order to consummate it in everlasting bliss.

THE *BERAKOTH*, THE RESPONSE TO THE WORD

It is to the Word so understood that the prayers of the *berakoth*
will bring their response. They are the gradually evolving response of obedient faith to the Word which progressively manifests itself in its mysterious fulness, loftiness and depth. They
are therefore the completed expression of the knowledge of God
in the heart of the people whom he knew, "alone among all the
peoples of the earth."[35]

It may be said that the Psalms, the canticles of the people of
God, which themselves have come to be acknowledged as inspired, as being part of the Word of God, have progressively nourished and prepared the full flowering of Israel's prayer in the
berakah. Let us note the significance of the fact that the Psalms,
the great prayers of Israel, have come to be accepted as an integral and central part at the very heart of the Bible, the Holy
Scripture in which the inspired Word has been set down. No
fact could better illustrate the significance of the Word of God
for Israel as a creative word. Its pre-eminent creative action is
that of placing a new heart in man, so that, upon the tablets of his
own flesh, the *Torah* has been engraved. The result is that man
responds in his whole being and above all in his heart to the great
design of the divine Word. By intervening in his life, it patiently
but all-powerfully pursues its plan which is the fulfilment of a
people in whom it has molded this design over the course of history. It has the intention of forming a man who knows God as

---

[34] Cf. Joel, 3 ff., which Peter will quote in Acts, 2, 17-21.
[35] Cf. the text of Amos cited in note 14.

he has been known by him, who responds to his Word with a response that is nothing but the final key to the Word uttered within man himself. Even if the translation of Psalm 27 in French Protestant Bibles: "My heart says to me on your behalf: Seek my face, I seek your face, my God," is only a conjecture, it translates marveleously the whole plan of the Word.

Considered in their variety and their totality, the Psalms constitute a great *berakah*, as it were, even though they go beyond the precise form that Jewish tradition defined only after they had been composed and arranged into their present collection. But the *berakah* schema, as a spontaneous schema of prayer responding to the Word, predates them. It is found in Israel's most ancient tradition. In turn, the Psalms nourish the *berakah* with their substance so that it may finally be said that the later tradition will evolve the fully explicated theory, out of their constant recitation. This explains why the Jewish liturgy always inserted the recitation of the *berakoth* within the continued recitation of the whole psalter, as the Christian liturgy was to do afterwards.[36] If the Jewish *berakoth* or the Christian liturgy as well were isolated from the psalter, they would be cutting themselves off from their roots. Before long both of them would see their sense weakened and watered down, and run the risk of being reduced to an empty framework.

The *berakah* schema makes its appearance already in Genesis and Exodus. The examples given to us by these books are already of such a surprising clearness that we should be tempted to see in them a reflection of the late piety of the priestly scribes who were the last editors or revisers of these writings. Yet the formulas there are so simple and so spontaneous that it is quite likely that they are rather remote models, retained and preserved, of the immediate response to the Word; models which the development of this Word would only have further substantiated. In the Psalms, where this enriching action of the primitive prayer by the increasingly revelatory word is everywhere evident, the *berakah* schema seems frequently to be subjacent, even though it is rarely clear-cut. We may say that it is like a crystal forming

[36] Cf. D. H., pp. 26 ff.

in its matrix, still invisible to a superficial glance, but ready to shape its whole substance into the form which it demands.

In Genesis, when Eliezer meets Rebekah and becomes aware of the way in which the God who revealed himself to Abraham managed everything, he cries out: "Blessed be the Lord, the God of my master Abraham, who has not forsaken his steadfast love and his faithfulness toward my master. As for me, the Lord has led me in the way to the house of my master's kinsmen."[37] In other words, God is praised for having kept his promises toward one who had believed in his Word. The object of this blessing of God, as rudimentary as it is, is already the gratitude about which St. Paul was to say: "In everything God works for good with those whom he loves."[38]

Perhaps even more striking is the *berakah* uttered by Jethro, Moses' father-in-law, especially if looked at in its whole context. Jethro sees as with his own eyes that God actually did speak to Israel through Moses and that he fulfilled his promises. Then he cries out: "Blessed be the Lord, who has delivered you out of the hand of the Egyptians and out of the hand of Pharaoh. Now I know that the Lord is greater than all gods, because he delivered the people from under the hand of the Egyptians." The text goes on: "And Jethro, Moses' father-in-law, offered a burnt of-fering and sacrifices to God; and Aaron came with all the elders of Israel to eat bread with Moses' father-in-law before God."[39]

This *berakah* from the mouth of a stranger to God's people is therefore the expression of his association with their faith. Jethro acknowledges here that the divine Word has made itself heard in Israel and that it kept its promises toward them. This pro-claiming of God, acknowledged in his *mirabilia*, resulted in the offering of the sacrifice, and as a consequence, his entrance into fellowship with the people which the Word has formed, in the presence of God.

A number of psalms are just amplified *berakoth* of this kind. They manifest the full sense of these expressions: bless (*bene-*

---

[37] Genesis, 24: 27.

[38] Romans, 8: 28.

[39] Exodus, 18: 9-10.

dicere), sing (*cantare*), avow (*confiteri*), proclaim (*praedicare*) when applied to the *mirabilia Dei*, as announced, manifested and produced by the almighty Word. Whether their specific object is creation in general or some benefit received by an individual, Israel's own experience is always implied in their praise: God who is first of all manifested in the history of his people and who will then be acknowledged everywhere and in all things. This is so true that everything for the believing Israelite is but an echo of his Word, the work that bears witness to it.

Those psalms which are prayers of petition always presuppose the background of this praise; it is the basis for every prayer: the God to whom Israel prays is in no way unknown. He is the God who is well known through his Word, the God who is acknowledged in the great deeds accompanying it and resulting from it. Even when this presupposition is still implicit, it always underlies the entreaty: the God who has done these wonders, in whom we believe, is the only one from whom we may expect everything.

But many of them already give a glimpse and often more than a glimpse of a development of the schema which was to become definite in the great liturgical *berakoth* of the Synagogue. Particularly in the psalms composed to accompany the sacrifices (and these seem to be one of the oldest and most constant types in its structure), there is a primary phase which joyfully evokes the great deeds God has performed in the past for his people in a confession of jubilant faith. Then, the sacrifice is offered amid supplications that he renew and thereby confirm his past wonderful works. Frequently, a priestly oracle, undoubtedly arising from omens detected during the course of the rite, appears at this point and promises deliverance or the hoped for favor. Therefore the psalm which begins in praise and develops in supplication, ends with a doxology: God is always the same; today and tomorrow, as in the past, he will gratify his people.[40]

---

[40] See Aage Bentzen, *Introduction to the Old Testament*, vol. I (Copenhagen, 1948), pp. 146 ff., and S. Mowinckel, *The Psalms in Israel's Worship* (Oxford, 1962).

This schema is particularly obvious in a psalm like the 40th. It opens with the announcement of past deliverances:

> I waited patiently for the Lord; he inclined to
>   me and heard my cry.
> He drew me up from the desolate pit,
>   out of the miry bog,
> and set my feet upon a rock,
>   making my steps secure.
> He put a new song in my mouth,
>   a song of praise to our God.

Then comes the sacrificial offering with the prayer that God always show himself in a like manner, that he continue to do and to accomplish what he began for the person who invokes him. But at the same time it is a consecration of the one praying, in his sacrifice, and above and beyond the material oblation which merely represents the gift or rather the abandonment of self to the divine will.

> Sacrifice and offering thou dost not desire;
>   but thou hast given me an open ear.
> Burnt offering and sin offering
>   thou hast not required.
> Then I said, "Lo, I come;
>   in the roll of the book it is written of me;
> I delight to do thy will, O my God;
>   thy law is within my heart.
> I have told the glad news of deliverance
>   in the great congregation;
> lo, I have not restrained my lips,
>   as thou knowest, O Lord.
> I have not hid thy saving help within my heart,
>   I have spoken of thy faithfulness
>   and thy salvation; ...
> Do not thou, O Lord, withold
>   thy mercy from me,
> let thy steadfast love and thy faithfulness
>   ever preserve me!

It is on this basis of a consecration to God's will that the prayer is sent up to him. It does so with such certitude that the supplication, of itself, turns into renewed and definitive praise.

... Be pleased, O Lord, to deliver me!
O Lord, make haste to help me!
Let them be put to shame and confusion altogether
who seek to snatch away my life;...
But may all who seek thee
rejoice and be glad in thee;
may those who love thy salvation
say continually, "Great is the Lord!"

The core of this psalm is a thought which recurs many times
in the psalter, and which is a central teaching of the prophets,
and Isaiah in particular. It is not the material substance of any
offering that can satisfy the Lord, but the offering of one's self.
Only a consecration of our will to this, acknowledged in his Word,
gives meaning to our sacrifices.[41]

Under the influence of Protestant prejudices, nineteenth-cen-
tury exegesis wished to see a repudiation of sacrifice in these
formulas, which would be expressed with greatest clarity in the
phrase of Hosea which Jesus was to use again: "I desire steadfast love, and not sacrifice."[42] But as the contemporary Scandinavian school has well shown, this is false literalism, and mis-
understands the deliberately paradoxical style of the prophets.
They are not premature Protestants or anticlericals who wished to substitute the idle dream of a secular religion for the un-
avoidably ritual reality of the actual religion. They simply state
the meaning that sacrifice must assume in the religion of the
Word: a consecration of man and his entire life through the ritual
itself.[43] The result is not a morality into which religion is absorbed
to the point of disappearance, but a religion which consecrates
moral requisites in such a way that it makes one's whole life one
act of religion.

What remains true in this perspective is that the consecratory
prayer accompanying the sacrifice assumes a place of increasing

[41] Cf. Isaiah, 1.
[42] Cf. note 23.
[43] See in particular A. Haldar, "Associations of the Cult Prophets among
the ancient Semites," 1945, and J. Pedersen, "The Role played by inspired
Persons among the ancient Semites," in *Studies in Old Testament Prophecy
presented to T. H. Robinson* (Edinburgh, 1950).

importance in proportion as it expresses more forcibly the consecration of man himself. There is nothing more typical in this
regard than the evolution of the sense given to a liturgical expression: *shevah todah* ("sacrifice of praise," or "of thanksgiving").
In the beginning it designated a special kind of sacrifice whose
meaning was expressed by the accompanying psalm of praise.
But little by little the "sacrifice of praise" came to mean the praise
itself, which became not only an integral part of the sacrificial
ritual, but the pre-eminent sacrifice. Hence we have such telling
expressions as that which we find again in Hosea: "sacrifice of
our lips."[44] This "sacrifice of the lips" where the heart's oblation is expressed, is one with the "broken and contrite heart"
that the conclusion of Psalm 51 opposes to empty ritualism.

Nothing voices the sentiment that this is not an outgrowing
but an interiorization of sacrifice better than a particular expression of St. Paul. It comes so naturally to him that it must
have already passed into common usage among the Jews, despite
the fact that its very paradoxical character verges on misconstruction. In one of the oldest texts expressing the sacrificial
sense given by Christians to the cross, he says that Christ handed
himself over for us as a fragrant offering and sacrifice to God.[45]
The reference to the 40th psalm which we have quoted is obvious. But the psalm says literally: "sacrifice and offering thou
dost *not* want," but acceptance of the divine will. St. Paul translates, or rather transposes the sense by saying something which
in its expression is almost the contrary: this accepting of the
divine will *is* the offering that God desires.[46]

The progressive introduction into the heart of the sacrifice
of the prayer of offering of one's self, under the specific form of
a *berakah*, will draw its ultimate inferences in the Synagogue worship. Since the Jews of the exile and the diaspora could no longer
offer sacrifices, a prayer of this type, as a response to the reading

[44] Hosea, 14: 2.

[45] Ephesians, 5: 2.

[46] A more detailed discussion of this problem will be found in our book
The Spirituality of the New Testament and the Fathers (*History of Christian
Spirituality*), vol. I (London, 1963), pp. 175 ff.

of the Word, came to take the place of sacrificial worship. When the Temple was rebuilt, it accompanied the morning and evening sacrifices. And in all the synagogues it will be pronounced facing Jerusalem, or more precisely, facing the Holy of Holies where the high priest once a year brought the blood of atonement.[47]

All of this sheds light on the description given in the book of Nehemiah of the *qahal*, i.e. the liturgical assembly of the people back from captivity in the ruins of the Temple.[48] At the first *qahal* when the covenant was made on Sinai, the people had responded with unanimous acceptance of the ten sentences of the basic *Torah*, and then the first sacrifices of the covenant were offered. At the scarcely less solemn *qahal* which marked Josiah's reform, after the reading of Deuteronomy, i.e. the law enlightened by the prophets and renewing the prohibition of idols, this acceptance was similarly renewed, and the renewed covenant was sealed in the Passover sacrifice, the memorial of the deliverance from Egypt.[50] At the third great *qahal*, of the scribe Ezra, which the Synagogue of latter Judaism was to look upon as its foundation or consecration,[51] It is the whole priestly *Torah* of the scribes which is read, the Pentateuch completed in its definitive form in exile. At this time it was still not possible to offer sacrifices: there was no longer any Temple, nor altar, nor undoubtedly any victim that could be found to be offered. But in committing themselves to the rebuilding of the holy place and to the restoration of its service, the "elders" pronounced the *berakah* which is the most explicit in its form and the most exhaustive in its content found in the Bible.

The Levites began by exhorting the people to thanksgiving:

Stand up and bless the Lord your God from ever-
    lasting to everlasting.
Blessed be thy glorious name
    which is exalted above all blessing and praise.

---

[47] Cf. D. H., pp 81 ff.
[48] Nehemiah, 8-9.
[49] Exodus, 19 ff.
[50] 2 Kings, 22 ff.
[51] Cf. note 48.

Thereafter follows a great prayer which passes the entire history of creation in review and then the whole history of the people of God up to the present. It concludes with a formal consecration to God's plans together with an emphatic supplication that he accomplish his work for and in his people.

It may be said that here we have a model of the two great prayers of the Synagogue service: the blessings which lead to the *Qedushah* and the recitation of the *Shemah,* and later the great prayer of the *Amidah* or *Tefillah* (the pre-eminent prayer). Throughout the entire life of the pious Jew the piety of Judaism extends the ramifications of these *berakoth,* which are found in detail in the tractates with this title in the *Mishnah* and *Toseftah.* From the time he awakens, through each of his actions of the day, to the moment of his retirement and falling asleep, they consecrate the totality of his acts. And at the same time they consecrate the world in restoring it in praise to the Word which created it in the beginning, for each and every one of them are but so many acts of "acknowledgement" of this Word as being the beginning and the end of all things. As Rabbi Trypho, echoing the whole of rabbinical tradition, told St. Justin,[52] it is through the constant offering of these *berakoth* that the Jews in diaspora among the Gentiles are conscious of offering everywhere to God the "pure offering" spoken of by the prophet Malachi.[53] And it is thus that all of Israel believes it is accomplishing the promise of the book of Exodus: they will be made an entirely priestly people, a kingdom of priests, of consecrators of the entire universe to the one divine will revealed in the *Torah.*[54]

With this ultimate understanding that Israel came to have of its own role, it is certain that we have gone definitively past the old ritual borrowed from Canaan. Whatever transformations in meaning and content that it may have undergone, it has now been surpassed. And this is why the destruction of the Temple and its sacrifices in the year 70 of our era can no longer destroy Israel nor the *Torah* worship.

---

[52] Justin, *Dialogue with Trypho,* 116-117; P. G., t. 6, col. 745-746.
[53] Malachi 1: 10-12.
[54] Cf. Exodus, 19.

But, as we have emphasized, this means not so much a moralization of the sacrifices as a sacralization of morality, or rather of the "righteousness" of the *Torah*. It would be a mistake to believe that this religion of the ultimate Israel would have escaped every particular ritual act, and more especially every definite sacrifice. Nothing is more significant than to observe the new ritual which, on the contrary, was then to arise spontaneously, and to which the ritual communities awaiting the Messiah, the *haburoth* as they were later to be called,[55] were to give its full meaning. We mean the meal rituals, particularly the community meals on the evening of the Sabbath or a feastday. For the priests of Qumrân or Damascus, as for the Essenes or the Therapeutes mentioned by Philo or Josephus, this meal came to constitute not only a new equivalent of the old sacrifices, but ultimately the only sacrifice remaining in the expectation of the new and eternal covenant.[56] The great *berakah* pronounced by the president of the assembly over the last cup, which was to be shared by all, invoked the imminent coming of the Messiah and consecrated in this expectation the "remnant" which had remained faithful to the hoped-for Kingdom. With this new sacrifice we arrive at the Last Supper, and the immediate prehistory of the Christian eucharist.

[55] The term is attested in Hebrew only after the beginning of the Christian era.

[56] Cf. G. Vermès, *Les Manuscrits du Désert de Juda* (Paris-Tournai, 1953), pp. 59 ff.

The Jewish *Berakoth*

THE BEST MEDIEVAL COMMENTARY OF THE JEWISH LITURGY, the *Sefer Abudharam*, a work of Rabbi David ben Joseph Abudharam, who lived in Seville around 1340, rightly observes that there are two types of *berakoth* in Jewish tradition.[1] One type is a brief formula that became very soon stereotyped and is composed merely of a praise-thanksgiving, a "blessing" in the narrowest sense. The other is a more developed formula in which the prayer of supplication has its place, although always in a "blessing" context. The first is destined to accompany every action of the pious Jew from his awakening in the morning to the moment that sleep overtakes him in the evening. The second has its place either in the Synagogue service (in the morning, at noon and at night) or in the meal prayers, particularly those accompanying the final cup shared by all the participants.

THE TRANSMISSION OF THE TRADITIONAL FORMULAS

A whole chapter in the *Mishnah* and an entire corresponding section in the *Toseftah* (the two parts of the Talmud) are devoted

---

[1] *Sefer Abudharam* (Prague, 1784), 2B and 3A. There exists a modern re-edition which is incomplete, by C. L. Ehrenreich (Klausenberg, 1927).

to all these *berakoth*. The *Berakoth* chapter is the first in the *Mishnah* and the material it quotes and discusses is incontestably of the greatest age. There we find the formulas for the short *berakoth* in their entirety. On the other hand, since the long formulas were supposed to be known by everyone, they are generally cited or recalled merely by their first words. Yet, frequently the discussions of which they are the object allow us to have a sufficient notion of their content, and even about the debated details of their development.

The complete text of these formulas has come down to us through the prayer books, the *Siddurim* as they are called today.[2] But these collections only began to be assembled in the time of the *Gaonim*, the presidents of the Jewish academies which served simultaneously as courts of justice. In the ninth century the *Gaonim* and their academies were the successors of our era of the *Amoraim* who since the third century had been the commentators of the oldest oral traditions of Judaism, those of the *Tanaim*, of which the Talmud (in its two editions, Jerusalem and Babylonia) is the compilation.[3]

Moreover, these collections of the *Gaonim* are not and do not in any degree claim to be original works. As is forcefully expressed in the introduction of the most valuable of them, the *Seder Rab' Amram Gaon*, they were assembled only to fix an immemorial tradition whose origins were then considered to be inspired.[4] This stabilization, as is shown by the divergencies in the medieval manuscripts of the *Seder Amram Gaon* themselves, was never absolute. Elbogen thought it possible to conclude from this fact that in the beginning this *Seder* did not contain the text of the prayers, but only their explanation.[5] This view is rejected by most contemporary specialists, particularly by David Hedegard who provided the critical edition of the col-

[2] Cf. the introduction of D. H., pp. xx ff.

[3] *Ibid.*, pp. xvii ff.

[4] D. H., pp. 3 ff.

[5] I. Elbogen, article "Prayer Books", in *The Universal Jewish Encyclopedia*, (London, 1901-1906), vol. VIII, p. 620.

lection in question.[6] The text of Rabbi Amram's explanations, and even more so his introduction, suppose with utmost clarity that what he was asked to do by some Jewish communities (undoubtedly Spanish) was first of all to make an authorized edition of those prayers. Furthermore the text of these prayers is found also in a somewhat later book of the same type, the *Seder* of the famous Saadia Gaon.[7]

The divergencies in the text of the prayers are noticeable in each of the three principal manuscripts of the Seder Amram: the Codex 613 of the British Museum, dating from the end of the 14th or the beginning of the 15th century and serving as a basis for the Coronel edition (1865), the Codex 1095 of the Bodleian Library at Oxford, completed January 3, 1426, edited by Frumkin (1912), and the Sulzberger Codex of the Jewish Theological Seminary in New York, completed November 8, 1516, and edited (with a re-edition of the other two) by Hedegard in 1951. Let us point out immediately that these differences are almost insignificant and even non-existent, with regard to the principal texts which we shall be examining in greatest detail and which are of the greatest importance for our study: the meal prayers and the central prayers of the synagogue service. The texts that are still in use today in the various synagogues and given in the modern editions printed for liturgical use, like Singer's, follow the formulas of the *Gaon* very closely.

Still, the first thing to do is to explain these variations. In doing so, we shall be elucidating a basic problem for the correct understanding of the liturgical tradition of the Synagogue, a problem which at least has its analogy in the liturgical tradition of Christianity.

Frequently, modern historians of Synagogue worship, like those who study Christian worship, imagine that at a more or less late date a rigid written formulation must have been substituted for the original freedom of the prayer formulas, and that this for-

---

[6] Cf. D. H., p. xxvi; also G. Ginzberg, in *Jewish Quarterly Review, New Series*, vl. XXXIII, p. 321.

[7] Cf. *Siddur R. Saadia Gaon*, ed. I. Davidson, S. Assaf, B. I. Joel, (Jerusalem, 1941).

mulation consequently became *ne varietur*. This twofold presupposition is based on nothing but a ready-made view that reflects the Protestantism of the historians who first circulated it.

In the first place, it is a constant characteristic of oral tradition among the most varied of peoples, but especially among the Semites, that it be handed on in the form of a very definite schema, accompanied by well determined coupling formulas. With these as a basis a certain freedom of detail is maintained. But this freedom is strictly governed by the awareness of the underlying schema and controlled by religiously preserving the key expressions.[8] On the other hand, when a need came to be felt for setting the formulas down completely in written form, it was still felt for a rather long time that it was above all the schema and the key expressions that were to be fixed. The result, at least with texts thought to be more or less peripheral, was that the copyists, at least up to the age of the printing press, never had scruples about substituting oral variants which had persisted and with which they were more familiar, for the details in the formularies they were reproducing.

Thus we see a double chimera dissolving: the primitive improvisation of the prayers, and their ultimate crystalization in a rigid literalism. Whether or not they were fixed in their detail from the beginning and down to our own day, the Jewish prayers had a content, a structure and key terms that were perfectly defined from the outset. And, even in their set forms, these elements are the ones that first attracted attention. Of course, in Judaism as in every religion, there is the ever-present threat of formalism. Everyone who is accustomed to the "ex tempore" prayers dear to certain Protestant groups knows how easily they become mere catch phrases, a constant and tedious rehash of repeated clichés. On the other hand we must acknowledge that there is scarcely any religion in which the spiritual teachers have shown themselves to be more careful to avoid a formalism that empties the prayers of their meaning than in Judaism. This is one of the most constant themes of the teaching of the Rabbis in regard to the recitation of the prescribed prayers: they are

---

[8] Cf. Eduard Nielsen, *Oral Tradition* (London, 1954), pp. 18 ff.

bereft of any worth and are no longer prayers properly so-called, when they are recited without being accompanied by what they call *Kawannah*.[9] This rabbinical Hebrew term, corresponding to a verb with the root *kwn*, meaning "to be attentive," expresses the interior attitude of one whose intelligence and heart are kept constantly awake through an act of living faith, a cleaving of one's whole being to what is being said, and beyond the words themselves to the sacred realities they recall.

The Rabbis teach that to arrive at this state the prayers should be recited deliberately, with care to observe the pauses indicated, and by enunciating with vigor in order to rivet the attention. They insist that their formulas should be meditated upon and their meaning probed as deeply as possible. With this last objective in mind they encourage the practice of preceding the recitation, particularly of the great *berakoth* of the synagogue liturgy, with a moment of quiet meditation in which each person would think over by himself what is to be recited publicly. The result would be that the *kawannah halleb*, the "attention of the heart" becomes the soul and the fruit of liturgical prayer.

The whole teaching of the Sermon on the Mount on prayer, with its necessary introduction of the idea of being "alone" with God, the absorption in his presence, in order to offer a prayer worthy of the name, far from being a contradiction of the rabbinical tradition on this point is actually its purest expression. As has been rightly pointed out, Jesus' teaching against the Pharisees whose prayer deteriorates into an empty formalism coincides with the teaching of the most revered of the Pharisee doctors themselves.[10] Moreover it is quite noteworthy that Jesus' criticism leveled against a devitalized practice is never turned against the Synagogue prayer itself, which Christ undoubtedly made his own without a shadow of reticence up to his last hours on earth.

• [9] Cf. D. H., p. xxxix and the references he gives. To this we may add G. Sholem, "Der Begriff der Kawanna in der alten Kabbala", in *Monatschrift für Geschichte und Wissenschaft des Judentums*, vol. 78 (1934), pp. 492 ff.

[10] Cf. the work of R. Travers Herford cited in the first chapter.

But while the Rabbis multiply warnings and counsels in order that prayer may become the most personalized act possible, they are no less watchful to keep it from any sort of individualism. Collective prayer, in the midst of God's people assembled for that purpose, must be prepared for by personal prayer and meditation. But it is always and everywhere in union with the people that the faithful individual must pray, and it is in his heart's adhesion to the traditional expressions of collective, liturgical prayer that his prayer is to find its rule. Without this, they say, man would tend to ask for what his selfish impulses suggest to him.[11] He would bless God only in a perspective that focuses on his own self-interest, and he would ask God for his own satisfaction. In contrast to this, in adhering to the prayer of the faithful people, he will come to ask nothing which is not the sole accomplishment of God's will, and to praise God no longer for what touches him personally but for the fulfilment of His Plan alone. Every other prayer is but a masked idolatry. The only genuine prayer is that which makes us, within the people of God and by its teaching, the worshippers of the God who has spoken and never ceases to speak to us, worshippers who themselves never cease bringing to his Word the "fiat" of their exultant faith.

THE SHORT FORMULARIES

The study of the short *berakoth* enumerated and commented upon by the *Mishnah* and the *Toseftah*, especially if they are reread in the light of the interpretations constantly given to them by later rabbinic tradition, shows that they have no other tendency than this.[12] They contribute to making the whole life of the pious Jew an unceasingly renewed act of awareness of God in all things, and of his Word in all human actions. The classic form of these prayers begins with an invocation of the God of Israel which is practically always the same: "Blessed (art) thou,

[11] Cf. *Sefer Ha-Kuzari*, David Cassel, Ed. (Leipzig, 1853), pp. 233 ff., and S. Krauss, *Synagogale Altertümer* (Leipzig, 1922) p. 95.
[12] They will be found conveniently in the Lukyn Williams translation, cited in note 28 of ch. 3.

Adonai, our God, king of the ages (or "of the universe")." It is therefore the divine Name revealed to Moses on Horeb that is immediately evoked, under the traditional periphrase "Adonai" (Lord) since respect for the sacred name renders it unutterable. It is this revealed God, still the *Deus absconditus*, the hidden God, mysterious in his revelation, who is acknowledged in every circumstance as the master of our life as well as of the whole universe. In the exultant acknowledgement of his people, he is praised, "blessed" as their God, as the one who made a covenant with them in this exchange of ineffable "knowledge," which is implied by the revelation of the sacred Name and the correlative acceptance of the easy yoke and the light burden of the *Torah*. But it is not as an ordinary tribal divinity, one of the countless "lords of the covenant" of the Canaanites that this God is confessed by his people. It is as the hidden King of all things, the one who holds the ages in his hand by his almighty Wisdom: the Master of the world throughout all its history. And it can be said that the faithful soul who so confesses him, by that very fact, accomplishes the coming of his kingdom *here and now*.

The variable continuation of the prayer, usually through an explicit reference to a Scripture passage, proclaims the lordship of the God of Israel over the reality of the moment, the action in the world that is about to be undertaken. Thus the world, darkened by man's sin, rediscovers its original significance, and from now on man's action will be but the accomplishment of God's plan.

Upon awakening, the morning ablution will be sanctified by the formula:

> Blessed be thou, JHWH, our God, King of the universe, who hast sanctified us by thy commandments, and given us command concerning the washing of the hands.[13]

Once he has completely awakened, the faithful Israelite adds:

> Blessed be thou, ... who restorest the souls to the dead corpses (connecting awakening with the resurrection).

At cock-crow he says:

[13] D. H., p. 7.

Blessed be thou, ... who hast given the cock intelligence to distinguish between day and night.

Then come the three blessings in which the Israelite praises God for not having made him a pagan, a slave or a woman. Their sense, as the Rabbis have always explained, is not to gloat over a merit that others would not have, but to become again aware of the undeserved grace of knowing God, of being able and having to observe the prescriptions of the law.[14] The misogyny that a too imaginative antisemitism thought it could find in the last of these three formulas simply overlooks what the woman will be required to say:

Blessed be thou, ... who hast created me according to thy will.

The Rabbis explain both blessings by saying that it is a grace both for the man to be called to fulfill the ceremonial obligations and for the woman to be freed from them in order to attend to the chores of her home.[15]

The man then straightens up, saying:

Blessed be thou, ... who exaltest them that are lowly.

For the first time he looks at his surroundings and cries out:

Blessed be thou,... who openest the eyes of the blind.

He dresses and says:

Blessed be thou, ... who clothest the naked.

He gets up and puts his feet on the ground, saying:

Blessed be thou, ... who spreadest forth the earth above the waters.

And throughout the whole day there will be no object or being which will not remind him of God and his Word of love, who has created all things for his people, no action in which he will not surrender himself in the same way to the revealed will of God.

In the light of these hundred blessings and their symbolic number on which the Rabbis delight in commenting,[16] we can under-

[14] Cf. the note in D. H., p. 10.
[15] *Ibid.*
[16] D. H., p. 16 ff.

stand the exact significance of this passage from St. Paul: "For
everything created by God is good, and nothing is to be rejected
if it is received with thanksgiving (εὐχαριστία = *berakah*, blessing)
for then it is consecrated by the word of God and prayer."[17] The
constant practice of the *berakoth* actually becomes an all-embracing prayer, involving the life of man and the world, whereby
all things are brought back to the creative Word and restored
to the original goodness which it had conferred upon them. As
the Rabbis again tell us, this is how the whole faithful life of the
people of Israel, even in its apparently most mundane occupations,
is clothed with a character that is not only sacred but also priestly. They are thereby that priest-people spoken of in the book
of Exodus, because their whole life, taken in the framework of
the *berakoth*, reconsecrates the entire universe to its author through
the Word of God and prayer. Thus we can understand why Rabbi Trypho in the dialogue with Justin explains Malachi 1: 11 (on
the pure offering offered at all times and everywhere among the
pagans) by saying that this is what is accomplished by the Jews
of the diaspora, when they never cease to bless God in all things
in the midst of those who do not know him.[18]

Again, the same Rabbis who repeated that the *Shekinah* dwells
invisibly with every group of Jews that has come together to
meditate on the *Torah*, do not hesitate to say that by pronouncing
the *berakoth* over everything he sees or touches with his hands
every faithful Jew makes these same things a consecrated dwell-
ing-place for the *Shekinah* itself.[19]

THE *BERAKOTH* PRECEDING THE *SHEMAH*: THE *QEDUSHAH*

It is against this general background of the manifold *berakoth*
which make the entire existence of the pious Jew a universal
and constant sacrificial "blessing," that the great *berakoth* of
of the synagogue service and the meals (particularly in the com-

---

[17] 1 Timothy, 4: 3-4.
[18] Cf. note 52 of ch. 3.
[19] Cf. the beautiful text of the *Zohar*, attributed to R. Simeon, translated
by L. Gillet in *Communion in the Messiah* (London, 1942), p. 138.

munities awaiting the Messiah) stand out in high relief. They
lead us to the source of the priestly life of the people of God in
a detailed supplication for the hallowing of his Name, the coming
of his kingdom, the accomplishment of his entire will, between
a great *berakah* for the gift of light and another for the gift of
life. These then, respectively, are the three themes of the *berakoth* preceding the central act of synagogue worship: the recitation of the *Shemah*,—of the great *Tefillah*, the pre-eminent prayer
of the Eighteen (actually today, nineteen) Blessings that follow
it, —and finally the meal *berakoth*.

The morning service of the synagogue, as we have said, was
to be preceded by a prolonged moment (one hour say the Rabbis) of meditation and private prayer, in the synagogue itself
insofar as possible.[20] From the earliest, this preparatory prayer
was nurtured by the recitation of the psalter. It seems that some
particularly fervent communities of pre-Christian antiquity already knew the practice, renewed in modern times by the *Hasidim*
of Poland, of preceding the public service at least on some days
with a recitation of the whole psalter. But they were very soon
to introduce the custom of reserving the 145th to 150th psalms
that is, the great cosmic praise on which the psalter concludes,
especially to this hour of morning meditation.[21] In a parallel
way, after the evening meal, they soon introduced the custom
of reciting the entire *Hallel* (Psalms 113 through 118). This is
the "hymn" which as the Last Supper accounts tell us was sung
by the disciples after they had eaten.[22] There is scarcely any
need to point out that this is the origin of the Lauds and Vespers
of Christianity. Baumstark has correctly pointed out that all
the ancient Christian rites, whether Eastern or Western, made
use of these same psalms.[23]

The *Pesuqe de zimra*, i.e. the "passages from the psalms,"
still make up an obligatory prelude to the synagogue service of
today. Some *berakoth* precede their recitation, which are like

[20] Cf. *Mishnah*, tractate *Berakoth*, V, 1 and D. H., p. 32.
[21] D. H., pp. 32 ff.
[22] Cf. Matthew 26: 30 and parallels.
[23] A. Baumstark, *Comparative Liturgy*, pp. 106 ff.

a summary of the themes contained in the psalms that follow: praising God for his creation, and for the way that he has made all things be for the good of his elect, those whom God "knows" and loves.[24]

However interesting this preliminary service may be, we have to restrict our study to the synagogue service proper and to its characteristic *berakoth*, for, as we shall soon discover, they lead us directly to the eucharistic service of the Christian Church.

As we have said, the first group of *berakoth* that we find purposes to prepare for the central act of daily Jewish piety: the recitation of the *Shemah*, i.e. principally these words from Deuteronomy:

> Hear, O Israel: The Lord your God is the Lord alone; you shall love the Lord your God with all your heart, with all your soul and with all your thought, and him only shall you serve.[25]

In the repetition of this sentence, in its assimilation by the prayer of faith, the people of God renew themselves in this knowledge of God corresponding to the knowledge he has of his own, a knowledge which is at the heart of Israel's piety. The preceding prayers are aimed at expressing this very knowledge.

On the Sabbath day as well as Monday and Thursday of every week they originally followed the solemn reading of the law and the prophets.[26] Towards the patristic age, this reading was transferred from the beginning to the end of the service and it now constitutes its conclusion. It seems clear that this transfer came about as a reaction against the Christians who in the meantime had given this supreme place to the eucharistic banquet. It is possible also that prescinding from the Christians this reaction aimed at all the Jewish communities who had tended already to consider the community meals as the equivalent, and in their

---

[24] D. H., pp. 27 ff.

[25] Deuteronomy 6: 4-9, to which is added 11: 13-21 and Numbers 15: 37-41 (according to *Mishnah*, tractate *Berakoth*, II, 2). Cf. D. H., pp. 52 ff.

[26] Cf. Eric Werner, *The Sacred Bridge*, (London-New York, 1959), pp. 3 ff and 50 ff.

eyes a superior one, of the Temple sacrifices.[27] The *minim*, to which at this same period the 12th of the present prayers of the *Tefillah* refers (it was introduced at this time), are certainly indiscriminately both the Christians and those Jews whose messianic leanings were seen to be leading them straight to Christianity.[28]

Even today at the beginning of the Synagogue service there is a vestige of the reading that was once used here in the beginning. It is the *Qaddish* prayer which was the original conclusion of the *targum*, i.e. the paraphrastic Aramaic translation that followed the ritual Hebrew reading of the Holy Scriptures.[29] In fact, alone in this central composite of these immutably Hebraic prayers, it is still recited in our day in Aramaic. Its first part which is also the oldest and certainly anterior to the Christian era must be quoted. It is evident that it is the direct source of the first part of the Lord's Prayer:

> Magnified and sanctified be his great name, Amen. In the world which he has created according to his will. And may he establish his kingdom during your life and during your days and during the life of all the house of Israel, even speedily and at a near time. Amen.

After this begin the *berakoth* that introduce the recitation of the *Shemah*. As we shall see again in the final meal prayer, the *Sheliach sibbur*, i.e. the member of the community designated for saying the prayer in the name of all invites the community to the "blessing". (Today, and since the 6th century, it is always the *hazan*, the ὑπηρέτης mentioned in the Gospels, the "minister" who is the ancester of the Christian deacon.

Bless ye JHWH, who is to be blessed.

All answer:

Blessed be JHWH, who is to be blessed, for ever and ever.

---

27 Cf. D. H., pp. xxxviii-xxxix and 16.

28 Cf. O. Cullmann, *Le problème littéraire et historique du Roman pseudo-clémentin* (Paris, 1930), pp. 170 ff.

29 Text in D. H., pp. 41 ff., with commentary, p. 40. Cf. David De Sola Pool, *The Old Jewish Aramaic Prayer, the Kaddish* (Leipzig, 1909).

30 D. H., p. 43.

The *Sheliach sibbur* says, or rather chants, as is the rule for all these solemn prayers, this great blessing called *Yozer*:[31]

Blessed be thou, JHWH, our God, king of the universe, who formest light and createst darkness, who makes peace and createst all things: Who in mercy givest light to the earth and to them that dwell thereon and in his goodness renewest the creation every day continually. How manifold are thy works, JHWH. In wisdom hast thou made them all, the earth is full of thy possessions. King who alone wast exalted from aforetime, praised, glorified and exalted from days of old. Everlasting God, in thine abundant mercies have mercy upon us, Lord of our strength, Rock of our stronghold, Shield of our salvation, thou stronghold of ours. The blessed God, great in knowledge, prepared and formed the rays of the sun: it was a boon he produced as a glory to his name. He set the luminaries round about his strength. The chiefs of his hosts are holy beings, they exalt the Almighty, continually declare the glory of God and his holiness. Be thou blessed, JHWH, our God, in the heavens above and on the earth beneath. Be thou blessed, our Rock, our King and our Redeemer, Creator of holy beings, praised be thy name forever, our King, Creator of ministering spirits, and all of his ministering spirits stand in the height of the universe, and with awe proclaim aloud in unison the words of the living God and everlasting King. All of them are beloved, all of them are pure, all of them are mighty, all of them in dread do the will of their master, all of them open their mouths in holiness and purity and praise and glorify and sanctify the name of the great King, the mighty and dreaded One, holy is He. They all take upon themselves the yoke of the kingdom of heaven, one from the other, and give leave one to another to hallow their Creator: in tranquil joy of spirit, with pure speech and with holy melody they all respond in unison in fear, and say with awe ...

Here all join the *Sheliach sibbur* in chanting the *Qedushah*:

HOLY, HOLY, HOLY IS JHWH OF HOSTS; THE WHOLE EARTH IS FULL OF HIS GLORY.

[31] D. H., pp. 46 ff.

The *Sheliach sibbur* resumes:

And the Ophanim and the holy Chayoth with a noise of great rushing, upraising themselves towards them praise and say:

and again all chant:

BLESSED BE THE GLORY OF JHWH FROM HIS PLACE.

He continues and concludes:

To the blessed God they offer pleasant melodies, to the King, the living and ever-enduring God they utter hymns and make their praises heard, for he alone performeth mighty deeds and maketh new things, the Lord of battles, he soweth righteousness, causeth salvation to spring forth, createth remedies, is revered in praises, the Lord of wonders who in his goodness reneweth the creation every day continually, as it is said: (Give thanks) to him that maketh great lights for his grace endureth forever. Blessed be thou, JHWH, Creator of the luminaries.

Whereupon he immediately proceeds to the second *berakah*, *Ahabah*:

With abounding love hast thou loved us, JHWH, our God, with great and exceeding pity hast thou pitied us, our Father, our King, for the sake of our fathers who trusted in thee, and whom thou didst teach the statutes of life, be gracious also unto us. Our Father, merciful Father, have mercy upon us, and put it into our hearts to understand, and to discern, and to hear, and to learn, and to do all the words of instruction in thy Torah in love. And enlighten our eyes in thy commandments, and let our hearts cleave to thy fear, and unite our hearts to love thy name because we have been called by thy holy, truly great name. Do unto us for the sake of thy great and fearful name, soon in love exalt our horn and be thou our king and save us for the sake of thy name, for we have trusted in thee, that we be not put to shame, and we trust in thy name that we be not abashed nor stumble for ever and ever because thou, O God, art our Father, our God, and let not thy mercy abandon us for ever and ever. Let peace come over us from the four corners of the earth and cause us soon to go upright to our land, for thou hast chosen us from all peoples and tongues and hast brought us near unto thy great name in love. Blessed be thou, JHWH, who hast chosen thy people Israel in love.[32]

At this point there finally follows the collective recitation of the *Shemah* ...

This double *berakah* opens then with a praise of God the Creator, within the general perspective of the Jewish morning prayers. This is immediately specified in an act of thanksgiving for light. But from physical light we make the transition to the spiritual light of the knowledge of God and therefore to an act of thanksgiving for the gift of the *Torah* which will lead directly to the recitation of the *Shemah*. At the same time we go from the praise of God the Creator to that of God the Savior who has intervened in history to bring together the chosen people.

The transition from the *berakah* for visible light to the *berakah* for the invisible light of the *Torah* is promised by the mention of the Angels who unceasingly contemplate and praise the divine glory. This makes us aware that the two lights, visible and invisible, in the Jewish mind, are not separated and opposed as in the hellenistic notions. They are but two successive aspects of one reality into which we are only penetrating more profoundly.[33] For Judaism, faithful to biblical notions, the world, the creation of the unique God, is itself unique. The angelic world is not a world different from the material world. It is the same, although seen in its deepest or most exalted aspect. Or, better, if we may borrow an excellent expression of Newman's, what we call the visible world is but the fringe of a world the rest of which remains invisible for us.[34] Reciprocally as in the vision of the 6th chapter of Isaiah underlying the whole of this text, God himself is described as luminous in a sense which even though physical is not solely so. In the biblical and Jewish sense his

---

[32] D. H., pp. 50 ff.

[33] Vl. Lossky, in his book *The Vision of God* (London, 1963) shows very well what Eastern Christian tradition has preserved of this biblical and Jewish view.

[34] Cf. *Parochial and Plain Sermons*, vol. II and vol. IV, the two sermons for the feast of St. Michael.

glory is a radiation of his being which is reflected in all creation, visible as well as invisible.[35]   The higher Angels, the Seraphim, as their name indicates, are themselves products of a mysterious fire which is like a first reflection of the glowing hearth of the divine life, and the altar fire and sanctuary lamps act as a re-minder of it.   This fire recalls the illumination, the transfiguration of all things that is the product of the descent of the *Shekinah*, the divine presence, in the luminous cloud in which it is envel-oped.[36]   The glory given to God by the Seraphim's singing of the *Qedushah* is this reflection of divine glory returning to its source.   But in them it is a conscious reflection expressed in song, just as in God the igneous light is that of the Spirit expressed in the Word.   Man will be associated both with this revelation of glory and this glorification of praise responding to it, first by contemplating the visible light in creation, and then by making the conscious homage of the angelic *Qedushah* his own, thanks to the *Torah* he has received and accepted.

The second *berakah* develops this vision of the gift of the *Torah* and its acceptance, as a supreme act of divine love eliciting the reciprocal love of creatures for the one Holy One, the one Lord, whose lordship and holiness are those of love.   Hence the place given in this prayer to the heart, i.e. not the sense faculty but this core of man's whole being which is the loving intelligence, consumed by its adherence to the *Torah* in this knowledge of love which in man responds to that knowledge with which God has enveloped him.[37]   Moreover, this explains the place given by this same prayer to the divine fatherhood over Israel.

Dalman somewhat exaggerates when he states that the expres-sion "Our Father" is often applied to God in the prayers of the synagogue.[38]   This is true to a certain extent with the modern

[35] See the work of A. M. Ramsey, *The Glory of God and the Transfigura-tion of Christ* (London 1964).

[36] We once made a study of this notion in an article that appeared in *Bible et Vie chrétienne*.

[37] See the article καρδία in the *Theologisches Wörterbuch* of G. Kittel.

[38] See D. H., pp. 50 ff.

formulas but is less so in regard to the more ancient ones. On the other hand, there is no question that the insistence on this title, repeated twice in the climax of the *Ahabah* prayer, just before the recitation of the *Shemah*, is quite significant. These words addressed to God by Israel in such a context are far more than a formulation of a faith in a simple and commonplace adoption. They express the emergence of a faith in a genuine assimilation to his life, through his love creating our own, in the *Torah* given to believing hearts. Once again, and more now than ever, we find ourselves at this point on the brink, as it were, of evangelical revelation. And it is superfluous to conjure up some later Christian influence in order to account for the increased use of this expression "Our Father" in the Jewish liturgy. It must have been the natural result of a daily repetition and a constant meditation on the prayer we have just analyzed.

The *Qedushah* of the Seraphim, with its extension in the *berakah* of the Ophanim and the Hayoth, requires some special comment.

In the first place it must be pointed out that even in the time of *Amram Gaon* and probably for a very long time before, the *Qedushah* was not only sung at this point in the synagogue service, but in two other instances: before the third *berakah* of the *Tefillah* (as we shall see later), and after the reading from the Prophets which today comes at the end of the service.[39] Hence the classical distinction between the *Qedushah* of *Yozer* (the one which has its place in the prayer we have just studied), the *Qedushah* of the *Tefillah* and the *Qedushah* of *Sidrah*. The question has arisen as to whether the three recitations are all equally ancient, and if not, then which is the oldest? The majority of specialists (particularly Kohler and Ginzberg) consider the *Qedushah* of *Yozer* as certainly dating from the earliest antiquity. Elbogen is practically alone in holding another opinion and maintaining that the *Qedushah* of *Sidrah* is the most ancient. The argument is actually quite futile. What is sure is that the *Tannaim* already were familiar with the *Qedushah* of *Yozer* and considered it to be traditional, although they do not have such explicit re-

---

[39] See Hedegard's dissertation in D. H., pp. 47 ff.

ferences to the other two. The apocalyptic books attributed to
Henoch make the *Qedushah* the central element of heavenly worship, which they describe manifestly on the model of the synagogue worship as it was known to their authors.[40] From this Odeberg wanted to conclude—obviously wrongly—that in the beginning the *Shemah* itself would not have been the high point
of Synagogue worship, and could even have been absent from
it since this place originally belonged to the *Qedushah* of *Yozer*.[41]
Nevertheless, the rabbinical commentaries on *Yozer* underline
that this text presents the singing of the *Qedushah* by the angels
as the heavenly equivalent of the acceptance of the *Torah*, signified for the Israelites by the reciting of the *Shemah*.[42] In both
cases, the Kingdom of God is accomplished in the adoring and
loving acknowledgment on the part of creatures, and the entire
world becomes a harmony by attuning itself to God.

We must add that there are two zones or aspects of the spiritual
world corresponding to the angelic *Qedushah* and *berakah*. The
Qedushah, expressly associated with the leaders of the angelic
armies, represents the glorification of God in the heavenly world,
completely engrossed in and filled with his presence, either by
the Seraphim as in the vision of Isaiah or by the Archangels like
Michael or Gabriel whom later Jewish speculation tends to identify with them. The second chant brings to mind the initial vision of Ezekiel in an allusion to the spirits who sustain the visible universe: they are the four Cherubim or Hayoth, the "Living
Creatures," spirits of the element of the world (the στοιχεία
spoken of by St. Paul)[43] and the four Ophanim, the "Wheels" spang-
led with eyes, the spirits of the astral spheres. The song of these
other angelic spirits therefore expresses God's glory, no longer
considered in its inaccessible majesty as in the *Qedushah*, but in
its presence manifested in this world, especially in the Temple
of Jerusalem, the "place" where it dwells. This song which is

---

[40] Cf. H. Odeberg, *3 Enoch or the Hebrew Book of Enoch, edited and translated with Introduction, Commentary and critical Notes* (Cambridge, 1928),
pp. 184 ff. of the introduction.

[41] *Ibid.*

[42] Cf. the commentary of Odeberg on ch. XXXV, 6 of *3 Enoch*.

[43] Cf. Galatians 4: 3 and 9, and Colossians 2: 8 and 20.

presented by Ezekiel as the hymn of the Hayoth and the Ophanim
is an equivalent of the liturgical chant for the setting up of the
ark in the tabernacle mentioned in Numbers 10: 36. It is permissible to think that the *Qedushah* itself that Isaiah gives as the
song of the Seraphim must have already been a chant accompanying
the incense sacrifice in the Temple of his time, long before it was
taken into the prayer of the Synagogue.[44]

The importance of the themes of light and knowledge in all
these prayers must be emphasized.[45] At times people have wanted
to oppose Jewish piety to what is called hellenic mysticism, as
a spirituality of the Word nurturing life, opposed to a luminous
contemplation that satisfies knowledge alone.[46] It is beyond
question that the unfolding of the divine Word and the progressive
revelation of the God of Israel as the living God intervening in
the course of events to give life to those who hear him, are characteristics of biblical and Jewish religion. But the prayers we
have just examined and the biblical themes with which they are
woven give evidence that this unfolding of the Word of the living
God who gives life need not be opposed to a knowledge-light mysticism: one envelops the other both in Jewish piety and in the
Bible.

It is true that scholars have at times wanted to reduce these
developments of the igneous light theme in the Bible to late Ira-
nian influences. But to do so is to forget that possibly even the
latest of these developments of priestly themes, particularly the
divine presence in the luminous cloud, are connected with the
most archaic traditions of Israel concerning the Sinai covenant.[47]
The Lord who revealed himself to Moses on Horeb appears at
the very first as the God of the wild mountain where he revealed
himself in a thunderstorm in order to give the *Torah* of the covenant to his people. Similarly the "knowledge," explicitly a know-

---

[44] Cf. again what Odeberg says, *op. cit.*, p. 184.

[45] See our studies of these themes in Judaism and the New Testament in
our book *The Spirituality of the New Testament and the Fathers*.

[46] *Ibid.*

[47] Cf. our book *The Meaning of Sacred Scripture* (Notre Dame, 1958), the
chapter on Jewish mysticism, and in the second French edition, *La Bible
et l'Évangile* (Paris, 1953), the chapter on the problem of worship.

ledge of love, which is expressed in these *berakoth*, is evidently
the flower of the prophets' "knowledge of God." With these themes,
we therefore find ourselves at the heart of a Jewish mysticism
that remains basically biblical, even if it is true that we must expect from other texts, which we shall soon be examining, the
complementary aspects of Israel's piety where the Word and life
will come into the limelight.[48]

A final remark with regard to the *berakoth* preceding the *Shemah* should show how the last one of these, the *Ahabah*, already
manifests a tendency to pass from thanksgiving to supplication,
in order finally to return to praise in a brief doxology. This is
a movement which we have seen in the psalter and which reaches
its fulness in the *Tefillah* of the eighteen blessings. In accordance
with the last perspective of Israel's faith, the entire gift of God,
and most especially his love, has in one sense already been accorded us. Yet this gift is also awaiting its full eschatological
realization which will cause prayer to come to full flower in pure
praise forever. Supplication is therefore naturally introduced
to the praise itself, as a prayer that what is already the object
of praise may be accomplished fully so that this supplication
in its turn will be finally consumed in the praise from which it
proceeds.

We shall not dwell at this point on the *Shemah* since it was
to disappear in the Christian liturgy where, as we shall see, the
eucharistic banquet takes on its focal position. Let us simply
specify that the present three-part formula of the *Shemah*, adding
Deuteronomy 11: 13-21 and Numbers 15: 37-41 to Deuteronomy
6: 4-9, must have developed in three stages. It seems that the
first citation alone was already part of the Temple service from
which it must have passed over into the Synagogue service. The
two others were added in turn. A parallel development must
have followed for the concluding prayer that was added to it,
the *Gehullah* as it is called today in reference to the third citation, since each of its parts corresponds to each of the three
biblical texts to the point of quoting expressions from them.

[48] Cf. below, p. 78 ff.

On the other hand, in the beginning, at least in the Synagogue worship if not in the Temple, Deuteronomy 6: 4-9 was preceded by the recitation of the ten commandments. Their disappearance is another result of anti-Christian polemics, which is at least hinted at in the *Berakoth* tractate (12a) of the *Mishnah*. Undoubtedly there was the wish to counter the Christians' assertion that only the decalogue had any permanent importance among the legal prescriptions.[49]

THE *TEFILLAH* OF THE *SHEMONEH ESREH*

After the *Shemah* and the following prayer, which purposes merely to impress its meaning on the mind of the faithful, there comes the *Tefillah* of the 18 blessings (*Shemoneh Esreh*). Its name itself signifies that it is *the* prayer *par excellence*. It is actually the formula which gave gradual definition to the totality of the objects of prayer to which the Israelite was commanded and obliged to give his full attention.

Although basically a prayer of supplication (the substantive *tefillah* like the verb *hithpalpel* in rabbinical Hebrew is only used for this type of prayer), it is considered to be a series of "blessings" because three proper *berakoth* precede it and three others follow its twelve petitions. Furthermore each of these concludes with a short *berakah*. The *tefillah* has come down to us in two forms Babylonian and Jerusalemite. It is the Babylonian one that is given in the *Seder Amram Gaon* and which we shall reproduce. The Jerusalemite recension was edited for the first time by Salomon Schechter.[50] Which of the two most closely corresponds to the usage at the time of Christ is still being argued. But this dispute is perhaps not as important as might be thought. Even Abudharam pointed out that there were no two Jewish communities of his time where it was recited in exactly the same words.[51] Of the great prayers of the Synagogue, it seems actually to have been the one which in the details of its formulation retained for

[49] Cf. D. H., pp. 52-53.
[50] Cf. D. H., pp. 70 ff.
[51] *Ibid.*

the longest time the greatest elasticity, as is the case today in the Churches of Byzantine rite with the *ektenias* which seem, as we shall see, to have been directly derived from the *Tefillah*. Still, the content of these eighteen (or now nineteen) prayers became fixed at a very early date, as is evidenced by the abundant and manifold commentaries to which they have given rise in rabbinical literature.[52]

Contrary to the *berakoth* before the *Shemah*, it has always been the role of the *hazan* (like the deacon for the Christian *ektenias*) to recite them, standing before the ark of the Scriptures and facing Jerusalem.[53] But custom demands even today that the *hazan*, along with each of the faithful, recite it first mentally in silence, before he alone chants it from beginning to end. The faithful then answer *Amen* after each *berakah*, and the *Qedushah* is again sung between the second and third *berakoth* preceded by an introductory prayer of which we know three different forms.[54]

It seems certain that originally the period of quiet which préceded the recitation aloud was not accompanied by a first recitation in a low voice but by individual silent prayers, inspired by the familiar themes of the public prayer that was to follow, but without any special required formula. The disciples' request of Jesus to "teach them to pray" ($\pi\varrho o\sigma\varepsilon\acute{v}\chi\varepsilon\sigma\theta\alpha\iota$, usual translation of *hithpalpel*) seems precisely to be aimed at this personal *tefillah*, and the Lord's Prayer appears to constitute its synthetic formulation.[55] Later we shall return to this point. Here are the three initial *berakoth* as found in the *Seder Amram Gaon*, following the Babylonian tradition, with the *Qedushah* and its most solemn introduction which seems also to be the most ancient.

They are preceded by an introductory verse which was to pass over into the daily Christian office:

JHWH, open my lips,
and my mouth shall declare thy praise!

The three initial *berakoth* follow immediately:

---

[52] *Ibid.*
[53] D. H., p. 6.
[54] D. H., p. 114.
[55] Cf. D. H., p. 70.

1. (*Aboth*) Blessed be thou, JHWH, our God and God of our fathers, God of Abraham, God of Isaac and God of Jacob, the great, mighty and revered God, the most high God, who bestowest lovingkindness, possessest all things and rememberest the pious deeds of the fathers, and wilt bring a redeemer to their children's children for thy name's sake, in love, King, Helper, Saviour and Shield. Blessed be thou, JHWH, the Shield of Abraham.

2. (*Geburoth*) Thou art mighty forever, JHWH, thou quickenest the dead, thou art mighty to save, and thou causest the dew to fall (who causest the wind to blow and the rain to fall), who sustainest the living with lovingkindness, quickenest the dead with great mercy, supportest the falling, healest the sick, loosest them that are bound and keepest faith to them that sleep in the dust. Who is like unto thee, Lord of mighty acts, and who resembleth thee, King, who killest and quickenest and causest salvation to spring forth. And faithful art thou to quicken the dead, Blessed be thou, JHWH, who quickenest the dead.

(*Keter*) Unto thee shall the multitudes above with all the gatherings below give a crown,[56] all with one accord shall thrice repeat the holy praise unto thee, according to what is said through the prophet: *and one cried unto another and said*: HOLY, HOLY, HOLY IS JHWH OF HOSTS, THE WHOLE EARTH IS FULL OF HIS GLORY. Then with noise of great rushing, mighty and strong, they make their voices heard, and upraising themselves towards them, they say: BLESSED, BLESSED BE THE GLORY OF JHWH FROM HIS PLACE.

From thy place shine forth, our King, and reign over us, for we wait upon thee. When wilt thou reign? Reign in Zion speedily, even in our days and in our lives do thou dwell (there). Mayest thou be magnified and sanctified in the midst of Jerusalem thy city throughout all generations and to all eternity. And let our eyes behold thy kingdom, according to the word that was spoken in the songs of thy might by David, thy righteous anointed: JHWH shall reign for ever, thy God, Zion, unto all generations. Hallelujah.

---

[56] We are reminded of the "elders" of Revelation throwing down their crowns before God (4: 10).

3. (*Qedushat ha-Shem*) From generation to generation give homage to God for he alone is high and holy, and thy praise, our God, shall not depart from our mouth for ever, for a great and holy king art thou. Blessed be thou JHWH, thou holy God.[57]

The first *berakah* is therefore a commemoration of the Fathers with whom the covenant was made, essentially Abraham and the patriarchs (hence the name *Aboth*, "Fathers" which is given to it). At the same time it is an act of thanksgiving anticipating the future coming of the Messiah who will redeem their children.

The second (*Geburoth*) goes on to give thanks for life and its fecundity; similarly it unfolds into a blessing for the hoped for resurrection.

The third (the *Qedushat ha-Shem*) can be considered as *the* blessing, for it is the blessing of the divine Name, revealed to the fathers and kept upon the lips of the sons. Hence the solemnity of its introduction, with the chant of the *Qedushah*. In the divine Name it is actually God in person who communicates himself to his people, above and beyond all of his gifts.

After these we come to the twelve (now thirteen) prayers.

4. (*Binah*) Thou favourest man with knowledge and teachest a human being understanding. Favour us with knowledge, understanding and discernment from thee. Blessed be thou, JHWH, who graciously bestowest knowledge.

5. (*Teshubah*) Cause us to return, our Father, unto thy Torah, and draw us near, our King, unto thy service, and bring us back in perfect repentance before thee. Blessed be thou, JHWH, who delightest in repentance.

6. (*Selishah*) Forgive us, our Father, for we have sinned; pardon us, our King, for we have transgressed, for thou art good and forgiving. Blessed be thou, JHWH, who art gracious and dost abundantly forgive.

7. (*Geullah*) Look upon our affliction and plead our cause, and redeem us speedily for thy Name's sake; for thou art a mighty Redeemer. Blessed be thou, JHWH, the Redeemer of Israel.

---

[57] D. H., pp. 83 ff. for the first three "blessings", and pp. 114 ff. for the *Qedushah* and its introduction (*Keter*).

8. (*Refnah*) Heal us, JHWH, and we shall be healed; save us and we shall be saved, and grant a perfect healing to all our wounds; for thou, God, art a merciful Physician. Blessed be thou, JHWH, who healest the sick of thy people Israel.

9. (*Birkat ha-shanim*) Bless this year unto us, JHWH, our God for (our) welfare (and give dew and rain for blessing upon the face of the earth, and wind on the land, and satisfy the whole world by thy goodness and fill our hands from thy blessings and from the riches of the gifts of thy hands, and watch and rescue this year from all evil and from all destruction and from all calamity, and make it a hope, and let the end of it be peace. Spare us, and have mercy upon us and upon all the produce of it, and upon all the fruits of it, and bless it like (good) years with blessing of dew, and life, and plenty, and peace). Blessed be thou, JHWH, who blessest the years.

10. (*Qibbus galuyoth*) Sound the great horn for our freedom, and lift up the ensign, to gather our exiles, and proclaim liberty to gather us from the four quarters of the earth to our land. Blessed be thou, JHWH, who gatherest the dispersed of thy people Israel.

11. (*Birkat mishpat*) Restore our judges as at the first, and our counsellors as at the beginning, and reign thou alone over us, JHWH, in grace and mercy and righteousness and judgment. Blessed be thou, JHWH, the King who lovest righteousness and judgment.

12. (*Birkat ha-minim*) And for the slanderers let there be no hope, and let all the wicked perish in a moment and let all our enemies be speedily cut off, and the dominion of arrogance do thou speedily uproot and crush and humble in our days. Blessed be thou, JHWH, who breakest the wicked and humblest the arrogant.

13. (*Birkat saddiqim*) Towards the righteous and the pious and the true proselytes may thy mercies be stirred, JHWH, our God, and grant a good reward unto all who faithfully trust in thy name and set our portion with them, so that we may never be put to shame. Blessed be thou, JHWH, the stay and trust of the righteous.

14. (*Birkat Yerushalem*) To Jerusalem, thy city, return in mercy, and dwell in it as thou hast spoken; and rebuild

it as an everlasting building in our days. Blessed be thou, JHWH, who rebuildest Jerusalem.

15. (*Birkat David*) Speedily cause the offspring of David to flourish, and let his horn be exalted by thy salvation, because we wait for thy salvation all the day. Blessed be thou, JHWH, who causest the horn of salvation to flourish.

16. (*Tefillah*) Hear our voice, JHWH, have mercy upon us and accept our prayer in mercy and favour; for thou art a God who hearkenest unto our prayers and supplications: from thy presence, our King, turn us not empty away, for thou hearkenest to the prayer of every mouth. Blessed be thou, JHWH, who hearkenest unto prayer.[58]

The first prayer (called *Binah*, "understanding" or *Dehah'* "Knowledge," or *Birkat Hokmah*, "blessing of wisdom," echoing the blessing of the Name which precedes it) is quite naturally a prayer for the "knowledge of God." It obviously is first directed toward the knowledge of the Torah, the divine exigencies over man. But in this context it is clear that the knowledge of the Torah and of God himself are but one. It is a question of reaching this relationship of mutual intimacy which his revelation is aimed at producing, with the result that the Torah imprints the seal of the divine Name upon us, and that the sanctification of the Name sanctifies us by its own holiness.

The following prayer (*Teshubah*) is a prayer of repentance, or more precisely an entreaty that God himself grant us repentance, this *teshubah* which may also be translated as a return (to God), a conversion.

The third (*Selichah*, "pardon") consequently begs for forgiveness.

The fourth (*Geullah*, "redemption") then asks for redemption, i.e. the deliverance from the tribulations which have befallen the people on account of their sins. The Talmud sees an allusion here to the eschatological redemption by the expected Messiah.[59] Raschi, on the contrary, explains it as the present deliverance from particular evils that may be plaguing the faithful.[60] Zunz's

---

[58] D. H., pp. 87 ff.
[59] *Mishnah*, tractate *Megillah*, 17b.
[60] *Ad loc.*, in his *Commentaire du Talmud babylonien*.

supposition[61] that it was introduced at a time of national distress, either under Antiochus IV or perhaps later under Pompey, may undoubtedly be retained. Following this there is a plea for good weather during the year (the *Birkat ha-shanim*, "prayer for the years"—"good years" being understood), abundant harvests, and more generally "peace" (the Hebrew *shalom* includes material prosperity in this idea).

Then follows the *Qibbus galuyoth* (the gathering of the exiles) which is a prayer for the bringing together of the exiles of the whole diaspora of Israel.

Then comes the *Birkat mishpat* (the prayer for righteousness) which is a prayer for the authorities, asking that they be faithful to the divine will, so that the reign of the Lord over his people will be assured.

It is after this and prior to a prayer for proselytes that the *berakah* was introduced as a later addition which brought the number of traditional "blessings" from eighteen up to nineteen. It is the famous prayer against the apostates and slanderers of the people of Israel. These *minim* are certainly the Christians, especially the Jewish Christians, and all those among the Jewish people who were in league with them or thought to be. The formulas are more variable than any of the others, probably in part because of the censure that the Christian authorities could bring against it, or, simply out of fear of such a censure.[62]

The *Birkat saddiqim*, a prayer for the "righteous," is in fact a prayer conceived for the proselytes who have decided to become members of the people of God.

The *Birkat Yerushalem* which follows it is obviously, since the year 70 of our era, aimed at the rebuilding of Jerusalem which Titus has destroyed. But, as Abrahams points out,[63] the original formulas must have focused not on the rebuilding but on the building of Jerusalem and on her perpetual possession of the divine presence.

---

[61] *Die gottesdienstlichen Vorträge der Juden*, 2nd ed., (Frankfurt-am-Main, 1892) p. 381.
[62] Cf. D. H., p. 94.
[63] Abrahams, *op. cit.*, p. LXV.

After this the *Birkat David* expressly implores the coming of the Davidic Messiah.

A last and particularly solemn petition to which the name *Tefillah* ("prayer" par excellence) is given, together with the whole eighteen, beseeches God to hear all the prayers of Israel.

From here we come to the three final blessings where the theme of praise again becomes dominant.

17. (*Abodah*) Accept, JHWH, our God, thy people Israel and their prayer and restore the service to the Holy of Holies of thy house and receive speedily in love and favour the fire-offerings of Israel and their prayer, and may the service of thy people Israel ever be acceptable unto thee, and let our eyes behold thy return to Zion in mercy. Blessed be thou, JHWH, who restorest thy Presence to Zion.

18. (*Hodah*) We give thanks unto thee, our God and the God of our fathers; thou art the Rock of our lives, the Shield of our salvation through every generation. We will give thanks unto thee and declare thy praise for our lives which are committed unto thy hand, and for our souls which are in thy charge. Thou art all-good for thy mercies fail not, thou art merciful for thy lovingkindnesses never cease, we have ever hoped in thee. And bring us not to shame, JHWH, our God, abandon us not and hide not thy face from us, and for all thy name be blessed and exalted, our King, for ever and ever. Everything that liveth should thank thee, Selah, and praise thy name, All-good, in truth. Blessed be thou, JHWH, whose name is all-good, and unto whom it is becoming to give thanks.

19. (*Birkat kohanim*) Grant peace, welfare, blessing, lovingkindness and mercy unto us and unto all Israel, thy people, and bless us, our Father, even all of us together, with the light of thy countenance; for by the light of thy countenance thou hast given us, JHWH, our God, the Torah of life, love and grace, and righteousness and mercy, and may it be good in thy sight to bless thy people Israel in mercy at all times. Blessed be thou, JHWH, who blessest thy people Israel with peace.[64]

---

[64] D. H., pp. 96 ff.

Although the first of these last three *berakoth* does not begin with the classic formula "blessed be thou ...," it is considered to be a *berakah* of praise, for its sole object is the praise of God by Israel. It is called *Abodah*, "service" and it is generally admitted that it proceeds directly from the prayer that was recited in the temple of Jerusalem for the daily offering of the holocaust.[65] Later it was revised so that it could be applied to the restoration of the sacrifices interrupted by Titus.

It is followed by a prayer called *Hodah*, "thanksgiving" in a pre-eminent sense, for it sums up all the motives of the blessing of the Lord in a final doxology.

The last *berakah* is merely a preparation for the Aaronic blessing which in the beginning must have closed the service.[66]

We have already pointed out the close kinship between the first three petitions of the Our Father and the *Qaddish* which (in the beginning) concluded the scripture readings. We may now add that both are a kind of expansion of the principal initial *berakah*, the one which focuses on the Name. The rest of the Our Father seems in turn to be a kind of summary of the twelve central petitions. But we must still consider two facts which arise from the discussions of the Rabbis. The first is that the recitation of the Eighteen Blessings was required for everyone each day only by the school of Gamaliel (contemporary to the time of Christ). The second is that up to that time these Eighteen Blessings were used only during the week.[67] On the Sabbath and on holy days there was a formulary of only seven blessings. It seems that it is precisely in this framework that the version of the Our Father in St. Matthew's gospel, with its seven verses, is intended to be taken.[68]

THE MEAL *BERAKOTH*

We still have to examine another series of Jewish prayers whose importance for a study of the ancient eucharist is especially evi-

---

[65] Cf. I. Elbogen, *Studien zur Geschichte des jüdischen Gottesdienstes* (Berlin, 1907), p. 55.

[66] Numbers 6: 24-26.

[67] Cf. D. H., p. 67.

[68] Cf. Matthew 6: 9 ff.

dent: the meal liturgy. In principle, it was required, for every Jewish meal, even if it were merely a simple individual collation. But it took on its greatest importance in the family meals, especially the holy day meals, such as at Passover. We have already had occasion to say that in the Jewish communities, like Qumrân, it came to take on the place and significance of the ancient sacrifices. According to many modern exegetes such as Pedersen, the Passover meal in primitive Israel was probably the only sacrifice.[69] Similarly, since the community meal brought together in the expectation of the messianic banquet mentioned by the prophets, the "remnant" which thought of itself as forming the kernel of the future and eternal Israel, that meal became the supreme and unique sacrifice. On the other hand, it must be pointed out that the meal prayers, and particularly the great act of thanksgiving that ends the meal, have always been looked upon by the Jews as being especially venerable. The Rabbis attributed a legendary antiquity to them.[70] Yet even if there is some exaggeration here, these prayers are certainly among the most ancient of the Jewish rituals that have come down to us. Louis Finkelstein, who devoted a particularly thought-provoking study to them, observes with reason that this family liturgy was as important in sustaining the community religious life in Israel as the Synagogue service itself.[71]

The obligatory prelude of the meal was the ritual hand-washing with which the Jews also began their day. Then, in a ceremonial meal, each person upon arriving drank a first cup of wine, repeating for himself this following blessing:

> Blessed be thou, JHWH, our God, King of the universe, who givest us this fruit of the vine.[72]

This is the first cup mentioned by St. Luke in his account of the Last Supper, and which proved such an embarrassment to

[69] Cf. J. Pedersen, "Passahfeste und Passahlegende", in *Zeitschrift für alttestamentliche Wissenschaft*, LII (1934), pp. 161 ff.

[70] Cf. D. H., p. 139.

[71] Louis Finkelstein, "The Birkat Ha-Mazon", in *Jewish Quarterly Review*, New Series, vol. XIX (1928-1929), pp. 211 ff.

[72] *Mishnah*, tractate *Berakoth*, VI, 1 and *Toseftah*, tractate *Berakoth*, IV, 8.

the Christian exegetes who knew nothing about the Jewish meals.[73]
The words of Jesus cited by Luke in this regard on the fruit of
the vine which he would no longer drink with his disciples before
they met again in the Kingdom, are a transparent allusion to
this formula.

But the meal did not officially begin until the father of the
family or the presiding member of the community had broken
the bread which was to be given to the participants, with this
blessing:

> Blessed be thou, JHWH, our God, King of the universe, who
> bringest forth bread from the earth.[74]

It was looked upon as a general blessing for the whole meal
that was to follow, and no one who arrived later was allowed to
partake.

The courses and the cups of wine then followed, and each person
in turn pronounced a series of appropriate blessings. The Passover meal was distinguished simply by special foods, bitter herbs
and the lamb, which were used together with the special corresponding prayers and the dialogued recitation of the *haggadah*,
i.e. a kind of traditional homily on the origin and the ever fresh
sense of the feast.[75] We shall have occasion to speak again further
on about this *haggadah*.

In every case, however, the essential ritual act came at the end
of the meal. About that time, in the holy day meals celebrated
on the eve (like our first Vespers), the lamp was brought in, normally by the mother of the family who had prepared and lighted
it.[76] It was blessed in turn by a blessing that recalled the creation of the luminaries to light up the night.[77] This is the origin
of the ancient Christian use of the *lucernarium*, which has survived in our own day in the blessing of the paschal candle. Following this incense was burned with a proper blessing.[78] Then

---

[73] Cf. Luke 22, 17-18.
[74] Cf. the first reference of note 72 and D. H., p. 144.
[75] Cf. J. Jeremias, *The Eucharistic Words of Jesus*, p. 58.
[76] *Mishnah*, tractate *Berakoth*, VIII, 5 and 6.
[77] *Ibid.*
[78] *Mishnah*, tractate *Berakoth*, VI, 6.

a second general hand-washing took place; the one who presided received the water first from the hands of a servant, or in his absence from the youngest at the table.[79]

This explains to us the scene described by the fourth evangelist.[80] Probably in this function John, brought water to Jesus, who, conveying in an expressive gesture the teaching of humble love that he wanted to give his disciples, took the ewer from his hands, and beginning with Peter, who was considered the most worthy after himself, washed not the hands but the feet of his disciples.

It is after these various preliminaries that the president, with the cup of wine mixed with water before him, solemnly invited those assisting to join in with his act of thanksgiving.

"Let us give thanks to the Lord our God," he said, bowing over in the case where the assembly included the minimum number of participants to be equivalent to a Synagogue congregation (ten in principle).[81] They then answered him in a similar vein:

Blessed be he whose generosity has given us food
and whose kindness has given us life.

The Jerusalem Talmud assures us that this dialogue goes back at least to the time of Simon ben Shetah, who lived under Alexander Jannaeus—103 to 67 B.C.[82]

The president then chanted a series of *berakoth* which number four in all the *siddurim*, beginning with the *Seder Amram Gaon*.[83] But the *Mishnah* knows only the first three, and the rabbinical commentaries date the fourth from the rebellion of Bar Kochba.[84] We shall therefore limit ourselves to the study of the first three which were certainly used by Christ and seem to be quite anterior to the Christian era. According to the *Berakoth* tractate of the *Mishnah*, the first would go back to Moses, the second to

---

[79] Cf. D. H., p. 145.
[80] John 13: 3 ff.
[81] D. H., p. 146.
[82] *Mishnah*, tractate *Berakoth*, VII, 2.
[83] Cf. D. H., p. 139.
[84] *Ibid.*

Joshua and the third to David and Solomon.[85] As Dembitz has
pointed out, this means only that from then on their origin was
immemorial.[86] Finkelstein established that the third must go
back to the second century B.C., while the first two could be still
older.[87]

Neither the *Mishnah* nor the *Toseftah* give us the complete
text, which is not to be found before the *Seder Amram Gaon*. But
they multiply allusions to the content of the formulas from the
earliest times, which act as a guarantee for us of the substantial
conformity between the text still in use today and the ancient
practice.

"Blessed be thou, JHWH, our God, King of the universe, who
feedest the world with goodness, with grace and mercy, who
givest food to all flesh for thou nourishest and sustainest
all beings and providest food for all thy creatures. Blessed
be thou, JHWH, who givest food unto all.

"We thank thee, JHWH, our God, for a desirable, good and
ample land which thou was pleased to give to our fathers,
and for thy covenant which thou hast marked in our flesh,
and for the Torah which thou hast given us, and for life,
grace, mercy and food which thou hast lent us in every season.
And for all this, JHWH, our God, we thank thee and bless thy
name. Blessed be thy name upon us continually and for
ever. Blessed be thou, JHWH, for the land and for the food.

"Have mercy, JHWH, our God, upon thy people Israel,
upon thy city Jerusalem, upon Zion, the abiding place of
thy glory, upon the kingdom of the house of David thine
anointed, and upon the great and holy house that was called
by thy name. Feed us, nourish us, sustain us, provide for
us, relieve us speedily from our anxieties, and let us not stand
in need of the gifts of mortals, for their gifts are small and
their reproach is great, for we have trusted in thy holy, great
and fearful name. And may Elijah and the Messiah, the son
of David come in our life-time, and let the kingdom of the
house of David return to its place, and reign thou over us,

---

[85] *Ibid.*

[86] L. N. Dembitz, *Jewish Services in Synagogue and Home* (Philadelphia,
1898), p. 435.

[87] *Op. cit.*, pp. 220 ff.

thou alone, and save us for thy name's sake, and bring us
up in it and gladden us in it and comfort us in Zion thy city.
Blessed be thou, JHWH, who rebuildest Jerusalem."[88]

The first of these *berakoth*, as is emphasized by the Jewish commentators, is a blessing for nourishment received and it grows
into a cosmic blessing for all of creation, especially the continued
creation of life.[89]

Starting with the fact that the food of the Israelite is the fruit
of the promised land, the second is a blessing for this promised
country. Parallel to the first, it opens out into a blessing for the
covenant, sealed by circumcision and the gift of the Torah.[90] Thus
it becomes a blessing for the whole history of salvation. In fact,
in the formulas of the *siddurim* that are in use today, to the mention of the land, the covenant and the Torah, is joined the deliverance from Egypt.[91] This is not found explicitly in Amram
Gaon, nor in the somewhat later text of Saadia Gaon, but it can
be already observed in the *Machzor Vitry* of Rabbi Semchah
ben Samuel (ca. 1100 AD).[92]

The third *berakah* is a supplication that the creative and redemptive action of God in olden times be continued and renewed
today, and that it find its ultimate fulfilment in the coming of
the Messiah and the final establishment of the Kingdom of God.
Here we see the full development of this tendancy, noticeable
in all the extended *berakoth*, to be prolonged into a prayer for
the accomplishment of the divine works which are the object
of praise, before returning to the note of praise in the final doxology. The end of the prayer, with its allusion to a Jerusalem
rebuilt, may bear the mark of a Judaism that is posterior to the
catastrophe of the year 70. But here again the remark made in
regard to the fourth blessing of the *Tefillah* is applicable: the

---

[88] D. H., pp. 147 ff.

[89] Cf. J. H. Hertz, *The Authorised Daily Prayer-Book of the United Hebrew
Congregations of the British Empire*, vol. III (London, 1945), pp. 968 ff.

[90] Cf. D. H., p. 147.

[91] Cf. Singer, *op. cit.*, p. 280.

[92] Cf. *Machzor Vitry*, par. 83 (S. Hurwitz, ed., Berlin 1923). The same thing
in Maimonides, cf. S. Baer, *Seder Abodat Israel* (Jerusalem, 1927), p. 555.

idea of the construction of Jerusalem which is to be continued
until the fulness of messianic times is a fully traditional Jewish
idea. The Christian notion of the Church's continually being
built until the parouisa merely transposes it.

We must add that the *Seder Amram Gaon*, in conformity with
the oldest rabbinical tradition, prescribes certain variations in
the third *berakah*, either for the Sabbath or for a high holy day.[93]

The festive form is especially noteworthy, and all the more so
because it is the object of very specific allusions in the *Toseftah*.[94]
After the petition for the kingdom of the house of David to return to its place, it introduces this passage:

> "Our God, and the God of our fathers, may the remembrance
> of ourselves and of our fathers and the remembrance of Je-
> rusalem, thy city, and the remembrance of the Messiah, the
> son of David, thy servant, and the remembrance of thy people,
> the whole house of Israel, arise and come, come to pass, be
> seen and accepted and heard, be remembered and be men-
> tioned before thee for deliverance, for good, for grace, for
> lovingkindness and for mercy on this such and such a day.
> Remember us, JHWH, our God, on it for good and visit us on
> it for blessing and save us on it unto life by a word of salvation
> and mercy, and spare, favour and show us mercy, for thou
> art a gracious and merciful God and King."

What is remarkable in this text is the so abundant use made
of the term memorial (in Hebrew: *zikkaron*). It is impossible to
imagine a better confirmation than this text for the thesis already so solidly established by Jeremias in his book on the eucharistic words of Jesus.[95] The "memorial" here is not merely
a simple commemoration. It is a sacred sign, given by God to
his people who preserve it as their pre-eminent spiritual treasure.
This sign or pledge implies a continuity, a mysterious permanence
of the great divine actions, the *mirabilia Dei* commemorated by
the holy days. For it is for the Lord himself a permanent attestation of his fidelity to himself. It is therefore the basis for

---

[93] D. H., pp. 151 ff.

[94] Tractate *Berakoth*, III, 49 a. For the text, D. H., p. 152.

[95] *Op. cit.*, pp. 237 ff. See also B. S. Childs, *Memory and Tradition in Israel*
(Naperville, Ill., 1962).

a trusting supplication that the unfailing power of the Word which produced the *mirabilia Dei* renew them and accompany them in the present. It is in this sense that the "memory" of the divine actions which the people have kept faithfully can urge Adonai to "remember" his people. For our subjective commemoration is merely the reflection of an objective commemoration, established by God, which first of all bears witness to himself of his own fidelity. Hence this prayer formula, which is so characteristic and which was to pass over from the Synagogue into the Church: "Remember us, O Lord."

The meaningful expressions petitioning that "the remembrance of thy people, the whole house of Israel, arise and come, come to pass, be seen and accepted and heard, be remembered and mentioned before thee for deliverance, for good, for grace, for lovingkindness and for mercy on such and such a day ..." underline the objective character rightly attributed by Jeremias to the memorial understood in this sense. A pledge given by God to his faithful, precisely so that they will re-present it to him as the homage of their faith in his fidelity, and in thus becoming the basis of their supplication, the "memorial" therefore becomes, as Max Thurian emphasizes, a superior form of sacrifice,—the sacrifice that it fully integrated in the Word and the act of thanksgiving which it arouses as a response.

Nothing proves this better than the fact that this "memorial" formula was added similarly to the *Abodah* prayer, which originally consecrated the Temple sacrifices. Hence the sacrificial character attributed to the communal meal.[96] In blessing God for its meal and in acknowledging in it through this *berakah* the memorial of the *mirabilia Dei* of creation and redemption, the community acknowledges it as the efficacious sign of the perpetual actuality within itself of these *mirabilia*, and still more precisely of their eschatological accomplishment in its favor. The prayer for everything which leads to this accomplishment finds here the assurance of a pledge. In "acknowledging" the inexhaustible power of the Word that creates and saves, the faith of Israel, we may say, becomes one with its object. The people here

---

[96] Cf. J. H. Hertz, *op. cit.*, p 148 and p. 972.

is itself consecrated to the accomplishment of the divine plan, while it welcomes it in a mysterious and real anticipation.[97] Here we have, the source as it were both of the Christian notion of the eucharistic sacrifice, and more generally, of the efficaciousness of the sacraments, as this was understood by the first Christian generations. As we shall see, the sacramental-sacrificial power of the eucharist will actually find the basic development of its expression in this third *berakah*, which has become the eucharistic anamnesis, together with its further extension in what will be called the epiclesis.

In close correlation with all of this a final question must be raised in regard to the *berakoth* of the liturgical tradition of the Synagogue.

It has been asked whether the use of the word "blessing" to translate *berakah* might not possibly involve a misconstruction. By blessing (cf. the blessings of the Roman ritual) we have come to understand a prayer that a grace be given to the blessed person or, if it is a thing, that a grace be attached to the object's use. In both cases the object of "to bless" is a creature. On the other hand, as has been pointed out, "to bless," *barak* in the Hebrew *berakoth* has never any object other than God. The blessing is addressed to him not so that he will send his grace on us or on our goods but in order to thank him for them, to relate ourselves to him in a basically disinterested perspective.

This remark includes an observation of incontestable correctness. Yet we should not make it too rigid, nor even less draw too systematic consequences from it.

In the first place, we should point out that there are abundant examples in biblical usage where *barak* "to bless," has creation as its object, or in any case men. We need only think of Jacob's exclamation in his nocturnal struggle with the Angel: "I will not let you go, unless you bless me,"[98] or again in that very typical episode where the same Jacob supplants Esau in order to get

---

[97] Cf. Max Thurian, *The Eucharistic Memorial* (Richmond, 1960-61), pp. 18 ff.
[98] Genesis 32: 26.

his father's blessing for himself.[99] Many other analogous cases could be cited. But the most important is that of the Aaronic blessing:

> The Lord bless you and keep you:
> The Lord make his face to shine upon you, and be
>   gracious unto you:
> The Lord lift up his countenance upon you,
>   and give you peace.[100]

Let us recall that its repetition, ends the *Tefillah*. There is no question that the blessing is understood here as a prayer of a very special kind, reserved, it seems, to a man of God, a priest, a father or a spiritual teacher. Through it he is thought able to obtain from God a special grace for the one who is the object of the blessing with an authority that is in some way guaranteed by God himself.

On the other hand, the twelve central *berakoth* of the *Tefillah* even if it is true that the theocentric blessing concludes them in the sense of praise and thanksgiving, are first of all and directly prayers of blessing in the sense that we understand this word today. They are actually prayers aimed at obtaining a definite grace for certain men, and precisely in this case at blessing certain specific elements (some of which are purely temporal, such as food, welfare, peace) or, if we prefer, at blessing these men in and through these created realities.

What is true, in the view of the most evolved Judaism where the most profound action of the divine Word has been explicated is that there is no blessing which does not refer back to God from the very first and return to him ultimately. Any creature is blessed for our use and man himself is blessed in all that he does only if everything goes back to God as the principle of all man's actions, of his whole life, in order to acknowledge that everything comes from God alone, and that he preserves a sovereign power over all things. Nor will the blessing reach its full development without a consecration of man's whole being to God, together with all the beings with which his life is associated. This conse-

[99] Genesis 27.
[100] Numbers 6: 24-26.

cration will reach its climax in an ultimate homage in which all
things will be brought together and in a certain sense absorbed
in pure doxology.

In spite of this it is, however, a characteristic line of development of the *berakoth*, unfolding in prayers of supplication,
to arrive precisely at this point. What remains true is that their
supplication itself proceeds from the act of thanksgiving, from
the confession of the one divine kingship. And the supplication
also tends to pervade everything and to immerse everything in
this confession and consecration. Again, there is no consecration either of man or the world except in the free "acknowledgement" by man of God's sovereignty which is at the very foundation of creation.

This certainly excludes any magical deviation which would
reduce a blessing to the infusion of a power into an object which
man might use or enjoy as a master. Nor does this any less exclude all idea, even apparently more spiritualized, of a blessing
of man which would be aimed at something other than his own
good. But, from the authentic biblical view of the best of Judaism, this does not involve any sort of quietistic "disinterest."
Quite the contrary is true. It is one of the most basic convic-
tions of Jewish piety and of the Bible that man will find his total
happiness, even his physical happiness, in the unreserved adhesion to God's will through his exclusive consecration to his
glory alone. There is no blessing of man or of the world except
in an act of thanksgiving, a homage of praise and confession,
that turns all things solely to God. But this is indeed the most
substantial blessing conceivable for man and for the world in
which God has placed him.

THE DIFFERENT STRUCTURES OF THE CHRISTIAN EUCHARIST

Before concluding this chapter, we must make one further observation which will appear as of the utmost importance for the
rest of our study. It involves the respective structure of the two
groups of *berakoth* which have just been studied: that of the Synagogue service and that of the meals. In this latter case we have
three *berakoth*. The first concerns creation, and more especially

the creation of life. The second refers to redemption, brought to mind by the promised land whose fruits have just been eaten. The third develops the *berakah*, which is most precisely a praise of God for his *mirabilia* that have already been accomplished, into a supplication for the eschatological fulfilment of the people of God in that Kingdom where he will ever be praised for the definitive building of Jerusalem.

It is obvious that the two *berakoth* before the *Shemah* and the following *Tefillah* present a development that is closely connected with the latter. The first of these other *berakoth* is also "blessing" for creation, and in this case for the creation of light whether visible or invisible ("knowledge"). In turn, the second is a "blessing" for redemption which this time is concretized in the gift of the Torah. The totality of the "eighteen" blessings similarly represents, although this time by a series of detailed intercessions, a development of the *berakah* for past gifts into an entreaty for future gifts, considered as the continuation and the fulfilment of the *mirabilia* commemorated in praise. But here, just as in the third meal *berakah*, despite the multiplicity of objects which it now includes, the prayer is still unified in the dominant idea of the building of Jerusalem which is to be fully accomplished in the eschatological kingdom. And it is in this light that the prayer of supplications returns once again to a prayer of praise in the final doxology.

For simplicity's sake, we may use letters for each of these prayers. A for the first *berakah* before the *Shemah*, B for the second and C for the whole *Tefillah*. In the same way we shall call the three final meal *berakoth* respectively D, E, and F. The point we are going to make, then, is that A is parallel to D, B to E and C to F, while the development ABC constitutes an organic whole by itself parallel to what happens with DEF.

If, as we shall see, the development of the primitive Christian liturgy seems to have come about within a framework inherited from the Jewish liturgy, we can expect to find a schema that closely follows DEF in the most ancient prayers of the Christian eucharistic liturgy. From the moment that the Christian eucharistic meal was no longer celebrated *after* a service of readings and prayers, where the early Christians still continued to be associated

with the Jews in the Synagogue, but on the contrary after such
a service, still more or less analogous to that of the Synagogue but
now proper to the Church, we may also expect to see a Christian
prayer develop where a DEF schema appears following the ABC
schema. But this interconnection, which never happened in Judaism since the meals were never immediately tied to the Synagogue service, will give rise to a problem that has yet to be posed.
The parallelism between ADC and DEF will be all the more noticeable since the disappearance of the *Shemah* (whose place was
taken by the eucharistic meal) will bring ABC into immediate
proximity with DEF. We may then expect to witness a more or
less successful and more or less forced fusion between ABC and
DEF.

All of this, as we shall point out, corresponds exactly to the
history of the eucharistic liturgy. The oldest formulas of the
eucharist we have contain exclusively a prayer (or rather a series
of three prayers) of the DEF type. From the moment that the
Christian service of reading and prayer and the eucharistic meal
became soldered together, we see the appearance of a eucharistic
prayer where an ABC schema becomes more or less easily fused
with a DEF schema.

But quite soon more or less important modifications can be
observed that synthesize the two groups so that doublets or too
evident repititions might be avoided. Once this remodeling produced a completely new mold, a new schema was arrived at, which
we might characterize by the formula AD-BE-CF.

It is now time to see how the Christian eucharistic prayer was
in fact to be born from the Jewish *berakoth*, which were first simply re-used with a few slight modifications, and then progressively
transfigured.

From the Jewish *Berakah*
to the Christian Eucharist

CARDINAL SCHUSTER SAID THAT IN THE PSALTER CHRIST HAD found a ready-made sacerdotal book in which he had only to read the liturgy of his sacrifice.[1] It would be even more exact to say this about the Jewish liturgy and its *berakoth*, even though it is true that they merely express what has remained latent in the psalter. As has been often pointed out, Christ's words suppose an unequaled knowledge of the Hebrew Bible, with the absolute understanding that it was his function, and his alone, to interpret it. Nor is Jesus any less the predestined heir of synagogal piety. It can be said that it was reserved for him to reveal to the whole world everything that it contained germinally and to bring it to flower in his own piety. But it is in the context of the Jewish piety of the Son of Mary that the piety of the Son of God was to be humanly expressed.

---

[1] I. Schuster, *The Sacramentary* (London, 1924-30) Cf. 2nd French edition, *Liber Sacramentorum* (Brussels, 1938), p. 191.

JESUS' USE OF THE *BERAKAH*

Just as it can be said that Jesus of Nazareth is the Word made flesh, it could also be said of his humanity that in it man has come to pronounce the perfect "blessing," the blessing in which everything human gives itself over as a perfect response to the God who speaks. In the human life of Jesus the divine Word finds its perfect creative and salvific fulfilment. The perfect blessing that Jesus pronounces will be fulfilled in the supreme act of his existence, the Cross.

With the exception of a few short invocations, the Synoptic Gospels give us only one prayer as Jesus' own and the same is true of St. John.

It is worthy of note that the prayer mentioned by Matthew and Luke after the first mission of the Twelve is a typical *berakah*. It is all the more so since its theme is the one which we have seen grow into the major and ultimately the dominant theme of the *berakoth*: the "knowledge of God" in us, responding to the knowledge he has of us, in the blessing which his own Word provokes in response.

The *berakah* for knowledge reaches its completion in this text since in Jesus God reveals himself perfectly to man and elicits man's perfect response. At the same time this *berakah* for the knowledge that the Father has of the Son and the knowledge that the Son receives from the Father opens out into a *berakah* for the communication of this singular intimacy to the "poor," in the sense that Israel understood the term, that is, those who live by faith alone.

Here is the text that we find in St. Luke which is undoubtedly the form closest to the formulas that Jesus must actually have used:

> In that same hour he rejoiced in the Holy Spirit and said, "I thank thee, Father, Lord of heaven and earth, that thou hast hidden these things from the wise and understanding and revealed them to babes; yea, Father, for such was thy gracious will. All things have been delivered[2] to me by my

[2] παρεδόθη

Father; and no one knows who the Son is except the Father
or who the Father is except the Son and any one to whom
the Son chooses to reveal him.[3]

There is not a detail in this text which is not filled with meaning.
To begin with, Jesus' rejoicing expresses the joy which is the
soul of every *berakah*. It is the rejoicing of one who through divine
revelation is discovering the meaning of all things, and of the
very life of man. Indeed, everything takes on its meaning in our
knowledge of God as the one who first knows us. Before we have
any consciousness of anything, before we exist, he knows us. He
knows us with a knowledge that is love. Once we discover it,
all things become resolved in his love.

But Jesus' own exultation infinitely surpasses that of every
old covenant believer. His prayer is the prayer of one who knows
not only that he is known by God, but that he is in some way
the unique object of divine knowledge: the one in whom the knowledge proper to God (not only as sovereign Lord of heaven and
earth, but as Father) takes perfect delight. God began to reveal
himself to and for Israel. But now, Jesus is the only-begotten
Son, the "beloved" Son, in whom all Israel reaches fulfilment,
is summed up, and also surpasses itself.

Yet the recognition by Jesus of this unicity of "knowledge"
of which he is the object, far from being restrictive, actually flows
out into the world and into men. This is why, when he pronounces
the *berakah*, it is a confession and a proclamation *par excellence*
of the divine wonder works. But it is above all the communication
of that unique wonder work which is both the basis and the entirety of divine knowledge. And, reciprocally, this communication
is but a radiation of the permanent "eucharist" which is at the
very root of the soul of Christ.

In this regard let us note how the sense of this inseparability
of Gospel proclamation and "eucharist" remained very much
alive in early liturgical tradition. With the Syrian fathers, the
homily spontaneously took the form of a eucharistic hymn.[4]

---

[3] Luke 10:21-22; cf. Matthew 11:25-27.
[4] Cf. in particular the homilies of St. Ephrem.

Nevertheless, this communication of the supreme Wisdom presupposes the humiliation of all human wisdom, as St. Paul was to explain in his first Epistle to the Corinthians. It is accessible only to the little ones, to those who have been touched by the spirit of supernatural childlikeness which is the Spirit of the Father in whom alone Jesus himself can rejoice in knowing the Father as the Father knows him. These are the people whom the piety of the last psalmists called the "poor,"[5] those who have nothing but faith which unreservedly surrenders them to this Spirit. Such is the "good pleasure," the εὐδοκία, the Father's plan of gratuitous love, which will find its realization in all men in and through the Son.

Indeed, it is to the Son alone that all things are "handed over"; he is the source for everyone else, and at the same time the content of the supreme tradition. In this tradition the knowledge that God has eternally of his work is revealed as contained in a unique knowledge. His εὐδοκία, his entire good pleasure rests in the Son as the one "beloved" of the Father. For the Father finds in him alone this reciprocal knowledge which is the perfect "acknowledgement" of his love. Yet, this knowledge which he alone has of the Father is given to us by the Son in accordance with the Father's plan. He reveals it to us in glorifying the Father by his "confession" in which both God's Word and man's response to it are accomplished.

Harnack had a very good point when he said that this text in the Synoptics stands out like a Johannine meteorite.[6] Not only do we sense here a surprising foretaste of the tone and atmosphere proper to St. John: we already have the announcement of the theme whose development will be the core of the fourth Gospel: the unique intimacy between the Father and the Son, and the Gospel, the "Good News," directed towards bringing us into this intimacy.[7] It is astonishing, however, that Harnack and his con-

---

[5] See A. Causse, *Les pauvres d'Israël* (Strasbourg-Paris, 1922).

[6] It is an historical irony that the Johannine gospel which had been reputed by nineteenth - century criticism to be the most hellenized seems to us today to be at least as Jewish as Matthew's.

[7] Cf. in St. John, the whole of the discourses after the Last Supper (ch. 13 ff.).

temporaries in general, were so little capable of understanding the reverse of this analogy. Better than any other argument this text of Luke and Matthew alone shows the error that has been with us for such a long time and which searched for the secret of Johannine christology in a supposed hellenization of the primitive Gospel. Indeed, there is nothing which is more primitive, more Semitic, more specifically Jewish in the sense of Synagogue Judaism, than all the terms and even the form of this prayer.[8] The theme it unfolds is perhaps the most central theme of the Bible, and it arrives at its final realization here following its most autonomous line: knowledge which is also love, the knowledge one has of God, which is always the fruit of the knowledge God has of us. The modes of expression are just as completely biblical as the thought, with their antithetical parallelism, an absolute assertion which is immediately shaded by a corrective that seems to contradict it while actually extending its meaning. Finally, the framework in which it is written is precisely that of a prayer shaped in the mold of the synagogue *berakoth*.

What Matthew adds to the text which is substantially the same as Luke's is no less Jewish in its form and basic sense.

Come to me, all you who labor and are heavy laden,
and I will give you rest.
Take my yoke upon you . . .
For my yoke is easy
and my burden is light.[9]

This yoke which is a light burden is the very expression that designated the acceptance of the *Torah* for the Rabbis, as we saw in regard to the *berakah* for light and knowledge.[10] Similarly for them, the Sabbath rest was a figure of the entry into the promised land, likened to an entry into God's rest which terminated the work of creation.[11] The new *Torah*, and the eternal covenant

---

[8] In addition to the general form of the *berakah*, note the parallelism and the typically Hebrew fashion of balancing off an absolute negation with a defined affirmation.

[9] Matthew 11:28-29..

[10] Cf. above, p. 61.

[11] See below the prayers for the Sabbath, quoted on pp. 130 ff.

which is its consequence, bring us into the true Sabbath: this
rest filled with joy that follows upon the full completion of God's
work, the work, as St. John tells us, which is that we should believe.[12]

For his part, St. John, places a great prayer on Jesus' lips after
the Last Supper at the moment when he is about to give himself
over to his Passion.[13] It merely resumes and explicates what
already was there germinally for his followers in the *berakah* in
St. Matthew and St. Luke where Christ told of the meaning of his
mission which the apostles were to continue.

It is true that in the 17th chapter of St. John, following a tendency we have already pointed out in the Jewish *berakoth*, the supplication flows back somewhat over the act of thanksgiving. But
the thanksgiving, the "confession" in praise, is underlying throughout. This whole "sacerdotal prayer," as it has been called,[14] arises
out of a contemplation of the glorification of God which was the
earthly work of Jesus, in order to ask for his own glorification,
in which the Father's glorification will be achieved in the salvation of believers.

If the Matthew-Luke prayer was set in a *berakah* for the communicated divine "knowledge," the communication of the divine
life is asked for here, as the supreme glorification of God.[15] Christ
will be glorified in his resurrection which will perfect the divine
glory by becoming the source of life for his people. But from the
very first words this life is defined: "And this is eternal life, that
they know thee the only true God, and Jesus Christ whom thou
has sent."[16] This will be expressed in the unity of love among
the faithful, flowing from the unity between the Father and the
Son: a unity of reciprocal "knowledge" rooted in the unity of life.
In them it will be the effect of their "sanctification," i.e. their
consecration, in the "sanctification" of Christ which is about to
be fulfilled—in other words his sacrifice.[17] This sanctification

---

[12] John 6:29.

[13] Ch. 17.

[14] The name was given to it by the exegete David Chytraeus.

[15] Cf. vv. 1 to 5.

[16] V. 3.

[17] Vv. 17-19. Cf. the article ἁγιάζειν in Kittel's *Theologisches Wörterbuch*.

will be fulfilled in them as it is fulfilled in him: in "truth," i.e. the communication of the "knowledge" of God in a communion in his life.[18]

The object of the knowledge of life which is shared with his people by the Son is expressly the divine Name. This Name was given to the Son in the substantial communication that the Father makes of himself in giving existence to the Son, and through the Cross it will be extended to men. Hence the final convergence of all these themes in the dominant theme of the divine glory, radiating in the Saviour's own glorification by his cross: knowledge of God, sanctification of his people, communicated life, a union in love in which is expressed the outpouring of this incomparable life which is God's life.[19]

These are the thoughts which the Last Supper was to convey to the first Christians, and which were to impregnate their later eucharistic celebrations.

THE MEAL *BERAKOTH* AND THE INSTITUTION
OF THE EUCHARIST

The undoubtedly insoluble argument whether the last meal Jesus took with his followers was the Passover meal or not need not delay us too much at this juncture, since it focuses on a secondary point. While the majority of modern exegetes have been inclined to answer negatively, Jeremias, in an extraordinarily ingenious way, seems for the moment to have reversed the tide.[20] Nevertheless the fact remains that St. John expressly tells us that the Passover was to be celebrated on the very evening of Jesus' death which implies, it seems, a negative answer.[21] At first sight, the Synoptics seem to suggest the contrary, since they describe the evening meal after having stressed the preparation of the Cenacle for Passover.[22] But it is at least curious that they tell us nothing

[18] V. 17.
[19] Vv. 22ff.
[20] *The Eucharistic Words of Jesus*, first chapter.
[21] Cf. John 18:28 and 19:31.
[22] Cf. Matthew 26:17 ff. and parallels.

about this meal that would allow us to conclude that we are actually dealing with a Passover supper. The phrase quoted by St. Luke: "I have earnestly desired to eat this passover with you ..." seems at first sight to remove any ambiguity.[23] But, it actually carries the problem to its most difficult stage, since it may just as well express the idea of sorrow at not being able to eat the Passover as it can the satisfaction of leaving them at the time of this celebration. And the vow of abstinence that Jeremias himself very well acknowledged[24] in the following words: : "For I tell you I shall not eat it until it is fulfilled in the kingdom of God ... " and somewhat further on: " ... I shall not drink of the fruit of the vine until the kingdom of God comes," becomes practically unthinkable if it should imply an abstention on Jesus' part with regard to Passover over which he would preside nevertheless ! On the other hand, among the details, cited by the Synoptics themselves that seem to be opposed to the idea that the Passover coincided with the very day that Jesus died (the Passover meal, in this case, having taken place on the preceding night), the fact that Simon of Cyrene had come in from the fields—to mention it only—resists Jeremias' explanations.[25] It is quite unlikely that by these words the evangelists meant not that he had returned from his morning's work, but that he was simply returning from a lawful outing, even on a holy day, to one of those rural enclaves near the city. Everything which precedes the meal however, if not all that follows in the first three Gospels, still makes us think of a Passover celebration, even though very little in the meal itself leads to this conclusion.

Mademoiselle Jaubert's attempt[26] at harmonizing all of the divergencies and thereby preserving the Passover character of the Last Supper is so ingenious that it has delighted many a troubled exegete, but the consequences of her hypothesis make it unlikely. The disciples, she believes, merely followed a different calendar

---

[23] Luke 22:15-16.

[24] *Op. cit.*, pp. 207 ff.

[25] Mark 15:21 and Luke 23:26.

[26] Annie Jaubert, *La date de la Cène; calendrier biblique et liturgie chrétienne* (Paris, 1967).

from the Jews as a whole. But, supposing that they actually
did use this other way of reckoning that she mentions, they would
have had their last evening with their master not on Thursday
but on Tuesday. Both from the point of view of the Gospel accounts
and unanimous tradition, this displacement which is without a
trace in either of these sources would appear impossible. And
especially, we do not see how in Jerusalem itself, where all the
Passover lambs had to be immolated together in the Temple,
one or several dissident groups could have celebrated the feast
on any other day without causing a riot.

But all of these arguments, however interesting they might
be from the viewpoint of the Gospel story, are of no importance
for the interpretation of the Last Supper and the eucharist to
which it was to give rise. Actually, people usually are so concerned
about them because they suppose that the paschal references of the
cross and the eucharist are all dependent upon the paschal character that may or may not be attributed to the Supper. Now this
a priori is totally foreign to the reality. In the first place, the
Passover setting is no less relevant to the Last Supper whether it
preceded Passover (the immolation of the lambs coinciding in
time with the death of the Savior in this last case), or was actually
the Passover meal. But—and this is of especial importance—the
paschal references were present not only in the prayers of this
one night but in all the meal prayers. And in fact, whether the
Supper was this special meal or another, there is no doubt that
Jesus did not connect the eucharistic institution of the new covenant to any of the details that are proper to the Passover meal
alone. The connection is solely with what the Passover meal had
in common with every meal. That is, the breaking of bread in
the beginning and the rite of thanksgiving over the cup of wine
mixed with water at the end. And, we may add, this is what made
it possible for the Christian eucharist to be celebrated without
any problem, as often as one might wish, and not only once a year.

However interesting the significance of the paschal lamb may
be for an understanding of Christ's death,[27] we must not look to

---

[27] Cf. Jeremias, *op. cit.*, pp. 220 ff.

the rite of the eating of this lamb, and even less to the secondary rites like the unleavened bread or the bitter herbs, for the source of the Christian eucharistic prayer. For an understanding of this prayer our starting point is with the broken bread at the beginning of the meal, the shared cup at the end, and the blessings which were traditionally connected with them.

According to the Rabbis, the bread whose blessing as it was broken began the ritual meal, represented the supreme food, the life that is given and sustained by the Creator.[28] The blessing of the Didache, about which we shall soon be speaking and whose Jewish origin is incontestable, manifests the fact that certain Jewish communities of the time already looked upon the breaking of this one bread and its being eaten in common as a figure of the diaspora of Israel and of their reunion in this resurrected body mentioned in the vision of Ezekiel.[29]

The association of the cup and the wine that filled it seems to have been still more meaningful and especially more explicit. The Johannine simile develops the new meaning that the wine is to take on in the atmosphere of a eucharistic interpretation of the Passion.[30] But since the time of the prophet Isaiah,[31] and undoubtedly long before him, it had already been for Israel the symbol of the people of God which had been uprooted in Egypt in order to be replanted in Zion by David. The meaning of the vine of gold which Herod had represented on the front of the Temple was evident to all who looked upon it. The shared cup implied further the ideas of the covenant as in the 23rd psalm, of a libation of thanksgiving as in Psalm 116, and of affliction accepted from the hand of God as in Psalm 80 (which is echoed in the discussion with the sons of Zebedee).[32]

More generally along with the remembrance of Passover and the Exodus, behind the whole meal and its blessings there lie the prophetic promises of the messianic banquet.[33] Jesus alluded to

---

[28] Cf. Jeremias, *op. cit.*, pp. 233 ff.
[29] Cf. below, p. 116.
[30] John 15.
[31] Cf. Isaiah 5.
[32] Matthew 20: 22-23.
[33] Cf. Jeremias, *op. cit.*, pp. 233 ff.

them when he spoke of the banquet in which the righteous who have come from all corners of the earth would be sitting at table in the Kingdom along with Abraham, Isaac and all the prophets.[34] Maurice Goguel was right in pointing out that the accounts of the multiplication of the loaves insist on the anticipation of the messianic banquet more than on the wondrous aspect of the miracle.[35] Jesus, through his blessing of the bread that was broken and distributed among his hearers, was to begin to shape the community of the covenant from the crowd attracted by his word. Even if the discourse given by the fourth Gospel after one of these meals did bring together and develop later teachings,[36] it is at least likely that such meals were connected with a sermon of Jesus that had been a primary preparation for what he was to announce at the Last Supper.

All of this, and no doubt many other acts and words, which we do not know, all of the meals which he had taken with the small group of his disciples, coming in the wake of practices in more or less similar communities such as Qumrân, seem to flow into the preliminaries of this last meal. When Jesus takes the first cup, his words mentioned by St. Luke portend what is to follow.[37] Having repeated the blessing which we have quoted, a blessing which already calls the vine of David to mind, that vine which is the people of Israel, he proclaims in barely disguised words the end of the old order which was only preparatory, and the imminent renewal of Israel in the Kingdom (or Reign) that his death was to establish: "I tell you that I shall not drink of the fruit of the vine until the Kingdom of God comes."

Prepared undoubtedly by the teachings of the sermon on the bread of life, his words after the blessing and breaking of bread will announce the sacrificial meaning of his death and also define how he will give his flesh, not only for the life of the world (on the cross) but as the food of life for his people (in their eucharistic banquets).

[34] Matthew 8:11 and Luke 13:28.
[35] Maurice Goguel, *Jésus et les origines du christianisme*, I. *La vie de Jésus* (Paris, 1932).
[36] Cf. C.H. Dodd, *op.cit.*, pp. 333 ff.
[37] Luke 22:16.

There is no room for supposing that Jesus otherwise modified the traditional blessing of the bread, as we have quoted it according to the *Seder* of Amram Gaon, who again gives it as it was in the *Mishnah*:

Blessed be thou, JHWH, King of the universe,
who bringest forth bread from the earth.[38].

The disciples answered their *Amen*, and then he broke the bread and passed it to them, saying most probably:

Take, this is my flesh,
(or perhaps,) Take, here is my flesh.

Jeremias' analysis concerning the various New Testament formulas seems to demonstrate conclusively that they are all liturgical formulas that had become consecrated by various local usages. They all have an Aramaic or Hebrew formula behind them, and John 6, almost certainly, is alone in retaining the exact term used by Jesus.[39] As a parallelism with the blood, for a Semite, it is flesh (*bashar-bišra*) and not body that seems to be required both by rabbinical tradition and by properly biblical tradition. "This is my body" is a kind of hellenizing *targum* made necessary by the transition to a liturgy in Greek.

Similarly, at the end of the meal, Jesus took the prepared cup in his hands and pronounced the three customary blessings. As Finkelstein has established,[40] at that time they must have included at least the following elements, although the formula that was actually pronounced was probably still closer to the liturgical eloquence of Amram Gaon's formularies if not in every detail at least in its religious tonality;

1. Blessed be thou, JHWH, our God, King of the universe, who feedest the world with (thy) goodness, (thy) grace and (thy) mercy.
2. We thank thee, JHWH, our God, for a good and ample land which thou wast pleased to give (us).

---

[38] Cf. the preceding chapter, p. 80.
[39] Jeremias, *op. cit.*, pp. 173 ff. and 196 ff.
[40] Cf. L. Finkelstein, *op. cit.*

3. Have mercy, JHWH, our God, upon thy people Israel,
upon thy city Jerusalem,
upon Zion, the abiding place of thy glory,
upon thy altar and thy Temple.
Blessed be thou, JHWH, who rebuildest Jerusalem.

While passing around the cup, Jesus (still according to Jeremias, to whose analyses we would refer the reader) would have used the Hebrew expression *dam berithi*, or in Aramaic, *adam keyami* (literally *blood of my covenant*). They are the only expressions possible in the Semitic languages. Greek correctly translates them as: This is my blood, of the covenant, shed for you.

THE MEANING OF THE "MEMORIAL"

The words that follow are generally translated:
Do this in memory of me.
They have been the object of endless discussions among modern exegetes, depending on whether they did or did not admit the likelihood that Jesus could have instituted a ceremony that was to be repeated, in such an explicit formula. Dom Gregory Dix deserves the credit for showing that the question is badly put.[42] The repetition of the religious meal could cause no problem, since for Jews the eucharist was not a novelty in its ritual form (which they would have kept in any case after Jesus' death as before) but in its content. The stress then is laid not on the prescription: "Do this" but on the specification: "Do it (*from now on* is understood) *in memory of me*." More exactly, as Jeremias has shown these words should be translated:

DO THIS AS MY MEMORIAL.

and this word must be given the sense that it always has in the rabbinical literature and especially the liturgical literature of the period.[43] It in no way means a subjective, human psychological act of returning to the past, but an objective reality destined to

[41] Jeremias, *op. cit.*, pp. 193 ff.
[42] Cf. *The Shape of the Liturgy* (London, 1945), pp. 55 ff.
[43] Cf. above, p. 84 ff.

make some thing or some one perpetually present before God and for God himself. As Max Thurian so well showed, this notion of "memorial" is not only an essential ritual element of certain sacrifices, but one that gives ultimate significance to every sacrifice, and eminently to the Passover sacrifice.[44] It is an institution, we may say, established by God, given to his people and imposed on them by him, in order to perpetuate forever his salvific interventions. Not only will the memorial assure the faithful subjectively of its permanent effectiveness, but above all it will assure this very effectiveness through a pledge which they can and must represent to him, a pledge of his own fidelity.

We have pointed out how the feast-day interpolations in the third *berakah* at the end of the meal, precisely multiply the use of this word *zikkaron*, "memorial," with certainly the meaning we have just mentioned.[45] We have assurance that these interpolations, focusing on the "memorial," were already the practice before the beginning of our era. We may then rightly suppose that they suggested his formula to Jesus directly. And in the case where the Last Supper would not have been the Passover meal, we may well ask whether in the third *berakah* Jesus may not have improvised an explicit memorial of his blood shed for the new covenant.

Let us repeat that the fact that the expression of this "memorial" is found in the same terms both in the *Abodah* prayer for the consecration of the Temple sacrifices and in the third meal *berakah* underlines its sacrificial character.

It is in this way above all that the sense of a sacrifice was decidedly attached to the cross which would sum up all previous sacrifices in itself and abolish them. This sense is given by the *berakah* of the bread and wine, as his body and blood, which are forever to be the substance of the "memorial" left by Jesus to his followers, to be represented unceasingly to God by them, as the definitive pledge of his redeeming love. It may be said that at

---

[44] Max Thurian, *op. cit.*, the whole first chapter. See also N. Dahl, *Anamnesis: mémoire et commémoration dans le christianisme primitif* in *Studia Theologica* (Lund, 1948), pp. 69 ff.

[45] Cf. above, p. 85.

the Last Supper the cross of Christ and the Christian eucharist
have inseparably received a sacrificial character from Jesus,—
the cross of Christ because he handed himself over to it at the
Last Supper as an immolated oblation, like that of the Passover
lamb, in order to effect the new and eternal covenant conforming
to the divine plan "acknowledged" in his eucharist,—the Christian eucharist, because it becomes at the same moment the "memorial" of Jesus and of his salvific act. Every time Christians
celebrate it, as St. Paul says, they "announce" or "proclaim" this
death, not first to the world, but to God, and the "recalling" of
Christ's death is for God the pledge of his fidelity in saving them.[46]

It seems that we must follow Jeremias one step further and add
with him that the hoped-for fruit of this representation to God
of the "memorial" of the redemptive death is, in Jesus' own intention, the ultimate accomplishment of his work in his parousia.[47] The invocation, which in the Jewish liturgy is connected
with the recalling of the memorial, is always actually the realization of the eschatological experience.[48] This is surely what St.
Paul has in mind when he says: "For as often as you eat this
bread and drink the cup, you proclaim the Lord's death *until
he comes*," this latter phrase most certainly implying "so that he
will come."[49]

It is understandable then how the juxtaposition of the traditional hope focusing on the fulfilment of the definitive people of
God in the definitive "building" of Jerusalem, and the hope of the
parousia produced in the early Church the invocation of a fulfilment of Christ in us. Will not this fulfilment be not only promised but also prefigured in the eucharistic celebration in which
we become the "body" of Christ by being nourished with his
"flesh" and his "blood," believing in his resurrection?

---

[46] 1 Corinthians 11:26.
[47] Cf. Jeremias, *op. cit.*, pp. 237 ff.
[48] Cf. above, p. 88.
[49] Cf. Jeremias, *op. cit.*, *ibid.*

THE JEWISH *BERAKOTH* AND THE PRAYER
OF THE FIRST CHRISTIANS

From this point on we can understand that we must place what we call today the "words of institution" of the eucharist back into their own context which is that of the ritual *berakoth* of the Jewish meal, so that we may perceive the sense and the whole import of their expression. The words announcing everything that was to follow in the Last Supper, as preserved for us by St. Luke, are connected with the preparatory *berakah* over the first cup. The blessing over the body (or the flesh) of Christ is connected with the initial *berakah* of the breaking of bread, and that over the blood of the new covenant with the second and the third final *berakoth*. Finally the sentence about the "memorial" corresponds to the feastday interpolations in the third *berakah*.

We must go further. These words of Christ which were to give rise to the Christian eucharist arise from a whole structure underlying the Gospels, the Jewish liturgy in which they were inserted. If we separate them from it, we misunderstand the whole movement which inspired them. Reciprocally, their exact meaning risks being lost once we no longer perceive all that they accomplish and complete. Early Christianity was preserved from ever committing such an error by the fact that Christian prayer continued to develop within the forms of the Jewish *berakah* and the *tefillah*, i.e. the prayer of petition which evolves without ever becoming actually detached from it. The first formulas of the Christian eucharist, in imitation of what Christ himself had done, are but Jewish formulas applied by means of a few added words to a new content, which however was already prepared for by them.

That the expression of the first Christian prayers was molded spontaneously on the Jewish *berakoth* and their own developments is shown in a particularly striking way by the Pauline Epistles. Practically every one opens with a *berakah* and passes to the *tefillah*, to the supplication that the gift which is the object of the act of thanksgiving be perfectly fulfilled. The teaching and the exhortation which make up the body of the Epistles remain dominated by this preamble. They are merely the explication of what the preamble includes. They therefore retain the imprint of this exultant contemplation, and are replete with the suppliant yearning for the accomplishment of this acknowledged and confessed mystery.

These introductions are generally built on the two terms εὐχαριστία (or εὐλογία) and προσευχή, which in Greek Judaism already translated the two Hebrew terms *berakah* and *tefillah*.

In the first epistle to the Thessalonians we have:

We give thanks (εὐχαριστοῦμεν) to God always for you all, constantly mentioning you in our prayers (προσευχῶν), remembering before our God and Father your work of faith and labor of love and steadfastness of hope in our Lord Jesus Christ.[50]

And in the second we have similarly:

We are bound to give thanks (εὐχαριστεῖν) to God always for you, brethren, as is fitting, because your faith is growing abundantly, and the love of every one of you for one another is increasing ... To this end we always pray (προσευχόμεθα) for you, that our God may make you worthy of his call, and may fulfill every good resolve and work of faith by his power, so that the name of our Lord Jesus may be glorified in you, and you in him, according to the grace of our God and the Lord Jesus Christ ... [51]

That this initial formula was telescoped in the case of the Epistle to the Galatians shows how vehement were the anxiety and indignation that cause St. Paul to write them. But the spontaneous impulse still remains like a watermark beneath his salutation:

Grace to you and peace from God the Father and our Lord Jesus Christ, who gave himself for our sins to deliver us from the present evil age, according to the will of our God and Father; to whom be the glory for ever and ever. Amen.[52]

But to the Romans, even though he does not yet know those to whom he is writing, and therefore his salutation loses some of its customary warmth, he says formally:

[50] 1 Thessalonians 1.
[51] 2 Thessalonians 1.
[52] Galatians 1.

First, I thank my God through Jesus Christ for all of you, because your faith is proclaimed in all the world. For God is my witness, whom I serve ($\lambda\alpha\tau\varrho\varepsilon\acute{v}\omega$: a pre-eminently liturgical term) with my spirit in the gospel of his Son, that without ceasing I mention all of you always in my prayers, asking that somehow by God's will I may now at last succeed in coming to you.[53]

In the introduction to the two Epistles to the Corinthians it is only the $\varepsilon\acute{v}\chi\alpha\varrho\iota\sigma\tau\acute{\iota}\alpha$ that is formally expressed, although the $\pi\varrho\sigma\sigma\varepsilon\upsilon\chi\grave{\eta}$ underlies it at least at the end of the first.

I give thanks to God always for you because of the grace of God which was given you in Christ Jesus, that in every way you were enriched in him with all speech and all knowledge — even as the testimony to Christ was confirmed among you — so that you are not lacking in any spiritual gift, as you wait for the revealing of our Lord Jesus Christ; who will sustain you to the end, guiltless in the day of our Lord Jesus Christ. God is faithful, by whom you were called into the fellowship of his Son, Jesus Christ our Lord.[54]

And in the second, we have:

Blessed ($\varepsilon\acute{v}\lambda\sigma\gamma\eta\tau\acute{o}\varsigma$) be the God and Father of our Lord Jesus Christ, the Father of mercies and God of all comfort, who comforts us in all our affliction, so that we may be able to comfort those who are in any affliction, with the comfort with which we ourselves are comforted by God.[55]

To the Philippians he says with that note of peaceful and joyful trust that is so characteristic of his relations with this Church:

I thank my God in all my remembrances of you, always in every prayer of mine for you all making my prayer with joy, thankful for your partnership in the gospel from the first day until now. And I am sure that he who began a good work in you will bring it to completion at the day of Jesus Christ ... And it is my prayer ($\tau\sigma\tilde{v}\tau\sigma$ $\pi\varrho\sigma\sigma\varepsilon\acute{v}\chi\sigma\mu\alpha\iota$) that your love may abound more and more, with knowledge and all dis-

---

[53] Romans 1.
[54] 1 Corinthians 1.
[55] 2 Corinthians 1.

cernment, so that you may approve what is excellent, and may be pure and blameless for the day of Christ, filled with the fruits of righteousness which come through Jesus Christ, to the glory and praise of God.[56]

In the Epistle to the Colossians, the blessing and the accompanying prayer burst out into a great exposition of the whole plan of God and its accomplishment, not only in the case of the apostle and those to whom he is writing, but in the entire world:

We always thank God, the Father of our Lord Jesus Christ, when we pray for you, because we have heard of your faith in Christ Jesus and of the love which you have for all the saints, because of the hope laid up for you in heaven. Of this you have heard before in the word of the truth, the gospel which has come to you, as indeed in the whole world it is bearing fruit and growing—so among yourselves, from the day you heard and understood the grace of God in truth, as you learned it from Epaphras our beloved fellow servant. He is a faithful minister of Christ on our behalf and has made known to us your love in the Spirit.

And so, from the day we heard of it, we have not ceased to pray for you, asking that you may be filled with the knowledge of his will in all spiritual wisdom and understanding, to lead a life worthy of the Lord, fully pleasing to him, bearing fruit in every good work and increasing in the knowledge of God. May you be strengthened with all power, according to his glorious might, for all endurance and patience with joy, giving thanks to the Father, who has qualified us to share in the inheritance of the saints in light. He has delivered us from the dominion of darkness and transferred us to the kingdom of his beloved Son, in whom we have redemption, the forgiveness of sins.

He is the image of the invisible God, the first-born of all creation; for in him all things were created, in heaven and on earth, visible and invisible, whether thrones or dominions or principalities or authorities—all things were created through him and for him. He is before all things, and in him all things hold together. He is the head of the body, the church; he is

[56] Philippians 1.

the beginning, the first-born from the dead, that in everything he might be pre-eminent. For in him all the fulness
of God was pleased to dwell, and through him to reconcile
to himself all things, whether on earth or in heaven, making
peace by the blood of his cross.

And you, who once were estranged and hostile in mind, doing
evil deeds, he has now reconciled in his body of flesh by his
death, in order to present you holy and blameless and irreproachable before him, provided that you continue in the faith
stable and steadfast, not shifting from the hope of the gospel
which you heard, which has been preached to every creature under heaven, and of which I, Paul, became a minister.[57]

Finally, in the Epistle to the Ephesians, this same initial "eucharist" is repeated, aimed at the perspective of building the Church
as the fulness of Christ. It thus becomes a hymn to the whole
divine plan and its accomplishment in us, with a particularly
liturgical color.

Blessed be the God and Father of our Lord Jesus Christ, who
has blessed us in Christ with every spiritual blessing in the
heavenly places, even as he chose us in him before the foundation of the world, that we should be holy and blameless
before him. He destined us in love to be his sons through
Jesus Christ, according to the purpose of his will, to the praise
of his glorious grace which he freely bestowed on us in the
Beloved. In him we have redemption through his blood, the
forgiveness of our trespasses, according to the riches of his
grace which he lavished upon us. For he has made known
to us in all wisdom and insight the mystery of his will, according to his purpose which he set forth in Christ as a plan
for the fulness of time, to unite all things in him, things in
heaven and things on earth.

In him, according to the purpose of him who accomplished
all things according to the counsel of his will, we who first
hoped in Christ have been destined and appointed to live for
the praise of his glory. In him you also, who have heard the
word of truth, the gospel of your salvation, and have believed
in him, were sealed with the promised Holy Spirit, which is the

[57] Colossians 1.

guarantee of our inheritance until we acquire possession of it, to the praise of his glory.

For this reason, because I have heard of your faith in the Lord Jesus and your love toward all the saints, I do not cease to give thanks for you, remembering you in my prayers, that the God of our Lord Jesus Christ, the Father of glory, may give you a spirit of wisdom and of revelation in the knowledge of him, having the eyes of your hearts enlightened, that you may know what is the hope to which he has called you, what are the riches of his glorious inheritance in the saints, and what is the immeasurable greatness of his power in us who believe, according to the working of his great might which he accomplished in Christ when he raised him from the dead and made him sit at his right hand in the heavenly places, far above all rule and authority and power and dominion, and above every name that is named, not only in this age but also in that which is to come; and he has put all things under his feet and has made him the head over all things for the church, which is his body, the fulness of him who fills all in all.

And you he made alive, when you were dead through the trespasses and sins in which you once walked, following the course of the world, following the prince of the power of the air, the spirit that is now at work in the sons of disobedience. Among these we all once lived in the passions of our flesh, following the desires of body and mind, and so we were by nature children of wrath, like the rest of mankind. But God who is rich in mercy, out of the great love with which he loved us, even when we were dead through our trespasses, made us alive together with Christ (by grace you have been saved), and raised us up with him, and made us sit with him in the heavenly places in Christ Jesus, that in the coming ages he might show the immeasurable riches of his grace in kindness toward us in Christ Jesus. For by grace you have been saved through faith; and this is not your own doing, it is the gift of God—not because of works, lest any man should boast. For we are his workmanship, created in Christ Jesus for good works, which God prepared beforehand, that we should walk in them.[58]

[58] Ephesians 1 and 2.

Here more than ever, the instructions and the exhortations that follow immediately, form one body with the *berakah* to the extent that its echoes are felt practically to the end of the epistle. The account of the mystery of Christ seems to be borne on the waves of the eucharist, which in turn seems to be developed for the sole purpose of explaining that mystery.

The parallelism of these texts, with their progression leading to the ultimate expansiveness of the great christological epistles, is no less indicative of St. Paul's theology than of his prayer. It becomes manifest here that his theology is basically eucharistic in the sense that it is only a meditation on what comprises the substance of the Christian eucharist. For this reason, proceeding from the thanksgiving, into the prayer for the realization of the mystery, its tendency is only to doxology, to the ultimate glorification of God in all things. It is a *theologia*, in the sense that this word had in hellenistic antiquity: an encomium, a glorification in praise of the God about whom we are speaking. It can be said that the Greek Fathers, especially the Cappadocians and eminently St. Gregory of Nazianzum, who above all has received the title of theologian, never lose sight of this direction, this primary orientation of theology even in their most extreme speculative developments. It is permissible to think that the working out of the anaphoras, which were in the process of being completed at that time, and were destined to become classic, contributed in no small way towards their authors' keeping alive an "orthodoxy" which is both right glorification and right doctrine.[59]

But, to return to the Pauline texts, we see how they all are merely resumptions of the *berakah* for the knowledge of God, under this knowledge's twofold aspect of faith and love. In the Epistle to the Colossians, within the προσευχή, the *tefillah* for the complete achievement of this knowledge, its object's definition takes on prominence. In the context proper to the Epistle—to counter the warped Jewish gnoses—the unity between creation and redemption is therefore affirmed. There is but one creator

---

[59] This theme, familiar to modern Orthodox authors, rests upon a play of words between δόξα in the biblical sense of glory, and δόξα in the classical sense of opinion.

and redeemer: Christ in whom the world, since he created it in the beginning, must be reconciled with its author in the mystery of his Cross. This mystery is also that of the Church brought together in his crucified body in order to become the fulness of his resurrected body.

This terminal vision in the Epistle to the Ephesians fills the whole horizon. It is already present in the *berakah* proper, the thanksgiving. From the very first, the all-embracing plan of God is recalled, the plan whereby, in the ἀνακεφαλαίωσις, the ultimate "recapitulation," he will resume his impaired and divided work in accordance with the original plan. The fulness of the original plan, implied for all time in Christ, will be made explicit at the end of time in the Church in which he himself is fulfilled. Thus the knowledge, to which all are predestined and which is given to them by the Gospel, will be the discovery and the realization of this unique "perfect man" in whom the dead, risen and ascended Christ is completely fulfilled.

Here, we would be tempted to say, we discover the progressive pressure of the Christian vision that had been prepared by the Jewish formulas: it pervades them in turn and impregnates them to the point of remodeling them. The reorientation is decisive: from the *Torah* to Christ, from the first covenant to the mystery of the new covenant, the mystery of his Cross which is also the mystery of Christ in us, the hope of glory, to borrow a key expression from the Epistle to the Colossians.[60]

From the first Christian generations, this continuity and this metamorphosis are equally in evidence in the prayers which give us the most glowing witness borne to Christ: the prayers of the martyrs. Throughout their authentic acts, at the moment when their offering is consumed in that of Christ himself, it is noteworthy that it is still the Jewish *berakah* that continues to express it.

It is Carpus who cried out from the stake at Pergamum, under Marcus Aurelius:

---

[60] Colossians 1:27.

Blessed art thou, Lord, Son of God, for despite my sins thou hast judged me worthy of your inheritance.[61]

It is Theodotus of Ancyra, under Diocletian, whose *berakah* leads into a *tefillah*, like that of many others:

Lord Jesus Christ, who hast created heaven and earth, thou dost not abandon those who put their hope in thee. I give thee thanks for having made me worthy of becoming a citizen of the city of heaven, and of inheriting thy Kingdom.

I give thee thanks for allowing me to vanquish the dragon and to crush its head.

Give rest to thy servants and turn aside from me the furor of thy enemies.

Give peace to thy Church, and snatch it from the tyranny of the demon. Amen.[62]

We see the same thing in a certain Irenaeus of Sirmium, also under Diocletian:

I give thee thanks, Lord Jesus Christ, for having given me endurance in different trials and torments, and for having judged me worthy to share in thy eternal glory. Lord Jesus Christ, who hast deigned to suffer for the salvation of the world, open thine eyes that the Angels may receive the spirit of thy servant Irenaeus, who endureth these torments for thy name's sake and for the people that groweth in the catholic Church of Sirmium. I pray thee and I beseech thy mercy that thou deignest to gather and strengthen the others in the faith.[63]

But of all these prayers, the most interesting and the most ancient is that of Polycarp of Smyrna who died towards the end of the second century. The account of his martyrdom shows us this bishop handing himself over to the fire exactly as if he were going to celebrate the eucharist for the last time. And in this supreme celebration where he identifies himself with the victim

---

[61] In the critical edition of the *Acta Martyrum* of Knopf-Kruger (Tübingen, 1929), pp. 12-13.

[62] Ruinart, *Acta primorum martyrum sincera* (Paris, 1689), in the re-edition of 1859, p. 384.

[63] *Ibid.*, p. 313.

which is Christ, we can think that his prayer derives from the eucharist which he was accustomed to offer. But it espouses the whole development of the Jewish *berakah*: praise of the creator, then of the redeemer, the presentation of the "memorial" with the supplication that the offering be accepted, and the final doxology.

> Lord, Almighty God, Father of Jesus Christ, thy beloved and blessed child, through whom we have known thee, God of the Angels and the powers, God of all creation and of the whole family of the righteous who live in thy presence: I blessed thee for having judged me worthy of this day and this hour, for being counted among the number of thy martyrs and for sharing the cup of thy Christ, that I may rise to the everlasting life of the soul and the body in the incorruptibility of the Holy Spirit.
>
> May I today, together with them, be received into thy presence as a precious and acceptable offering: thou hast prepared me for it, thou hast shown it to me, thou hast kept thy promise, God of faithfulness and truth. For this grace and for all things, I praise thee, I glorify thee through the eternal and heavenly high priest, Jesus Christ, thy beloved child: through him, who is with thee and the Spirit, may glory be given to thee, now and in the ages to come. Amen.[64]

THE FIRST EUCHARISTIC LITURGIES: THE *DIDACHE*

Yet it still seems that it is the *Didache* which has preserved for us the most ancient example of these formulations of the eucharist where the Church, like Christ at the last Supper, still used the Jewish formulas, merely giving a new sense to their expressions with the help of a few insertions.

We need not argue at this point about the origin of the *Didache*, which has been placed either at the very beginning of the Church or else after the year 180 at the time of the Montanist crisis.[65]

Let us say once again—and this will not be the last time— that the date and the origin of a liturgical prayer must not be

---

[64] *Martyrum Polycarpi*, P.G.., t. 5, col. 1040.
[65] Cf. Audet, *La Didachè* (Paris, 1958).

confused with that of the collections in which it is found. What now interests us in the *Didache* for our study is only the prayers themselves. That these are of Jewish origin, as Dibelius was the first modern scholar to acknowledge,[66] is obvious once we connect them with the traditional Jewish meal prayers. We must even go further than Dibelius who thought that he had found here a prayer of hellenistic Jews. Let us recall that the Synagogue of Dura-Europos has given us a fragment of papyrus where we read a Hebrew prayer which is the central element of the *berakah* of the *Didache*.[67]

But in the *Didache*, it is clear that the prayer used by the Christians has undergone a few additions, not without some awkwardness, which are intended to specify the renewed sense given to it.

Concerning the Eucharist, give thanks in this way.
First for the cup;
   'We give thanks to thee, our Father, for the holy vine of David thy servant, *which thou madest known to us* through thy servant ($\pi\alpha\tilde{\iota}\varsigma$) Jesus.
To thee be the glory for ever.'
And for the broken bread;
   'We give thanks to thee, our Father, for the life and knowledge, which thou madest known to us *through thy servant Jesus.*
To thee be the glory for ever.'
As this broken bread was scattered upon the hills, and was gathered together and made one, so let thy Church be gathered together into thy kingdom from the ends of the earth; for thine is the glory and the power *through Christ Jesus* for ever.' ...
And after ye are filled, give thanks thus:
   'We give thee thanks, Holy Father, for thy holy name, which thou hast made to tabernacle in our hearts, and for the knowledge, faith and immortality which thou hast made known to us *through thy servant Jesus.*
To thee be the glory for ever.
Thou, Lord Almighty, didst create all things for thy name's sake, and gavest food and drink to men for their enjoyment, that they might give thee thanks; and to us thou didst grant spiritual food and drink and life eternal, *through thy servant.*

---

[66] Cf. Audet, *op. cit.*
[67] Cf. above, p. 27.

Above all we thank thee that thou art mighty.
To thee be glory for ever.
Remember, Lord, thy Church, to deliver her from all evil
and to make her perfect in thy love, and to gather from the
four winds her that is sanctified into thy kingdom which thou
didst prepare for her; for thine is the power and the glory
for ever.
Let grace come, and let this world pass away.
Hosanna to the God of David.
If any is holy, let him come:
if any is not holy, let him repent.
Maran atha.
Amen.'[68]

We have italicized the obviously Christian additions. Their
small number and their laconicism will be noted. It will also
be noted that we have not italicized the mentions of the Church.
The rediscovered Hebrew text shows that ἐκκλησία in our text
simply corresponds to the Hebrew *qahal*, which for the first com-
posers and users of the prayer simply designated the expected
foregathering of the diaspora of Israel.

Arguments are still in vogue among Christian critics, who are
ignorant (willingly or no) of the parallel Jewish texts, about whether we have here a eucharistic prayer in the strict sense or a prayer
for the agape meal which they suppose to have already been separated from the eucharist, or again two groups of texts to be used
in different celebrations. They are rendered useless once we are
aware of the Jewish parallels. The whole is in continuity, and follows the traditional succession of the meal *berakoth* (blessing over
the initial cup, blessing over the broken bread, threefold blessing
over the last cup). But, in their final state, they obviously apply
to a sacred meal of a Christian community that is still very close to
Judaism, and it could only be its eucharist. It can be all the better understood that the Christians kept the Jewish prayers practically intact since this form of those prayers certainly represented
a special form of them proper to the communities dominated by
the expectation of the Messiah. What particular community was

[68] *Didachè*, 9 and 10. For the translation, cf. Henry Bettinson, *Documents
of the Christian Church* (London, 1959), pp. 90 ff.

its author? This is undoubtedly an unanswerable question. But from these texts we can get some idea of what must have been done with the traditional Jewish prayers, before the first Christians, by Jews such as those from Qumrân or the Zadokite community of Damascus.

The mention of the hills where wheat was scattered indicates a Palestinian origin, or at least a Syrian one. The connection between life and knowledge, and even the mention of the spiritual food and drink, can belong just as well to this messianic Judaism as to primitive Christianity, like the insistence on the revealed divine Name and even the title "our Father" given to God. But for Christians all of this was so easily charged with a more precise content that they could hardly have felt the need at the moment to say anything more. Jesus, as Daniélou has so well shown, was this revealed divine Name for them,[69] just as he was spiritual food and drink as well as life and knowledge, which were found in faith in him and procured immortality through participation in his resurrection.

Up to the final invocation ("Let grace come, and let this world pass away") there is nothing which may not have been Jewish before being taken over by the Christians. On the other hand, "Hosanna to the *God* of David" seems a cryptic expression, typical of primitive Christianity, of belief in the divinity of Jesus. It seems to be an echo, by its correction of the formula repeated by the gospels: "Hosanna to the *son* of David," of the discussion Jesus had with the scribes about the 110th Psalm.[70]

The following words are an invitation to communion which seems to be the most ancient expression that we have of the need for penance on the part of Christians who wish to approach the holy table after having sinned. But we might also wonder if the disciples of the Baptist, for example, could not have used them as well.

Maran atha, the expression of the expectation of the parousia, which St. Paul has preserved for us,[71] confirms what he himself

---

[69] J. Daniélou, *The Theology of Jewish Christianity* (Chicago, 1964) p. 189 ff.
[70] Matthew 22:41-45 and parallels.
[71] 1 Corinthians 16:22.

has allowed us to see of the eschatological orientation of these first Christian eucharists, where they "proclaimed" the death of the Lord, "until he comes." As many an appearance of the risen Lord must have been in relation to the first celebrations, they were done in the expectation of his return. But we may indeed wonder, particularly if we consider that the entreaty for the coming of the Messiah was already, at least on feast days, to be found at the conclusion of the Jewish *berakah* over the cup, whether the formula *Maran atha* itself was not borrowed by the first Christians from other earlier groups of pious Jews.

THE *APOSTOLIC CONSTITUTIONS*

We have the opportunity of being able to see in other texts, hardly less archaic, the transition from this first state of Christian liturgical prayers to a more mature form that was destined to continue. From a Jewish prayer that was christianized by a few minor insertions we can follow the transition to a prayer that has been entirely recomposed in a Christian perspective. But along with the traditional Jewish schema this will always retain literal re-uses of prechristian formulas. It is another archaic or archaizing collection which is scarcely less difficult to date and to localize that gives that clue to us: the *Apostolic Constitutions*.[72]

The seventeenth and eighteenth centuries, particularly in certain Anglican milieus (especially among the Non-Jurors), were enchanted by them. As a consequence of their attribution to St. Clement of Rome, sustained by the text, but untenable historically, people thought that in the liturgy of the 8th book, the Clementine liturgy as it was to be called, they had found an almost immediate trace of the liturgy of the apostles. In fact, as we shall see, however interesting the text remains, it betrays not only a very advanced stage of composition but also a systematic remodeling. It represents more a final phase in the evolution of the eucharistic prayer. than a primitive state. The totality of the compilation seems to have been arranged at the end of the fourth century, certainly

[72] F.X. Funk, *Didascalia et Constitutiones apostolorum*, vol. I (Paderborn, 1905).

by a Syrian, as is shown by the close relationship of the liturgy
of the 8th book to the Jerusalem liturgy called the liturgy of St.
James. But some divergencies of detail in the pseudo-Clementine
liturgy remain typical of the Antiochene liturgy. From what
we see of his christological and trinitarian formulas, the author
must have belonged to the semi-Arian milieu of this region. We
shall return at length to all of this.

But there is another part of this collection which has an undeniable and even exceptional interest for our knowledge of the
primitive eucharist, even though scholars have been very slow to
realize it. It is the 7th book. We find there a series of prayers
which give us not only primitive Christian material but also,
undoubtedly, Jewish material used at a very early period by
Christians. The way that certain of these elements were taken
into the much later synthesis of the liturgy of the 8th book allows
us to have a vivid grasp of the process through which a systematized Christian eucharist developed out of elements that came
not only from archaic Christianity but from Christianized Judaism.

It is Wilhelm Bousset who deserves the credit for having brought
these Jewish prayers used by Christians to our attention.[73] Goodenough specified, undoubtedly in a rather definitive way, the transformations (quite analogous to those we observe in the *Didache*)
that this re-use brought about.[74] The fantastic hypothesis of this
remarkable scholar, who for once has been led astray by too vivid
an imagination, is that these texts would have been composed by
Alexandrian Jews who cast their Judaism in the form of a "mystery religion" whose high priest would have been Philo. The
hypothesis is absolutely indefensible.[75] The "mystery" language
of Philo, which he shares with all sorts of contemporaries and not
only those concerned with religious questions, is precisely nothing
more than a language. It is mere fancy to look for any sort of ritual to which it should apply.[76] In fact, as we shall see, these texts
merely represent a local form of the Synagogue prayers which

---

[73] *Op. cit.*, note 20 of ch. 2.
[74] *Op. cit.*, note 8 of ch. 2.
[75] *Op. cit.*, pp. 235 ff.
[76] Cf. our book *Rite and Man*.

we have already studied. If it is a form that was obviously developed in a Greek-speaking area, it owes nothing more than its language to hellenism, and this language bears no appreciable trace even of that "mystery" jargon dear to Philo.

A study of these texts shows that they were composed in Greek by someone whose knowledge of Hebrew was rather rudimentary. The way in which he stumbles over expressions like Phelmoni is revealing. But it does show at the same time that the hellenized Jews who worked on these texts before the Christians who were to take them over and remodel them (if only slightly), were working with Hebrew sources. It manifests the fact that there never was an Alexandrian Judaism, no matter how hellenized, that became really independent from the Palestinian traditions.

When we are familiar with the text of the Palestinian or Babylonian *Tefillah*, it is enough to read these prayers to realize immediately that the first three are just a more wordy equivalent of its first three blessings. The following one is a prayer for the Sabbath which was later (and rather awkwardly) arranged into a prayer for the Christian Sunday. The last two of the series are respectively a prayer synthesizing the 14th, 15th, 16th and 17th *berakoth* of the same *Tefillah*, and an amplification of the 18th. It is therefore very likely that below their surface there was originally a *Tefillah* for the Sabbath, formed of seven prayers, according to a schema whose existence, as we have seen, is attested at the age of the beginning of Christianity. The seventh, connected with the Aaronic blessing, must have purely and simply disappeared once the liturgy was Christianized, along with the blessing itself.

Here is the first of these prayers which is obviously only a targumizing form of the *Aboth* blessing, the first of the Eighteen. It will be noted that Christians could use it, it seems, without having to change or add even a word. The idea, which appears at the end, that in the vision of the heavenly ladder Jacob had seen the Messiah in advance was already part of Jewish tradition.[77]

---

[77] Cf. L. Cerfaux, *La théologie de l'Église suivant saint Paul*, new edition (Paris, 1965).

Our eternal Savior, King of the gods: the only Almighty One
and Lord, the God of all that exists, and God of our holy and
irreproachable fathers who were before us, the God of Abraham, Isaac and Jacob, merciful and compassionate, patient
and abounding in mercy, to whom all hearts are open, and every
hidden feeling is revealed: the souls of the righteous cry to
you, in you the saints have placed their hope. The Father
of the irreproachable, he who hears those who call upon him
in righteousness, and who even knows the unspoken supplications, for your foreknowledge extends to the bowels of
men, and through the conscience you probe the thought of
each, and in every region of the earth incense goes up to you
through prayers and words—O you who have set up this present
world as the stadium of justice and who have opened to all
the almsgate, you who have shown to each of men, through
an innate knowledge and a natural judgment, and in accordance
with the expression of (your) law, that the possession of riches
is not eternal and that the beauty of a pleasing appearance
does not last, that physical strength easily disappears, and that
all (that) is but vapor and vanity, while only a consciousness
of an unerring faith passes through the heavens where, rising
up with truth, it receives (from your) right hand the future
delights; at the same time and even before it receives the
promise of the resurrection, the exultant soul rejoices in it.
Indeed, from the beginning, while our ancestor Abraham
gave himself to the way of truth, you led him by visions, and
you taught him what this world is, so that (your) knowledge
traced out the path for his faith, and that faith followed knowledge, and the covenant followed faith. Indeed, you have said:
"I shall make your seed like the stars of heaven and like the
sand on the shore of the sea". But again, having given him
the gift of Isaac, and knowing that he would behave likewise,
of him also you called yourself the God, saying: "I shall be your
God, and of your seed after you".[78] And as our Father Jacob
went off into Mesopotamia, you spoke to him through the
Christ whom you showed to him and you told him: "Here
I am with you, and I shall increase you and multiply you
abundantly".[79] And to Moses, your faithful and holy servant,

---

[78] Genesis 22:17 and 17:7.
[79] Genesis 26:24 and 48:4.

you spoke likewise in the burning bush: "I am who am, this is my eternal name, and my memorial for generations unto generations." O, Defender of the race[80] (γένους) of Abraham, you are blessed for ever.[81]

Let us limit ourselves to linking it to the condensed text of the first of the *Eighteen Blessings* as found in the Seder Amram Gaon.

Blessed be thou, JHWH, our God and God of our fathers, God of Abraham, God of Isaac and of Jacob, the great mighty and revered God, the most high God, who bestowest loving-kindness, possessest all things and rememberest the pious deeds of the fathers, and wilt bring a redeemer to their children's children for thy name's sake, in love ... Blessed be thou, JHWH, the Shield of Abraham.[82]

The second of our prayers is also an amplification of the second "blessing," *Geburoth*. It will be noted that its development is influenced by Psalm 104. As in the Jewish connected prayer that has remained traditional, we find there two different notions: the accent on the blessing of the seasons, good weather, assuring the faithful of their subsistence, and the transition from the present life to the life of resurrection. This feature which the Jewish commentators on *Geburoth* rightly attribute to a Pharisaic influence,[83] furnished a very natural starting point for the Christian developments that we are emphasizing. But this time we shall first quote the Jewish prayer that has remained within Hebrew tradition to show all that already belonged to the Jewish tradition, since we might be quite wrongly tempted to see in it merely Christian interpolations.

The second prayer of the *Gaon* says:

Thou art mighty forever, JHWH, thou quickenest the dead, thou art mighty to save, and thou causest the dew to fall (who causest the wind to blow and the rain to fall), who sustainest the living with lovingkindness, quickenest the dead with great mercy, supportest the falling, healest the sick,

---

[80] Exodus 3:14-15.
[81] *Apostolic Constitutions*, 1, VII, c. 33; F. X. Funk, *op. cit.* pp. 424 ff.
[82] Cf. above, p. 72.
[83] Cf. above, p. 73.

loosest them that are bound and keepest faith to them that
sleep in the dust. Who is like unto thee, Lord of mighty acts,
and who resemblest thee, King, who killest and quickenest
and causest salvation to spring forth. And faithful art thou
to quicken the dead. Blessed be thou, JHWH, who quickenest
the dead.[84]

Here now is what became of that prayer in the tradition used
by the 7th book of the *Apostolic Constitutions*:

Blessed are you, Lord, King of the ages, who, *through Christ*,
have made all things, and *through him*, at the beginning, have
brought order out of chaos, you who have separated the
waters from the waters by the firmament, and who have poured
out a spirit of life, who have strengthened the land, spread
out the heavens, and adorned both with appropriate creatures.
For it is by your power, O Master, that the world was established in its beauty, the heavens planted as a tent, lit up with
stars as a comfort in darkness; the light and the sun were
begotten to give the day and to bring forth fruit, the moon
to mark the seasons, according to its wax and wane, thus the
night was called forth and the day named and the firmament
appearing in the midst of the abysses. You have said also
that the waters come together and dry land appear. As for
the sea, who would describe it? The sea which ebbs, turbulent
with waves, but flows out again, pushed back from the shores
by your command, for you have said that the floods would sub-
side. Moreover, you have made a place there for the animals,
great or small, and for ships. Then, the earth has made the
many-colored flowers come forth and trees with every adorn-
ment, and, sustained by the variations of the luminaries,
they grow without ever varying from your prescriptions,
but, at your command, they are born or fade away, as a sign
of the seasons and the years, serving alternatively the needs
of men. Then the different types of animals were established,
on the land, in the sea, in the air and also the amphibians,
and the craftsmanlike Wisdom of your foreknowledge gives
to each of them what you have foreseen, for it does not neglect to provide for their divers needs any more than it failed
to produce their diversity. And, as the final stroke of your

[84] Cf. above, p. 72.

work, having disposed in your Wisdom an animal endowed
with reason, the citizen of the world, you formed him, saying:
"Let us make man in our image and likeness," establishing
him as a world within this world, with the help of the four
elements, modeling for him a body out of the elementary
bodies and fitting him with a soul created from nothing, gra-
tifying him with five senses, and placing in the soul a mind
(νοῦν) to be the guide of the senses. And, above all that,
Master, Lord, who will worthily tell of the course of the winds
which bring showers, the glitter of lightning, the rumbling of
thunder, all of which furnishes food for all men, and harmoniously tempers the atmosphere? Yet, man disobeyed you,
and you deprived him of the reward of his life, without an-
nihilating him, but with the result that after falling asleep for
a little while, you called him forth to rebirth by your sworn
promise. You have abolished the decree of (our death), you
who give life to the dead *through Jesus Christ our hope.*[85]

We can notice again in this formula the expressions borrowed
from the philosophers. We shall find still more of these in those
that follow. Once again, this is a feature that was already noticeable
in the Wisdom writings of the Greek bible, with which the following
prayers are even more closely related, as it will be shown later.
But borrowings of this kind, particularly from popularized stoicism,
are also to be found in St. Paul, despite the Palestinian character
of his Judaism.[86]

The third prayer is the most interesting of the series for our
study. In the third *berakah* of the *Shemoneh Esreh*, together with
the *Qedushah* that preceded it in the public recitation, as we said,
it incorporates the substance of the prayer that introduced the
Qedushah (*Keter*, "crown"), which is so notable for its stress on
the divine Kingdom. For the first time we find in the *Qedushah*
in this text the formula *heaven and earth* (and not only *earth*),
which will pass over into all the Christian liturgies. It comes
evidently from the *Yozer* prayer and the anticipated commentary
of the *Qedushah* which it contains. We must believe that the

---

[85] *A.C.*, VII, 34; Funk, *op. cit.*, pp. 426 ff.
[86] Cf. above, p. 20.

Alexandrian Jews incorporated it in the text before the Christians.[87]

Another significant characteristic of this third prayer of the 7th book is the way in which it also includes the recitation, if not of the *Shemah*, at least of a text which is its equivalent, taken from the same book of Deuteronomy. It seems that here we have a supplementary confirmation of the thesis common to the Jewish commentators, maintaining that the original place of the *Qedushah* would have been just before the *Shemah*, with the result that the *Qedushah* of the *Tefillah* would come from a later transposition of the *Qedushah* of *Yozer*. Indeed, as we see here, did it not actually bring the *Shemah* along with it, which would be a proof that it was originally connected with it?[88]

In order to facilitate comparison, here once again is the *Keter* prayer, the *Qedushah* which it introduces, and the third *berakah* as we find them in the *Seder Amram Gaon* to be recited straight through by the *hazzan*.

> (*Keter*) Unto thee shall the multitudes above with all the gatherings below give a crown, all with one accord shall thrice repeat the holy praise unto thee, according to what is said through thy prophet: *and one cried unto another and said*: HOLY, HOLY, HOLY IS JHWH OF HOSTS, THE WHOLE EARTH IS FULL OF HIS GLORY. Then with noise of great rushing, mighty and strong, they make their voices heard, and upraising themselves towards them, they say: BLESSED BE THE GLORY OF JHWH FROM HIS PLACE.
>
> From thy place shine forth, our King, and reign over us, for we wait upon thee. When wilt thou reign? Reign in Zion speedily, even in our days and in our lives do thou dwell (there). Mayest thou be magnified and sanctified in the midst

---

[87] Cf. Eric Werner, *The Sacred Bridge*, pp. 284 ff., who shows well the foolhardiness of too many Christian commentaries on this difference even though they are ignorant of its origin.

[88] Cf. above, p. 64. For the first time we find here in the *Qedushah* the formula *the heavens and the earth* (and not merely the *earth*) which will pass into all Christian liturgies. It comes evidently from the *Yozer* prayer and from the anticipated commentary of the *Qedushah* which it constitutes. We must believe that the Alexandrian Jews, incorporated it in the text, before the Christians.

of Jerusalem, thy city throughout all generations and to all eternity. And let our eyes behold thy kingdom, according to the word that was spoken in the songs of thy might by David, thy righteous anointed: JHWH shall reign for ever, thy God, Zion, unto all generations. Hallelujah.

(*Qedushat ha-Shem.*) From generation to generation give homage to God for he alone is high and holy, and thy praise, our God, shall not depart from our mouth for ever, for a great and holy king art thou. Blessed be thou JHWH, thou holy God.[89]

And here now is the synthesized text of the *Apostolic Constitutions*. It will be noted that, preceding the introduction of the themes that we have just re-read, there are other themes whose provenance we shall attempt to point out.

You are great, Lord almighty, and great is your might, and your intelligence cannot be calculated: Creator, Savior, rich in grace, patient, *choregos*[90] of mercy, you who in no way neglect the salvation of your creatures, for you are good by nature and even so, you spare sinners, inviting them to penance, for your instruction is compassionate. Indeed, how would we subsist, if you were to call us suddenly to judgment, while we have difficulty in catching our breath in our weakness when you have patience with us? The heavens have announced your power, and the earth, shaken in its self-assurance, is suspended over the abyss. The sea, swirling with waves, which nourishes an innumerable flock of living beings, is held back by the sand, dreading your will, and forces all to cry out: "How wonderful are your works, O Lord, you have done them all in (your) Wisdom; the earth is filled with your creation" And the zealous Army of Angels, with the intelligible spirits, says: "One alone is holy (for whoever it may be)"[91], and the holy six-winged Seraphim, with the Cherubim, singing to you the hymn of victory, cry out with (their) voices

---

[89] Cf. above, p. 72.

[90] The *choregos* in classical Greece was the one who paid for all the expenses of a public holiday.

[91] The Greek translator did not understand the sense of the Hebrew *Phelmon* and transcribed it in this way, like the Septuagint, Aquila and Theodotion.

that are never silent: *Holy, holy, holy, the Lord Sabaoth; the heavens and the earth are full of your glory.* And the multitude of the other orders, the Angels, the archangels, the thrones, the dominations, the principalities, the authorities, the powers say in a loud voice: *Blessed (be) the glory of the Lord and of his place!* Moreover, Israel, your earthly Church, *taken from the nations*, vying with the heavenly powers, night and day, with all its heart and with all the desire of its soul, sings: "God's chariot, through myriads and thousands, rejoices, the Lord is in them, in Sinai, in the sanctuary." The heavens know the one who spread his tent without founding it upon anything, like a cube of stone, who joined the earth and the waters, who diffused the air to foster life, and who surrounded it with fire to warm (it) and to comfort (us) in the darkness. The choir of the stars amazes (us) in telling of him who counted them out and in manifesting him who named them, like the living creatures (who manifest) him who gave them life, and the trees, him who planted them. Moreover, all things, made by your Word, represent the force of your might, wherefore every man must, in dominating over all of this because of you, from the depth of his heart send up to you *through Christ* the hymn of all of this. For you are good in your benefits and munificent in your compassion, the one Almighty one, for whenever you wish you have the power, and your eternal might cools the flame, shuts the mouth of lions, tames the sea monsters, raises the sick, and overturns the powers: when they become too haughty, it subdues an army of enemies, a numerous people. You are the one who, in heaven, on the land or upon the sea, is never limited by any boundary. And this does not come from us, Master, but it is the oracle of your servant who said: "And you shall know in your heart that the Lord your God is God on high in heaven, here on earth, and that there is none other than he."[92] Indeed, there is no other God but you; no other is holy but you. Lord God of (all) knowl-

---

[92] As Baumstark emphasized, it is remarkable that precisely this verse and not 6:4 ff, was used by the liturgy of the Samaritans. This fact allows us to suppose that this must have been the case with the archaic forms of the Synagogue liturgy and that it is to them and not to a Christian revision that we owe this presence in this prayer of a text other than the *Shemah*, but with an equivalent meaning.

edge, God of the saints, holy above all the saints, for the sanctified are made so by your hands. Glorious and superexalted, invisible by nature, unfathomable in your judgments, you whose
life has need of nothing, immutable and indefectible in (your)
continuity, tireless in (your) operation, indescribable in (your)
greatness, established forever in your tabernacle, you whose
knowledge is without beginning, truth without change, work
without intermediary, whose might is incontestable, whose
monarchy inseparable, whose Rule is without end, whose
force unrivaled, whose army is uncountable. For you are
the Father of Wisdom, the demiurge of creation *made by a
mediator, but* whose beginning you are, *choregos* of providence,
giver of laws, the satisfaction of want; (you are) the one who
punishes the ungodly and who rewards the righteous, *the
God and the Father of Christ and the Lord of those who venerate
him, whose promise is without deception, whose judgment is incorruptible, whose decision is impossible to decline, whose piety
is unceasing, whose eucharist is eternal, through whom there
is owed a worship that is worthy of you, on the part of all holy
and rational nature.*[93]

We may wonder from where the initial developments on penance
come from in this text since they are not found in the third blessing
neither as we have it in the *Gaon* nor in the other medieval or
modern prayer-books. We must stress that they correspond to the
respective contents of the fourth, and especially the fifth, as well
as the sixth, seventh and even the eighth of the *Shemoneh Esreh*
blessings: on the knowledge of God, repentance, forgiveness, redemption, and finally the healing of all evils, particularly those
illnesses that are looked upon as a consequence of sin.

There is nothing among the *berakoth* of the *Shemoneh Esreh*
which corresponds to the fourth of our prayers. Yet it is nonethe-

---

[93] *A.C.*, VII, 35; Funk, *op. cit.*, pp. 428 ff. This text explains to us how the
Sanctus was part of the Christian liturgy from the beginning, before taking its
place in the eucharistic meal itself. The fact is attested by Clement of Rome,
Epistle to the Corinthians, 34, and by Tertullian, *De Oratione*, 3 ; P.L., t. 1, col.
1156-1157. But by itself our text allows us to assert that it was still, as in the
Synagogue, to the prayers of the service of readings that its recitation belonged.
Origen, it seems, gives us the first example of its transition into the eucharistic
prayer of the sacramental meal: *De Principiis*, IV, 3, 14.

less the most Jewish of all with its stress on the Sabbath, to the
point that the particularly emphatic Christian additions were not
able to apply it to Sunday and its original focus was completely
erased. At this point we should recall that the Eighteen Blessings,
in their most ancient use, were not recited on the Sabbath, but
were replaced by a formula of seven *berakoth*, which was to be
the Jewish model of our own prayers. Because it fell into disuse
at an early date, no text of this special Sabbath formulary has
been preserved for us. The sequence of the prayers of the 7th
book of the *Apostolic Constitutions* give us an idea of what this
shortened formula may have been, and the following text helps
us to conceive how the praise of the Sabbath must have been
its pivotal point.

Lord almighty, you have created the world *through Christ*,
and you have established a memorial of it in the Sabbath
for on that day you have caused us to rest from our labors
in order to meditate upon your laws, and you have prescribed
festivals for the joy of our souls and that we might commemorate the Wisdom which you have created: *how, on our behalf,
it accepted to be born of a woman, it was manifested in life,
showing itself in the baptism as God and man; it suffered for
us by your leave, it died and was raised by your might. Wherefore, we, celebrating on Sunday the feast of the resurrection,
rejoice on account of him who has conquered death, and brought
life and incorruption. Indeed, through him you have led the
nations to you, in order to make them the people you have acquired for yourself, the true Israel, the friend of God, the one
who sees God.* For you have caused our fathers, Lord, to come
out of the land of Egypt, you delivered them from the fiery
furnace, and from the mud and the bricks that they were
obliged to make; you redeemed them from the hand of Pharaoh and his subjects, and you led them across the sea on
dry land, and you made them sojourn in the desert by virtue
of your benefits of every kind; you gave them the law, the
Decalogue, which your voice pronounced and your hand
wrote, you prescribed the Sabbath for them, not as a pretext
for idleness but as an occasion for devotion, for the knowledge of your power, to prevent them from doing evil by surrounding them with a holy barrier, to teach them and to
gladden them during the week. Wherefore (you established)

a week, seven weeks, the seventh month and the seventh year, and upon its seventh return, the jubilee, in the fiftieth year, for forgiveness, so that men might have no excuse to cover up their ignorance; (the law) prescribed that they rest each Sabbath, so that no one would even dare to utter one word of anger upon the Sabbath day. Indeed, the Sabbath is the repose of creation, the fulfilment of the world, the study of the law, the eucharistic praise to God for the gifts he has made to men. *But Sunday surpasses all of this in that it manifests the mediator himself, the provident one, the lawgiver, the principle of the resurrection, the first born of all creation, God the Word, and the man born of Mary, the only one (who was so born) without the help of man, the one who lived in a holy manner, who was crucified under Pontius Pilate, who died and who rose from the dead. Wherefore, Sunday, O Master, invites (us) to offer you the eucharist for all things (πάντων): for it is itself the grace that comes from you and whose greatness has hidden beneath it every (other) benefit.*[94]

In the absence of a more direct term of comparison, we may connect this prayer with the insertion that was introduced into the third *berakah* for the end of the meals on the Sabbath. There we can see the same sabbatical theology:

> Comfort us, JHWH, our God, in Zion, thy city, and in establishing thy Temple, and be merciful, JHWH, our God, unto thy people and upon thy city Jerusalem and upon Zion, the dwelling place of thy glory ...
>
> Be pleased, JHWH, our God, to fortify us by thy commandments, and (especially) by the commandment of the seventh day. This (day) is great and holy through thy holiness and thy rest, and we will rest on it in accordance with the commandment of thy will, and let there be no trouble and grief in our rest. And let the kingdom of the house of David speedily return to its place ... [95]

The fifth of our prayers begins by combining the content of the fourteenth and fifteenth *berakoth*: the *Birkat Yerushalem* and the *Birkat David*:

<hr>

[94] *A.C.*, VII, 36; Funk, *op. cit.*, pp. 432 ff.
[95] D.H., p. 151.

(*Birkat Yerushalem*) To Jerusalem, thy city, return in mercy, and dwell in it as thou hast spoken; and rebuild it as an ever-lasting building in our days. Blessed be thou, JHWH, who re-buildest Jerusalem.

(*Birkat David*) Speedily cause the offspring of David to flour-ish, and let his horn be exalted by thy salvation, because we wait for thy salvation all the day. Blessed be thou, JHWH, who causest the horn of salvation to flourish.[96]

Here is what we find in the first paragraph of the fifth prayer given by the *Constitutions*:

You who have accomplished the promises of the prophets, who have had mercy on Zion, who took pity on Jerusalem by exalting the throne of David your servant in its midst, through the birth of Christ, who is born according to the flesh from the seed of David, of the one who alone remained a virgin ... [97]

What follows will similarly combine the 16th *berakah* (*Tefil-lah*) for the granting of prayers, with the 17th (*Abodah*), which according to the Rabbis resumes the prayer that accompanied the offering of sacrifices in the Temple.

They are formulated in this way by *Amram Gaon*:

(*Tefillah*) Hear our voice, JHWH, have mercy upon us and accept our prayer in mercy and favour; for thou art a God who hearkenest unto our prayers and supplications: from thy presence, our King, turn us not empty away, for thou hearkenest to the prayer of every mouth. Blessed be thou, JHWH, who hearkenest unto prayer.

(*Abodah*) Accept, JHWH, our God, thy people Israel and their prayer and restore the service to the Holy of Holies of thy house and receive speedily in love and favour the fire-offerings of Israel and their prayer, and may the service of thy people Israel ever be acceptable unto thee, and let our eyes behold thy return to Zion in mercy. Blessed be thou, JHWH, who restorest thy Presence to Zion.[98]

---

[96] Cf. above, p. 74.
[97] *A.C.*, VII, 37; Funk, *op. cit.*, pp. 436 ff.
[98] Cf. above, p. 77.

The prayer of the *Apostolic Constitutions* synthesizes these two prayers into one. It reintroduces a detailed recall of the fathers, this time in relation to the sacrifices that the Bible speaks about.

... And you, now, Master, O God, accept the prayers which are upon the lips of your people, *taken from the nations*, of those who call upon you in truth, as you have accepted the gifts of the righteous in their generations. You have looked in the first place upon the sacrifice of Abel and you accepted it, that of Noah upon leaving the ark, that of Abraham when he had left the land of the Chaldeans, that of Isaac at the well of the oath, that of Jacob at Bethel,[99] that of Moses in the desert, that of Aaron between the living and the dead, that of Gideon on the rock and the fleece before his sin, that of Manoah and his wife on the plain, that of Samson who thirsted before his transgression, that of Jephthah in the battle, before his rash promise, that of Barak and Deborah in regard to Sisara, that of Samuel at Mishpah, that of David on the threshingfloor of Ornan the Jebusite, those of Solomon at Gibeon and at Jerusalem, that of Elijah on Mount Carmel, that of Elisha at the dried up spring, that of Jehoshaphat during the war, those of Hezekiah in his illness and in regard to Sennacherib, that of Manasseh in the land of the Chaldeans after his transgression, that of Josiah for the Passover, that of Ezra upon his return (from exile), that of Daniel in the lions' den, that of Jonah in the belly of the sea monster, that of the three children in the fiery furnace, that of Anna in the tabernacle before the ark, that of Nehemiah and Zorobabel at the time of the rebuilding of the walls, that of Mattathias and his sons in their zeal towards you, that of Jael in his blessings. Now, also, receive the prayers which your people offer you, with (their) knowledge, *through Christ in the Spirit.*[100]

Several of these names should be remembered. Abraham and Abel, particularly, we find mentioned again, and more than once, in a Christian eucharistic prayer at the moment that it implores the acceptance of the sacrifice.

---

[99] The text, through a copyist's error, has Bethlehem.
[100] A.C., VII, 38; Funk, *op. cit.*, p. 438.

The last of our prayers, finally, corresponds to the 18th "blessing," the *Hodah*, which concludes the whole of the *Tefillah* in a classic return to the initial act of thanksgiving.

Here they are, one after the other:

(Hodah) We give thanks unto thee, our God and the God of our fathers: thou art the Rock of our lives, the Shield of our salvation through every generation. We will give thanks unto thee and declare thy praise for our lives which are committed unto thy hand, and for our souls which are in thy charge. Thou art all-good for thy mercies fail not, thou art merciful for thy lovingkindnesses never cease, we have ever hoped in thee. And bring us not to shame, JHWH, our God, abandon us not and hide not thy face from us, and for all thy name be blessed and exalted, our King, for ever and ever. Everything that liveth should thank thee, Selah, and praise thy name, All-good, in truth. Blessed be thou, JHWH, whose name is all-good, and unto whom it is becoming to give thanks.[101]

We give you thanks for all things, almighty Master, because you have not taken away your mercies and your compassion from us, but in every generation you save, deliver, assist, and protect. For you were helpful in the days of Enos and Enoch, in the days of Moses and Joshua, in the days of the Judges, in the days of David and the kings, in the days of Samuel, Elijah and the prophets, in the days of Esther and Mordocai, in the days of Judith, in the days of Judas Maccabaeus and his brothers. In our days, also, help us, *through your great High priest Jesus Christ, your Servant.* Indeed, *he* has delivered (us) from the sword, *he* has snatched us from famine by giving (us) food, of sickness *he* has healed (us), from the evil tongue *he* has protected (us).[102] For all of this, *through Christ,* we give thanks to you who have given us a voice disposed to confessing (you), having fortified us with a harmonious tongue, as with a plectrum. (You have also provided us) with taste for appreciation, with touch for distinguishing, with eyes to see, with ears to hear, with the sense of smell, with hands for working, with feet for walking. And all of this,

---

[101] Cf Cf. above, p. 77.

[102] We underline the *"he's"*, which are inserted in order to attribute to Christ all that in the original prayer was to have been attributed to God.

you form from a particle in the maternal womb, you grant it after it has taken shape an immortal soul and you make it see the light of day. This rational animal, man, you have instructed by (your) laws, you have enlightened by (your) judgments, and, bringing him for a short time into decomposition, you promised him resurrection. What life will suffice then, what length of ages will be such that man can give you thanks? But what is impossible for us to do as we should do, we must still perform in so far as it is in our power. *For you have delivered us from the ungodliness of polytheism, you have snatched us from the sect of Christ's murderers, you have freed us from the ignorance in which we had wandered. You have sent Christ as a man among men, the one who is God the Only-Begotten Son; you have made the Paraclete dwell in us, you have placed us in the care of the Angels, you have reduced the devil to shame; you have made to be what did not exist, you preserve what exists, you give to life its measure, you procure food for us, you have promised penance. For all that, to you (be) glory and veneration, through Jesus Christ, now and always and forever and ever.* Amen.[103]

Once again, the differences bear especially on detailed enumerations, substituted for the global formulas of the Jewish prayers which prevailed. In each case, as we have been able to observe in the foregoing prayers, these exhaustive encomia (which are traditional in the Wisdom writings whose kinship with the Alexandrian Judaism of our formulas is obvious), that are also found in the Epistle to the Hebrews, furnish for the Christians who used them a final and ready-made place to insert the mention of Christ and his work.

Jewish as these prayers still are beneath their Christian overlay, entire portions of them will enter integrally into the eucharistic prayer of the 8th book, which is decidely Christian as we shall soon show. With these prayers, we see the Christian prayer being formed within the context of the Jewish prayer. When it finally becomes separated, it will appear very naturally that it was composed not only in a Jewish mold but of its very substance.

---

[103] *A.C.*, VII, 38; Funk, *op. cit.*, pp. 438 ff.

The Patristic Eucharist
and the Vestiges of the Primitive Eucharist:
the Liturgies of Addai and Mari
and of St. Hippolytus

THE SETTING DOWN IN A WRITTEN FORM OF THE LITURGICAL
prayers in both Judaism and Christianity is a relatively late phenomenon. In both cases, it came about only after it was felt that
tradition was in danger of being changed as long as it was not
cast in forms that were set even to their last details. Because
of the reaction the heresies brought about, they were a particularly important factor in this evolution. This is indeed the reason
why we see Christian texts of this type becoming common only
until after the great crisis of Arianism, i. e. after the second half
of the fourth century.

THE CONSTITUTION OF THE TRADITIONAL FORMULARIES
OF THE EUCHARIST

Still, a document like the *Apostolic Tradition* of St. Hippolytus
gives evidence that typical models had begun to be composed be-

136

fore that date. But the same document shows evidence that it was as examples to guide the celebrants rather than *ne varietur* formulas that they were first proposed.[1] Inversely, for a long time after the appearance and the generalization of relatively set formularies, variations on their basic themes managed to continue almost to our own day. In the Roman liturgy itself, as conservative as it seems to be, the composition of variable eucharistic prefaces practically never ceased. For as long as it continued to remain alive the Mozarabic liturgy experienced this plasticity with all the parts of the eucharist.[2] The Eastern liturgies, for their part, particularly among the Copts, the Ethiopians and the Maronites, continued up to the end of the Middle Ages to work out more or less new formulas.

It is true, however, that the great development of the eucharistic formularies coincides with the high-point of the patristic period, which extends approximately from the middle of the fourth century to the middle of the sixth, or from the Cappadocian Fathers to St. Gregory the Great. Since the liturgical manuscripts were destined for liturgical use and were then destroyed or scrapped once they were no longer used, we have but very few precious fragments from an earlier age. On the other hand, since the compositions of this period came to dominate and to be accepted, we are overwhelmed by the abundance of texts it has produced. We may say that it was at this time that the eucharist found its classic expression. We should not be sorry that a rather strong discouragement of improvisation soon set in. For, we must admit the following centuries produced little else but more or less successful variations on the themes which at that time were beginning to be defined and take shape. Or else they were lost from sight and men very quickly became sidetracked in prattle and fancy. When what we shall call for simplicity's sake the Middle Ages did not hold to the patristic texts, the eucharistic prayer was in perpetual danger of being debased or fragmented.[3]

---

[1] Cf. *Apostolic Tradition*, the end of par, 10.
[2] Cf. below, pp. 319 ff.
[3] Cf. below, pp. 338 ff.

On the other hand, when we look at what this great age produced, we are struck by its vigor and its richness. But at first
sight at least, we are also disconcerted by the variety of forms.
Certain constant factors can be observed. But the multiplicity
of the forms which surround them is such that we have difficulty
in classifying these documents and even more so when it comes
to making up their genealogy. Still, a consensus has been gradually established among comparative liturgists connecting this
vast proliferation with five great principal centers, or better,
with five areas of composition and initial diffusion. Three are situated in the East and two in the West. We may therefore say
roughly that there are five basic schemas for the eucharistic prayer
which are still found today in the most venerable texts that have
remained in use. Going from East to West, they are the East
Syrian, the West Syrian, the Alexandrian, the Roman and the
Gallican-Mozarabic types.

We must not disguise the fact that there is some oversimplifica-
tion in this commonly accepted division. For example, we have
to admit that the so-called West Syrian type has more or less
affected both the East Syrian and the Alexandrian, in practically
all their formulas which are available to us directly. Moreover,
upon closer examination, the West Syrian type itself has two
profoundly different varieties that may be connected with Antioch and Jerusalem respectively.[4]

In the West, similarly, the Roman type is accompanied by a
whole series of secondary types like that of Lyon and especially
the Milanese (which is called Ambrosian).[5] It is very hard to determine whether they are Gallicanized Roman types or rather
preserved archaic Roman forms. It is so difficult that some people
have come to maintain that the Roman type in the beginning
was not clearly distinct amidst a tangle of local forms. All of
these would be more or less analogous to the forms we call Gallican or Mozarabic. The latter would have simply continued to

---

[4] Cf. below, pp. 350 ff.

[5] Cf. Archdale A. King, *Liturgies of the Primatial Sees* (London, 1957),
pp. 1 ff. and pp. 286 ff.

evolve elsewhere, while the others would have been statically fixed in Rome.[6]

It is certain, in any case, that we must allow for unexpected exportations and local metamorphoses that are not always easy to explain. It is not in Byzantium that we can best discover the characteristics of the ancient Byzantine rite, but rather in remote Armenia, despite the original and particularly proliferous overlays that they underwent.[7] In the capital itself there were influences, particularly from Palestine, which did a great deal to alter and even abolish ancient local customs.[8] Similarly, it is not in Cappadocia, nor in neighboring Syria, nor even in Constantinople, but only in Egypt that we find the eucharist of St. Basil in what seems to be its original form.[9]

In addition to these more or less global interchanges, there are some erratic elements, and it is still harder to explain just how they could have ended up where we find them. To give but one example, how does it happen that in the middle of the Ambrosian canon we come up against a phrase that seems to have come straight out of a West Syrian anaphora?

In all of these interchanges two facts are so obvious that people have been too often tempted to explain all the apparent assimilations by them. It is the imperialism of Rome and that of Byzantium. Contrary to what many modern scholars would tend to imagine, as a result of a romantic notion of Orthodox liberalism (or anarchy) and Roman authoritarianism, Byzantine imperialism, particularly in what interests us, seems to have been much more systematic (and much more rigorous) than the imperialism of Rome. For a long time, the Roman liturgy spread rather by a whole process of spontaneous lendings, or desired (or encouraged) adoption on the part of the secular authorities, than by any effort from pontifical authority. People have been bewildered for so long by a St. Gregory the Great's liberalism on this point when he advises St. Augustine of Canterbury in a letter to shape a liturgy

---

[6] Cf. for example, Dom Gregory Dix, *The Shape of the Liturgy*, pp. 563 ff.

[7] Cf. A. Baumstark, *Comparative Liturgy* (London, 1958), p. 30.

[8] Baumstark, *op. cit.*, p. 4.

[9] Baumstark, *op. cit.*, p. 51.

for the Anglo-Saxons that would be adapted and borrowed from whatever sources seemed best to him, that they have tried to think that the letter was counterfeit.[10] Today, everyone is practically agreed on its authenticity. It is true that a few examples of the contrary attitude are found, such as a particularly narrow and acrimonious letter of Pope Innocent to Decentius of Gubbio.[11] But this is much more an indication ot the personal temperament of its author than an evidence of any coherent political notion on the part of the Roman See at that time. In fact, ancient ecclesiastical Rome seems for a long time to have remained indifferent to the spread of its own liturgical tradition. And it subsequently showed itself very receptive to the traditions, Gallican and others, that came to it with editions of its own books that had been copiously interpolated by the "barbarians" for their own use.[12] We have to wait for Gregory VII for this political outlook, or rather its absence, to be modified. Actually, in a few years, this pope was to effect the almost complete annihilation of the Mozarabic rite and its replacement by the Roman rite in Spain.[13] Yet, it must not be forgotten that the Mozarabic rite had been dogmatically discredited by the support that adoptionist theology thought it could find there. Then, too, the Spanish kings who were more or less under the influence of the Cluniac monks, had already precipitated the more or less spontaneous movement that led to this substitution.

Byzantium, on the contrary, from the fifth century pursued a politic of pure and simple suppression of the local traditions and their replacement by the so-called Byzantine liturgy, which actually was merely the special form that the West Syrian liturgy came to take in the new Rome on the Bosphorus. The defections that followed, which were blamed on the Nestorian or Monophysite heresies, seem today to have rather been reactions of cultural nationalism, exacerbated by the imperial desire for unification at

---

[10] Cf. *Epist. 64*, lib. XI.; P. L., t. 77, col. 1187.
[11] Cf. Gregory Dix, *op. cit.*, p. 564.
[12] Cf. below, pp. 318 ff.
[13] Cf. below, p. 317.

any price.[14] The absolutism which it was to reach in the twelfth century was expressed undisguisedly in a famous opinion of the great canonist Theodore Balsamon. The Orthodox Alexandrian patriarch at the time asked him what should be thought of and done with the liturgy of St. James and this high authority answered him that there were no other Orthodox liturgies except those said to be of John Chrysostom and St. Basil, and of course, in the form in which they were known and practiced in the imperial city. The response is all the more characteristic since Balsamon himself was originally from Antioch, yet the idea, incontestable in itself, never seems to have touched him that the liturgies of New Rome were merely sub-products of the liturgy of his native province.[15]

Nor must we forget that the victories of these two imperialisms proved many times to be merely Pyrrhic. We have already said enough about the evolution of the Roman liturgy and the very beginnings of the Byzantine liturgy for it to be easily understood. If the so-called Roman liturgy was finally imposed on the whole of the West, it was under a composite form in which the only thing Roman remaining is a certain framework and certain formulas. These were fairly well swallowed up by an onrush of foreign formulas and submerged by a whole veneer of rites, vestments and chants that had nothing Roman about them. Similarly, the Byzantine liturgy, which was born not in Byzantium but at Antioch, and which had been remodeled at Antioch or elsewhere before it was transported to Byzantium, was to receive there first a considerable monastic overlay coming from Jerusalem, and more precisely from the laura of St. Sabbas. The Stoudios monastery in the capital was the home of this genuine remolding, at least the main one. Nor were these allogenic elements the last that the city of the *basileis* would continue to receive, before re-exporting them under the imperial seal together with what remained of its most ancient features.

[14] Metropolitan Seraphim in his work *L'Église orthodoxe* (1952) brings this point out.

[15] Cf. P. G., t. 119, col. 1033 ff. The liturgy of St. Mark is, of course, similarly condemned by Balsamon.

These few reminders were doubtless necessary so that we might
have no illusions about the distinctness or the autonomy of the
five great types of the eucharistic liturgy that are generally acknowledged. Actually they are merely families which in many
ways are interrelated and which in any case still remain part of
one and the same race.

Independently from the later interbreeding which may have
been able more or less to obliterate the original differences among
the types enumerated, it seems that we have to acknowledge
certain original points of kinship. But once again they defy the
most rooted prejudices. We have become accustomed to see Chris-
tendom as having been divided for a long time into two blocs,
the East centering around Byzantium and the West around Rome.
That a large part of this division is artificial is particularly, if not
uniquely, evident in the realm of liturgy. Actually, the West
Syrian liturgy (i.e., in this case, the liturgy of Antioch) seems
more directly related to the Gallican and Mozarabic liturgies than
to its neighbors in the East, if we keep to what seems most basic.
And, still more clearly, the Roman and Alexandrian liturgies
seem to be very close cousins, if not sisters. In other words, if we
wish to trace a line of demarcation between the different paths of
liturgical tradition, and especially the tradition of the eucharist,
among the different models of prayer which first formed along these
paths, this line cannot be vertical. It does not know the customary
sectioning off of East from West. It tends to reveal another division which cuts in two both the East and the West.

Let us hasten to add that the fact is undoubtedly so little in
conformity with our mental habits that many scholars still find
it repugnant to accept it completely. They cannot deny either
the surprising analogies or the common differences for they are
patent. But they would like to explain them by more or less late
influences rather than by some community of origin. This is particularly the case with regard to rites from what we may call the
Far West (the Gallican and the Mozarabic), compared to West
Syria.[16] Many people admit that the analogies are secondary and
not original. We shall see further on a few reasons that seem to

---

[16] Cf. Archdale A. King, *op. cit.*, pp. 457 ff.

militate against such an opinion. It remains tenable, however, in view of the relatively late date of all our detailed documents on the rites of the Far West. On the other hand, it becomes much more difficult to uphold the thesis of later influences in order to explain the analogies between Rome and Alexandria. Actually it is clear that the more ancient the texts to which we can go back, and which are certain witnesses of a local usage, the more striking are the analogies.

Whatever the case in the texts as they are presented to us, and whatever way we may wish to account for them the analogies are there. They are mainly structural, but there are also frequently analogies even more striking (which does not necessarily mean more convincing) in the detail of the formulas.

THE WEST SYRIAN AND GALLICAN-MOZARABIC TYPES

To begin with the West Syrian rite, whose structure seems to be of a very special clarity, we have successively:

1) The first part of an act of thanksgiving, leading to the hymn which we call the *Sanctus*.

2) The second part of the thanksgiving, leading to the narrative of the eucharistic institution.

3) A prayer of a special but practically universal type which is called the "anamnesis", and which seems to be a resuming and an amplification of the words: "Do this in memory (or as a memorial) of me."

4) Another prayer of a very definite type, but which actually is scarcely found in its fulness elsewhere but in the West Syrian rite and the rites influenced by it: the "epiclesis," i.e. an invocation petitioning the descent of the Holy Spirit to consecrate the bread and wine and to make them the body and blood of the Lord, and, secondarily, a petition that God accept the sacrifice offered and that he communicate his grace to the participants.

5) A series of detailed intercessions for all the needs of the Church and the world, and of commemorations of saints.

6) A final doxology in a trinitarian form.

Let us add, as a characteristic proper to the West Syrian rite
that (1) is dominated by the divine person of the Father and is
more or less purely an act of thanksgiving for creation, while (2) is
dominated by the Son and gives thanks for the redemption; (3) (4),
and to a certain extent (5) introduce the Spirit and develop the
theme of the sanctification of the Church and the whole universe,
in a clearly eschatological perspective.

All of this can be found again, in the same order, in at least a
certain number of Gallican or Mozarabic formularies, with the
exception of (5) which is never present. But the content of the
the different parts in the Far West is often much more nebulous
in its details, and it is not rare for it to wander more or less completely from this schema, although there is always first an initial
act of thanksgiving ending with the *Sanctus*, secondly its renewal,
in a form more or less explicit ending with the words of institution,
thirdly a continuation in which we must admit that the anamnesis
and the epiclesis are often intermingled and more often tapered
down or even watered down completely into almost any kind of
prayer whatsoever, and fourthly a doxology which is generally
stunted.

THE ALEXANDRIAN AND THE ROMAN TYPES

If we go on to Rome, we have a very different order and, after
the simplicity and harmony of the foregoing, it may seem disconcerting. We have first of all (1) which is also an act of thanksgiving leading to the *Sanctus*, but here redemption and creation
are mingled (most often creation is little more than merely mentioned); (2) a first prayer recalling the sacrifice; (3) a first series of
intercessions for the living and commemoration of the Saints;
(4) a prayer—in two distinct but connected formulas—petitioning
for the acceptance of the sacrifice together with a formal invocation for the consecration of the eucharistic elements, (5) the words
of institution, (6) an anamnesis which is rather similar to the West
Syrian, although more sober, (7) a last invocation—at present
also in two joint prayers—that the sacrifice offered be accepted,
and more precisely, today, that it have in us its whole effect of
grace; (8) a new intercession which is first for the departed and

then again for the living, combined with a new commemoration of the Saints, and (9) the final doxology.

At Alexandria, especially if we refer to the most ancient documents, we find an analogous order, except that all the intercessions were grouped together at the beginning as well as the commemorations, and that this whole section together with the prayer that precedes it in the Roman rite is placed even before the *Sanctus*. We therefore have the following order:

1) initial act of thanksgiving;

2) first prayer recalling the sacrifice;

3) copious intercessions and commemorations ending with a prayer for the acceptance of the sacrifice.

4) resumption of the thanksgiving, leading to the *Sanctus*;

5) a new prayer petitioning for the acceptance of the sacrifice with a formal invocation for the consecration of the elements;

6) the words of institution;

7) the anamnesis;

8) a last invocation that the sacrifice offered be accepted, and more precisely that it have its effects of grace in us, and

9) the final doxology.

It is fitting to add that neither at Rome in the text which has come down to us nor at Alexandria in the most ancient forms of the texts known to us, is there any trace of a special attribution of the major sections of the anaphora to the three divine persons in particular, as referred to in turn. It is particularly only in the formulas that are visibly influenced by West Syria that we find in Egypt a special invocation of the descent of the Holy Spirit, either in the second or in the third prayer. Between these two in Alexandria as in Rome the whole content of the Syrian epiclesis seems at first sight to have been scattered. In other words, the "epiclesis" as it is ordinarily understood seems to be no more primitive in Alexandria than in Rome, where it seems simply to be lacking. Or, if you prefer, at Alexandria as in Rome, there are not one but at least two epicleses (if we take the word in its broad sense), one before and the other after the words of institution, not to mention what could be called a pre-epiclesis which comes well before the institution. But none of these prayers, at

Rome today nor, it seems, at Alexandria in the beginning, implores the intervention of the Holy Spirit.

THE SURVIVAL OF A MORE ANCIENT TYPE
IN THE EAST SYRIAN TRADITION: ADDAI AND MARI

Before seeking to unravel this apparent tangle, despite the partial analogies which may suggest an initial path for the investigations to follow, it is worthwhile to proceed to the fifth type of the patristic eucharist, that of East Syria. Until now we have left it aside because it obviously refuses to be classed with either of the two preceding groups. From its general framework, at least at first sight, it would rather connect with the other Syrian type, but not from its plan which differs on a capital point: the intercessions and commemorations, all grouped together in one whole as in West Syria, instead of following the epiclesis, are inserted in a manner that is found nowhere else, between the anamnesis and the epiclesis. We have then the plan that we first gave, except that (4) and (5) are inverted:

1) the first act of thanksgiving leading to the *Sanctus*;
2) the second thanksgiving leading to the words of institution;
3) the anamnesis;
4) intercessions and commemorations;
5) the epiclesis, and
6) the final doxology.

Yet, when we examine the most ancient example of this schema, the so-called eucharist of the Apostles, or of Addai and Mari, it is immediately evident that the schema in question is artificial.[17] It was obtained, and furthermore very imperfectly, only by the addition of elements that are visibly from different times, at the price of splitting up a prayer or a series of prayers that are more ancient. But, undoubtedly by reason of its great age, the original text of these prayers was practically entirely respected. We may say that their artificially separated extremities always tend to reconnect over and above the adventitious elements. It is enough

---

[17] Cf. E. C. Ratcliff, "The Original Form of the Anaphora of Addai and Mari," in *Journal of Theological Studies*, vol. 30, 1929, pp. 23 ff.

to leave out these latter for us to see a prayer arise which is undeniably continuous. And everything leads us to believe that this prayer is the most ancient Christian eucharistic composition to which we can have access today. It represents a model that is quite different from the prayers of the patristic period. On the other hand, although all these expressions are Christian, it is still molded after the pattern of the Jewish prayers for the last cup of the meal.

Let us first see how the primitive anaphora, encased in the liturgy of Addai and Mari, evidently suggests its presence out of the hybrid composition which bears this name today in the liturgical books of the Nestorians, the Catholic Chaldeans and of all those influenced by them, in Malabar and elsewhere.

The following is the text of the Nestorian liturgy given in Brightman and arranged in accordance with the order of Dom Botte:

I. Worthy of praise from every mouth and of confession from every tongue and of worship and exaltation from every creature is the adorable and glorious name of thy glorious Trinity, o Father and Son and Holy Ghost, who didst create the world by thy grace and its inhabiters by thy mercifulness and didst save mankind by thy compassion and give great grace unto mortals.

II. Thy majesty, o my Lord, thousand thousands of those on high bow down and worship and ten thousand times ten thousand holy angels and hosts of spiritual beings, ministers of fire and spirit, praise thy name with holy cherubin and spiritual seraphin offering worship to thy sovereignty, shouting and praising without ceasing and crying one to another and saying: "Holy, Holy, Holy Lord God Hosts, heaven and earth are full of his praises and of the nature of his being and of the excellency of his glorious splendour. Hosanna in the highest and Hosanna to the son of David. Blessed be he that came and cometh in the name of the Lord. Hosanna in the Highest."

III. (And with these heavenly hosts), we give thanks to thee, o my Lord, even we thy servants weak and frail and miserable, for that thou hast given us great grace past recompense in that thou didst put on our manhood that thou mightest quicken it by thy godhead, and hast exalted our

low estate and restored our fall and raised our mortality
and forgiven our trespasses and justified our sinfulness and
enlightened our knowledge and, o our Lord and our God,
hast condemned our enemies and granted victory to the weakness of our frail nature in the overflowing mercies of thy grace.
And for all thine helps and graces towards us let us raise
to thee praise and honour and confession and worship now
and ever and world without end. Amen.

IV. O Lord God of hosts, accept this offering for all the
holy catholic church and for all the just and righteous fathers
who have been wellpleasing in thy sight and for all the prophets and the apostles and for all the martyrs and confessors
and for all the mourners and distressed and for all the needy
and tormented and for all the sick and afflicted and for all
the departed who have been severed and have gone forth from
amongst us and for this people that looketh for and awaiteth
thy mercies and for my frailty and misery and poverty.

V. Do thou, o my Lord, in thy many and unspeakable
mercies make a good and acceptable memorial for all the
just and righteous fathers who have been wellpleasing in thy
sight, in the commemoration of the body and blood of thy
Christ which we offer unto thee on thy pure and holy altar
as thou hast taught us, and grant us thy tranquility and thy
peace all the days of the world.

VI. Yea, o our Lord and our God, grant us thy tranquility
and thy peace all the days of the world that all the inhabit-
ants of the earth may know thee that thou art the only true
God the Father and that thou hast sent our Lord Jesus Christ
thy Son and thy beloved. And he our Lord and our God
came and in his lifegiving gospel taught us all purity and
holiness ...

VII. (Be mindful) of the prophets and the apostles and
the martyrs and the confessors and the bishops and the doctors and the presbyters and the deacons and all the children
of the holy catholic church, even them that have been sign-
ed with the living sign of holy baptism.

VIII. And we also, o my Lord, thy weak and frail and
miserable servants who are gathered together in thy name,
both stand before thee at this time and have received the
example which is from thee delivered unto us, rejoicing and
praising and exalting and commemorating and celebrating

this great and fearful and holy and lifegiving and divine mystery of the passion and the death and the burial and the resurrection of our Lord and Saviour Jesus Christ.

IX. And may there come, o my Lord, thine Holy Spirit and rest upon this offering of thy servants and bless it and hallow it that it be to us, o my Lord, for the pardon of offences and the remission of sins and for the great hope of resurrection from the dead and for new life in the kingdom of heaven with all those who have been wellpleasing in thy sight.

X. And for all this great and marvellous dispensation towards us we will give thee thanks and praise thee without ceasing in thy church redeemed by the precious blood of thy Christ, with unclosed mouths and open faces, lifting up praise and honour and confession and worship to thy living and holy and lifegiving name now and ever and world without end. Amen.[18]

The great Anglican liturgist E.C. Ratcliff, who devoted to this text one of the most profound studies, emphasizes from the first the absence of the words of institution. Would this not have been a unique example of the survival of a type of primitive eucharistic prayer where these words did not enter in, any more than they are found in the *Didache*? Moreover, the whole of paragraph II, with the *Sanctus* and the first words of paragraph III (they are furthermore not to be found in the Maronite anaphora of St. Peter, which is called *charar* and which incorporates a good part of our text), interrupts the sequence of development. On the other hand, it regains its continuity if we connect paragraph III with paragraph I. The same should be said of paragraph IX, which can be looked upon as an epiclesis (at least in the broad sense: let us note that if it requests the descent of the Holy Spirit upon the oblation, it does not explicitly petition for the consecration of the bread and wine into the body and blood of Christ).

[18] Dom Bernard Botte, "Problèmes de l'anaphore syrienne des apôtres Addaï et Mari," in *L'Orient Syrien*, vol. X, fasc. 1, 1965, pp. 89 ff. The text is translated into French on pp. 91 ff., after the *Missale Urmiense* (Rome) 1906. Brightman, *op. cit.*, pp. 283 ff. A better form of the text was published by W. F. Macomber, "*Orientalia Christiana Periodica*, vol. XXXII, fasc. 2, 1966, pp. 336 ff.

If it is kept, the beginning of paragraph X is left hanging in mid air. But once it is suppressed, we see that this paragraph X is connected directly with the end of paragraph VIII, which constitutes the anamnesis.

The result is that the *Sanctus* and what is connected with it, on the one hand, and the epiclesis on the other, seem to have to be looked upon as later insertions.

The same thing seems to be true of paragraphs IV to VII. Not only do the intercessions here appear in a form that, according to all the parallels we have, seems to be late, but they are disjointed. Paragraph VII particularly seems out of place, even if we add to it the words which Renaudot thinks are missing and which we have placed in brackets: "Be mindful."

Once we have made these eliminations, we find ourselves with a rather well formed prayer in three paragraphs. God is extolled 1) for his work of creation, 2) for his redemptive work accomplished in Christ and 3) the memorial of this redemption is presented to him, on which basis glory is given to him.

Dom Botte, however, has written two articles in which he brought to bear a series of remarks on this reconstruction and which we cannot overlook.[19]

He is fully in agreement with Ratcliff in eliminating all of paragraph II, including the *Sanctus*.

But he doubts that the absence of the words of institution is original. His objection rests on the fact that the beginning of the anamnesis (paragraph VIII): "And we also, o my Lord, thy weak and frail and miserable servants who are gathered together in thy name ... " still remains up in the air after the eliminations suggested by Ratcliff as before. These words seem to require a foregoing sentence, but this phrase is no more the conclusion of III than it is the final words of VII.

But these same Nestorians who still use the anaphora of Addai and Mari have two others which they attribute to Nestorius and Theodore of Mopsuestia, respectively. Now the latter anaphora,

---

[19] Add to the article mentioned in the preceding note "L'Anaphore chaldéenne des Apôtres," in *Orientalia christiana periodica*, vol. 15, 1949, pp. 259 ff.

especially, contains an anamnesis that presents close analogies with that of Addai and Mari (and the same is true for the intercessions which, today at any rate, are found in both anaphoras in obviously related forms). But the anaphora of Theodore does have the words of institution in a rather peculiar text that must be quoted:

> ... And he, together with his apostles, on the night he was betrayed, *celebrated this great, awesome, holy and divine mystery* (in Syriac: *rozo*): taking bread, he blessed it, and broke it, gave it to his disciples and said: This is my body which is broken for you in remission of sins. Likewise the cup: he gave thanks and gave it to them and said: This is my blood of the New Testament, which is shed for many in remission of sins. Take then all of you, eat of this bread and drink of this cup and do this *whenever you are gathered together* in memory of me.[20]

If we connect this text with the anamnesis of Addai and Mari, its first words: "*And we also ... who are gathered together in thy name ...* " appear to be a direct echo of the conclusion of the words of institution given under a form similar to that which was set down by Theodore of Mopsuestia. This impression is re-enforced when we see this other phrase a bit further on, in the anamnesis "*celebrating this great and fearful and holy* and lifegiving *and divine mystery.*" This seems another echo of the same narrative, this time of its first sentence. The coincidence becomes irresistible when we note further, still following Dom Botte, that the ancient commentators on the Syrian liturgy had knowledge of a formulation of the words of institution which ended not, as with Theodore, with: "whenever you are gathered together *in memory of me,*" but rather with: "whenever you are gathered together *in my name,*" which follows the formula of the anamnesis of Addai and Mari exactly.

We must admit that this demonstration seems to be so clear that it comes close to being irrefutable. In fact, many years have gone by since Dom Botte presented it and no one has risked re-

---

[20] Cf. Renaudot, *Liturgiarum orientalium Collectio*, (Paris 1712), t. 2, p. 619.

futing it. Undoubtedly it will be asked if the words of institution
were originally in our text, just how could they have subsequently
disappeared? Dom Botte rightly answers that the liturgical manuscripts where these words do not appear are legion, even in cases
where there is not the least doubt, if only according to the commentators of the period, about their compulsory presence in the
celebration. This is actually the case in the West, with all the
texts of the Gallican liturgy, with all the earliest texts of the Mozarabic liturgy, and in the East with many Syriac manuscripts,
particularly among the Maronites. We should simply suppose
that every celebrant knew the customary formula in a given rite
by heart.

Let us go on to the epiclesis. Without denying the soundness
of Ratcliff's remark that its introduction breaks an obvious connection between the end of VIII and the beginning of X, Dom Botte
points out rightly that it too is no less archaic and that the parallelisms of its structure furthermore attest to the fact that it was
composed directly in Syriac and cannot be a later translation of
some Greek original. For our part, we shall be permitted to point
out that the entire suppression of IX would eliminate from the
original text an element that is found in the Jewish meal prayers,
precisely between the anamnesis in the strictest sense (the mention of the memorial) and the final doxology. This is the purpose
for which the memorial is presented to God, that he bring about
the ultimate fulfilment in his people of the *magnalia* commemorated.
But this is exactly what we have if we simply drop the beginning
of IX, i. e. the express invocation of the Spirit.

We then have a text in which the theme development is exactly
the same as the corresponding part of the meal *berakoth*:

> ... commemorating and celebrating this great and fearful
> and holy and lifegiving and divine mystery of the passion
> and the death and the burial and the resurrection of our Lord
> and Saviour Jesus Christ for the pardon of offences and the
> remission of sins and for the great hope of resurrection from
> the dead and for new life in the kingdom of heaven with all
> those who have been wellpleasing in thy sight.

In this case, far from being interrupted by the invocation of the
Spirit, the thought of the memorial continues to underlie the whole

end of the phrase. Since the eschatological hope is therefore directly connected with the passion and glorification of the Savior, paragraph X no longer gives the impression of being disconnected: "this dispensation" is perfectly applicable to the whole of the foregoing prayer.

At the same time, this answers Dom Botte's last objection to Ratcliff: that the absence of any element of intercession in an ancient anaphora would be something quite singular and hard to explain. But once the conclusion of IX is restored to the original text, there is no longer any room for including other intercessions. We shall speak again about this point when we come to the developments of the fourth century eucharist, in order to acknowledge furthermore, once again following Dom Botte, the relative antiquity of this same element as it is presented in the present state of our anaphora.

One final remark seems to have to be made before we propose the reconstruction of the primitive text at which we are aiming. At the beginning of paragraph I, "the adorable and glorious name of thy glorious Trinity, o Father and Son and Holy Ghost ... " seems to be an insertion that could scarcely be earlier than the end of the fourth century. The expression "name of the Trinity" is furthermore bereft of meaning. The parallelism with the conclusion of paragraph X lets us suppose that the original text, at the beginning as well as the end, mentioned simply: "thy adorable and glorious name, which created the world by thy grace, etc." Once we have made this last elimination, the beginning and the end of the prayer become fully consonant. They furnish, it seems, one more example of the use familiar to early Christians of the expression: "the divine Name" to designate the person of Jesus.[21] The transition immediately afterwards of the eucharistic prayer, to a direct invocation of Jesus is now much better understood.

We can now attempt to present a reconstitution of the original form of the eucharistic prayer of Addai and Mari. We shall italicize the words of institution, whose presence after Dom Botte's demonstration seems to be required, even though the exact form remains a matter of conjecture:

[21] Cf. above, pp. 118.

1. Worthy of praise from every mouth and of confession from every tongue and of worship and exaltation from every creature is the adorable and glorious Name who created the world by his grace and its inhabiters by his mercifulness and saved mankind by his compassion and gave great grace to us mortals.

2. We give thanks to thee, o my Lord, even we thy servants weak and frail and miserable, for thou hast given us great grace past recompense in that thou didst put on our manhood that thou mightest quicken it by thy godhead and hast exalted our low estate and restored our fall and raised our mortality and forgiven our trespasses and justified our sinfulness and enlightened our knowledge and, o our Lord and our God, hast condemned our enemies and granted victory to the weakness of our frail nature in the overflowing mercies of thy grace. And for all *thine* helps and graces toward us let us raise to *thee* praise and honor and confession and worship now and ever and world without end. Amen.

3. *Our Lord Jesus Christ, together with his apostles on the night he was betrayed, celebrated this great, awesome, holy and divine mystery: taking bread, he blessed it, and broke it, gave it to his disciples and said: This is my body which is broken for you for the remission of sins. Likewise the cup: he gave thanks and gave it to them and said: This is my blood of the New Testament which is shed for many for the remission of sins. Take then all of you, eat of this bread and drink of this cup, and do this whenever you are gathered together in my name.* And we also, o my Lord, thy weak and frail and miserable servants who are gathered together in thy name, both stand before thee at this time and have received the example which is from thee delivered unto us, rejoicing and praising and exalting and commemorating and celebrating this great and fearful and holy and lifegiving and divine mystery of the passion and the death and the burial and the resurrection of our Lord and Saviour Jesus Christ, for the pardon of offenses and the remission of sins and for the great hope of resurrection from the dead and for new life in the kingdom of heaven with all those who have been wellpleasing in thy sight. And for all this great and marvellous dispensation (Syriac: *indabrânuthâ*) towards us we will give thee thanks and praise thee without ceasing in thy church redeemed

by the precious blood of thy Christ, with unclosed mouths and open faces, lifting up praise and honor and confession and worship to thy living and holy and lifegiving name now and ever and world without end. Amen.

Restored in this way to what must have approximately been its original form, this prayer appears obviously with a character that is still fully Semitic. It bears no trace of theological developments, even those prior to Arianism, which were to come about in the Christianity of the hellenized churches. The way in which it is dominated by the notions associated with the divine Name, identified, it seems, with Christ, and the idea of "dispensation" or "economy," that is, the plan which found its fulfilment in Christ, brings us to what Fr. Daniélou has described as Jewish-Christian theology, which barely survived the missionary development in hellenistic areas.

The way in which the transition from the Father to the Son is made in several instances in connection with this notion of the divine Name, is one more evidence of a very undeveloped theology, such as is reflected in the discourses and the prayers in the Acts of the Apostles.

The redundancies we observe, and the accumulation of synonyms called for by parallelism, are characteristic traits of Jewish prayer. Evidence of the themes of Jewish prayer is striking throughout. The first two paragraphs which are still two distinct prayers, treat successively, in praise, of creation, preservation and then redemption. In the second paragraph the mention of "knowledge" corresponds to the Jewish mention of the Torah. Similarly, in the third prayer, as we have proposed to reconstruct it, the presentation of the "memorial" by the faithful recalls in God the inseparable remembrance of the Messiah and themselves. They await his ultimate fulfilment in them of what is the object of the memorial, exactly as in the Jewish prayer. And in the same way this supplication returns to praise in the final doxology.

Very primitive also seems to be this translation of the memorial by the "typos," the "example" as we have translated it following Baumstark and Dom Botte. But we could equally well say the "sacrament," for, given by God and handed down by tradition, it evidently communicates to us the "mystery" of Christ which we "praise, exalt, commemorate and celebrate" (the last word itself could be translated perhaps more exactly by "accomplish").

But the most primitive trait of this eucharistic prayer is the fact that we do not yet find in it any technically sacrificial formula. There is no mention of either sacrifice or offering. On the other hand, it is clear that the notion of "memorial" which is the core of the *Christus passus* and its "sacrament" which he has given us, retains all the pregnant significance, so typically Jewish, which Jeremias has pointed out. Through this "memorial" we can call upon God to have the fulfilment of his wonderworks in us, just as the memorial, in that it was given by God, preserves their permanent actuality for us. In this way the eucharistic memorial appears as the equivalent of the sacrifice, taken in the most exalted sense that the Old Testament had evolved, in what is evidently the paramount Christian sacrament. We must therefore expect to see arise in the anamnesis, as we shall soon point out, the first explicitly sacrificial formulas of the eucharist. They will be nothing other than the translation of all that the Jewish memorial implied into a more immediately accessible language for non-Jews. And at this place in the eucharistic prayer most especially, their explication will go hand in hand with a more and more formal expression of the fact that the eucharistic celebration is, on the other hand, sacrificial only in so far as it unites us to the Cross of Christ on which it impressed this character in the beginning.

In this regard it is fitting to shed light on the connection between the anamnesis and the institution narrative. In the eucharist of Addai and Mari, if Dom Botte is right as we believe, we already see this narrative incorporated in the eucharistic prayer and through its conclusion giving rise to the formulation of the anamnesis. Dom Botte himself does not hesitate, after Leitzmann,[22] to posit as a principle: "no anamnesis without the institution narrative." We should rather be inclined to say: "no institution narrative without the anamnesis." Actually, we have seen and can now verify that the Christian anamnesis has its pre-history

---

[22] Cf. Dom B. Botte, "Problèmes de l'Anamnèse," in *Journal of Ecclesiastical History*, vol. 5, 1954, pp. 16 1 f., and H. Lietzmann, *Messe und Herrenmahl*, 3 ed., (Berlin, 1955).

and its primary source in the "memorial" formulated in the first
part of the third of the final *berakoth* for the Jewish holy day meals.
But it is clear that this "memorial" in the Jewish prayers was
not directly attached to any narrative of this kind. And, as the
formulas of the Didache seem to demonstrate, at the origin of
the Christian eucharist, it was not to be found either, at least at
this place. Yet this should not surprise us, for it does not seem
that Jesus himself sought to incorporate what we call the words
of eucharistic institution into the *berakoth* themselves which he
must have left unchanged. Still it does seem that Jeremias was
right in explaining the divergencies of detail in the institution accounts that the New Testament has handed down to us by the
fact that these were already different local liturgical formulations.
But in the beginning, while the eucharist was still inseparable
from the whole of a complete community meal, it seems that they
must have been recited during the meal, as was the *haggadah* of
Passover and as an explanation of it. When the eucharist became
detached from the meal, the initial blessing of the bread became
confused with the first of the three *berakoth* over the final cup,
since both had the same object: a blessing for food, giving rise to a
more general blessing for the creation and preservation of life.
At this time, we think, the new *haggadah* of the renewed sacred
meal was incorporated in the eucharistic prayer, It came quite
naturally to be attached to the words of the anamnesis in the third
blessing, both because it furnished a justification for it and because
the words: "Do this as a memorial of me" were directly called forth
by the formulation of this memorial in this part of the prayer.
For this fact, we can find twofold evidence in liturgical tradition.
Even where the whole eucharistic prayer was being organized
and redistributed, many examples subsisted where the Last Supper narrative was not incorporated into the detailed recall, in the
praise for the redemption, of the *mirabilia* of Christ, but was returned to, after the mention of his death and glorification, as
the starting point of the anamnesis. And, elsewhere, particularly
in Egypt, it is not before the anamnesis properly socalled begins,
but within it that the narrative appears. This is also what may
explain the fact, at first sight so disconcerting, that there is a eucharistic liturgy (that of St. John Chrysostom) where the words

"Do this, etc." have simply disappeared from the narrative. This is a case where we can so well verify the remark of Fr. de Vaux that there is no need to recite a rubric once it is in operation.

RESURGENCE OF THE ARCHAIC TYPE IN THE
APOSTOLIC TRADITION OF ST. HIPPOLYTUS

The evidence given by the liturgy of Addai and Mari of a primitive type of eucharist, directly and exclusively modeled on the Jewish meal prayers, is corroborated by a whole group of other texts. Not one of them seems as ancient. But they are all witnesses to the subsistence, which lasted for a more or less long time depending on the place, of a eucharistic prayer whose schema was worked out in a period when the eucharist was celebrated in a community meal, without any direct connection with the service of readings and prayers either of the Synagogue or the primitive Church.

The most interesting of these texts is the eucharistic prayer which the document generally known as the *Apostolic Tradition*, attributed to St. Hippolytus, advises a newly consecrated bishop to use.

The problems posed by this document and its author are extraordinarily involved and particularly thorny. Here we shall merely speak about what is necessary for an intelligent reading of the text that concerns us, and shall reserve for later an account of its latter influence and especially its connection with the properly Roman liturgical tradition.

In regard to this text and its interpretation if one does not wish to fall into vicious cycle reasoning, arising from unconscious question begging, then one has to start by making a distinction between questions that are brought up in its regard. However interconnected they may be, and all the more because they are, it is important not to confuse them. The first is the establishment of the text, either of the whole document, or—and this is our principal concern here— simply of the eucharistic prayer found in it. We have only translations of this text which must have been composed in Greek and they are all incorporated in other documents in which it is not always easy to distinguish what is a quote and what an adaptation. Hence the title of prudent modesty that Dom Botte gave to the last edition he made: *Essai de reconstitution.*[23]

The second question is that of the title. A curious thing is that most, not to say all, modern commentators seem to forget that the title itself is a conjecture that depends upon the answer given to the third question.

This concerns the author of our text. Here again, every one agrees that it concerns a certain Hippolytus and tradition on this point is sufficiently unanimous to obviate any doubt. But we have hardly progressed beyond this point, since neither the ancient scholars nor those of our own day agree as to who this Hippolytus was and, more especially, what body of works should be attributed to him.

Finally, should this question itself be resolved indisputably, there would remain a last question which is perhaps the most important of all: to what extent are we dealing with a personal work, to what extent does it reflect a particular local tadition, and which tradition was it?

Let us attempt, if not to answer each of these questions, at least to disentangle the chief elements of a solution which we have at hand.

Let us first see how our text can be re-established. Its first appearance is in H. Tattam's London edition of 1848 of a collection in Bohairic-Coptic, which unluckily he called *The Apostolical Constitutions.* In reality, it was simply a particularly interesting example from the canonical collection of the Patriarchate of Alexandria, called *Sinodos.* Only the third part had any relation to the collection called the *Apostolic Constitutions*, and it reproduced in an abridged version the prayers of the 8th book. The second part contained an analogous but different document that was still unknown. It was called the *Constitution of the Egyptian Church.* D.B. von Haneberg published in 1870 an Arabic text of the latter at Munich, under the title *Canones S. Hippolyti arabice*

---

[23] Dom Bernard Botte, "La Tradition apostolique de saint Hippolyte, essai de reconstitution," in *Liturgiewissenschaftliche Quellen und Forschungen*, vol. 39 (Münster-Westfalen, 1963).

e codicibus romanis. This was to be found again in a new text, this time in Sahidic-Coptic of the Alexandrian *Sinodos*, published by P. de Lagarde in 1878, then in Arabic and Ethiopic texts, published by G. Horner in 1904. In the meanwhile, Msgr. I. Rahmani in 1899 had published at Mainz a Syriac text, a translation of a Greek original that had been lost,. the *Testamentum Domini nostri Iesu Christi*, in which fragments of the same document (and particularly of its eucharistic prayer) were to be found. They were sometimes reproduced literally and sometimes were the object of prolific personal developments.[24]

Finally, in 1900, E. Hauler published a Latin palimpsest text, deciphered from a manuscript from Verona of the *Sententiae* of Isidore of Seville. Among other ancient canonical collections, this palimpsest reproduced a Latin version of this same text of which Bohairic, Sahidic, Arabic and Ethiopic versions were already known in the different editions of the Alexandrian *Sinodos*. But we must point out that this new example of the text, which is more valuable than all the others since the manuscript itself goes back to the fifth century, has a title that is completely obliterated and illegible today.

This brings us straight to our second question: the original title of the collection, which up to this point has been generally called the *Constitution of the Egyptian Church* simply because it was first discovered in various versions of the Alexandrian *Sinodos*. There are two studies, one by E. Schwartz, published in 1910 and the other by Dom R.H. Connolly in 1916 which have convinced modern scholars that it was in fact the *Apostolic Tradition*, (’Α)ποστολικὴ παράδοσις; this title figured in a list of works

---

[24] Elsewhere, F. X. Funk, in 1905, added to his edition of the *Apostolic Constitutions* (vol. II, pp. 72 ff.) another Greek text that was first called the *Constitution by Hippolytus*, even though this title in the text itself was given only to its second part, and is now called preferably an *Epitome* (i.e. a "summation") *of the Apostolic Constitutions*. In fact, for a prayer of this second part, in the episcopal consecration, it is actually not the text of the *Apostolic Constitutions* that the text reproduces, but 'that of the hypothetical *Constitutions of the Egyptian Church*, as we have it in the Ethiopian version, corroborated by the Verona Latin text. Similarly, for the ordination of lector, like these same sources, it prescribes nothing but the handing on of the book.

reproduced on the pedestal of an anonymous statue found in Rome in the sixteenth century. After having remained in the Lateran Museum for a long time, it has been installed today at the foot of the stairway leading to the Vatican library.[25]

This identification is made probable by the fact that a prologue of the composition in question (a prologue which is to be found both in the Latin and Ethiopian versions, and which has a parallel in the 8th book of the *Apostolic Constitutions*) makes the statement that the author, after having spoken of charisms, is now about to explain the tradition (although he himself does not specify the *apostolic* tradition). Now since this title on the pedestal of the statue follows immediately the mention of a work $(\pi)\varepsilon\varrho\grave{\iota}\ \chi\alpha\varrho\iota\sigma\mu\acute{\alpha}$-$\tau\omega\nu$ the coincidence is obviously striking. It can be demonstrated completely once we admit that the anonymous person represented by the statue is the Hippolytus to whom our text is attributed in the Arabic version of the *Sinodos*.

On the other hand, this last point was generally admitted until quite recently, both because the statue had been discovered on the Via Tiburtina at a place where a martyr by this name had been buried and honored, and because it was thought that this would enable the establishment of a connection between various other works that have come down to us under this same name Hippolytus and one or other of the titles figuring on the pedestal.

But even when we have reached this point, we must admit that there are still some difficulties. Eusebius, who attributes seven works to Hippolytus and in particular an Easter computation which could correspond to the one mentioned on the pedestal of the statue, merely knows that he was a bishop but does not know of what place.[26] Though St. Jerome enlarges Eusebius' lists in his *De Viris Illustribus*, and makes particular mention of a commentary on the psalms and a treatise on the resurrection, both of which could correspond to two other titles on the statue, he knows nothing more, except that, according to the content of another

---

[25] Cf. E. Schwartz, *Über die pseudoapostolischen Kirchenordnungen.* (Strasbourg, 1910) and R. H. Connolly, *The So-Called Egyptian Church Order and Derived Documents* (*Texts and Studies*, VIII, 4) (Cambridge, 1916).

[26] Eusebius, *Ecclesiastical History*, VI, 20-22.

work he attributes to him, Hippolytus would have spoken once in the presence of Origen.[27] Elsewhere, in a letter to Pope Damasus, he calls him a martyr.[28] Theodoretus, who quotes Hippolytus several times, calls him also bishop and martyr, but without any further qualification.[29] But none of these authors seems to think he was a Roman.

From the end of the fifth century, some of those who still mention Hippolytus do attribute a definite locality to him. Unfortunately they do not agree. There is very little to be got from what Gelasius says (that he would have been bishop of Arabia) since this probably resulted from too hasty a reading of Eusebius, hence a misconception.[30] From this time on, others speak of him as bishop of Rome, while still others attribute the see of Porto to him (which, however, seems not to have existed before a much later date).[31] On the other hand, Photius who makes him a disciple of Irenaeus always refrains from attributing any localization to him.[32]

In the nineteenth century, the discovery of the *Philosophoumena* (or *Elenchos*), attributed to Hippolytus first by Jacobi, then by Bunsen, and finally by such fine scholars as Doellinger, Volkmar and Harnack, brought with it a recasting of all the hypotheses on Hippolytus. In accordance with the content of this text he would have been a Roman priest in difficulties with Pope Zephyrinus, and for some time an antipope against Callixtus, Zephyrinus' successor. He would be supposed to have been reconciled with Pontianus, the second successor of Callixtus, before their common martyrdom, since despite everything he was to come to be listed among the martyrs venerated at Rome.

This whole delicate construction, in which many elements remain purely conjectural, was roundly shaken by a thesis main-

---

[27] Jerome, *De viris inlustribus*, 61.

[28] *Epistulae*, 36, 16, Vienna Corpus, vol. I, 1910, p. 283, 7.

[29] Theodoretus, *Eranistes*, I, II, III; P. G., t. 83, col. 85D, 172c, 284D.

[30] E. Schwartz, "Publizistische Sammlungen zum acacianischen Schisma," 'in *Abhandlungen der Bayerischen Akademie der Wissenschaften, Philosophisch-historische Abteilung*, Neue Folge, Vol. 10 (Munich, 1934), p. 96, 28.

[31] Cf. P. Nautin, *Hippolyte et Josipe* (Paris, 1947), p. 16.

[32] Photius, *Bibliotheca*, 121; P. G., t. 103, col. 401.

tained by M. Nautin in 1947.[33] According to him, the *Fragment against Noetus*, which seems assuredly by Hippolytus, according to the testimony of Theodoretus, would certainly have used some elements from the *Elenchos*. But this use itself would attest to the fact that the two works have two different authors from the standpoint of theology, heresiological method, mental formation and style as well. Yet, since the *Elenchos* attests that its author also wrote a tract *On the Universe*, a title that is also mentioned in the statue's catalogue, we should have to conclude that this statue is not of Hippolytus, but of another person who alone would have the qualifications of Roman and antipope. M. Nautin particularly relied on a passage of Photius attributing an *On the Universe* to "Josephus," and therefore thinks that we are dealing with a confusion of names; the Roman antipope would in fact have been a certain Josipus (᾿Ιώσιπος, a name that Photius declared to have been found in the manuscripts but which he attributes to a copyist's error).

In this case, Hippolytus would remain the author of our collection as well as of a whole series of works attributed to him by antiquity, works which show obvious kinship of style and ideas with this collection. But there would no longer be any reason to make him a Roman and we must be resigned to looking upon him merely as a bishop, undoubtedly from the East, but impossible to localize. The weakest point of this new theory is that we are not to attribute to this Hippolytus at least two consecutive tracts with the titles: *On Charisms* and *Apostolic Tradition* that follow one another on the pedestal of the statue of the hypothetical Josipus, to say nothing of the other writings that may correspond to the same list. Simple coincidence, replies M. Nautin. But Dom B. Capelle for one, by reason of the style of the two works which M. Nautin intends to separate, and Dom Botte for another, by reason of their content, both seem to have shown that the arguments of M. Nautin are not at all as decisive as they may appear at first sight.[34] The coincidence, which is at least disturbing, between the

---

[33] *Op. cit.*, in note 31.

[34] Cf. Dom Bernard Botte, "Note sur l'auteur du De Universo attribué à saint Hippolyte," in *Recherches de Théologie ancienne et médiévale*, tome

two consecutive titles and the content of the two connected works (which M. Nautin himself attributes unhesitatingly to Hippolytus), together with the place where the statue was discovered, does not seem to Dom Botte, especially, to be in any way deprived of its probative force in favor of one author. He therefore maintains:

1) The author of the *Apostolic Tradition* (by this let us understand our collection) is indeed the subject of the Roman statue.

2) This author lived in Rome and enjoyed a certain prominence since a statue was erected to him.

3) This author was called Hippolytus: the indications of literary tradition (*Epitome, Canons of Hippolytus*) are in agreement with the archeological data concerning the statue.

4) The ambiguous position of Hippolytus, as a head of a dissident community, explains the fluctuations in tradition: but he is indeed the Roman martyr commemorated on the 13th of August along with Pope Pontianus."[35]

This seems to us again to suppose too many conjectures which are probable or merely possible, and to raise too many imperfectly resolved difficulties for us to consider it a proof. Yet it still seems to us to be the most likely hypothesis that can be made at present.

But even if we admit it, this is not enough to solve the question that most concerns us here. Must the document, to which we shall continue to give the title *Apostolic Tradition*, and which we still intend to attribute to Hippolytus, a Roman priest and sometime antipope, therefore be looked upon as a simple reflection of the Roman liturgy of the period? Or would it rather represent its author's own notions? And, if so, where would he have got them? Dom Botte, in the first edition which he made of it some time ago for the collection *Sources chrétiennes*, gave an affirmative answer. Our document would be typically Roman, both by reason

---

XVIII, 1951, pp. 5 ff., and Dom Bernard Capelle, "Hippolyte de Rome" and "A propos d'Hippolyte de Rome," *ibid.*, t. XVII, 1950, pp. 145 ff. and t. XIX, 1952, pp. 193 ff.

[35] *Op. cit.*, p. 35.

of its content and its style, and would therefore attest to the pure "Romanness" of its acknowledged author.[36]

In his new edition, he uses terms that seem to be less definite. After the lines that we have already quoted, he writes: "We may therefore look upon the *Apostolic Tradition* as a Roman writing. Is this to say that it represents exactly the discipline and the liturgy of Rome in the third century? We must take care not to be too intransigent in our positions, and to be guilty of an anachronism. We cannot look upon the *Tradition* as a third century equivalent of what the Gregorian Sacramentary was at the end of the sixth. At the time of St. Gregory, the Roman liturgy had taken on its definitive shape. In the third century we are still at a time when the first liturgies were being formed. We have not yet passed the improvisation stage, and Hippolytus gives his prayers as models and not as set formulas. On the other hand, it is not likely that since he was writing in Rome he would have presented as genuine tradition things which would have had nothing to do with Roman usage. Undoubtedly he did make specifications on certain points on his own authority. But, in its entirety, we are right in thinking that the *Tradition* does represent the Roman discipline of the beginning of the third century."[37]

It is useless to emphasize that in this context "the improvisation stage" and the "time when the first liturgies were being formed" are expressions that ought not to be taken too literally. Otherwise how would there be any question of rediscovering, at a similar period, in such a stage, "Roman usage" and the "Roman discipline of the beginning of the third century"?

On the other hand, the unavoidable question is to what extent Hippolytus, since he was writing at Rome (supposing that this was the case), could have given us "as genuine tradition things which would have had nothing to do with Roman usage." Precisely, if the author of what we believe to be the *Apostolic Tradition* is also the author of the *Elenchos*, as Dom Botte convinces us, it seems certain that he was hardly scrupulous in other areas,

---

[36] Hippolyte de Rome, "La Tradition apostolique," in *Sources chrétiennes*, n°. 11, (Paris) p. 9 and p. 24.

[37] In the volume cited, note 23, p. xiv.

and that it was precisely for that reason that he could have become antipope. The trinitarian theology current in Rome (which the popes of his time certainly had not invented!) seemed to him to be a crass heresy.[38] That marriages between freemen and slaves could have been contracted with the approval of the Church seemed loathsome to him,[39] an incomprehensible scandal for a Roman, Christian or no. Finally, that penance was practiced with mollifications that seemed to have been a practically constant local tradition was particularly inadmissible for him.[40] Considering this, we should not be too surprised if the local liturgy also had an intolerable effect upon him. And it does seem, actually, that, because the liturgies he saw celebrated where he was displeased him just as much as all the rest, he judged it necessary to make up one of his own.

What does he tell us about it?

> Now, motivated by charity towards all the saints, we have come to the essentials of tradition which befits the Churches, in order that those who are well instructed may keep the tradition which has lasted until the present, according to the explanation we are giving it, and in order that, as they take cognizance of it, they might be strengthened, on account of the fall or the error which has come about recently through ignorance, and (on account of) the ignorant—the Holy Spirit conferring perfect grace upon those who have a right faith, so that they might know how they should teach and preserve all (those) things, those who are at the head of the Church.[41]

Is it not likely that he is aiming here at the same people (Zephyrinus, Callixtus and their followers) whom he attacks by name elsewhere? And is it not also quite clear consequently that, in this case no more than in the others, the genuine Roman customs are not his own, but those of his adversaries?

Does this mean that he is inventing what he is claiming to make obligatory? It is quite as unlikely with such an out-and-out con-

---

[38] Cf. *Philosophoumena*, 9. 12.
[39] *Ibid.*
[40] *Ibid.*
[41] *Apostolic Tradition*, 1.

servative as he was. We should rather believe that he holds as
the sole lawful customs, some which are different from those he
sees in Rome (and elsewhere), customs which he knew from another less evolved area, from which he must have originated. He is
attempting to make these customs obligatory in his present home
under the guise of a restoration. How many Romans in general,
at this period in particular, how many Roman Christians and even
ecclesiastics were "Roman" only by adoption? There is reason
to believe that Hippolytus belonged to this latter category.

Are we able to pinpoint his origin? Fr. Hanssens thought it
possible and judged that he should be looked upon as an Alexandrian who became a Roman priest, seeking to transport from
Alexandria to Rome those forms which he judged ideal. Not
without reason Dom Botte refuses to see anything but pure fiction in this hypothesis.[42] It is actually true that in Hippolytus
we can find absolutely nothing of the peculiarities of the Alexandrian liturgy, or more generally of Alexandrian Christianity.
Nor is it further proof that the *Sinodos* of the Alexandrian patriarchs
found it so easy to include his writings, for this collection like all
the canonical and liturgical legislation of Alexandria, admitted
also all kinds of material which we know to be foreign, and particularly an abundance of Syrian elements.

If we must opt for a particular localization for Hippolytus' origin, then it may well be Syria, as Tillemont thought. He gave
the greatest evidence leading to that conclusion.[43] His class prejudices, his penitential rigorism, his theology everywhere reeking of
Sabellianism, to which must be added his systematic suspicion
of the philosophers, are traits that set him apart from Alexandria
and connect him with Syria, especially with its most Semitic elements. Now it is precisely in Syria that the most archaic Christian forms were to survive the longest, as the liturgy of Addai and
Mari has already shown.

---

[42] J. M. Hanssens, *La liturgie d'Hippolyte*, (Rome, 1959). Cf. Dom Botte's
judgment in the introduction to his edition of the Münster *Traditio*, p. xvi.
[43] Lenain de Tillemont, *Mémoires pour servir à l'histoire ecclésiastique*,
t. III (Paris, 1701), p. 674.

Even if we adopted what is still merely an hypothesis, we need not conclude that Hippolytus in Rome would have attempted to acclimatize a completely foreign liturgy. Wherever Christianity was introduced in the first generation of Christians, and more particularly through the local Jewish communities, a liturgy of this type must have existed, and even after a century or more it could not have been completely lost from memory. We shall see that in fact both in Italy and elsewhere more than one other trace is to be found. But it is permissible to believe that Hippolytus, on this point as on the others, must have collided with the Roman authorities in following a policy of deliberate archaism which was above all the product of a backward provincialism. His liturgy is no mere survival, like that of Addai and Mari. We shall see that it betrays the artificiality of its pretentions to being original. But it is still likely that these pretentions themselves were nurtured by a provincialism which focused on a past that it still retained without any longer being able to keep it intact. Hippolytus seems to be from such a background, as were many provincials and the Syrians above all.

This long introduction was hard to avoid. Perhaps it may help us to read Hippolytus' eucharist without imposing upon it an aspect it does not possess. It probably tells us very little about what had become of the eucharistic liturgy at Rome and even elsewhere in the middle of the third century. It shows us what this liturgy may have remained in a few remote areas and that it was still possible to attempt restoring and maintaining elsewhere forms that were in the process of disappearing. Once more, we shall make use of Dom Botte's translation (and in this case his preliminary reconstruction) of the text:

> Let the deacons present the oblation (to the bishop) and let him, while laying his hands upon it with the whole *presbyterium*, say in giving thanks:
> The Lord be with you.
> And let all say:
> And with your Spirit.
> —Lift up your hearts.
> We lift them up to the Lord.
> —Let us give thanks to the Lord.

It is right and just.

And then let him continue in this way:

We give you thanks, O God, through your beloved Child (*puerum*) Jesus Christ, whom you have sent us in the last times (as) savior, redeemer and the messenger (*Angelum*) of your plan; who is your inseparable Word, through whom you have created all things and whom, in your good pleasure, you have sent down from heaven into the womb of a Virgin and who, having been conceived, became flesh and was shown to be your Son, born of the Holy Spirit and the Virgin. It is he who, fulfilling your will and acquiring for you a holy people, stretched out his hands while he was suffering that he might free from suffering those who have trust in you. While he was being betrayed to his voluntary suffering, in order to destroy death and break the chains of the devil, tread hell underfoot, bring forth the righteous into light, set the guiding principle (*terminum*) and manifest the resurrection, taking bread, he gave thanks to you and said: Take, eat; this is my body which is broken for you.

Likewise the cup, saying: This is my blood, which is shed for you. When you do this, do it in memory of me.

Wherefore we, being mindful of his death and his resurrection, offer you this bread and this cup, giving thanks to you that you deemed us worthy to stand before you and to serve you as priests.

And we beseech you to send your Holy Spirit upon the oblation of Holy Church. And in bringing (them) together, grant to all those who partake of your holy (mysteries) (to partake of them) in order that they might be filled with the Holy Spirit, and for the strengthening of (their faith) in truth; that we may praise you and glorify you through your Child Jesus Christ, through whom be to you glory and honor with the Holy Spirit in the Holy Church, now and for ever. Amen.[44]

This text has practically no correspondence in wording with the eucharist of Addai and Mari, but the analogy of their structure and the commonness of their themes are considerably more

---

[44] Dom Botte's Münster edition, pp. 11 ff. (n°. 4). On the introductory dialogue, cf. C. A. Bouman, "Variants in the introduction to the Eucharistic Prayer," in *Vigiliae christianae*, t. 4 (1950), pp. 94 ff. DDC - p. 1067.

striking in their common adhesion to the Jewish schema of the table prayers. There is the same transition from the act of thanksgiving for creation to thanksgiving for the redemption, and the same notion of the anamnesis as a recalling of the memorial given by God, to beseech him for the final gathering together of his chosen in the Church for the purpose of his glorification. In the paragraph preceding the anamnesis and the institution narrative introducing it, we note the insistent presence of the themes of the formation of the people of God and the covenant (*terminum*),[45] keynotes of the development of the Jewish prayer.

On the other hand, if the institution narrative is undoubtedly part of the text here, the *Sanctus* and its appendages together with the intercessions and commemorations that developed are still absent.

Again we must point out the theological archaisms, particularly in christology, which bring us back not only to Judeo-Christian theology, with Christ considered as the "Angel", but to the discourses in Acts with the expression puer ($\pi\alpha\tilde{\iota}\varsigma$) that is twice attributed to him.

In the text we have given there is an epiclesis: "we beseech you to send your Holy Spirit upon the oblation of Holy Church." It is striking that it agrees almost exactly with the one inserted into the eucharist of Addai and Mari. Like the latter, it is most rudimentary, in the sense that it does not request the acceptance of the sacrifice, nor even its consecration through the transformation of the elements. Here again, it is directly the gathering together of the people into the Church that is envisioned.

But here again, we may wonder if this epiclesis formula belonged to the original text. Dom Gregory Dix, in his edition of the *Apostolic Tradition* puts it in doubt.[46] He first of all pointed out the incoherence of the Latin text at this place, which appears to betray an awkward remodeling. In addition, he suggests that the original text might well have been the one reproduced by the

---

[45] The Ethiopian has *ser'et*, which means testament. It is likely that the Greek had $\acute{o}\varrho o\varsigma$ (cf. Botte, p. 15, note 4).

[46] Dom Gregory Dix, *The Treatise on the Apostolic Tradition of Saint Hippolytus of Rome*, (London, 1937), pp. 75 ff.

Testamentum Domini. It does indeed mention the Holy Spirit but it could not be called an epiclesis even in taking the word in its broadest sense, for his coming *into* the sacrament (or upon it) is not sought. Let us quote this formula in Rahmani's Latin translation: *Da deinde, Deus, ut tibi uniantur omnes, qui participando accipiunt ex sacris (mysteriis) tuis, ut Spiritu Sancto repleantur ad confirmationem fidei in veritate ...*

In English, this can read:

Therefore grant, O God, that all may be united to you who receive of your holy (mysteries) by partaking of them, that they may be filled with the Holy Spirit for the strengthening of their faith in truth ...[47]

Richardson brought up a few minor difficulties in regard to the idea that this text could have lent itself to the final transformation, attested to by both the Latin and Ethiopian versions.[48] But above all Dom Botte, who had at first maintained that even if the form given by the *Testamentum Domini* was original, it would be no less the equivalent of an epiclesis (which, again, seems to be a misuse of the term), revised his opinion and thought that he had found a trace of the *Apostolic Tradition's* epiclesis not in this final sentence of the prayer of the *Testamentum*, but in a previous formula.[49] At first sight, we must admit that it offers nothing resembling an epiclesis. But we must follow Dom Botte step by step in a demonstrative proof that is perhaps the master-work of this most discerning scholar's genius.

Here first of all is the text upon which his analysis and reconstruction depend. It immediately follows the anmnesis and Rahmani translates it in this way:

Offerimus tibi hanc gratiarum actionem, aeterna Trinitas, Domine Jesu Christe, Domine Pater, a quo omnis creatura et omnis natura contramiscit in se confugiens, Domine Spiritus Sancte, adfer potum hunc et escam hanc sanctita-

---

[47] Rahmani, *op. cit.*, p. 45.

[48] Cf. C. C. Richardson, "The So-Called Epiclesis in Hippolytus," in *Harvard Theological Review*, vol. 40 (1947), pp. 101 ff.

[49] Cf. *Sources chrétiennes*, n° 11, p. 23 and "L'Épiclèse de l'anaphore d'Hippolyte," in *Recherches de theologie ancienne et médiévale*, t. 14 (1947), pp. 241 ff.

tis tuae, fac ut nobis sint non in judicium, neque in ignomi-
niam vel in perditionem, sed in sanationem et in robur spiritus nostri.[50]

Dom Botte has no trouble in stressing the apparently disconnected and clashing character of this text. The trinitarian formula in which the Son is named first seems bizarre to him. It is
connected then with the phrase: *Domine Spiritus Sancte, adfer
potum hunc et escam hanc sanctitatis tuae,* which is particularly
clumsy and incoherent. He then wonders what we would get by
re-working the Syriac text back into Greek the original language
of both the *Testamentum* and the *Traditio.* This is his answer.
"*Domine Spiritus Sancte*: the translation can cause no difficulty:
κύριε πνεῦμα ἅγιον. But let us point out that πνεῦμα ἅγιον
can be an accusative as well as a nominative-vocative. But the
Syriac took it for a vocative; otherwise it would not have kept it
in this position, or else it would have preceded it with a particle.

"*Adfer*: in Syriac it is the imperative of the *afel* form of the
verb *eto*, to come, a causative form (*aytoy*) which means: cause
to come. But what is remarkable is that the *yod* terminating this
form indicates that the subject is feminine; spirit, in Syriac, is
feminine. The same is true for the verb translated by *fac*. If we
translate it into Greek, we need an imperative of the second person singular; but in Greek the gender of the subject is not important. We can translate it by πέμψον or a compound form of πέμψον.
Potum hunc et escam hanc: since there are no cases in Syriac, the
determinate object of the verb is preceded by the particle *l*; but
this same particle also has the value of a preposition of motion.
The Syriac text is equivalent to an accusative, preceded or not
by ἐπί. This gives us: (ἐπί) τοῦτον τὸν πότον καὶ ταύτην τὴν
βρῶσιν. *Sanctitatis* here is another idiomatic expression. The
noun, preceded by the particle *d*, the sign of the genitive, is equivalent to an adjective. We must therefore suppose ἅγιος which
naturally agrees with the last noun: ταύτην τὴν βρῶσιν ἁγίαν.

"*Tuae*: in Syriac, it is again the particle *d*, with the second person pronoun, and again in the feminine. It is the equivalent of

---

[50] Rahmani, *op. cit.*, p. 43.

σοῦ, relating to *potum* and *escam* and not to *sanctitatis*. If we bring what we have analyzed together we obtain the following: κύριε πνεῦμα ἅγιον πέμψον (ἐπὶ) τοῦτον τὸν πότον καὶ (ἐπὶ) ταύτην τὴν βρῶσιν τὴν ἁγίαν σου[51]."

This is not yet fully suitable for an epiclesis, and the beginning of the sentence remains still up in the air. But, let us remember, this trinitarian formula, where the Son was invoked first, seems suspect. We might then put a period after *Trinitas* and suppose that it was followed by: *Domine Pater Domine Jesu Christe*, ... a form which is found in an Ethiopian anaphora that is also dependent on Hippolytus. If we admit that once again the Syriac translator was confused, we shall finally end up with a completely satisfactory epiclesis:

> Lord, Father of Our Lord Jesus Christ, etc ..., send the Holy Spirit upon this holy drink and this holy food ...[52]

This is so dazzling that all we can ask is to be convinced of it. We undoubtedly would be if we did not reread two sage pieces of advice in the same article by Dom Botte which he addresses to students of these texts. The first is never to isolate one passage from the whole. The second is not to work with translations but always on the texts themselves, which would indeed require one to be an orientalist. We can only applaud at this point... But we are equally astonished to note that Dom Botte himself, in this instance, seems blithely to violate the first piece of advice, by isolating the section *Domine Spiritus sancte adfer potum hunc et escam hanc sanctitatis tuae*. If he shows himself to be an orientalist without peer by re-creating the Greek text, did he not also allow himself to be taken in by the clumsiness of Rahmani's Latin, a frequent consequence of excessive literalism? Therefore, before isolatedly working this part of the sentence into Greek would he not have done better to re-read the whole sentence in Syriac, and ask himself whether it causes difficulty as to impute to the translator a whole series of mistakes? We must confess that in reading it from beginning to end—leaving Rahmani's

---

[51] Botte, *op. cit.*, p. 246.
[52] *Ibid.*, p. 247.

translation aside—it seems very clear. Since we are surely not an orientalist of such stature as to stand up to Dom Botte, we have given the text to some unquestionable specialists in Syriac, who moreover are accustomed to the daily use of this language in their own liturgy. None of them saw any more difficulty than we, and all understood it in the same way as we did:

> We offer you this thanksgiving, eternal Trinity: Lord Jesus Christ, Lord Father before whom every creature trembles and draws back, Lord Holy Spirit, obtain for us this food of your holiness, so that it may not turn to our judgment, nor to our shame or our condemnation, but to the healing and the consolation of our own spirit.[53]

Let us simply point out that the feminine of the verb is explained by the invoking of the Trinity. We could admit Dom Botte's correction of "food of your holiness" to "your holy food." But probably, it would be best to understand it as "the food of your sanctification." That aside, the principle that a text should be corrected only when it appears necessary to do so should keep us from modifying a sufficiently coherent formula. This is a typical example of those apologies which, as we shall soon see, were introduced at a very early date into the Syrian liturgies before making their entrance into our own medieval liturgies in the West. Unless we submit the text to a reworking that it does not seem to require, it does not seem possible to us that any sort of epiclesis can be produced from this text. We must conclude that the author of the *Testamentum*, who would certainly not have suppressed it had he found it in St. Hippolytus, actually did not find it there. And this comes down to saying that the epiclesis in the *Apostolic Tradition*, just as in the eucharist of Addai and Mari, is probably not original. The striking similar-

---

[53] If we should wish a re-translation into Greek, it hardly presents any difficulties: προσφέρομέν σοι τὴν εὐχαριστίαν ταύτην, αἰωνία Τριάς, Κύριε Ἰῆσου Χρίστε, Κύριε Πάτερ, ἀφ' οὗ πᾶσα κτίσις καὶ πᾶσα φύσις συμφρίττει, εἰς ἑαυτὴν ἀποφυγοῦσα, Κύριε Πνεῦμα ἅγιον, ἐπένεγκε (or : ἐπιχωρήγησον) τοῦτον τὸν πότον καὶ ταύτην τὴν βρῶσιν τοῦ ἁγιασμοῦ σου, ἵνα μὴ γενηθῇ εἰς κρίσιν ἢ αἰσχύνην ἢ ζημίαν ἀλλὰ εἰς ὑγίειαν καὶ στερέωσιν τοῦ νοῦ ἡμῶν.

ity between the formula found in most of the texts of Hippolytus' liturgy that have come down to us and what figures in all of the Addai and Mari texts would incline us to believe that this was an epiclesis formula popular for some time in the East. It is certainly a very archaic formula, since once again it does not ask for the consecration of the elements, nor even the mere accepting of the sacrifice, but only a descent of the Spirit, in and through the sacrament, which must have for its purpose the sanctification of those partaking, and more particularly, their fulfilment in the unity of the body of Christ that is the Church.

The text of the *Testamentum* which, as we think, Dom Gregory Dix was right in preserving as a vestige of Hippolytus' original text, enables us to understand how the epiclesis of the Spirit was introduced at this place in the eucharistic liturgies of the East. Let us recall the formula that it gives at the conclusion of the lengthy development, in the form of an apology that it adds to the anamnesis:

> Da deinde, Deus, ut tibi uniantur omnes, qui participando accipiunt ex sacris (mysteriis) tuis, ut Spiritu sancto repleantur ad confirmationem fidei in veritate, ut tribuant tibi semper doxologiam et Filio tuo dilecto Jesu Christo, per quem tibi gloria et imperium cum Spiritu sancto in saeculum saeculorum.[54]

We may admit here that the composer of the *Testamentum*, separating the end of Hippolytus' sentence from its beginning, added the invocation (Deus), modified the word order, substituted a passive (uniantur, which supposes ἐνοῦσθαι) for the active which is presupposed by the Verona Latin translation *in unum congregans*, confirmed by the Ethiopian and which must have been εἰς ἕν συνάγων. On all of these points, Richardson is probably right.

The text that this translator had before him must then have been something very close to the following:

> ...gathering them together, grant to all those who partake of your holy mysteries for the fulness of the Holy Spirit, for the strengthening of the faith in truth, that they may

---

[54] Rahmani, *op. cit.*, p. 45.

praise and glorify you through your Child Jesus Christ, through whom to you be glory and honor with the Holy Spirit, in the Holy Church, now and for ever. Amen.[55]

Dom Botte points out that in the text as given to us by the Verona palimpsest and confirmed by the Ethiopian version, this mention of the Spirit whom the communicants are to receive in fulness is explained, and can only be explained as a consequence of the previous invocation of the same Spirit.[56] Agreeing with Dom Aidan Kavanagh,[57] we should rather think the contrary. How did it happen that there was an insertion, after the anamnesis, or more exactly within its conclusion and before the return to praise in the final doxology, of an invocation of the Spirit which had no precedent either in the Jewish prayers or in the most ancient Christian eucharistic prayers, as is proved in any case by the original text of Addai and Mari? This seems to have developed in two stages. The mention of the Holy Spirit here was brought about both by the idea of the gathering of all together in the body of Christ in its fulness, and by their unanimity in the glorification of the Father through the Son. This eschatological fulfilment of the Church brought about in unity, and the con-

---

[55] In this case the word "grant," which otherwise remains up in the air, no longer causes any difficulty for the construction.

[56] Op. cit., p. 247. Dom Botte, in *Recherches de theologie ancienne et medievale,* jul. dec. 1966, pp. 183 ss. has reproached us for a few misprints (corrected in this edition) and raised objections against our attempted retroversion of the *Testamentum Domini.* These objections probably, will not be considered as very decisive by many scholars (a glance at Liddell and Scott is enough to dispel most of them.) More serious appears his emphasis on the fact that both the Latin and the Etiopic versions give the same text for the epiclesis in Hippolytus, although they are independent witnesses. This would be indeed a strong argument in favor of its authenticity ... if the epicleses given were really the same in both. However, such is hardly the case: only the first words are the same, but that does not prove much, since they can be found more or less literally in all the known epicleses. What follows is not the same in both texts, and is very uneasy in both. We persist therefore in thinking that we may well have there a witness of the later introduction of an epiclesis, which, occurring at different places, has produced different but equally unsatisfactory rehandlings of the end of the text.

[57] Aidan Kavanagh, "Thoughts on the Roman Anaphora," in *Worship,* vol. 39, n° 9, 1965, pp. 515 ff.

secration of mankind to the glory of the Father through the Son are actually two inseparable parts of the work of the Spirit in primitive Christian pneumatology: he is the seal of unity in the body of Christ, and he is the "Spirit of glory," the one who glorifies the Son and thereby perfects his own glorification of the Father.[58] Sooner or later, at the conclusion of the Christian anamnesis, at the precise point where it was leading to the doxology, the mention of the Spirit had to be made. It is this mention that we see appear for the first time, it seems to us, beneath the original text of Hippolytus, as the author of the *Testamentum Domini* must have read it. Somewhat later, at the time when theology became concerned with specifying the role of the Spirit, it would be natural that his coming would be sought more expressly at the point where mention of him had already been introduced. But, at this first stage of an epiclesis properly so-called, it is also natural that the aim of the petition be only to produce the fruit of their communion in the communicants. This is exactly what we find in the epiclesis that was certainly at an early date, introduced into the liturgy of Addai and Mari and Hippolytus as well.

Let us note that he is still not asked to consecrate the eucharist by having its sacrifice accepted; it is even less a question of the transformation of the elements. He is asked to come "in the oblation." This formula is most valuable, for by associating the Spirit and the "oblation" for the first time, it prepares the way for these further developments.

This brings us to a vocabulary trait that betrays a primary doctrinal development whereby the text of the *Apostolic Tradition*, even in its first and unretouched form, is clearly shown to be later than that of Addai and Mari. And this is a first instance, and, with the exception of the epiclesis which to us seems to be an addition, of technically sacrificial terms into a text of a eucharistic prayer. Let us recall what the text of the anamnesis of Hippolytus actually says:

Wherefore we, being mindful of his death and his resurrection, *offer* you this bread and this cup, giving thanks to you in that you deemed us worthy to stand before you and *to serve you as priests.*

In the anamnesis of Addai and Mari we did not yet find anything similar. Nevertheless it was clear there that the anamnesis expressed the whole and specifically Semitic content, of
the Jewish "memorial": a pledge given by God of his saving action that we can re-present to him with the assurance that our
prayer for the accomplishment in us of this action will be heard
since this pledge also signifies for us its permanent actuality.
For Judaism contemporary with the beginnings of Christianity,
in the communities bound together by the Messianic expectation,
this turned the meal *berakah* once again, not only into an equivalent of a sacrifice but also into the sacrifice itself in all its purity.
This is what a Christian community which was still Semitic, like
that of the anaphora of Addai and Mari, could continue to express in the same terminology. But, when we pass over to Greek-
speaking Christians, an anaphora of this type had to make clear
that the "remembrance" we make of Christ in the eucharist is
not simply a subjective, psychological recall but above all a representation to God of his own gift. In this case, it was inevitable
that sacrificial expressions make their appearance, and it is at
this point in the eucharist that they were to arise in order to interpret the content of the Jewish "memorial" in a hellenized
anamnesis.

After the appearance of the term "oblation" in the anamnesis
itself—a kind of "unveiling" of its deepest meaning—it was not
long before other terms associated with this meaning make their
own entrance into the liturgy. In particular, people became aware
that to celebrate the eucharist was to fulfil the paramount priestly ministry. But, just as the eucharistic sacrifice whose substance
is found in the "memorial" of God's own blessings which he places
in our hands so that we may re-present that memorial to him,
appears as the pre-eminent gift of God, so this priestly character
of the action in which his people re-present it to him is but the
effect of consecration to God which itself is his supreme grace.
Therefore the people add: we give thanks, ultimately and above
all, for having been made this priestly people that can "give thanks"
in fulness. This is what the Fathers of this period, like Justin
in his *Contra Tryphonem*, never tired explaining: the Jews said
that they had realized their vocation as a priest-people by filling

their existence with the traditional *berakoth*, but in fact, it is the Christians alone who can respond fully to such a vocation through the eucharist of Christ Jesus.[58]

But here, it seems, we have already taken one further step. Without excluding a reference in these words, to the whole people of God celebrating the eucharist together, it does seem that we must see in them more specific allusion to the ministry of the one pronouncing the eucharistic prayer, in the name of all, but by virtue of a mission, a special consecration coming from the Head of the whole body. In other words, in this prayer which—we must not forget—is suggested to a newly consecrated bishop for the eucharist he is celebrating at the conclusion of his consecration, "to serve you as a priest" applies undoubtedly, once again not in an exclusive but an eminent sense, to the interior of the "body," and *for* the whole "body" to the one presiding over the eucharist, who is evidently the representative of the "Head" in the midst of his people.

There is one other characteristic in Hippolytus' eucharist that sets it off from Addai and Mari, despite their close parallelism. At first sight this difference may appear purely literary. But, in fact, it portends a change in the eucharist which was to turn out to be more substantial than the appearance of sacrificial terminology. This latter merely transposed already present realities in a different manner of expression, since these realities already contained the meaning which terminology merely made more explicit. As Dom Botte pointed out, the eucharist of Addai and Mari is basically Semitic, in that it is obvious that its wording is not a translation from Greek into Syriac, but a composition that was originally produced in a Semitic idiom. There is a constant play of parallelisms of which we find no equivalent in the text proposed by the *Apostolic Tradition*. This is not all. The eucharist of Addai and Mari remains based on the Jewish meal *berakoth*, to the point that like them it is still composed not of one but three prayers, each having its own conclusion (the second is even punctuated by a first *Amen*). On the other hand, Hippolytus' eucharist as faithful as it is in following the plan

---

[58] Cf. above, p. 48.

of Addai and Mari, with the development of the themes which already followed one another in the *berakoth* of the Jewish meals, now forms only one continuous prayer. We shall soon have to return at length to this characteristic, and contrary to what most Christian liturgists still imagine, it does not attest to its primitive character. Far from it, it actually manifests its relatively late origin. Addai and Mari is an archaic formula of indisputable authenticity. On the other hand, the *Apostolic Tradition* is the work of an archaizer. It cannot be doubted that Hippolytus knew full well everything that was to be included—and that alone—in a primitive eucharist, and what order these elements were to follow. But this does not mean that he could go on formulating it as the apostles would have done, even though he zealously claims to follow them, quite simply because his customary language, and with it his way of writing and even of thinking, were no longer those of a Semite but rather of a citizen of the hellenistic empire.[59] The fine unity in the unfolding of his prayer would undoubtedly not have been possible if he did not have as a basis an organic progression that was already present in the ancient models which he wanted to retain. But this does not go so far as to be expressed in the logical and rhetorical unity of his composition, except as a result of a formal and conceptual ideal which primitive Christianity, as long as it remained Semitic, did not know. His eucharist is no longer a series of Jewish *berakoth* following one upon the other, but rather one hellenistic periodic sentence that fuses them into a continuous whole. As is illustrated by comparison with the liturgy of Addai and Mari, between what he wished to produce and what he in fact came up with, there is undoubtedly the same difference as between an authentic piece of Louis XIV furniture and a good imitation by a craftsman from the Faubourg Saint-Antoine. At first sight, they are the same. But examine them more closely and we spot the glue and the nails that ought not to be there.

Moreover, we may add that his hand all the more betrays him since he interlarded his combination with deliberate archaisms.

---

[59] This is what he means when he calls the Roman Empire "our kingdom" in his Commentary on Daniel, IV, 9.

With him they are so deliberate precisely because we can recognize them at first sight. For, by introducing them at every turn, he cannot restrain from intermingling his own elaborate style. Like the first Christians he affects calling Christ the Child (*puer*, translating παῖς) or the Servant of the Father, the Messenger, or more precisely the "Angel" of his will. As we shall also see further on, this is a survival of very old Judeo-Christian christology that can be found in other texts. But at the same time, in a way that is proper to his own theology, and much more thought through than that of the first Christians, he stresses Christ's freedom in handing himself over to death. And, if the use of the image of Christ extending his arms (on the cross), as if to draw us all to him, is a reference also to an old apocalyptic image that may be anterior to St. Paul, it merely forms a frame for the elaborate systematization of his thought.

Before leaving Hippolytus, we must observe the form in which he gives us the introductory dialogue to the Christian eucharist. This is certainly the oldest evidence we have of it since the Liturgy of Addai and Mari has come down to us merely with a dialogue that is common to the Syriac anaphoras, and it does not seem as primitive. The salutation: "The Lord be with you.— And with your spirit," although we have no evidence of it in the forms of the Jewish liturgy that we know, can be scarcely anything but Semitic in origin. In Greek it must already have had the rather bizarre and enigmatic effect it produces on people today. The invitation: *Sursum Corda—Habemus ad Dominum*, which is also Semitic (since "heart" has only a physiological meaning for the Greeks and Latins), seems to be a properly Christian creation, stressing, as the symbolic orientation substituted in the prayer directed toward the Jerusalem sanctuary, both the transcendent and the eschatological character of the Christian eucharistic prayer. It is directed toward the *heavenly* Jerusalem which is actually the future Jerusalem. But the last exchange: *Gratias agamus Domino—Dignum et justum est* is textually the Jewish formula that precedes the three *berakoth* at the end of the meal. We must be even more specific and emphasize that it is the formula that was to be used for a meal of less than ten people, that is a group which did not form the minimum required for

Synagogue worship. Is this not an indication of the fact that Hippolytus sought to reduce a Christian eucharist, which practically everywhere in his time had emerged from its primitive framework, to the forms it had when it brought together in a meal proper to them, a handful of Jewish Christians, who had first had their service of readings and prayers with the other Jews in the Synagogue? This goes along with the fact that he systematically ignores the direct connection between a service of this type, which for a long time had been customary for the Christians of his time, and the eucharist. The evidence given us by Justin assures us moreover that this connection was already a current fact one century earlier.[60] Nothing imaginable depicts what is factitious and fantastic in Hippolytus' archaism. He in no way describes for us the liturgy of his time either at Rome or elsewhere. He attempted desperately to resurrect the liturgy of the past insofar as he was capable of doing so, even though at the time of his writing there were probably merely rare survivals in more or less remote areas.

THE TRANSFORMATION OF THE ANAMNESIS AND THE BIRTH OF THE EPICLESIS

Addai and Mari through its indisputable archaism and Hippolytus by his intentional archaism give us two convergent examples of what the Christian eucharistic prayer must have been in its very first stage,—all the more remarkable for their convergence since they come from such different sources. Not only is it a prayer still wholly modeled on the Jewish prayers whose content and order it respects integrally, but it is a prayer modeled exclusively on the three final meal *berakoth*. With Addai and Mari their separation remains. With Hippolytus, it has disappeared, but the themes remain in their original position (although the first thanksgiving, for creation, already shows a tendency to be reduced to one for redemption under the pressure of the Christian developments of the second.) Of course, neither one has the *Sanctus*, nor any mention of Angels and their cult, any more than we can

---

[60] Cf. Justin, *First Apology*, 67.

find any development of the theme of divine light and divine knowledge, or the long intercessions and commemorations of the "Saints." All these themes appeared only when the eucharist had become joined with the service of prayers and readings and the prayers which preceded the Jewish prayers that mentioned them came to be combined or blended with the prayers proceeding from the meal *berakoth*.

Still, it would be wrong to conclude that the ancient eucharist was nothing more than pure praise of the creator and the redeemer. Through its third paragraph, proceeding from the third and last *berakah* of the Jewish meals, this eucharist in primitive form already makes the transition from praise to prayer by recalling the "memorial" of the *mirabilia Dei*. It does so within the logic itself of this "memorial": that the wonder-works of God, re-presented before him, have their whole eschatological fulfilment in us, that is to say: that we all achieve the perfect unity of the definitive people of God in the whole Christ, Head and members perfectly united. In this way, just as with the third Jewish *berakah*, the prayer, originating in praise, could return to praise in the final doxology: that God be glorified by Christ in his whole body, the Church, animated by his Spirit.

From this, we see what twofold development was to follow, which this study has allowed us to grasp in its nascent state.

On the one hand, the necessity to translate, or to "targumize", for the "Greeks" the pregnant sense of the Jewish "memorial" would lead in the anamnesis itself to explicitly sacrificial formulas: the "oblation" which the anamnesis of Hippolytus is the first to mention. This oblation is nothing but the re-presentation to God of the pledge of salvation that he has given to his people in the "memorial." It acts as a basis for the prayer that the "mystery" of Christ, which is the soul of this memorial, may have its fulfilment in us. This comes down to our consecration as a people of priests, dedicated to the sole praise of the Father, through the Son, in the power of the Spirit.

Hence, in addition, we have the second development, not so much in the heart of the anamnesis as at its conclusion, the one which was to end up in what we call the epiclesis. This being gathered together in Christ, in his body, in order to form the Church,

on the part of all his people and their consecration to the glory
of God, was for Christians the work of the Spirit. An extension
of the prayer's conclusion, including the mention of the Spirit,
was therefore quite natural at this point. In what we should
come to consider the original form of the eucharist of Hippolytus,
still visible beneath the conclusion of the *Testamentum* in our
opinion, it seems that we witnessed the appearance of this notion
in this context and for this reason.

It is easy then to understand that at a time when it was thought
necessary to stress the equal divinity and personality of the Spirit,
in the second half of the fourth century, and probably, as we
shall see, in Syria, there developed what at first was merely a
subordinate clause making up the first epiclesis: an express invocation of the descent of the Spirit, today, upon the eucharistic
celebration, parallel to the invocation of the Son in the incarnation in order that its effect might be fulfilled in us. Hence the
precise form of this original epiclesis, as we find it both in the
remodeling of Addai and Mari and in what seems also to be a
remodeling of Hippolytus: the Spirit's coming is not yet invoked
to consecrate the sacrifice (even though it is in immediate proximity to the first sacrifical formulas that he is invoked); nor is
he invoked to transform the elements, but to cause our celebration
of the eucharist to produce its fruit in us: the completion of the
Church in unity in order to glorify for ever the Father, through
the Son, in (or with) the Spirit. At this first stage, the epiclesis
inevitably betrays its late character, either because of the simple
break in continuity that it causes, as in the case of Addai and
Mari, or by the redundant effect it produces, as in the case of
Hippolytus where it is added to another and probably earlier
mention of the Spirit without yet managing to absorb it.

OTHER EVIDENCES OF THE SAME TYPE

We have a few indications, it seems, of a survival of this primitive type of the eucharist, at least up to the fourth and perhaps
up to the fifth century in local liturgies: without the *Sanctus* and
what accompanies it, and doubtless also without the intercessions
and commemorations that nevertheless are found everywhere

at this period. The first is in a text cited in favor of his own ideas
by an Arian of the West. He must have found it in a liturgical
compilation of Northern Italy at the end of the fourth or the beginning of the fifth century, for Cardinal Mai found this example
in a Milanese manuscript.[61]

Here is the text which unfortunately is incomplete, but which
does seem to lead us to an anamnesis in which the institution
narrative seems on the verge of appearing in the midst of sacrifical terms which apply directly to the "thanksgiving":

> It is right and just, equitable and just, that we give you
> thanks for all things, Lord, Holy Father, almighty and ever-
> lasting God, who (by the light) of your incomparable good-
> ness have deigned to shine in the darkness, in sending us
> Jesus Christ as the Savior of our souls, who in humbling him-
> self for our salvation gave himself up to death that, by giving
> us the immortality which Adam had lost, he might make
> us his heirs and his sons. We cannot worthily give thanks
> to your great mercy nor praise you with such goodness, but
> we pray you, out of your great and compassionate love, to
> accept this sacrifice that we offer you, as we stand before
> your divine love, through Jesus Christ, our Lord and our God,
> through whom we pray and beseech ...

This is certainly an interesting formula both for the archaism
of its schema and for the details of its wording which are very
close to the style of the Roman canon. And it undoubtedly permits us to form some idea of the really archaic forms of the Roman liturgy or related liturgies, better than by having a questionable recourse to Hippolytus.

More recently, a fragment of another anaphora, attributed
to St. Epiphanius, has been rediscovered which shows these same
peculiarities: the absence of the *Sanctus* and of the mention of
the cult of Angels, the absence of any commemoration of the
saints and of any intercession. Dom Botte devoted an article

---

[61] A. Mai, *Scriptorum Veterum Nova Collectio*, t. III, (1827), 2nd part,
pp. 208 ff. Dom Gregory Dix, *op. cit.*, p. 540, rightly called attention to this
text. Cf. since then, L. C. Mohlberg, *Sacramentarium Veronense* (Rome,
9176), p. 202.

to it in the review *Muséon*.[62] This is one more evidence of the survival up to the same era, and now in the Greek world, of eucharists that developed after the pattern that we find both in liturgy of Addai and Mari and under the surface of Hippolytus' liturgy. As rare as they are, these valuable relics would be enough to assure us, if any doubt could remain, that our reconstruction of the primitive formula of Addai and Mari is not in any way imaginary, just as Hippolytus' archaism, as false as it might be, was still not illusory.

Still, the fact is that once we are faced with set texts of widely attested usage, a usage that has been retained more or less in its entirety up to our own day, they come from models that are quite different from those we have been treating. And, whatever the differences they show among themselves, these different models which we have schematized at the beginning of this chapter, all present the same series of additional elements, in addition to those that were already present in the type of the eucharist that we may look upon as primitive, despite some variations which can be observed in their arrangement. It is to these other types, the only ones which were to survive in Catholic and Orthodox tradition, that we must now address ourselves. The first question that will obviously arise in their regard will be to explain how they so quickly and universally came to be substituted for the ancient type that we know now merely through a few traces.

---

[62] Dom Bernard Botte, "Fragments d'une Anaphore inconnue attribué à saint Épiphane," in *Muséon*, t. 73 (1960), pp. 311 ff.

The Alexandrian and Roman Eucharists

THE CANON OF THE ROMAN MASS MADE ITS APPEARANCE
with St. Gregory the Great in the sixth century practically as
it is today, with the exception of a few secondary details that
we still use.[1] This canon shows a structure quite different from
Hippolytus' eucharist and a treatment of its subject that is
no less different. Again, as in the case of the liturgy of Addai and Mari, we are confronted not with a continuous prayer,
but with a series of connected prayers. Not one of its expressions shows any recognizable kinship with any formula from
Hippolytus. For those who wish to maintain that the *Apostolic Tradition* represents the Roman usage of its time, there is
only one conclusion that can be drawn: the canon of the present
Roman mass is the result of an unlikely reshuffling, where everything was broken up, disorganized and disfigured by the introduction of adventitious elements that ruined the beautiful unity
which the Roman eucharist supposedly had in the beginning.
This catastrophic notion of the evolution of the eucharist at Rome
since the patristic period, has been put forth articulately by Anton

---

[1] Cf. Dom Bernard Botte, *Le Canon de la Messe romaine* (Louvain, 1935).

187

Baumstark.[2] It is good to remember that P. Drews and Baumstark himself, when he was still hypnotized by the West Syrian liturgies (not to mention W.C. Bishop), had admitted it beforehand on the supposed grounds of an origin for the canon which no one any longer would think of looking for in this area.[3] Some Anglican scholars, like Walter Frere,[4] had gleefully seized upon this theory, finding in it an unexpected justification for the relinquishment of the Roman liturgical tradition of the eucharist in their own Communion. A. Jungmann[5] and Th. Klauser[6] have popularized it with some self-assurance. And in our own day, as might have been expected, some dauntless reformers have taken it over as an excuse for unburdening us of this monster and returning us finally to the true Catholic and Roman tradition which had been lost for at least fifteen centuries.[7]

IS ST. HIPPOLYTUS A WITNESS OF THE ORIGINS OF THE ROMAN LITURGY?

In all of this, it seems to us, we fall far short of our goal, and on grounds that are incredibly shaky. Upon the mere examination of Hippolytus' personality and his work in general, we have already mentioned the positive reasons we have for doubting that he represented true Roman tradition even if he was a member

[2] Cf. A. Baumstark, "Das 'Problem' des römischen Messkanons" in *Ephemerides liturgicae*, t. 53 (1939), pp. 204 ff.

[3] On all of this, see the article of Dom Cabrol, "Canon romain," in the *Dictionnaire d'archéologie et de liturgie chrétiennes.*

[4] Walter H. Frere, *The Anaphora or great Eucharistic Prayer* (London, 1938).

[5] Andreas Jungmann, *The Mass of the Roman Rite*, 2 vol. (New York, 1950-1955).

[6] Th. Klauser, *The Western Liturgy and its History* (London, 1952).

[7] Let us cite only, as one example among many others, an article of Leo Mahon that appeared in *Commonweal*, 1965, pp. 560 ff., who called the Roman canon disdainfully a Gallican pot-pourri that was a latecomer to the Roman mass, and proposed purely and simply to discard it. His taking apart and reassembling of it on the West Syrian plan is no small work of the imagination.

of the Roman clergy. But, if we come to compare his eucharist with everything else that we know for sure about the Roman eucharist after him, it becomes not simply questionable, but, it must be said, quite unlikely that the liturgy of Hippolytus could have engendered the present Roman liturgy, even after all the debasements that one might wish to imagine are removed. Granting the total absence of any community in structure, treatment or details of expression, to speak of a dislocation produced by the introduction of alien material into the original model would be plainly insufficient. The Roman canon, since St. Gregory in any case, is certainly the Roman liturgy. If the Roman liturgy, two and a half or three centuries earlier, was that of Hippolytus, it must then be said that the same is true for the Roman liturgy as for Jack's knife; it is always the same knife, even though handle and blade had both been changed in turn. It is not one or multiple modifications that would have intervened between the two, it is the total substitution of one text for another.

When, how and why did this substitution take place? We have no information about this at all. Once we accept that Hippolytus represents the Roman eucharist in the middle of the third century we should have to accept the fact, but without being able either to situate it or to explain it. That we should allow for such a mutation, which neither any thing or any person seems to have recorded in any way, and this in a Church which of all Churches was quite singular for its conservatism, is, let us admit it, so difficult that it makes the supposition very doubtful that Hippolytus may be giving us a description of the third-century Roman liturgy. On the other hand, as we have seen, the intrinsic reasons that are present for so thinking—we mean those that can result from a knowledge of his work and personality—are so flimsy, not to say non-existent, that it seems that this alone ought to be enough to dispel the curious illusion to which the majority of modern scholars have succumbed. To explain the evolution that might have produced the canon of the Roman mass of St. Gregory with Hippolytus' liturgy as a starting point, is to set a task for ourselves that has no chance of success. Without sufficient reason, even without any probability of success we should be committing ourselves to an impossible route. By continuing to follow this course, we will be fated to end up with the idea that the canon of the Roman mass is inexplicable, unjustifiable and unacceptable, merely because we have wished at all costs to impose upon it an explanation that does not stand up.

But this is not all. As unlikely as the total mutation and not merely a more or less profound alteration may be *a priori*, which would have had to take place in the Roman mass for the transition from St. Hippolytus to St. Gregory, we cannot take refuge behind the two and a half or three centuries that separate them and imagine a slow decomposition and then a recomposition which at any event would remain imaginary in the absence of any precise historical evidence. Although we have no complete text of the canon before St. Gregory, we do have some references as to what it was some time before: precisely in the second half of the fourth century. The *De Sacramentis*, which is generally acknowledged today as the work of St. Ambrose, does contain a series of allusions to the eucharist which he used. For the whole central part, they even give an express and more or less literal quote. This cross-check that a happy chance allows us to make, assures us that in any case, just before the institution narrative, and just after the anamnesis, formulas were to be found that must have been the same as in the time of St. Gregory, if not word for word, at least very close to it. Moreover, even at his time, a series of intercessions followed the initial praise. This suffices to state that St. Ambrose was already familiar with a canon whose whole development practically coincides with that of St. Gregory, while there is nothing other than this last text in what he tells us that could be connected with St. Hippolytus.

We would therefore not be dealing with a slow break up, but rather with a cataclysm that came about within the space of hardly a century, substituting one eucharist for another.

Just one theory which has at times been maintained would allow us to explain the matter. The canon which we call Roman today would have to be not Roman at all, but Ambrosian or, in any case, Milanese, and the prestige of the great bishop would have had to induce Rome to scrap its own rite and adopt his

in its stead.[8] The matter seems to involve such a tremendous
step that it becomes unlikely. We must add that it would go
directly counter to what we know with greatest certainty about
the relationships between the liturgy of Milan and that of Rome
at the time of Ambrose. For a long time it seemed impossible
to attribute the *De Sacramentis* to him because the *De Mysteriis* (which is unquestionably his work) supposes a liturgy different from the *De Sacramentis* for baptism. And the liturgy of
the *De Sacramentis* is opposed to the other rite explicitly described
as being the Roman rite. Since then, a careful examination of
the thought and style of the two writings, like the one made
by Dom Botte in particular, has convinced practically everyone
that they can have only one and the same author.[9] We are thus
obliged to accept the conclusion that between the composition of
the *De Sacramentis* and that of the *De Mysteriis*, Milan had adopted
the liturgy of Rome on some points where it differed from it. In
other words, what happened must have been exactly the opposite
from the preceding supposition: it is not Rome that in Ambrose's
time tended to take on the Milanese liturgy (in those areas where
they still differed) but Milan which tended to take on the Roman
liturgy.

We should therefore do better to abandon all these hypotheses
and simply give up any idea of dislocation, dismemberment and
metamorphosis of the Roman eucharist. We should give up the
groundless idea that is at the basis of all of these notions. If Hippolytus can give us some information about certain characteristics of an archaic eucharist, which at his time must already have
long diappeared from Rome, and doubtless from many other
places, we must still not look to him for the origin of the Roman
eucharist, at least as we have it since the time of St. Gregory and
in its very advanced formulation at the time of St. Ambrose.

[8] See Th. Klauser, *The Western Liturgy and its History, Some Reflections
on Recent Studies* (London, 1952), pp. 20-21.
[9] See Dom Botte's introduction to his edition and translation of the *De
Mysteriis* and the *De Sacramentis* in *Sources chrétiennes* (Paris, 1950).

THE ALEXANDRIAN LITURGY AND THE PRESENCE
OF THE INTERCESSIONS IN THE FIRST PART OF THE
EUCHARIST

Must we therefore give up any idea of understanding the genesis of the Roman canon? Certainly not. If Hippolytus cannot be of any help to us, and risks waylaying us, we still have other evidence, some of which goes back before the time of Ambrose, of a rite related to the Roman rite as we know it, and whose evolution is somewhat better known to us. There is every reason for thinking that it would be much more profitable to follow this other track. The rite we are speaking of at the moment is that of Egypt, and more particularly of the archbishopric of Alexandria. Once again, the analogies of content, structure and even similarities of expression are manifold between the solidly attested forms of the Roman eucharist and those of the Alexandrian liturgy. If we consequently wish to bring together all the elements capable of shedding light on the genesis of the present Roman eucharist, it is in relation to the Alexandrian eucharist that it is fitting to study it. Here, we are on solid ground. And, instead of the principle of explanation multiplying insoluble problems and rendering ultimately inexplicable the evolution which we must try to outline, with its final result before our eyes, bringing the two together will shed a great deal of light. This will contribute, as we shall see, toward making perfectly comprehensible what too many people are set on claiming to be absurd.

It is quite true, however, that on first sight the Alexandrian rite even more than the Roman rite, gives us a eucharist whose complexity could pass for incoherence. When compared to its neighbor, the West Syrian rite, which at a very early date influenced it to the point finally of practically substituting itself for it, the Alexandrian rite seems like the Roman to present exactly the same elements, but in a curiously disparate order. But we need not pursue the comparison for too a long time before we see that it would be getting us again off the track if we were to wish to explain the Alexandrian eucharist from the starting point of a West Syrian eucharist where everything would have been disorderly scattered about. As we shall soon see, the order of the West Syrian eucharist, as admirable as it is, is obviously an order that was intentional, systematic and obtained by a procedure of elaborate rhetoric. And furthermore, it was conceived within the framework of a trinitarian theology that was itself very evolved. It is this order then that was evidently introduced later into the elements that we have the good fortune to find in the Alexandrian eucharist in an earlier, if not original, state. We can understand quite well what processes and principles worked towards the transformation, made from a state of the eucharist like the one that subsisted for a long time in Egypt to the one which was later established in West Syria, before imposing itself on Egypt herself. We absolutely do not understand how one could have conceived the idea of dismembering the Syrian order, if it were actually original (and once again, it seems impossible for it to have been) in order to arrive at the Egyptian order. And precisely, in Egypt herself, we can observe the transition taking place in the opposite order.

Ultimately, we have to start with the Alexandrian liturgy, in order to connect it up with the Roman liturgy, if we wish to have some success in discovering these new types of eucharistic liturgy in their nascent state, which were to become widespread in the fourth century, and definitively established in tradition, even though their beginnings are most probably quite prior to that date.

In the Greek liturgy, called the liturgy of St. Mark, which had long been classical in Alexandria (the Coptic liturgy of St. Cyril is hardly more than a translation of it,[10]) the eucharist follows a plan which we have already outlined and which we shall now recall:

1) initial thanksgiving;

2) a first prayer evoking the sacrifice (we shall call it the *pre-epiclesis*);

3) copious intercessions and commemorations, concluding with a prayer for the acceptance of the sacrifice (the starting point of the first epiclesis);

4) resumption of the thanksgiving leading to the *Sanctus*;

---

[10] On these liturgies, see I. M. Hanssens, *Institutiones liturgicae de ritibus orientalibus*, t. III, pars altera (Rome, 1932), pp. 632 ff.

5) a new prayer beseeching with greater insistence the acceptance of the sacrifice, along with a formal invocation for the consecration of the elements (the first epiclesis in this rite);

6) the institution narrative;

7) the anamnesis;

8) the last invocation for the offered. sacrifice to be accepted
and more precisely for it to have in us its effects of grace (second
epiclesis), and

9) the final doxology.

The section from 6 through 9 obviously corresponds to the
whole conclusion of the eucharistic prayer as it was from the beginning, and hardly poses any new problems for us. It is the origin and the structure of section 1-5 which must now occupy our
attention.

Let us first point out that the introductory dialogue is the same
as in the eucharist of Hippolytus, with the one exception that
instead of "The Lord be with *you*," we have "The Lord be with
all" at the beginning.

After that, 1 develops an act of thanksgiving which is interrupted
by the following prayers and commemorations, but it is taken
up again in 4 and ends in the *Sanctus*. This thanksgiving makes
a transition from the creation theme to that of the redemption,
with which we are now familiar. Man is made in God's image,
then falls. He is raised up by the redemptive incarnation of Christ,
given Wisdom and light, and is at the center of these perspectives,
which is very Alexandrian, an extension into Christianity of the
Wisdom train-of-thought which we have observed in the Jewish
prayers of the 7th book of the *Apostolic Constitutions*. When
the thanksgiving is resumed, it concentrates on the divine Name,
in accordance with another theme with which we are already
familiar. It is glorified above all "powers" in the present world
and in the world to come. This leads to the evocation of the angelic cult and the *Sanctus*.

Here is St. Mark's text. as given in Brightman:

It is truly right and just, holy and proper, and helpful
for the salvation of our souls, that we praise you, you who
are Master, Lord, God, almighty Father, and hymn you,
give you thanks and tell of your great deads (ἀνθομολογεῖσ-

θαι)), night and day, with untiring mouths, lips that do not keep silent, hearts that are not mute, you who have made heaven and what is found in heaven, the earth and what is upon the earth, the seas, the springs, the rivers, the pools and all that is found therein, you who have made man after your own image and likeness and who gave to him the enjoyment of paradise. But when he committed the transgression, you did not despise or abandon him, but in your goodness you called him back through the law, you instructed him through the prophets, you re-formed him and renewed him through this awesome, life-giving and heavenly mystery, and all (this) you have done through your Wisdom, the true Light, your only-begotten Son, our Lord, God and Savior Jesus Christ, through whom, with him and the Holy Spirit, giving thanks to you, we offer to you this reasonable (λογικόν) and unbloody worship, (a worship) offered to you, Lord, by all the nations from the rising of the sun to the going down thereof, from North to South, for great is your Name among all the nations and in every place incense is offered to your holy Name and a pure sacrifice, as an immolation and an oblation ...[11]

... For you are the one who is above every principality, authority, power and domination, and above every name, not only in this world but also in the world to come: a thousand thousands and ten thousand myriads of holy Angels and armies of Archangels assist you, your two very venerable living creatures attend you, as well as the many-eyed Cherubim and the six-winged Seraphim, who with two wings cover their faces, with two wings their feet and with two others fly, and cry out to each other with untiring mouths and with divine hymns (θεολογίαις) that are never silent, sing, exclaim, glorify, cry out the victory hymn and the trisagion, saying to your supereminent glory: *Holy, holy, holy, Lord Sabaoth, heaven and earth are full of your holy glory.*[12]

Once again this text is particularly close to the Jewish prayers of the 7th book of the *Apostolic Constitutions* through its Wisdom

---

[11] F. E. Brightman, *Liturgies Eastern and Western*, vol. I, *Eastern Liturgies* (Oxford, 1896) (only this volume ever appeared), pp. 125 ff. This text comes from the twelfth century *Codex Rossanensis*. Cf. *op. cit.*, p. 112.

[12] Brightman, *op. cit.*, pp. 131 ff.

references, although its "logical" humanism is very characteristic of Alexandrian Christianity, just as the emphasis on the waters, the springs, the rivers and the pools, in the evocation of creation, is typically Egyptian. But its primary origin is unquestionable: it is a Christian remodeling of the Synagogue *berakoth* associated with the *Sanctus*. It will be seen that the *Qedushah* here is given without the verse from Ezekiel, blessing the divine presence in the place of his dwelling. Doubtless this omission is a result of the fact that the Christians who used this prayer still understood that it was a question of a blessing for the divine presence in the Jerusalem sanctuary, which now was no longer relevant. Later they substituted another benediction in its place, signifying that for them the *Shekinah* is now in the manhood of the Savior.

Also very interesting, and typical of the Christianity of the patristic period, is the reference to the "pure sacrifice" offered to God in all places among the nations. As we have already pointed out, this citation of Malachi 1, after St. Justin, was invoked by the Rabbis as applying to the *berakoth* of the Jews of the diaspora rising up to God. But against this interpretation the same text sets off the Christians' own: this "pure sacrifice" offered among all the nations is rather the Christian eucharist.[13]

Let us go on to the intercessions and commemorations. These texts, in all Eastern liturgies, always had the tendency to develop progressively, and even to expand considerably. But in the present case of the liturgy of St. Mark, as we shall see momentarily, we have proof that the text of its eucharist, even if it too underwent progressive amplifications, remains substantially faithful in this section to its very ancient schema.

Between the two invocations of the divine Name which place the supplication within the act of thanksgiving, we find successively prayers for the Church in general, for peace in heaven and in this life, for the healing of all ills, death and sin, for Christians away from home, for rain, good weather, a fruitful earth, and for the authorities. There is then a commemoration of the dead, in which the saints and all the faithful who have died are the object

---

[13] Justin, *Dialogue with Trypho*, 116-117.

of one prayer (an indication of great antiquity), to which, at the end, the living are associated, so that all together might have their "part and inheritance with the saints."

At this point the diptychs are introduced, i.e. the list of names of those whom the people wished especially to commemorate.[14]

Then comes a recommendation of the offerings and an invocation for the acceptance of the sacrifice, which leads to a series of particularized invocations for those offering, or those in whose intention the offering is made: first the bishops and priests and the whole clergy, the Christian city, and finally a petition against the enemies of the Church. Ultimately, after a sort of general recapitulation of all the objects of intercession that were enumerated, there is a return to the act of thanksgiving through the repeated invocation of the divine Name.[15]

Let us note here that the prayer that follows the *Sanctus* merely resumes the theme of the recommendation of the sacrifice, to ask again, and more formally, that God himself consecrate it. Thus, we may say, just as the totality of the intercessions is enclosed within the thanksgiving, so the conclusion of the thanksgiving, together with the *Sanctus*, is in turn enclosed within the final petition for the acceptance of the eucharistic sacrifice. A first evocation of this in the initial act of thanksgiving introduced the intercessions.

If we now recall the content and the order of the blessings in the *Tefillah*, we shall be astonished to see that the themes of the prayer correspond exactly, taking into account some inevitable transpositions. Only their order is somewhat though not complepletely changed.

---

[14] We cannot at this point involve ourselves in all the problems posed by the diptychs. See the dissertation of E. Bishop, printed at the end of the edition of the *Homilies of Narsai*, by R. H. Connolly, *Texts and Studies*, vol. VIII (Cambridge, 1909), pp. 97 ff.

[15] Cf. Brightman, *op. cit.*, pp. 128 ff. We will give later what we possess as certain of the primitive forms of the Egyptian intercessions and commemorations. Since all these prayers are very variable, often even from one manuscript of the same liturgy to another, we shall give the integral text only for the *Apostolic Constitutions* and the part of the text of the liturgy of St. James that seems to be original.

In the *Tefillah*, the first blessing evoked the holy deeds of the "fathers" of the people of God and their expectations of a redeemer. Then the second gave thanks for life, its preservation and the resurrection. The third blessed the divine Name. With the evocation of the definitive worship offered today, because of the Redeemer, returning to us the gifts lost through sin, and then the blessing of the divine Name, something of this seems indeed to have passed over into the end of the first part of our thanksgiving.

Then came the beseeching blessings of the *Tefillah* prayed successively for penance, forgiveness, redemption, healing, rain and good weather bringing peace and prosperity, the liberation of captives and people who have been dispersed, the authorities, against the *minim*, for the faithful, and finally for the eschatological construction of the holy city and the coming of the Messiah.

After this came the *Tefillah* and *Abodah* blessings, beseeching the hearing of prayers and the acceptance of the sacrifices of Israel.

Finally, the *Hodah* blessing praised the divine Name again, while the *Birkat ha-kohanim* recapitulated the themes of the intercessions.

The correspondence between the themes is striking, and there is a conspicuous analogy, if not in the whole succession of the development, at least in its framework, between an evocation of the worship given to God by the faithful people (in the expectation, and now as a result of the coming, of the Redeemer) and a final supplication for the acceptance of the prayers and the sacrifices of this people. There is in both series of prayers also the invocation of the divine Name which opens and closes the intercessions and commemorations.

But the similarity becomes even closer if we do not base our comparison on the formula of the *Shemoneh Esreh* which ultimately came to be imposed upon the Synagogue service (although it was in a more fluid state at the time of the beginning of Christianity), but rather on the special formula of the *Tefillah* that we found in the 7th book of the *Apostolic Constitutions*, where it already bears the marks of its use by Christians, and which we have every reason to believe is also Alexandrian.

Here, as in the liturgy of St. Mark, not only the *Qedushah* but also the blessings preceding its first recitation before the *Shemah*, came to be inserted in the middle of the *Tefillah*. Similarly, this formula initiates a process of attraction, before the whole of the *Qedushah*, in the content of the prayers that follow in what has become the classical *Tefillah*. The 4th, 5th, 6th, 7th, and 8th are thus incorporated into the third: the blessing of the Name. Likewise, this Alexandrian *Tefillah* brought together the 14th, 15th, 16th and 17th blessings (for the building of Jerusalem, the coming of the Messiah, the acceptance of the prayers and sacrifices of Israel) into one great final invocation. Moreover it introduced into this final supplication a list of the sacrifices of the past which had been accepted by God. We have the same thing in the eucharist of St. Mark, and the two righteous men of the Old Testament who are mentioned are Abel and Abraham who were also at the head of the list in the prayer given by the *Apostolic Constitutions*.

This analysis, it seems, from now on allows us to conclude that the universal presence of the *Sanctus* and the thanksgiving preceding it, and of the detailed intercessions and commemorations of the saints in the set texts of the eucharist that appear from the fourth century on comes from the now customary conjunction of the service of readings and prayers with the eucharistic meal. In the first of these services, all these elements of the Synagogue service remained, although, obviously, in an evolved state. When this service was joined with the eucharistic meal, these prayers which concluded it, as in the Jewish usage, were combined with the eucharistic prayer of the sacred meal into one whole. Their character, which in the etymological sense of the word was already "eucharistic," made this fusion completely natural. It is likewise natural that it was to give rise to certain unavoidable compressions, from the fact that both included the same elements of thanksgiving for the creation and redemption, and of prayer for the accomplishment of the great deeds of God which were the object of the *berakah-eucharistia*.

It remains for this study now to see what became of the elements of the eucharistic prayer proper to the sacred meal in the Alexandrian liturgy.

But, before we do so, it is fitting to give a few archaic examples of the Egyptian eucharist. They will assure us of the substantial antiquity of the schema of the intercessions and commemorations preserved in the latest forms of the liturgy of St. Mark. And they will allow us also to distinguish in its final part the ancient forms from the evolved forms that the *textus receptus* gives us.

THE *DER BALIZEH* ANAPHORA AND THE ANDRIEU-COLLOMP PAPYRUS: THE ANAPHORA OF SERAPION

The *Der Balizeh* anaphora which has come down to us through a sixth century papyrus is unfortunately incomplete. The text begins with the end of the intercessions, and it has a gap of at least 16 lines at the end of the anamnesis and at the beginning of the epiclesis that follows it. But another papyrus, from the fourth century, published by Andrieu and Collomp, does give us the beginning of an anaphora of the same type, which, when brought together with the preceding text, allows us to verify the continuity of the Alexandrian tradition for this first part.

Here first is this latter text, in which it is clear that the very first words are missing:

(It is truly meet and right ...) to bless Thee night and day ... (Thanks) to Thee Who hast made heaven and earth and all therein, the earth and all that is on the earth, the seas and rivers and all that is in them; to Thee Who didst make man to Thy image and likeness; and hast created all things in Thy Wisdom, Thy true Light, Thy Son our Lord and Savior Jesus Christ, through Whom unto Thee and with Whom together with the Holy Spirit we give thanks and offer this reasonable sacrifice, this bloodless worship, which all peoples offer to Thee from the rising of the sun even to its going down, from the north even to the south, because great is Thy name among all nations and in every place incense is offered to Thy holy name and a pure sacrifice and oblation.

We beg and beseech Thee, remember Thy Holy, One, Catholic Church, all Thy people and all Thy flocks. Give peace which is from heaven to all our hearts, but give to us as well peace even of this life. (Watch over) the king of the earth; and (see to it that he entertains thoughts) which are peaceful toward us and toward Thy Holy Name ...[16]

With the exception of a few abbreviations, all of this agrees practically word for word with the text of St. Mark that has become classic. Again we must not conclude from these differences that they suppose later amplifications, for several of the more developed formulas of St. Mark follow the text of the Jewish *berakah* before the *Qedushah* more closely.

And here now is the fragment of the *Der Balizeh* anaphora. It is obvious that it reproduces a formula of the same type, starting from the last petition against unbelievers and for the faithful.

... Those who hate you. May your blessing be upon your people who do your will. Raise up those who fall, bring back the wayward to the right path, strengthen those who lack courage.

For you are above every principality, authority, power and domination, and above every name, not only in this world but in the world to come. The thousands of the holy Angels and the innumerable hosts of Archangels attend you, as well as the many-eyed Cherubim and the six-winged Seraphim, who with two wings cover their face, with two wings their feet, and with two others fly: all proclaim in every place that you are holy. With all those who acclaim you, receive our offering of today while we repeat: *Holy, holy, holy, Lord Sabaoth; heaven and earth are full of your glory.*

Fill us as well with your glory, and deign to send your Holy Spirit upon these offerings which you have created, and make this bread the body of Our Lord and Savior Jesus Christ and the cup the blood of the new covenant of our same Lord

---

[16] Cf. M. Andrieu and P. Collomp, "Fragments sur papyrus de l'Anaphore de saint Marc," in *Revue des Sciences religieuses* (Strasbourg, vol. 8, 1928), p. 500. Translation in *Sacraments and Worship*, P. F. Palmer, S.J., ed. (Westminster, 1955), p. 45.

and Savior Jesus Christ. And as this bread which was once dispersed upon the heights, the hills and in the valleys, was brought together as to make but one body, as also this wine, which gushed forth from the holy vine of David, and this water, which came from the spotless lamb, mixed together, have become but one mystery, so also bring together the catholic Church of Jesus Christ.

For our Lord Jesus Christ, on the night in which he was betrayed, took bread into his holy hands, gave thanks, blessed it, sanctified it, broke it and gave it to his disciples and apostles, saying: Take, and all of you eat of it: This is my body, given for you for the remission of sins. Likewise, after the meal, he took the cup and gave thanks, drank of it, gave it to them, saying: Take, and all of you drink of it; This is my blood, shed for you, for the remission of sins. As often as you eat of this bread and drink of this cup, you announce my death, you proclaim my resurrection, you make remembrance of me.

The people:

We announce your death, we proclaim your resurrection, and we pray.

... to us, your servants, grant the power of the Holy Spirit, the strengthening and increasing of our faith, the hope, of the everlasting life to come, through our Lord Jesus Christ, with whom, to you, Father, be the glory, with the Holy Spirit, for ever. Amen.[17]

This gap here obviously puts historians of the liturgy in the position of Tantalus' torture. Did we have here a second epiclesis addressed to the Spirit, following the anamnesis, and, supposing that were the case, what did it petition him to accomplish? Or did we on the other hand, as in what seemed to us to have been the original state of the text of Hippolytus, have here merely a prayer for the union of Christians in order to build up the body of Christ, including the mention of the Spirit as the seal of this unity? Undoubtedly we shall never be able to answer these questions, unless a happy chance uncover a second manuscript in the sands of Egypt, and this time a complete text of the same

[17] Cf. C. H. Roberts and B. Capelle, *An early Euchologium. The Dêr-Balizeh papyrus enlarged and reedited* (Louvain, 1949).

prayer. While we await this unlikely stroke of good luck, we still may have some possibility of conjecturing a still older form of the Egyptian epiclesis, or rather epicleses. The most interesting indication we have in this regard is furnished for us by a mid-fourth-century document. It is the euchologium of Serapion of Thmuis, the bishop who was a friend and correspondent of St. Athanasius. The commentators on the eucharistic prayer it contains rightly emphasize all that is so evidently personal in the composition of this prayer. We find in it a curious mixture of Johannine imagery, tending towards a kind of harmless Gnosticism and a vaguely mystagogical philosophical jargon which was already present in Clement of Alexandria in the preceding century, and which flourished very much in the following century with Synesius of Cyrene.[18] The result was that themes essential to the traditional eucharist have more or less vanished into thin air. Yet, the schema of the Alexandrian eucharist is found everywhere, even if it is often no more than a trace. And, as we shall see, it is not so certain that all of Serapion's peculiarities are merely a reflection of his own theological or rhetorical fancy.

It is meet and needful to praise, you, to hymn you, to glorify you, uncreated Father of the only-begotten Son, Jesus Christ.

We praise you, O God, uncreated, inscrutable, ineffable, incomprehensible to all created nature.

We praise you, you who are known by the only-begotten Son, you who through him are announced, interpreted and known by created nature. We praise you, you who know the Son and reveal to the saints the glories that concern him, you who are known by the Logos whom you have begotten, you who are revealed to the saints. We praise you, invisible Father, *choregos* (i.e. possessor and dispenser) of immortality. You are the source of life, the source of light, the source of all grace and truth.

Friend to men, friend to the poor, kind to all, you draw all to you by the coming of your beloved Son.

[18] See the *Hymns* of Synesius in N. Terzaghi's edition, 2nd ed. (Rome, 1949).

We beseech you, make living men out of us. Give us the Spirit of light that we may know you, you the true one, and him whom you have sent, Jesus Christ. Give us the Holy Spirit, that we can tell and recount your unspeakable mysteries.

Let the Lord Jesus, together with the Holy Spirit, speak in us: let him celebrate you through us. For you are above every principality, authority, power and domination, above every name, not only in this world but in the world to come.

A thousand thousands and ten thousand myriads of Angels, Archangels, Thrones, Dominations, Principalities, Powers attend you and especially the two most venerable six-winged Seraphim who with two wings veil their faces, with two their feet, and who fly with the other two; they sing of your holiness; receive our acclamation with theirs when we say: *Holy, holy, holy, Lord Sabaoth, heaven and earth are full of your wonderful glory.*

Lord of the powers, fill this sacrifice with your mighty participation. For to you do we offer this living sacrifice, this unbloody oblation. To you do we offer this bread, a figure of the body of your only-begotten Son.

This bread is the figure of the holy body, because the Lord Jesus, on the night he was betrayed, took bread, broke it and gave it to his disciples saying: Take and eat of it all of you: This is my body broken for you for the forgiveness of sins.

Wherefore we, celebrating the memorial of his death, offer this bread and we pray: through this sacrifice, be propitious to us all, be propitious to us, O God of truth.

And like this bread which once was scattered over the hills and brought together as one, do you also bring together your holy Church, from every race, from every land, from every city, from every town, from every house and make her the one, living and catholic Church.

And we offer this cup, a figure of the blood, because the Lord Jesus Christ, having taken a cup after the meal, said to his disciples: Take, drink, this is the new Covenant, this is my blood, shed for you for the remission of sins. Wherefore we offer this cup, a figure of the blood.

God of truth, may your holy Logos come upon this bread, that the bread may become the body of the Logos, and upon this cup, that the cup may become the blood of truth. And

cause all those who partake to receive the remedy of life, for
the healing of every infirmity, for the strengthening of all
progress and every virtue, and not for their condemnation,
O God of truth, nor for their shame or their abashment.
We have called upon you, you the Uncreated One, through
the only-begotten Son, in the Holy Spirit. May this people
receive lovingkindness, and be found worthy of progress. May
the angels attending the people crush the Evil One and build
up the Church.

We beseech you also for them that rest whom we commemorate.

Here the names are recalled.

Hallow these souls for you know them all. Hallow all them
that sleep in the Lord.

Number them among your holy Powers. Grant them a
place and a dwelling in your Kingdom.

Receive also the thanksgiving of the people. Bless these
who have brought the oblations and the eucharists.

Grant health, wholeness, joy and every progress of soul
and body to all this people, through your only-begotten
Son, Jesus Christ, in the Holy Spirit, as he was, is and shall
be from age to age, world without end. Amen.[19]

The absorption of almost the whole prayer in knowledge and
life can be attributed to the Alexandrian or rather the Clementine philosophism of Serapion, although these were also biblical
themes that were already central to the Jewish *berakoth*, and the
development he gives them is quite Johannine. More characteristic of this "gnosis," however orthodox it basically is, is perhaps the disappearance, of the "logical" worship and the unbloody oblation. Their mention at the end of the first part of
the thanksgiving seems to be traditional in Egypt. Moreover
we find them again in Serapion after the *Sanctus*, but without

---

[19] Discovered by Wobbermin, who published it in 1898 in the second volume of the new series of *Texte und Untersuchungen* of Gebhardt and Harnack, the *Euchologium of Serapion* was reissued by Funk in a second volume, adding to his edition of the *Apostolic Constitutions* some *Testimonia
et Scripturae propinquae* (Paderborn, 1905). The text of the anaphora is
found on pp. 172 ff. Dom Bernard Capelle devoted an article to it, "*L'Anaphore de Sérapion*," in *Muséon*, t. 49 (1936), pp. 1ff. and 425 ff.

the first recommendation of the oblation, which customarily comes at the end of the enclosed intercession. Undoubtedly, in his mind, "to tell and recount your unspeakable mysteries" (obviously, in the eucharistic prayer) was a sufficient equivalent of it.

Yet, should we believe that the reduction of the whole prayer of intercession to the one paragraph asking for life and knowledge, the first apparent curious note of this eucharist, also comes from a theology that is peculiar to its author? This is perhaps true as far as the formulation that he gives it is concerned. But we shall see shortly that we have good reason to suppose that he might have thought himself authorized, by a tradition with which he was familiar, to condense in this way the intercessions of the beginning into one prayer.

What can we say then of the peculiarities of the two epicleses, the one that precedes the institution narrative and the one that follows? In a moment we shall see, by going back to the anaphora of St. Mark that this twofold epiclesis is a characteristic trait of Alexandrian tradition. But, in the *Der Balizeh* text, the first one already sought the transformation of the elements into the body and blood of Christ, and sought it through a descent of the Spirit. Once again the fragmentary character of the text perhaps allows us in this text also, on account of the length of the lacuna, to suppose a second epiclesis, but it does not allow us to guess its content. Whatever the case, neither Serapion's first epiclesis nor the second contains any mention of the Spirit, and it is in the second alone that the transformation is sought (only it is through a descent of the Logos that it is expected).

Must we also attribute this last peculiarity to Serapion's fancy? This is what a number of commentators tell us, but it is quite unlikely. In the first place, just from a reading of his text, it is obvious that he tends everywhere to introduce the Holy Spirit. His prayer, even though it is relatively short, mentions him four times in places where no other known eucharistic liturgy does. If in the middle of the fourth century in Egypt such a tradition had existed, it would therefore be very strange for him to have removed it in a place where tradition would have placed it. But if we take into account what we know on the other hand about

Serapion's personality, this becomes highly unlikely.[20] With the exception of this euchologium, what we actually know with the greatest certainty about him is that he was concerned with fighting the Arians, or Arianizers, who questioned the divinity of the Holy Spirit. It is precisely to answer his request on this point that Athanasius composed the doctrinal letters he addressed to him. How then could Serapion have made such a mistake, directly opposed to his own concerns, that is attributed to him? If there already existed in the tradition of the eucharist a prayer beseeching the Spirit to bring about the consecration, he would have been the last one to remodel it in order to attribute to the Logos alone this properly divine intervention!

All that we can suppose is that the Alexandrian epiclesis of his time did not mention any divine person in particular (we shall soon see that this is not unlikely), and it is he who had the idea to attribute at least one of them to the Logos (an idea, as we shall see, which may have come also to others besides).

Another peculiarity of Serapion's eucharist is in what follows this last epiclesis: the mention of the Angels, the remembrance of the departed, and a last development of a prayer for the offerers and the whole people of God. This again we shall soon find elsewhere, and there is every reason to think that Serapion is not its originator.

But the most important peculiarity of his text is that the institution narrative does not precede the anamnesis, but overlaps it. We find in the Ethiopian liturgy and elsewhere other examples of this peculiarity that seems so curious to us. In any case, it manifests the closeness of the bond that antiquity felt existed between the anamnesis and the introduction of the narrative

---

[20] See J. Lebon's introduction in his edition and translation of St. Athanasius' *Letters to Serapion* in the *Sources chrétiennes* collection. Dom B. Botte, in an article in *Oriens Christianus*, Band 48 (1964), pp. 80 ff., "L'Eucharistie de Sérapion est-elle authentique?", has attempted to show that the author must have been a *"pneumatomachos"*, and that this could explain the absence of the Spirit in his epiclesis. The greatest difficulty faced by this supposition is that we cannot understand how a *pneumatomachos* could, on the other hand, have introduced the Spirit in a number of places where he does not figure in any other eucharistic liturgy.

in the eucharistic prayer itself. We may wonder if such an arrangement is not also ancient, indeed perhaps more ancient than what finally prevailed and which comes down to coordinating the narrative with the anamnesis, while still keeping them distinct.

A final peculiarity of this eucharist must be pointed out: like the liturgy of Addai and Mari, and like the great Jewish prayers which are the source of our Christian prayers, it is not truly *one* prayer, but a series of short prayers, connected by their sense, but completely separate in their composition. This will furthermore remain true, at least to a certain extent, even with the latest forms of the Egyptian eucharist. But it is of singular interest to observe this fact from the pen of a writer like Serapion, who was obviously molded from a background of hellenic culture. If, despite this, he held himself to a form of composition that is so obviously Semitic, we must really believe that the models of the eucharist which are considered to be normal at his time, at least where he lived, remained completely faithful to this pattern.

Let us add something more which is not only relevant to Serapion but also to the Der Balizeh anaphora, which it does not seem to have influenced: the use that both make of the Didache formulas though in different places. People have sometimes wished to conclude from this that the Didache was of Egyptian origin. This is completely unlikely: never would an Egyptian have had the idea to speak of bread "scattered over the hills," which, on the other hand, would be very understandable from the lips of a Palestinian or a Syrian. This is so true that the composer of the Der Balizeh manuscript thought he had to add valleys to the mention of the hills!

On the other hand, we might ask whether, like Serapion, this author had first-hand familiarity with the text of the prayer of the Didache. The use made of it leads one to think that it resulted from remodeling found in the 7th book of the *Apostolic Constitutions*, causing the prayer for the first cup to be placed after that for the bread, and introducing it thereby into a synthetic eucharist which supposed that the ritual meal was already separated from the real meal.

After what we have learned from the most archaic forms of the Egyptian eucharist, we can finally arrive at the stage where we have the last part of the eucharist in what has become the classical text of St. Mark.

ANAMNESIS AND EPICLESIS IN THE EGYPTIAN LITURGY

What we call the first epiclesis follows the *Sanctus*. Its connection with it is found in all the examples of the Egyptian tradition: the resumption of the idea of fulness, taken from the last words of the *Sanctus* in this tradition: "heaven and earth are *full* of your glory." The presence of this connecting link gives an indication that there was a cut-off at this point. Actually, as we have already said, the epiclesis is already begun before the intentions for which the sacrifice is offered, in the first formula of its recommendation to God:

Accept, O God, the sacrifices of those who offer (their) offerings, (their) eucharist upon your altar, which is holy, heavenly and spiritual (*νοερόν*) in the heights of heaven, through the archangelical liturgy, of those who have offered much or little, in secret or publicly, of those who would wish (to offer) but have nothing to offer, the offerings of today, as you have accepted the gifts of the righteous Abel, the sacrifice of our father Abraham, the incense of Zachary, the alms of Cornelius and the two groats of the widow, accept their eucharists also, and render to them, in exchange for corruptible (realities) those that are incorruptible, for earthly (realities) those that are heavenly, for temporal (realities) those that are everlasting ...[21]

This is obviously the idea of this exchange which leads to a prayer for the transformation of the gifts, and this is why the presence of this idea in the Der Balizeh anaphora as in another text which we shall soon be treating, is found in the second part of this first epiclesis and must be actually in its original place. In the text of St. Mark, however, this petition was put back after the anamnesis, in the second epiclesis. We may wonder if this

[21] Brightman, *op. cit.*, p. 129.

transfer, and perhaps also the attribution to the Holy Spirit of the requested transformation, are not the first signs of a West Syrian influence on the liturgy of Alexandria. It is true that Serapion is already a witness to this transposition, even though he does not know an epiclesis calling for the descent of the Spirit. But the use he makes of the Didache shows that he is nonetheless influenced by the Syrian formularies.

The present first epiclesis of St. Mark does mention the Holy Spirit, but this seems to be a result of the idea of fulness, and it is not the transformation of the elements but the accomplishment of the sacrifice that is expected of him:

> Heaven and earth, truly, are full of your holy glory through the epiphany of our Lord, God and Savior Jesus Christ: fill also, O God, this sacrifice with the blessing that comes from you through the visitation (ἐπιφοιτήσεως) of your all-holy Spirit. For our Lord and God and great king (παμβασιλεῦς) Jesus, the Christ, on the night that he delivered himself over on account of our sins, and suffered death for us all in the flesh, being at table with his holy disciples and apostles, having taken bread into his holy, pure and spotless hands, and raising his eyes to heaven to you, his Father, our God, and the God of all things, giving thanks, blessing (it), sanctifying it and breaking it, distributed it among his holy and blessed disciples and apostles, saying: Take, eat, this is my body broken for you and distributed to you for the remission of sins (*the people answer*: Amen).
>
> Likewise, having taken the cup after having supped, and having mixed wine and water in it, raising his eyes to you, his Father, our God and the God of all things, giving thanks, blessing it, sanctifying it, filling it with the Holy Spirit he gave it to his holy and blessed disciples and apostles, saying: Drink of it all of you, This is my blood, of the new covenant, shed for you and for many and distributed to you for the remission of sins (*the people answer*: Amen).
>
> Do this as a memorial of me, for as often as you eat of this bread and drink of this cup, you announce my death and you proclaim my resurrection and my ascension until I come.
>
> Master, Lord, almighty One, heavenly King, announcing the death of your only-begotten Son, our God and Savior Jesus Christ, and proclaiming his blessed resurrection from

the dead on the third day, as well as his ascension into heaven and his sitting at your right hand, God the Father, and waiting his second, awesome and dread parousia, in which he will come to judge the living and the dead in justice, and render to each according to his works—spare us, Lord our God!—, we have presented what comes from your own gifts before you, and we pray and beseech you (God) friend of men and good, send from your holy height, from the place where your dwelling is established, from your indescribable bosom, the Paraclete himself, the Spirit of truth, the Lord, the Life-giver, who has spoken through the prophets and the apostles, who is everywhere present and fills all things, who, of himself and not as a servant, shows sanctification to whom he will according to your good pleasure, who is simple by nature, manifold in his activity, the source of divine gifts, who is consubstantial with you, who proceeds from you, who shares the throne of your Rule with our God and Savior Jesus Christ; look upon us and send upon these loaves and these cups your Holy Spirit, that he might sanctify them and perfect them since he is the almighty God and that he might make this bread the body (Amen *of the people*) and this cup the blood of the new covenant, of our Lord and God and Savior and great king Jesus Christ himself, that they might be for us who are partakers (a source of) faith, watchfulness, healing, prudence, sanctification, renewal of soul, body and spirit, for the communication of the blessed eternal and incorruptible life, for the glorification of your all-holy name, for the remission of sins, that in all this and in all your Name, which is all-holy, precious and glorified, you may be glorified, praised with hymns and sanctified, together with Jesus Christ and the Holy Spirit, as it was, is and will be from generation to generation, and world without end. Amen.[22]

This text, which is obviously overworked in its last part, seemingly cannot be earlier than the council of Constantinople in 380 nor later than that of Chalcedon in 450, since the Monophysite Copts translated it practically as it stands in their liturgy of St. Cyril, while its litany of the titles of the Holy Spirit is obviously in great part borrowed from the Constantinopolitan creed.

[22] Brightman, *op. cit.*, pp. 132 ff.

Yet, as developed as it is, the epiclesis is still closely attached to the anamnesis, and even incorporated into its final part. But we may speculate that it developed from a formula that was very close to this, since the transformation was sought earlier:

> We have presented what comes from your own gifts before you and we pray and beseech you (God) friend of men and good, look upon us and send upon these loaves and these cups your Holy Spirit, that they may be for us who are partakers (a source of) faith and of renewal of soul, body and spirit, for the communication of eternal life and the glorification of your holy Name, etc.

Later we shall be wondering whether we cannot go back to an earlier state of this epiclesis. For the moment, let us be content with observing that the anamnesis that leads to this epiclesis now includes, after the resurrection, not only the ascension but the parousia itself, a remarkable explanation of the vividly felt unity of the mystery "commemorated," whose accomplishment will be sought, not as an after thought, but as the simple manifestation of the virtualities of the death and resurrection of Christ.

Very remarkable too is this formula for the presentation of the sacrifice: "we have presented what comes from your own gifts before you." More or less word for word, it will be kept by all the liturgies of the East. We could not better describe how the "memorial" is sacrificial: as the gift that God himself has made to us of the pledge of his saving mystery, so that we might represent it to him in the thanksgiving, and thus surrender ourselves to the whole permanent effect of this mystery, tending to its own accomplishment, in the glory of God.

For the first time also, we find here the phrase: "Do this as a memorial of me," developed in the words of St. Paul, but placed on Christ's lips, and furnished with a development that we should like to stress:

> ... As often as you eat of this bread and drink of this cup, you announce my death, *and you proclaim my resurrection and my ascension,* until I come.

This will also be found elsewhere in the East, and we may think, as we shall soon establish, that it is again from Syria that this formula, like the preceding one, passed into Egypt.[23]

The influence of the Pauline institution narrative, another characteristic common to the whole East, is very clear in the narrative reproduced in the eucharist of St. Mark. But, as in all the classic liturgies, three factors in its evolution can be observed: a tendency to accentuate the parallelism between what is said over the bread and over the cup, a tendency to harmonize the four New Testament narratives, and finally a tendency to accompany the description of the actions of Christ with adjectives and other formulas expressing devotion ("raising his eyes *to you his Father* ... ," " ... in his *holy, pure and spotless* hands", etc.)

But the great question facing us is how people came to introduce into the prayer coming from the *berakah Abodah* for the acceptance of the sacrifices of Israel, a mention of the transformation of the elements into the body and blood of Christ, absent from all the most ancient liturgies.

Let us repeat that this petition seems called for in the formulas of St. Mark, or at least prepared for, by the end of the first part of the prayer for the recommendation of the sacrifice, which introduces the idea of an exchange between the material, earthly, temporal gifts that we are presenting and the spiritual, heavenly, eternal gifts which we expect from God. But this merely takes the problem one step back, for there was nothing in the Jewish prayers that was directed toward that idea. We should be tempted to think that in order to understand its appearance at this point, we must look for a first consolidation which must have come about through the conjunction of the prayers derived from the *berakoth* before the *Shemah*, which were already combined with those derived from the *Tefillah*, and now with those coming from the *berakoth* at the end of the meal. It might have seemed admissible to retain a general and detailed intercession at the beginning of the eucharist and at the end a shorter supplication that was more immediately focused upon the building up of the body of Christ, an idea that underlies all the petitions at the

---

[23] Cf. below, pp. 272 ff. and 310.

beginning. But the repetition of a blessing for creation and then
for redemption, a short distance way, the first time centering on
life and "knowledge" and the second on life and the covenant,
must have very soon seemed to be an unendurable doublet.

Moreover, the Jewish prayers themselves, and particularly those
of the Didache, already tended to mingle the themes of life and
knowledge, just as the covenant was concretized in the Torah.
Quite naturally then, and especially under the influence of a theology strongly inspired by the fourth Gospel, as we see in the case
of Serapion, a transposition to the first part of the thanksgiving
was made of the theme of life side by side with the theme of the
light of truth. They fused together into one evocation of the
redemption, combining our deliverance from the ignorance of
idolatry and our liberation from death. But in this case, what
would be substituted for the double blessing which, in the still
autonomous sacred meal, immediately preceded the anamnesis?
A connection was needed between the whole last part of the prayers taken from the *Tefillah* on God's acceptance of our prayers and
sacrifices and the evocation of the memorial. This connection,
as a comparison of the first Alexandrian epiclesis with the *Abodah*
prayer shows, gives us, it seems, an indication of how it came
to be established. The *Abodah* prayer concluded with an invocation of the manifest return of the *Shekinah* to Zion. Likewise,
the first Egyptian epiclesis asks that the glory of God fill us (Der
Balizeh), or that his mighty participation (Serapion) or his blessing
and his visitation (classic St. Mark) fill our sacrifice. It is therefore this petition for the return of the *Shekinah*, which for primitive
Christians is always in the risen Christ, that must have elicited the
final request for the consecration of the elements into the body
and blood of Christ.

THE KINSHIP BETWEEN THE EGYPTIAN AND ROMAN
EUCHARISTS AND THE PRIMITIVE FORM OF THEIR EPICLESES

We think that study of the Egyptian eucharist has made available to us most of the elements necessary for elucidating the canon of the Roman mass. Their general structural analogy alone
invites us to connect the two. Actually, if we compare the plan

of the eucharist of St. Mark with that of the Roman eucharist, prescinding from the memento of the dead and the *Nobis quoque* we can see that they agree exactly, with the exception of this one difference, that instead of coming before the *Sanctus* the body of intercessions and commemorations immediately follows it. The schema of this body itself is exactly the same as in the Alexandrian rite: first, what we have called the pre-epiclesis (*Te igitur*), then the intercessions (*Memento of the living*), then the commemorations of the saints (*Communicantes*), and finally the first epiclesis. As at Alexandria, this latter is composed of two prayers (*Hanc igitur* and *Quam oblationem*). But obviously, since the *Sanctus* was already recited, they follow one another immediately.

To this structural analogy, we must add a whole series of verbal parallelisms, which exclude any assumption that it could be merely coincidental. Only in Egypt and Rome does the introductory dialogue begin with: "The Lord be with you" (or, in Egypt: "with all"). Similarly in both of these rites there follows simply "Sursum corda." At Rome the eucharist begins with: "It is truly meet and right, equitable and availing unto salvation," and at Alexandria: "It is truly meet and right (Alexandria adds: holy), equitable and availing unto salvation ... " Only in these two cases do we make the immediate transition from the motives for the thanksgiving to the expression of the worship given to God with the words: "Christ, through whom ... " The same is true for the mention of the Angels which follows, without connective, and the introduction of the *Sanctus* by a petition that our own praise be accepted together with theirs. Similarly, only in these two cases are the gifts of the faithful from this moment on called sanctified gifts (*qui tibi offerunt hoc sacrificium laudis* ...τῶν προσφερόντων τὰς θυσίας ..., τὰ εὐχαριστήρια), in the intercession preceding the consecration. In the Roman institution narrative, the mention that Jesus raised his eyes *ad te Deum patrem suum* has an exact parallel in the narrative of the liturgy of St. Mark. In the anamnesis, the formula *offerimus praeclarae majestati tuae de tuis donis ac datis* corresponds exactly and exclusively with τὰ σὰ ἐκ τῶν σῶν δόρων προεθήχαμεν ἐνώπιον τῆς δόξης αγίας σου. The parallelism that is most striking is that the first part of the first Egyptian epiclesis asks for the presentation upon the heavenly altar "through the archangelic liturgy (service)" of the sacrifice offered on earth, and it continues "as you have accepted the gifts of your righteous man Abel, the sacrifice of our Father Abraham," expressions which are found exactly in the *Supra quae* and the *Supplices* (we shall see that they furthermore were to form one sole prayer in the fourth century) of the Roman mass, where they constitute the equivalent of the second epiclesis.

Furthermore, with the exception of the special position of the body of intercessions in the Roman canon, it seems indeed that the other apparent differences between Rome and Alexandria are merely differences between two variants of the same tradition, and the "Roman" tradition must have existed at Alexandria at an early time just as it did at Rome. Actually, if we compare not the eucharist of St. Mark but that of Serapion with the Roman canon we discover: 1) that as at Rome, at Alexandria two epicleses must have been known (although they were not preserved after the fourth century) and neither of them expressly evoked the Holy Spirit, 2) that Alexandria also knew a mention of the Angels at the end of the last epiclesis, 3) that Alexandria also had a *Memento* of the dead, with the reading of their diptychs after this epiclesis and 4) that Alexandria ultimately connected this *Memento* with its conclusion through a formula coming from the prayer for those who offer the sacrifice, in a manner that is very similar to what we still have in the *Nobis quoque*. Let us then re-read the end of the eucharist of Serapion:

> ... May the Angels attending the people crush the Evil One and build up the Church.
>
> We beseech you also for them that rest whom we commemorate.
>
> *Here the names are recalled.*
>
> Hallow these souls for you know them all. Hallow all them that sleep in the Lord. Number them among your holy Powers. Grant them a place and a dwelling in your Kingdom.
>
> Receive also the thanksgiving of the people. Bless those who have brought the oblations and the eucharists. Grant health, wholeness, joy and every progress of soul and body to all this people, through your only-begotten Son, etc ...

Not only is the parallelism in the succession of ideas striking, but here again there are analogies, if not identity, in the wording. The dead are those "who rest," "those who sleep," or *qui dormiunt in somno pacis.* Their admission into beatitude in both cases is expressed as a spacial transfer: God is asked to give a "place" for them in his Kingdom, or to put them *"in loco lucis, refrigerii et pacis."*

The "also" connecting a final evocation of the offerers with that of the dead also has its parallel in the *"quoque"* of the *nobis quoque peccatoribus.* Similarly, earlier in the text, the petition for the graces expected from the communion was connected in Serapion with a κοινωνοῦντες, which seems to be echoed in the Roman *ex hac altaris participatione*; in addition, perhaps the words *haec plebs tua sancta* in the Roman anamnesis correspond to the two mentions of "this people" which appear somewhat further on in Serapion.[24] It is not true that the fact that the *Memento* of the dead was sometimes present and sometimes absent at this place in the manuscripts of the Roman canon indicates that there did not seem to have been a parallel situation in Alexandria, as the divergence between the usages of Serapion and St. Mark shows.

For its part, the comparison with the Der Balizeh anaphora shows that at Alexandria also the petition for the transformation of the elements could be attached to the first epiclesis as well as the second, just as at Rome.

Finally, there is perhaps one last apparent difference between Rome and Alexandria, although Serapion allows us to suppose that it corresponds to what could have been also the practice at Alexandria at an earlier period. The intercessions for the living at Rome are all brought together in one prayer, which is furthermore very compact, while at Alexandria, as in all of the East, they are extended into a long series of petitions which are in a state of constant expansion. But with Serapion, as in the Roman canon, we find them compressed into one prayer, one that is even shorter in Serapion than the Roman *Memento.*

---

[24] These analogies have often been pointed out, in particular by Baumstark and Jungmann.

The only major difference remaining then is the position of the intercessions and commemorations. The problem of the original place and of the exact interpretation of the prayer invoking the bringing of the offerings to the heavenly altar by the Angels will also concern us, but from now on we can observe that the mention of the Angels at the end of the last epiclesis in Serapion leads us to think that this mention could have been found at that place in Egypt as well as in Rome.

The difference between the respective positions of the *Sanctus* and the group of intercessions and commemorations, at Rome or at Alexandria, seems necessarily to be explained simply by the two different places in which the *Qedushah* was recited in the Synagogue ritual, either with the *Shemah* before the *Tefillah* or in connection with the *Tefillah*. We have already seen in the 7th book of the *Apostolic Constitutions*, the reasons for believing that the Jews of Alexandria were already reciting it only once, in the *Tefillah*, but with the *Shemah* along with it. This seems furthermore to justify the Jewish liturgiologists who think that its recitation in conjunction with the *Shemah* is the most ancient. At Rome, where there must have been a large proportion of Alexandrian Jews, it is likely that the Synagogues used a liturgy translated into Greek together with the Septuagint, as in Egypt. The Christians, who took over the Septuagint, before it served as a basis for the old Latin versions, built their own liturgy upon it, based on the same version of the Jewish liturgical texts as at Alexandria. This explains the common origin of the Christian liturgies of Alexandria and Rome in the beginning. The constant contacts between the two capitals were to continue. This state of affairs throughout the whole development of the liturgies up to the fourth century, when the Roman liturgy (like the other liturgies of the West) passed from Greek to Latin.

But undoubtedly the presence of a considerable number of Eastern and particularly Palestinian Jews in Rome preserved there a greater conservatism than at Alexandria. The *Qedushah* with the *Shemah* following it, was kept in its original place before the *Tefillah* and not right in the middle of it. It is from such a custom that the only marked difference in the structure of the eucharist in Rome and Egypt must have resulted.

All that remains for us to do is to examine the problem posed by the original place of the mention of the heavenly altar, with the Angels who are called upon to bring our sacrifice to it, and the resulting recall of the previously accepted sacrifices of "Abel the righteous" and our "father" or "patriarch" Abraham. This question, which would appear to be minimal, actually raises the whole problem of the meaning and the content of the original epiclesis or rather epicleses. The evidence from Alexandria coincides with what we have in the most ancient remodelings of the most archaic eucharists, and shows us that there was indeed an epiclesis, following the anamnesis, which if not original was at least relatively ancient. This epiclesis, however, even when we see it already directed to the Holy Spirit, began by being merely a development added to the conclusion of the anamnesis, which was always, even in Judaism, a petition that the object of the "memorial" might have its fulfilment in those who celebrated it: either the eschatological construction of the eternal Jerusalem or the building up of the Church as the body of Christ. We have seen what good reasons there are for thinking that this idea, the unity of the body of Christ being fulfilled in the final glorification of the Father, through the Son, in the Spirit, causes the first mention of the Spirit at this point. In a second stage, it developed into a formal invocation of his descent upon us and upon our celebration. As is shown in what we have today in the liturgy of Addai and Mari and of Hippolytus, the epiclesis in the beginning was nothing else but this, and not a word was said about the transformation of the elements.

Moreover, this idea seems to have arisen in the first epiclesis with the *Quam oblationem*, as we have it both in the Der Balizeh liturgy and the Roman canon. As we have seen, this prayer is but the result of an evolution of the *Abodah* prayer (combined with the preceding prayer, *Tefillah*) which concluded the impetrative part of the *Shemoneh Esreh*, and which in the beginning was a prayer for the acceptance of the sacrifices of Israel, which the Rabbis tell us was itself taken from the Temple liturgy. Let us notice here the outcropping of a second source of sacrificial expressions in the Christian eucharistic liturgy, starting from the moment that it acquired its full development. Even at the time when it was still necessary to translate the "memorial" for non-Semitic Christians, sacrificial expressions had made their appearance in the anamnesis in order to explain its meaning. In this case they were present from the very beginning in the prayer in question. Encouraged by the fact that this prayer follows the *Tefillah* blessing, which recommends *the prayers* of Israel, there was a tendency even in the Synagogue usage to understand this also as the acceptance of her sacrifices, and not only the ritual sacrifices of the Temple, but also, and perhaps even more so, the manifold *berakoth* which made the entire life of the Jewish people one priestly action.[25] Taken over and adapted by the Christians, as we see so well in the liturgy of St. Mark, not to mention Serapion, this recommendation of the sacrifices is understood as a recommendation of the eucharist, seen again primarily as a consecratory prayer, not only of the elements of the sacred meals, but along with them and through them, of the whole life of the Church.

Nevertheless, it is in this first epiclesis, it seems, that the petition for the acceptance of the sacrifice came to be specified as a petition for the transformation of the elements. This idea, as we saw, in the first Egyptian epiclesis, was prepared for by the idea of an interchange between the material, earthly, temporal gifts that we bring and the spiritual, heavenly, eternal gifts we await from God. This first idea is formulated here in terms that come from St. Paul, not in regard to the eucharist, but in regard to offerings of charity.[26] The transpositions are perfectly explained by the fact that he himself interpreted these offerings in a liturgical sense. Then too, with the Christians the eucharistic celebration was also connected from the beginning with a common meal, a fulfilment of charity through the community of the faithful's offerings.

But the first part of the prayer of recommendation of the eucharistic sacrifice, what precedes the *Sanctus* in the liturgy of St. Mark, where this basic idea is expressed, expresses in a parallel way another notion whose roots are still more ancient and come directly from Judaism. It is the idea that our offerings are accepted

[25] Cf. what we have said above, p. 57.
[26] Cf. Romans 15: 27.

by God if they are joined to the angelic worship: hence the petition made to God to send an Angel to bring our prayers and sacrifices from earth to heaven. In Revelation, the Elders (who are heavenly priests, in other words, Angels) offer to God cups of gold filled with perfume, which are the prayers of the saints.[27] Peterson saw very well the importance of the notion for the early Christians following in the steps of the Jews, that the earthly worship which God accepts joins us with the heavenly worship of the angelic powers.[28] This is obviously what is behind the visions of Isaiah 6 and Ezekiel 1, connected with the *Qedushah* and the accompanying blessings in Jewish worship. Even earlier, we have the ancient priestly tradition, recorded in the Pentateuch, according to which the Mosaic worship with its altar and sacrifices was only a copy of the worship of heaven, and therefore a means of associating men with it.[29].

But Peterson gets completely off the track when he asserts that the idea that the Angels themselves present our own prayers and sacrifices to God is a purely Christian notion unknown to Judaism.[30] It is true that it is not mentioned in the most ancient Jewish prayers. But it is already quite evident in the book of Tobit. Raphael said to Tobit: "And so, when you and your daughter-in-law Sarah prayed, I brought a reminder of your prayer before the Holy One," i.e. God (12, 12), and he added a few verses later: "I am Raphael, one of the seven holy angels who present the prayers of the saints and enter into the presence of the glory of the Holy One." In the text of St. Mark this evocation is in all likelihood the direct result of the citation from Malachi 1:11, on the pure sacrifice offered in every place to God among the nations. What follows shows that this is not the case with the present sacrifices of Israel which were defiled by the unfaithfulnesses of the people. But chapter 3 adds: "Behold, I send my messenger to prepare the way before me, and the Lord whom you seek will suddenly come to his temple ... And he (it is still the messenger or angel

---

[27] Revelation 5: 8, Cf. also 8: 4.

[28] Cf. E. Peterson, *The Angels and the Liturgy* (New York, 1964).

[29] Cf. Exodus 25: 9 and 40.

[30] The same would be true of the glorification of God on earth *and in heaven* (cf. above p. 126).

to whom the text refers) will sit as a refiner and purifier of silver, and he will purify the sons of Levi and refine them like gold and silver, till they present right offerings to the Lord. Then the offerings of Judah and Jerusalem will be pleasing to the Lord as in the days of old and as in former years" (3:1-4).

This is evidently the source of the reference to the "service of the Angels and the heavenly altar on which they are to present our offerings. But the manner in which it is formulated in the text of the Roman canon has every chance of being the most primitive: i.e. the petition that an Angel (or the Angels) be sent by God to accomplish this transfer from earth to heaven. Before the notion of asking for the special sending of a divine person, whether the Logos or the Spirit, it was most naturally in line with primitive Christian thought, as well as with the Jewish thought from which it proceeded. With this purpose in mind it invokes the "angelic" ministry, that is spirits whose characteristic is precisely that of "being sent" in order to establish connection reciprocally between heaven and earth. It can be very well understood that it seemed necessary for a more evolved theology to appropriate a directly divine intervention to this consecration of the eucharist, and that a prayer for a mission of the Logos or the Spirit should be substituted for the petition for the sending of the Angels. On the other hand, it would be totally incomprehensible, if such a petition were original, that it would have been removed from the Roman liturgy and an angelic mission substituted in its stead.

This brings us to touch upon an aspect of a lively argument that was the subject of discussion some years ago. Dom Cagin, and then Fr. de la Taille, maintained that the Angel of the Roman epiclesis was in fact only a figure designating the Holy Spirit or the Word.[31] To this Dom Botte rightly replied that the known text of St. Ambrose mentioned not *one* particular "Envoy" but the *Angels* in general.[32] In any case, the fact that he speaks of Angels in the plural at this point shows very well that it was a question

---

[31] Cf. Dom P. Cagin, *Te Deum ou Illatio* (Solesmes, 1906), pp. 215 ff. and M. de la Taille, *Mystery of Faith* (New York, 1940).

[32] Cf. Dom Botte, *Le Canon de la Messe romaine*, p. 66.

of an angelic "ministry", for him as in the text of the liturgy of St. Mark.

Yet, we should not simply oppose the idea of invoking in a special way the Logos and then the Holy Spirit, which seems to have appeared in the fourth century to the idea of invoking the mission of the Angels which must indeed be more ancient and even very close to the beginnings. As we see from the text of Malachi 3 that we have quoted, and since it is a general fact in the Bible when the "Angel of the Lord" is mentioned, neither the Old Testament nor ancient Judaism ever established the clear-cut distinction which we make between the presence of the Angels and the presence of God himself. The "Angel" makes God present in a particular place, while still preserving his transcendence. This notion may seem strange to our modern theology, but—and this is the point—the theology of primitive Christianity was no more "modern" in this sense than the Judaism from which it emerged. Our Christian Apocalypse describes the Logos exactly as it describes the Angels.[33] What is perhaps even stranger, it enumerates a singular trinity in which the third term is "the seven spirits who are before the throne of God."[34] It is quite true that it elsewhere mentions the "Spirit" in the singular,[35] but, if we ask what its relationship to these "seven spirits" may be, the only possible answer is either that he is one of them or that for the prophet they are only one reality with him.

To present the matter in another way, in the eyes of the first Christians as for the Jews, the heavenly world was an inseparable whole. When the Angels came down to earth, the presence of the Shekinah came down with them, borne upon the wings of the Cherubim, the "wheels" of fire that are the Ophanim, and glorified by the flight and the singing of the Seraphim. Similarly, in the Gospel narratives, when the Son of God comes down on earth at the nativity, he is accompanied by all the angelic hosts.[36]

---

[33] Cf. Revelation 19: 11 ff.
[34] Cf. ibid., 1: 4-5 and 4: 5.
[35] Cf. ibid., 5: 2; also 22: 17.
[36] Cf. Luke 2: 8 ff.

In the tomb his body is accompanied by two Angels who must be the same as the Cherubim of the Temple who spread their wings on either side of the mercy-seat.[37] And at the Ascension it is again with the Angels that he returns to heaven.[38]

In evoking the angelic ministry to bear our offering to the Altar of Heaven, the ancients were therefore well persuaded that what they were petitioning was not only the analogue of Christ's going up to heaven and the correlative descent of the Spirit, but that it was in a certain way the very same thing. The Spirit, as the Paraclete sent to the Church between the Ascension and the Parousia, far from being in opposition to the descent of the Angels, was in their eyes preeminently the "Angel of the Lord," inseparable, moreover, from all those "who stand before the face of God" and who present our prayers and sacrifices, just as they comfort us on his behalf. According to certain forms of primitive christology, Jesus himself, as Barbel showed in a very informative book, is conceived as an "Angel", i.e. the "Envoy" of the Lord in whom the Lord himself would purify his temple and re-establish the identity between the sacrifices on earth and the worship in heaven, as in Malachi's vision.[39] Because he was a dyed-in-the-wool antiquarian, Hippolytus did not hesitate to designate Jesus with this title, in which an orthodoxy as suspect as his saw nothing reprehensible.[40]

Such expressions became suspect only after the struggles with Arianism. In the apparent confusion between the Angels and their ministry, Christ or the Spirit and their respective missions, we can discern an ambiguity that ran the risk of being useful to the heretics. It is at this time, during the first phase of the Arian conflict, as we see with Serapion, that the Logos must have been introduced into the epiclesis, as the only one in whom the earthly sacrifice can become one with the heavenly sacrifice. When the controversy turned from him and focused on the divinity of the Spirit, they came to pray that the Spirit be sent upon the elements,

[37] John 20: 12; cf. Luke 24: 4.
[38] Acts 1: 10 ff.
[39] Cf. Malachi 3.
[40] Cf. above, p. 169.

as he was sent to the Virgin's womb,[41] so that these elements might "manifest," as a number of epicleses say, the presence of the very body and blood of the redeeming Logos.

At this time, at Alexandria, the Angels were retained only in a general formula in the introduction of the first epiclesis, while its main import was reserved for a divine person who alone is capable, as was thought from then on, of effectuating the transition from the earthly to the heavenly sacrifice in the transformation of the gifts offered.

At Rome, the local conservatism always resisted this modification of the formulas. They did indeed allow the admission of the formal expression of the transformation of the elements in the first epiclesis where it must have originated, but they retained the invocation of the Angels or the Angel in operating the transfer of the sacrifice of our world to the heavenly world. The only thing further that they could do was to let the sought after transformation remain anonymous, although it was obviously looked upon as a specifically divine work and one that could not be attributed to any creature. They therefore transferred the Angels, from the first to the second epiclesis together with the remembrance of the sacrifices accepted in the past which must have been the cause of their being introduced in the first place. An examination of the different forms of the Alexandrian liturgy has shown how very frequent were the exchanges between the two epicleses. And this must have made it easy, first of all in Syria, it seems, to concentrate all the themes of the different epicleses into one, the last one. But that the original position of this recommendation of the eucharistic sacrifice, in reference to the ancient sacrifices, was certainly the first and not the second epiclesis, results from the fact that the first epiclesis had its origin in the *Abodah* blessing at the conclusion of he *Tefillah*. Given the character, of the notions about the Angels that we find there, which is not only primitive in Christianity but actually pre-Christian, we may even think that it comes from a Jewish formula that has not come down to us, in which the Angel (or Angels) accompanied Abel and Abraham. (In fact was not Abraham's sacrifice enough to evoke the Angel?) In the ancient

[41] Cf. Luke 1: 35.

Roman liturgy there is a likely chance that there was no epiclesis at all after the anamnesis, but that the anamnesis ended simply with the petition that our sacrifice be accepted, as the representation to God of what comes from him; and that we in turn be "filled with every grace and heavenly blessing". The removal of Abraham and the Angel along with Abel at this juncture may have been the cause of the fluctuations in the definitive composition of the formula, as evidenced by the divergencies between St. Ambrose's text and the one handed down to us in the final form of the canon. Since the *Quam oblationem* from now on specified the original prayer for the acceptance of the sacrifice as a prayer for the transformation of the elements, the transfer to heaven of the earthly sacrifice came fortunately to be presented as the counterpart of the "blessing" that "fills us," in the perspective of the exchange between the gift received from God and the one which we make to him, which is still his alone.

The liturgy of Serapion allows us to suspect that in Egypt also they might have transferred the Angels from the first to the second epiclesis, since he omits them in the first and reintroduces them after the second, but only to give them the role of repelling the incursions of the Demon in the people of God.

And Melchizedek? He appears in the Roman canon, it might be said, once again "without either father or mother," in the sense that it is not possible for us, contrary to the case of Abel, Abraham and the Angel, to outline the genealogy of his presence in this text from related and prior texts. We may believe that, as the Epistle to the Hebrews invites us to think, he was already an object of speculation for certain groups of Jews, contemporary to the beginnings of Christianity. In this light, then, he may have been introduced like the other names of the patriarchs into certain forms of the *Abodah* blessing. If, on the other hand, it is from the Epistle to the Hebrews itself that his introduction into Christian prayer comes, we do not know whether the Roman epiclesis was preceded by others in this regard. Up to the present, along with the eucharist of the *Apostolic Constitutions*,[42] it is the sole

---

[42] Cf. below, pp. 169-170.

prayer of this type that is truly ancient and where we see him make an appearance.[43]

These various interconnections and the enlightenment which they produced have cleared the way for a reading of the Roman canon which will require only a minimum of commentary. The economy of its structure and the exact sense of its formulas are now ready to be shown to us in all their particularly venerable antiquity.

THE STRUCTURE OF THE ROMAN CANON
AND ITS EXPLANATION

The Lord be with you.
—And with your spirit.
Lift up your hearts.
—We have lifted them up to the Lord.
Let us give thanks to the Lord our God.
—It is right and just.

This form of the introductory dialogue, whose first two verses and their responses are so purely Semitic, and which are found in this precise way only in Hippolytus and the Egyptian liturgy (the latter has the word "all" instead of "you"), must be considered as the most primitive form that has come down to us. Yet, it is quite meaningful that the third verse gives us the form "to the Lord *our God*," and not merely "to the Lord" as in Hippolytus. We have recalled that this latter formula seems to be a survival of the primitive eucharist which, according to the happy formula of Dom Gregory Dix was still a *private* meal of the Christians,[44] through which they were completing the *public* Synagogue worship which they still attended with the Jews. In accordance with Jewish use, it was suited to the meal of a small group which was less than the minimum number of participants required for a Synagogue congregation (the Rabbis say ten). On the other hand, the Roman

[43] See G. Bardy, "Melchisédec dans la tradition patristique" in *Revue biblique*, 1926, pp. 416 ff. and 1927. pp. 25 ff. M. Bardy points out that certain ancients wished to see in Melchizedek the Holy Spirit. Cf. Bardy, art. "Melchisédéciens," in *Dictionnaire de théologie catholique*.

[44] Dom Gregory Dix, *The Shape of the Liturgy*, see the first chapter.

formula is the one prescribed since Jewish days for an assembly
equivalent to that of the Synagogue. That it was preferred is
perhaps the indication that the joining of the sacred meal to the
service of readings and prayers came about rather early at Rome
so that the original meaning of the use of one formula rather than
another was still known.

For the beginning of the eucharist, we shall quote the text of
the "preface" reserved today for the Easter season:

> It is truly right and just, proper and helpful toward sal-
> vation, that we always praise you, O Lord, but more espe-
> cially so at this season, when Christ our Pasch was sacrificed.
> For he is the true Lamb who has taken away the sins of the
> world, who overcame death for us by dying himself and who
> restored us to life by his own resurrection. Therefore with
> the Angels and Archangels, the Thrones and Dominations,
> and all the militant hosts of heaven, we continuously praise
> your glory in song and say: Holy, holy, holy Lord God of
> hosts.
> Heaven and earth are filled with your glory.
> Hosanna in the highest.
> Blessed is he who comes in the name of the Lord.
> Hosanna in the highest.

The *preface*, as we are accustomed to call it in the Roman
liturgy,[45] remains variable as we know, like the *Communicantes*
to a certain extent, and the *Hanc igitur* itself has long displayed
this trait. We shall return more at length to this variability in
the eucharistic prayers when we speak of the Gallican and Hispanic liturgies, where it has been preserved for all and not only some
of the prayers of the eucharist. Certain liturgists suppose, quite

---

[45] The origin of this term is obscure. It is certain that the ancient Latin
language could have used *praefari* with the sense of "proclaim in a loud voice,"
and that the word therefore could have been first used of the singing of the
eucharist in this sense. But, as we shall see below, the term *praefatio*, in the
Gallican liturgy, designated on the other hand a kind of initial commentary
on the celebration that was to follow. It is likely that this sense passed into
our Roman "preface" when it passed, along with the liturgy of which it was
a part, into Gallican areas, and that this explains how it came to be looked
upon as a simple prelude to the canon.

gratuitously: that in fact at Rome and elsewhere there would have been a fixedness for the whole text of the eucharist, which followed the period of improvisation, and then with this fixedness hardly in operation, a new variability would have appeared in keeping with the liturgical year.[46] But, in the texts we possess of the Western liturgies, we cannot anywhere find this intermediary phase in which the whole had become fixed between two periods of variability. It seems then that we must rather say that the variability, which has been preserved integrally down to our own day for the preface (we still have a few vestiges in the *Communicantes*, and in some *Hanc igiturs* most of which have long ago fallen into disuse), is merely a survival of the ancient improvisation. Naturally, once the liturgical year developed, new compositions tended to be modeled on various phases. But the ancient Roman sacramentaries offer us a superabundance of "extras" which surely all do not come from a desire to express the characteristics proper to the various times of the liturgical year which by this time had become more or less fully developed. We must go even further and say that many of the prayers that are classified in our collections as belonging to the liturgical year are actually connected with it only by such a loose bond that there is every reason to believe that they were merely appropriate to it after the fact, with hardly any modifications or no modification at all. If we remove the phrase "but more especially ... " (which furthermore gives the effect of being an addition) from the preface just quoted, it could be perfectly applicable originally to any Sunday celebration, before having been reserved for the Easter season.

As a general rule, the more ancient the Roman prefaces are, the more the compact fulness of their wording makes them interchangeable. Let us again quote the present prefaces for Christmas and Twelfthnight:

It is truly right and just, proper and helpful toward salvation, that we always and everywhere give thanks to you, O Lord, holy Father, almighty and eternal God; for the brightness of your glory has made itself manifest to the eyes of

[46] This thesis is particularly developed by Gregory Dix in *The Shape of the Liturgy*.

our mind by the mystery of the Word made flesh, and we
are drawn to the love of things unseen through him whom
we acknowledge as God, now seen by men. Therefore, etc ...
... for your only begotten Son restored our human nature
by the new light of his immortality when he appeared in
the substance of man's mortal nature, etc ...

If we were accustomed to using the first for Christmas and the
second for Twelfthnight, there would be nothing unsuitable about
interchanging the two. Both express the restoration of creation
through the redemptive incarnation in terms where the inter-
weaving of the light of divine glory and the "knowledge" of God,
which is one with immortality, is a direct echo of the Jewish daily
prayers.

It seems that from these examples we can understand the reason
why the Roman liturgy, even after it had fixed the following
prayers in the canon, left the celebrants free to improvise in the
beginning. This is undoubtedly because they wished to stay close
to the brevity of the ancient prayers handed down from the Synagogue and their themes which are found just as they were in
the examples we have just given, while still wanting to preserve
the capacity for expressing successively the manifold aspects of
the one saving mystery. Far from the liturgical year's complexity being the cause of the variability of these prayers, it rather
grows out of the same cause that maintained it. This is why this
variability consequently came to be adapted to the themes that
were successively distinguished in the rhythm of seasons and holy
days. But in our opinion, in many relatively late prefaces this
process did not escape weakening this one and total expression of
the Christian mystery that is found in the most ancient prefaces,
to the great harm of the later Roman eucharist.

The *Sanctus* itself appears here for the first time in the form
that has become practically universal almost as it stands. In
the Alexandrian liturgy we have already witnessed the disappearance of the blessing taken from Ezekiel 1, and we have explained
it by the fact that the ancient Christians were still close enough
to the Jews to understand that in the Jewish liturgy it was a blessing for the divine presence in the Jerusalem sanctuary. Once
this blessing had been dropped at Alexandria, it was not possible

to substitute another one because the attaching of the epiclesis to the end of the *Sanctus* through the idea of fulness prevented it. Yet, wherever this connection did not exist, as at Rome or in Syria, we see the phrase: "Blessed is he who comes in the name of the Lord" being introduced very early between the two Hosannas. Of course, this formula was suggested by the disciples' use of it to hail Jesus' entry into Jerusalem. But in order to understand all its meaning, and especially the sense it has taken on in the Christian eucharist, we must go back to the 118th Psalm from which it was taken. For Christians, this became the paramount Easter Psalm. But for the Jews it was first a Psalm of enthronement, glorifying in the Messiah-King's entry into the Temple the entry of the Lord himself into his sanctuary.[47] On the lips of the celebrants of the eucharist then, it is a confession of the divine *Shekinah* entering into the eschatological sanctuary of the Church. The eucharistic consecration not only gives us the glorified body and blood of Christ, under the species of bread and wine but by this very means, the definitive divine presence of God with his people in the Church, the body of Christ.

Therefore, we come to you, Father most merciful, through Jesus Christ your Son, our Lord. Through him we beg and beseech you to accept and bless these gifts, these tokens, these holy and spotless offerings. We offer them for your holy catholic Church. Watch over it and guide it; grant it peace and unity throughout the world. We offer them for N. our Pope, for N. our bishop, and for all the orthodox and those who teach the catholic and apostolic faith.

Remember, Lord, the servants of your household N. and N., and all who are gathered around your altar. You know their faithfulness and their dedication. (We offer to you for them) or they offer to you this sacrifice of praise for themselves and for all whom they cherish. They pray to you for the redemption of their souls, for the hope of salvation and safety (*incolumitas*).

In the fellowship of communion, *celebrating the most holy day when Jesus Christ our Lord rose from the dead according*

[47] Cf. S. Mowinckel, *op. cit.*

to the flesh, we honor the memory first of all of the glorious Mary ever virgin, mother of the same Jesus Christ our Lord. Then we honor blessed Joseph, spouse of the same virgin and your blessed apostles and martyrs, Peter and Paul, Andrew, James and John, Thomas, James, Philip, Bartholomew, Matthew, Simon and Jude, Linus, Cletus, Clement, Sixtus, Cornelius, Cyprian, Lawrence, Chrysogonus, John and Paul, Cosmas and Damian, and all your saints. Through their merits and prayers help and guard us in all things. Through the same Christ our Lord. (Amen.)

This then is the offering which we your servants and your whole family owe and give to you, *also for those whom you have been pleased to bring to new birth by water and the Holy Spirit. Grant forgiveness of all their sins.* Establish our days in your peace, save us from eternal damnation, and count us among those you have chosen. Through Christ our Lord. (Amen.)

As for this whole offering, O God, please bless it; make it proper, perfect, spiritual (*rationabilem*) and acceptable: so that it may become for us the body and blood of your beloved Son, our Lord Jesus Christ.[48]

---

[48] Our purpose here is to comment on the Latin text of the Roman canon, and we have therefore given a translation that is more literal than the one in current use throughout the English-speaking world. As a point of comparison, here is the latter text:

"We come to you, Father, in this spirit of thanksgiving, through Jesus Christ your Son. Through him we ask you to accept and bless these gifts we offer you in sacrifice. We offer them for your holy catholic Church. Watch over it and guide it; grant it peace and unity throughout the world. We offer them for N. our Pope, for N. our bishop, and for all who hold and teach the catholic faith that comes to us from the apostles.

"Remember, Lord, your people, especially those for whom we now pray: N. and N. Remember all of us gathered here before you. You know how firmly we believe in you and dedicate ourselves to you. We offer you this sacrifice of praise for ourselves and all who are dear to us. We pray to you, our living and true God, for our well-being and redemption.

"In union with the whole Church, *we celebrate the day when Jesus Christ, our Lord, rose in the flesh*. We honor the memory of the saints. We honor Mary, the virgin mother of Jesus Christ our Lord. We honor Joseph, her husband, the apostles Peter and Paul, Andrew, James and John, Thomas, James, Philip, Bartholomew, Matthew, Simon and Jude, Linus, Cletus, Clement, Sixtus, Cornelius, Cyprian, Lawrence, Chrysogonous, John and

This group of five prayers forms a whole which is what became of the *Tefillah* in Roman tradition. We must go back to

Paul, Cosmas and Damian, the martyrs and all the saints. May their merits
and prayers gain us your constant help and protection. Through Christ
our Lord. Amen.

"Father accept this offering from your whole family *and from those born
in the new life of water and the Holy Spirit, whose sins are now forgiven.* Grant
us your peace in this life, save us from final damnation, and count us among
those you have chosen. Through Christ our Lord. (Amen.)

"Bless and approve our offering; make it truly spiritual and acceptable. Let
it become for us the body and blood of Jesus Christ, your only Son, our Lord.

"The day before he suffered he took bread, and looking up to heaven, to
you, his almighty Father, he gave you thanks and praise. He broke the bread,
gave it to his disciples and said: Take this and eat it, all of you; this is my
body. When supper was ended, he took the cup. Again he gave you thanks
and praise, gave the cup to his disciples and said: Take this and drink from
it, all of you; this is the cup of my blood, the blood of the new and everlasting
covenant—the mystery of faith. This blood is to be shed for you and for
all men so that sins may be forgiven. Whenever you do this, you will do
it in memory of me.

"So now, Lord, we celebrate the memory of Christ, your Son. We, your
people and your ministers, recall his passion, his resurrection from the dead,
and his ascension into glory. And from the many gifts you have given us
we offer to you, God of glory and majesty, this holy and perfect sacrifice:
the bread of life and the cup of eternal salvation.

"Look with favor on these offerings. Accept them as you did the gifts of
your servant, Abel, the sacrifice of Abraham, our father in faith, and the
offering of your priest Melchisedech.

"Almighty God, we pray that your angel may take this sacrifice to your
altar in heaven. Then, as we receive from this altar the sacred body and
blood of your Son, let us be filled with every grace and blessing. Through
Christ our Lord. (Amen.)

"Remember, Lord, those who have died, N. and N. They have gone before us marked with the sign of faith, and are now at rest. May these, and
all who sleep in Christ, find in your presence light, happiness, and peace
Through Christ our Lord. (Amen.)

"For ourselves, too, we ask a place with your apostles and martyrs, with
John the Baptist, Stephen, Matthias, Barnabas, Ignatius, Alexander, Marcellinus, Peter, Felicity, Perpetua, Agatha, Lucy, Agnes, Cecilia, Anastasia,
and all the saints. Though we are sinners, we trust in your mercy and love.
Do not consider what we truly deserve, but grant us your forgiveness, through
Christ our Lord. Through him you give us all these things. You fill them
with life and goodness, you bless them and make them holy. Through him,
in him, with him, in the unity of the Holy Spirit, all glory and honor is yours,

the more developed text of the pre-epiclesis in the liturgy of St. Mark and beyond it to the first prayer of the 7th book of the *Apostolic Constitutions*, in order to understand how the evocation of the "fathers" and their devout actions, in the expectation of the Messiah whom their children await, led first to the evocation of the pure and spotless worship offered in every place by the faithful Jews in their *berakoth*, and then by the Christians in their eucharist. Thus they came to beseech the "most merciful" Father (a modifier already used of him in the Jewish prayer at this point) to accept the present offering through this Messiah who has now been given to them, as the "pure and spotless" oblation. In the prayer from St. Mark the idea of man's renewal brought about by Christ led subsequently to the glorification of the divine Name, just as in the Jewish *Tefillah*, the evocation of the hoped-for resurrection of the fathers led to this same glorification. Here, the transition has disappeared (although a memory of it can be found in the gathering in of the Church which is mentioned straight away), and the invocation of the Name seems also to be absent. In fact, this is not the case. What this invocation signified for the early Christians, that is, the revelation of God as the Father, in his Son given to the world, is found in the solemn invocation at the beginning of the prayer, to God, as the Father, through Jesus Christ his son. The sense of this offering of the eucharist, materialized here in the elements (although they can be called "holy and spotless" offerings only by reference to the eucharist of which they are the object), is given to us by the goal assigned to it: peace, protection, and the final gathering of the whole catholic Church throughout the world, and no longer Israel alone. The pope is first named among those to whom the prayer will be explicitly extended. The name of the bishop, when this liturgy was celebrated outside of Rome, was included with him. Following them, the name of the emperor used to be mentioned, and when relevant, that of the king.[49]

---

almighty Father, for ever and ever. Amen." (Copyright 1967 by the International Committee on English in the Liturgy, Inc.)

[49] Cf. the variants given by Dom Botte on p. 32 of *Le Canon de la Messe romaine*.

The end of the formula does not refer, as it has at times been interpreted, to all the faithful, but rather to all the other heads of the Church who have a part in this work of gathering together the one people of God in the "orthodoxy" of the apostolic faith.[50] It can be said that here the episcopate and the Christian princes associated with it in leading the people of God to unity, insofar as they are successors of the apostles, take the place held by the "fathers" in the mind of the Jewish people.

The *Memento* makes the transition from the people taken in its totality and unity to all its members and their individual needs. Hence the introduction at this point of the diptychs mentioning the living for whom we wish especially to pray. We have put in brackets the phrase "We offer to you for them" since it does not appear before the ninth century.[51] It misrepresents the transition from a notion of the common offering of the eucharist, the "sacrifice of praise," on the part of all who surround the altar to that of an offering that the ministers make for "offerers" supposed to be absent or who are mere passive witnesses of the eucharist. What is asked for the members of the people of God is very interesting: it is redemption which includes penance, forgiveness and ransom, which were successively petitioned for in the fifth, sixth and seventh blessings of the *Tefillah*. The "salvation" that follows corresponds similarly to the healing which is the object of the eighth prayer and the "*incolumitas*" to the peace and prosperity which are the objects of the ninth. If we observe the prior reference to the faith and the devotion of the offerers, we see that the "knowledge" of God, the object of the fourth, has also left its trace. The "dispersed" who came right at this point (and whom the Egyptian prayer still mentioned) have disappeared, along with the persecutors (also found in Egypt) and the faithful who stood in opposition to them. The authorities (figuring in the eleventh blessing) were already mentioned, and therefore did not have to be mentioned again.

---

[50] Cf. *L'ordinaire de la Messe romaine*, French translation by Dom Bernard Botte and Christine Mohrmann (Paris, 1953).

[51] See Dom Botte's notes, p. 34.

The *Communicantes*, with the commemoration of the saints now follows the intercessions as in the Egyptian prayer. We might be tempted to ask why these commemorations were not introduced at the beginning in order to correspond to the detailed mention of the "fathers" given to us in the *Tefillah*, with Abraham, Isaac, Jacob, and all the other names which developed forms, like those of the 7th book of the Apostolic Constitutions, might have added to them. But we must not forget that these same hellenistic forms of the Jewish *Tefillah* introduced a second list of holy persons after the intercessions in conjunction with the prayer for the acceptance of the sacrifice. It is from this, undoubtedly, in both the Roman and Egyptian liturgies, that the commemoration of the saints came to have the same position. The mention of the apostles must be the most ancient, and that of the Virgin was very soon to be joined with it. The martyrs that follow are either Roman martyrs or martyrs venerated at Rome. We have inserted the reminder of the Easter commemoration, corresponding to the preface quoted.

In the ancient sacramentaries these statements of the aspect of the Christian mystery celebrated on this day, before the mention of the saints were much more numerous than today. To some extent they correspond to the variable forms of the "memorial" that the last of the "blessings" at the end of the meal also introduced on Jewish holy days. Perhaps these reminders, placed here, before the "memory" of the Saints, may help us to interpret this enigmatic *"Communicantes"* used at the very beginning of the prayer.[52] What makes the whole people of God live in one fellowship, with the living and the dead (which was already so strongly inculcated by the whole first part of the *Tefillah*), is that all together are made one in the eucharistic "memory" of the saving mystery, upon which has been grafted, so to speak, the "memory" of the apostles and martyrs. Thus, for the Jews, the "memory" of God's great deeds in the past, the "memory" of the "fathers" who were witnesses of these deeds, and the anticipated "memory" of the expected Messiah were all one "memorial" presented to God in the *berakah*.

[52] See Dom Botte's note, *op. cit.*, pp. 55 ff.

The last two prayers which we have quoted, *Hanc igitur obla-tionem* and *Quam oblationem* together, form the first epiclesis of the Roman liturgy. The first epiclesis of the Egyptian liturgy was also, as we have seen, formed from two distinct prayers, the first, like the *Hanc igitur*, developing in an enumeration of the more special intentions for which the sacrifice was being offered. But, in Egypt, the *Sanctus* and its introduction were inserted between the two, producing the need of the connection, taken from the idea of fulness, in order to link up with the second. Here the two prayers remain distinct, but they are joined immediately, as in the *Tefillah* where the sixteenth blessing (in which all of Israel's petitions were brought together to be recommended to God) was joined to the *Abodah* which recommended to him her sacrifices themselves.

We have given here once again the special formula, which is still preserved, for the eucharist offered for the intention of the neophytes who had just been baptized at Easter. It was in antiquity and even much later in the Middle Ages only one among innumerable other special intentions that could be formulated at this point.[53] "Establish our days in your peace" seems originally to have been a simple special intention of this kind which St. Gregory the Great permanently included.[54]

The *Quam oblationem* is properly the presentation of the eucharistic sacrifice to God for his acceptance. Among the adjectives with which it qualifies the oblation, *rationabilem* is obviously the translation of "logical worship," i.e. offered in the Logos who is the Word made flesh. But it also brings to mind the "word" with which man, in the same Jesus Christ, responds to it, here identified with the eucharist. Let us recall that at Alexandria it was in the pre-epiclesis that "logical worship" was mentioned.

In telling us that the praise at the beginning of the eucharist was followed by the intercessions, St. Ambrose gives evidences at least in its general lines, of the beginning of the Roman canon as it was in the second half of the fourth century. But with this last prayer, we arrive at the part of the canon which he quotes

---

[53] Cf. Dom Botte, *op. cit.*, pp. 58 ff. on this point.
[54] Cf. A. Jungmann, *The Mass of the Roman Rite*, vol. 2.

practically in its entirety and more or less literally. It seems, actually, that he is no longer merely willing to give an explanatory paraphrase, but that he is quoting textually in the midst of his explanation the very words that he used in the eucharistic prayer from then on.

The form he gives of the prayer corresponding to our *Quam oblationem* is this:

> Make this offering for us orderly (*scriptam*), spiritual (*rationabilem*), worthy to please you, this offering which is (or because it is) the figure of the body and blood of Our Lord Jesus Christ ...[55]

The rest of the commentary, which is of a most decided realism, shows very well that *figura* here, like τύπος in the Greek liturgies, instead of being opposed to the reality of the presence, means to indicate that the visible elements are becoming its efficacious sign. In this regard, our formula: "so that (this offering) may become for us the body and blood of your beloved Son, our Lord Jesus Christ" means the same thing in a form which is clearer for us, but which was not any clearer for the ancients.

If what we have suggested about the original place of the references to the heavenly altar, the Angel and the patriarchs, had to be the same at Rome as at Alexandria, it is from the first words of the *Hanc igitur oblationem* that these references must have arisen (moreover, St. Ambrose's text, while placing them after the anamnesis, has them connected with a repetition of the expression *Hanc oblationem*). In this case it appears that the petition for the acceptance of the sacrifice, enveloping the one for the transformation of the elements, flowed directly from this.

We now come to the institution narrative, the anamnesis and the second epiclesis, which make up one closely connected whole (with St. Ambrose the connection is so continuous that the last phrase, which includes the epiclesis within the anamnesis, be-

---

[55] *De Sacramentis*, IV, 5-6, ed. Botte (*Sources chrétiennes*, n° 25), pp. 84-86; see also what he says about the intercessions at the beginning (IV, 4; p. 81) following the praise of God.

comes very overloaded—which explains why the present version, cutting the epiclesis into two sentences and separating it from the anamnesis, was ultimately preferred).

And he, on the day before he suffered, took bread into his holy and venerable hands, looking up to heaven, to you, God, his almighty Father, he gave thanks to you, blessed it and broke it, and gave it to his disciples, saying: Take and eat this, all of you, for this is my body. Likewise when supper was ended he also took this glorious cup into his holy and venerable hands, gave thanks to you again, blessed the cup and gave it to his disciples, saying: Take this and drink from it, all of you: This is the cup of my blood, of the new and everlasting covenant, the mystery of faith, which will be shed for you and for many for the forgiveness of sins. Whenever you do this, you will do it in memory of me.

Wherefore, Lord, we your servants and also your holy people, recall the blessed passion of the same Christ, your Son, our Lord. We remember his resurrection from the dead and his glorious ascension. From among the gifts you gave us (*de tuis donis ac datis*) we offer to your radiant majesty (*praeclarae majestatis*), a victim pure, holy, spotless, the sacred (*sanctum*) bread of life eternal, and the cup of eternal salvation. Look with a pleased and serene countenance upon these gifts. Accept them as you did the gifts of your just servant Abel, the sacrifice of Abraham, our patriarch, and the offering of Melchisedek, your priest; a holy sacrifice and a spotless victim.

Humbly we ask you, Almighty God, to bid your holy angel to carry these gifts up to your heavenly altar, in the sight of your divine majesty. This we ask so that whoever shares in receiving the most holy body and blood of your Son from this altar here below may be filled with every heavenly blessing and grace. Through the same Christ our Lord. (Amen.)

We have already pointed out the peculiarities of the institution narrative in the Egyptian liturgy, where the amplifications and harmonizations customary in the formulas of this time come very close to our own text. The insertion *mysterium fidei* is a unique peculiarity of the Roman rite. All sorts of unverifiable hypotheses have been trotted out to explain how it could have come to be inserted into the formula relating to the cup.[56] Its meaning is clear: it is the Pauline mystery, which is one with the new covenant in Christ, that is referred to here.

The anamnesis concludes with the ascension, an indication of its antiquity. The mention "we your servants," as opposed to "your holy people," obviously refers to the officiants to whom all the faithful are joined in the presentation of the sacrifice to God. The formula explicating the "memorial" in sacrificial terms is practically word for word the one which we have explained in the liturgy of St. Mark. The two connected formulas which unfold the second epiclesis were already abundantly commented upon. It is enough to add to what was said before that the last words of the first: *sanctum sacrificium, immaculatam hostiam,* added by St. Leo, and which are a last allusion to the pure offering of the nations in Malachi, in their primary intention apply to the sacrifice of Melchizedek which is the last mentioned.[57]

Then, before the great concluding doxology, there comes a series of prayers which, after the mention of the Angels, shows an obvious parallelism with the end of the eucharist of Serapion, as well as with the end of the commemorations in that of St. Mark.

> Remember, too, Lord the servants of your household N. and N. who have gone before us with the sign of faith and who sleep the sleep of peace. Grant, O Lord, to these and to all who are at rest in Christ a refreshing place of light and peace. Through the same Christ our Lord. (Amen.)
>
> For ourselves, too, who are sinners, your servants who trust in the multitude of your mercies, give us part and fellowship with your holy apostles and martyrs, with John, Stephen, Matthias, Barnabas, Ignatius, Alexander, Marcellinus, Peter, Felicity, Perpetua, Agatha, Lucy, Agnes, Cecilia, Anastasia and all your saints. We beg you to let us share their company, not in view of our merits but because of your mercy, through Christ our Lord. Through him you make good, you make holy, you make alive, you make blessed, and you give to us all these things. Through him, and with him, and in him

---

[56] Cf. Dom Botte, *op. cit.,* p. 62.
[57] Cf. *L'Ordinaire de la Messe romaine,* p. 82, n. f.

is given to you, Father almighty, together with the Holy Spirit, all honor and glory, forever and ever. Amen.

Since the *Memento* of the dead is absent from many of the most ancient manuscripts, some have drawn the conclusion that it was only a late addition.[58] This is quite unlikely since the *Nobis quoque*, which is never missing, was obviously attached to it. This omission must be explained by the fact that at a certain time, as we know, it was not recited at Sunday mass. The sequence of ideas, so striking at this point where they are quite uncommon, is the same as in Serapion from the end of the epiclesis to the end of the eucharistic prayer. And the end of the commemoration of the liturgy of St. Mark, where there is also a transition from a prayer for the dead to a final supplication for the offerers themselves, presents still more emphatic coincidences in wording with our text.[59] As Dom Botte, among others, has pointed out, the make-up of this *Memento* is of a particularly archaic language, with its mention of the "sign of faith" (the seal of baptism), the *refrigerium*, and the passing over into everlasting life described as the transfer from one place to another.[60]

The *Nobis quoque*, with its felicitous final formula on the gratuitousness of our admission into the company of the saints, this heavenly Jerusalem in the vision of which the Jewish *berakoth* ended before returning to praise in a final doxology, has a final enumeration of the saints. It is very variable in medieval manuscripts, which include all those to whom local devotion might be more especially attached.[61]

In the Roman text, Ignatius is the martyr of Antioch, Alexander, Marcellinus and Peter, martyrs about whom we know little, Felicity and Perpetua the two famous African martyrs, Agatha and Lucy two Sicilian martyrs, Agnes and Cecilia two Roman

---

[58] Cf. Dom Botte, *op. cit.*, pp. 67 ff.

[59] *Καὶ τούτων πάντων τὰς ψυχὰς ἀνάπαυσον, ... ἡμῶν δὲ τέλη τῆς ζωῆς χριστιανὰ καὶ εὐάρεστα καὶ ἀναμάρτητα δώρησαι καὶ δὸς ἡμῖν μερίδα καὶ κλῆρον ἔχειν μετὰ πάντων τῶν ἁγίων σου* (Brightman, *op. cit.*, p. 129).

[60] *Loc. cit.*

[61] In the Frankish lands, particularly, St. Martin was ordinarily named.

martyrs, and Anastasia the possibly legendary person after whom the basilica at the foot of the Aventine hill was named.[62]

The blessings for "all these things" that follow, seem originally to have been directed toward all the gifts from which the matter of the eucharist had been drawn; what was left over would serve for the charitable distributions that in antiquity were always connected with the celebration.[63] It should be noted that in certain Hispanic formularies this blessing seems to have come to absorb the final doxology.[64]

If we wonder why the *Memento* of the dead at Rome and, in certain archaic cases at least, in Alexandria, came thus to be put between the end of the epiclesis and the doxology, it seems that the answer must be found in the character of this conclusion (which has been strongly eschatological from the beginning). Since those who have died in the faith have gone before us, as the prayer says, into the heavenly Jerusalem, it was logical that a final prayer be devoted to them, before asking for ourselves our own anticipated entry into the choir of everlasting glorification through the eucharist.

Finally, it may have been noted that we put the *Amens* within the canon in brackets because they appear only very late in the manuscripts.[65] In fact, this simply means that from the high Middle Ages there was no longer any way for the faithful to respond to prayers now said in a low voice, although the bizarre custom of having the celebrant answer himself was not yet introduced. But, once again, the distinctness of the prayers with their separate conclusions is perhaps the best indication of the very great antiquity of the Roman Canon. And when everyone was able to hear what was being read, there is every reason to think that the faithful punctuated these conclusions with an *Amen*, just as in the liturgy of Addai and Mari.

---

[62] Cf. Dom Botte, *op. cit.*, p. 12, and R. van Doren, "Les Saints du Canon de la Messe" in *Questions liturgiques et paroissiales*, t. 16 (1931), pp. 57 ff.

[63] The idea was first maintained by Duchesne. Cf. Dom Botte, *op. cit.*, p. 69.

[64] Cf. below, p. 329.

[65] The most ancient manuscript containing them is a ninth century manuscript from Reims. Cf. Dom Botte, *op. cit.*, p. 57.

Put back thus in its true context, the Roman canon appears then as one of the most venerable witnesses of the oldest tradition of the eucharistic prayer, at least contemporary in its totality with the most archaic forms of the Alexandrian eucharist. There is every reason to think that the succession of these prayers and their content with many key expressions go straight back to the assuredly very ancient time at which the eucharist at Rome as everywhere else was definitively connected with the service of readings and prayers. This is to say that Hippolytus, far from being its originator—a man who still wished to ignore this connection—, must have propagated his own rite in Rome, if he ever did so, only in a vain attempt to dislodge a rite which must have already been very like the one that has come down to us and which we still use, with the exception that the language was still Greek and not Latin.

The West Syrian Liturgy:
The Apostolic Constitutions
and the Liturgy of Saint James

STARTING WITH THE MOMENT WHEN THE SERVICE OF PRAYERS and readings and the eucharistic meal were combined into one, the type of liturgy that subsisted in Rome and Alexandria, except for a few local peculiarities, must have been practically universal in the Church. But in the fourth century, under the influence of Antioch, we see appearing in Western Syria a eucharistic liturgy of a profoundly different type, even though the same elements are found in it. The first modern scholars to discover it at the end of the Renaissance in the liturgy of the 8th book of the *Apostolic Constitutions,* and then soon afterward in the Jerusalem liturgy of St. James, were all quite literally dazzled. Among Anglicans particularly, a whole series of attempts at restoring of a traditional eucharist in the seventeenth and eighteenth centuries was inspired by it.[1] This was because the eucharist of the *Ap-*

---

[1] Cf. the book of Jardine Grisbrooke, *Anglican Liturgies of the Seventeenth and Eighteenth Centuries,* already mentioned. See below, pp. 424ff.

ostolic Constitutions, attributed to Clement of Rome (hence the name Clementine liturgy, by which it was known for a long time) was provided with the prestige of apostolic authority, like the liturgy of St. James which was attributed to the brother of the Lord. But it is also because these texts are compositions of an excellent arrangement, of great richness of thought and expression, and set in the eloquence of an accomplished rhetoric. These texts' claim to apostolicity has not been taken literally by anyone for a long time. But even so, they are far from having lost their prestige. In the twentieth century there are still theorists, like Drews,[2] who look upon it as the most ancient and pure form of the eucharist, and try to show the hypothetical evolutionary process by which the Roman liturgy itself must have originated from it. One of the greatest Anglican liturgists of the last century, Bishop Walter Howard Frere, in his book *The Anaphora*,[3] more subtly, and much more prudently maintained that this was the ideal liturgy, conceived and developed on a plan which is substantially primitive, even if its working form represents an undeniably advanced evolution. The continuity of its development and the logical unity of the trinitarian structure in which it is inscribed seem to him to be guarantees of the quasi-apostolic antiquity of this eucharistic schema, whatever we might say about the variation in detail of the formulas with which it may be clothed. Out of this conviction there grew, and are still growing more or less concordant attempts in the Anglican Communion but also in many other Churches, at constructing an ideal eucharist that is presented as basically original.

THE LATE CHARACTER OF THE WEST SYRIAN EUCHARIST
AND THE FACTORS IN ITS FORMATION

We will not deny that the West Syrian eucharist can be considered ideal, at least in the sense that nowhere else has the whole traditional content of the Christian eucharist been expressed with such fulness and in such a satisfying framework for a certain logical type of mind. But that this eucharist can be considered original, even with all the reservations possible on the details

[2] P. Drews, *Zur Entstehungsgeschichte des Kanons* (Tübingen, 1902).
[3] *The Anaphora or Great Eucharistic Prayer* (London, 1938).

of expression with which we find it clothed in the *Apostolic Constitutions* or the liturgy of St. James, is, we must say frankly, the most curious aberration conceivable. The unfailing logical unity, the continuity of its development, and the impeccable trinitarian schema in which people are so happy to find it inscribed, are all irrefutable signs not only of a late dating, but of a well thought-out structure, that remodeled the traditional materials with hardly believable daring. Actually, if ever the original eucharist were taken apart in order to be put back together again piece by piece after as untraditional as possible a pattern, it is here in the West Syrian eucharist. All of this work bears on its date and its original stamp. It supposes both the very advanced evolution which trinitarian theology only attained in the fourth century, and the last Greek rhetoric for which Antioch, as if by chance, was to be the home. There is no question of shedding doubt upon the legitimacy or even the excellence of the theology of the Greek Fathers of the fourth century. Nor would we dream of not acknowledging tne literary accomplishments of the hellenism of their time. As Aimé Puech so well said, we may judge that Libanios, the Antiochian teacher of Basil and of the two Gregorys, brought into focus a remarkable type of culture, and prepared literary forms of a stunning versatility and richness, which lacked only the content of a substantial thought that these Christian writers were to give them.[4] But, we must say all of this gets us further and further away from the world of thought and the forms of expression known to the first Christians.

The first Christian prayers, from their content, however renewed it may have been by the "newness" of the Gospel, and from their spontaneous form, are still deeply Semitic, even when they are formulated in Greek. Now, in this framework, even the possibility of a long and eloquent prayer, developed systematically, is impossible. The thought animating the Jewish prayers and the first Christian prayers in no way moves to the rhythm of the steps of Greek logic. And it would not have had at its disposal the liter-

---

[4] Cf. Aimé Puech, *Histoire de la littérature grecque chrétienne*, the chapter on the Cappadocians.

ary molds without which a thought of this other type could not even be formulated.

In the Bible or in the ancient Synagogue literature, there are no long prayers. And if there are none, it is because there hardly could be. Semitic languages, like Hebrew, which had only a few prepositions, two or three conjunctions, and no relative pronouns, do not permit them. Chains of prayers, connected by the themes running through them, can be composed, but not prayers that are developed logically and at length, since they demand a complex syntax provided with an abundant variety of connective terms.

The exceptions are quite apparent. Leaving aside the prayers of the book of Esther (which were added at a later date in its translation into Greek), most of the long Psalms are not long prayers at all, but rather, as the Scandinavian exegetical school has shown, liturgies arranging different prayers end to end. The prayers correspond to the successive phases of a sacrifice, a procession, or some other type of complex service.[5] Hence the seeming *non-sequiturs*, the abrupt transitions from one subject to another, that have been the despair of the exegetes, for as long as they stubbornly wished to analyze them as one might a hymn of Cleanthes or even a Homeric hymn.

The only long Psalms that cannot be put into this category are the sapiential Psalms which are later meditations on sacred history. With these we may connect the great prayer of Nehemiah that we have cited.[6] We find there a source of the developed eucharists, although it is not a true antecedent of them. For all these texts remain profoundly different from the forms that these eucharists were to receive in the hellenic world. Their meditations remain on a purely narrative plane. History is not reconstructed in accordance with a rational synthesis. As long as the sapiential meditation remained in a Semitic context, it limited itself to punctuating a series of facts, looked upon as typical in their diversity, with one refrain such as "For his steadfast love endures forever" in the 136th Psalm, or "Let them thank the Lord for his steadfast love,

[5] Cf. Aage Bentzen, *op. cit.*

[6] See above pp. 47-48.

for his wonderful works to the sons of men" in the 107th. Most often it does not even go that far in its organization, and merely accumulates successive evidences of God's steadfast love (Psalm 105) or renewed examples of man's unfaithfulness (Psalm 106). Or else, if it does outline a structure, it will be with a totally Eastern literary device, as in the composition of the alphabetical psalms.

We must arrive at a decidedly Greek form of thought in a literary world inherited from hellenism, before we can see the sapiential meditation become synthesized in the eucharistic framework in accordance with the articulated lines of a systematic theology. Here less than ever, can we separate content and form: this content involving a vision of salvation history organized from the starting point of a synthetic theology could appear only in a Greek form.

Yet even in the New Testament, we see a first indication of the transition in St. Luke which was to be made from one stylistic form (and at the same time from one form of thought) to another. The canticle of Zachary, at first glance, is still a Psalm. But when it is read carefully in Greek, we see that it is not. The use, however rudimentary, of particles and the employment of varied conjunctions turns it into a Greek period, collecting and fusing the independent parts of a Semitic Psalm.

The same thing can be observed, as we have pointed out, when the transition is made from the eucharist of Addai and Mari to that of St. Hippolytus. As Dom Botte rightly remarked, it is evident that the former was composed in a Semitic language. It is no less evident that Hippolytus, despite his careful concern to keep *ne varietur* the most ancient schema of the eucharistic prayer, composed his in Greek, and *as* a Greek, at least by adoption.

The great West Syrian eucharistic prayers exhibit still more clearly what the last Greek rhetoric could produce, when it was used to give the eucharist a formula that conformed to its canons. As a result, it began by rethinking the content itself in order to rewrite it. Once again, it was not by chance that these prayers were written at Antioch or its environs. They could never have been composed elsewhere, nor at any other time but when Libanios was teaching there.

Actually, the last Greek rhetoric is no longer merely an "Asiatic" rhetoric, but a Syrian one. Although it imagined itself to be only the ultimate perfection of the art of Demosthenes or Aeschines, in reality it had become something quite different.[7] It retained its concern for a rational deductive development of thought in a strict grammatical form, making full but discreet use of all the resources of Greek vocabulary and syntax. But to this it added an oriental taste for profuse and striking imagery, for balancing ideas and sonorities, and above all for a whole amplification of rhythm. Greek monody was transposed here into a kind of completely hellenistic symphony, which would have seemed the height of bad taste and barbarism, not only to Demosthenes but even to Cicero. The result was that no matter how long and obligingly the phrase was drawn out, it still could not contain the full periodic thought. This therefore took on an oriental and more definitely Semitic element, and became a torrent of successive sentences. But the whole still remained Greek, not only in the structure of each of its sentences, but also because they were chained together, if not by means of express syntactical connectives, at least by the continuity of a rhythm which by balancing words and images always retained the thread of one and the same directional thought.

To Greeks formed in the school of the fourth or fifth century before our era, Semitic literature would have seemed not only untranslatable but inassimilable. On the other hand, to these pseudo-Greeks it offered choice material for amplification, which was the last word of their evolved rhetoric. Were we to judge it in accordance with classical canons, we could call it decadent. But obviously, in order for its hellenic veneer not to fall to pieces, it was necessary for them to assimilate this literature at the cost of a digestive process that rendered it unrecognizable.

The first condition *sine qua non* would be a redistribution of the matter which would conform it to the development of Greek thought and language, through an analysis of each idea in its parts in order to reconstitute a whole in which particular and partial

---

[7] See E. Norden, *Die Antike Kunstprosa*, 4 Abdr. (Leipzig-Berlin, 1923).

ideas would become synthesized of themselves into one general idea.

The trinitarian schema, as it was worked out in the fourth century by a Greek-speaking Christian theology, supplies the desired framework in which to display the most sumptuous rhetorical orchestration of the traditional eucharistic themes. The result was the liturgy of Antioch and Jerusalem. It was inevitable that it charmed the whole Byzantine Church, even to the extent that Byzantium adopted the whole rhetoric (and more generally the esthetics) of Antioch, along with the theology of Basil and that of the two Gregorys.[8]

It seems that we found the first and most exuberant product of this work in the eucharistic liturgy of the 8th book of the *Apostolic Constitutions* probably at Antioch itself. Somewhat later, at Jerusalem, an analogous composition, but one that was more sober and more polished, appeared with the so-called liturgy of St. James. The liturgies attributed to St. Basil and St. John Chrysostom were reworkings and by-products of this which brought this prototype to its classical form.

THE STRUCTURE AND THE SOURCES OF THE EUCHARIST OF THE *APOSTOLIC CONSTITUTIONS*

It is customary for the commentators on the eucharist of the 8th book of the *Apostolic Constitutions* to assert that it is a liturgy-on-paper which could never have been used as it stands on account of its prolixity.[9] This would mean forgetting what St. Justin tells us about the ancient celebrants who gave thanks "as much as they could."[10] There is every reason for believing that at Antioch in the fourth century, more than in any place in the world at any other time, there were men who "could" very well. Uttered by a celebrant in a hurry the eucharist of the 8th book of the *Apostolic*

---

[8] Cf. Gervase Matthew, *Byzantine Æsthetics* (London, 1964).

[9] Actually, the catecheses of St. Cyril of Jerusalem show that it is a question of a form of liturgy which must have been used, if not as it stands, at least in its major lines, before the one called after St. James (cf. especially the 5th *Mystagogica*).

[10] *First Apology*, 67,

Constitutions would take hardly more than a quarter of an hour. If the modern liturgists were not generally clergymen belonging to Churches where liturgical improvisation was nothing more than a memory, they would know by experience that a prayer of such length is not unusual in Churches where *ex tempore* prayer is still the practice. The faithful are too accustomed to it to bother complaining, and the pastors would never dream of asking their opinion, even though these Churches generally consider themselves among the most democratic. We may think that this was the case in the ancient Church for as long as improvisation remained the rule. We may even assume that the unspoken dissatisfaction of the faithful in regard to the verbal intemperance of certain clergy might have been behind the progressive disappearance of this wordy freedom. This factor, at the very least, must have added to the fears of the authorities, in the face of many improvisations where prolixity of formulas may have been on a par with inconsistency in thought. The liturgy of the 8th book of the *Apostolic Constitutions* seems to be the result of an attempt at delimiting as exactly and as widely as possible the content and the progression which were considered ideal by its author for a good eucharist. But it profits thereby from a loquacity of which people must have begun to tire, but which must not yet have appeared as intolerable as we might imagine.

Despite its loquacity, it is still one of the most beautiful eucharistic texts of antiquity, and is undoubtedly in any case the one which expresses as completely as possible everything that the ancient Christians could find in, or put into, a eucharistic prayer. It is generally admitted that its author must have been an Arian, or at the very least a Semi-Arian. Yet, we should not forget that many expressions which today might appear to be the result of this school are found with many Antenicean fathers, as Petau was the first to tell us. There is hardly anything that can express an embryonic theology so well as a positively defective theology. The Semi-Arians were so numerous only in so far as the Arians, when their language was prudent, limited themselves to using expressions which were current for a long time without anyone seeing anything wrong in them. These Semi-Arians, surrounding Basil of Ancyra, would have had no difficulty in accepting Nicean

orthodoxy when the consubstantiality of the Son was sorted out
from a declaration that was equally strong on the distinction
of hypostases and lost any appearance of Sabellianism.

It is clear that the author made an attempt to bring together all
the traditional materials that might have come into his hands
and to incorporate them into his text. As we look, we find expressions reminiscent of Hippolytus (a number of whose prescriptions, moreover, were textually incorporated in the other parts
of the *Constitutions*). But his major source was in the ancient
Alexandrian Jewish prayers which were Christianized through a
few interpolations, and which he himself has preserved for us in
his 7th book. We are therefore in a position to appreciate both
the fidelity with which he enshrined what he found in his sources
within his construction and the freedom with which he redistributed and recomposed everything in a whole that is his very own.

When we compare the end result with the liturgies we have found
in Egypt or in Rome, there are two things which we note immediately. The first is that this pseudo-Clementine liturgy is made up
of the same elements as the Roman or Alexandrian liturgy. Everything we have found in these, and only that, is also found, merely
in a more generally (although not universally) detailed form, as
if the compiler had wished to leave nothing implicit. The second
is that it is impossible to suppose that the Egyptian or Roman
type could proceed from this Antiochian type. This latter represents a maturely conceived and deliberately applied synthesis and
it would be inconceivable that one could have ever dreamed of
taking it apart in order to rebuild it in accordance with the other
order. As we have seen, this other order is explained very well
historically, if we begin with the antecedents supplied by the
Jewish Synagogue and table prayers. But on the other hand,
we do not see how it could have resulted from a dissociation from
the eucharist of the *Apostolic Constitutions*. It seems incontestable, furthermore, that this Syrian liturgy is an intentional rearrangement of an earlier local liturgy which must have been
very analogous to the Roman and Egyptian liturgy. We shall
see its verification later, when we return to the lengthy form of
the liturgy of Addai and Mari, in which it seems that we find a
complete Syrian liturgy that is slightly or not at all re-arranged.

We shall give the text of the 8th book of the *Apostolic Constitutions* in three successive fragments, and comment on it. The division corresponds to the trinitarian plan of the whole composition. But it seems suitable to delay once again over the introductory dialogue.

> The grace of almighty God and the love of our Lord Jesus Christ and the fellowship (κοινωνία) of the Holy Ghost be with you all.
> — And with your spirit.
> Lift up your minds (τὸν νοῦν).
> — We lift them up to the Lord.
> Let us give thanks to the Lord.
> —It is meet and right.

Here as with Hippolytus, and perhaps under his influence, we find again the short formula: "Let us give thanks to the Lord," whose origin and first meaning we have seen. But the two preceding verses have been completely hellenized. The replacing of the salutation: "The Lord be with you" with the blessing drawn from 2 Cor. 13:13 became universal in the Syrian East and in all the countries to which its liturgy was transported. But it was not adopted without a significant transformation. There was a concern for establishing the trinitarian hierarchy in it by placing the "almighty God" first and qualifying him with "grace," while Christ takes the second place and consequently received the attribute of ἀγάπη (which is a marked departure from the constant use of St. Paul). Similarly, it is no longer the "hearts" that are to be lifted up to God but the νοῦς, the most spiritual part of the soul in hellenic anthropology (as we have pointed out, for the Greek mind the heart is only the seat of the emotions).

Then comes the first part of the eucharist, which leads us up to the *Sanctus*:

> May it be truly[11] meet and right before all things to hymn thee who art indeed the living God, who art before the beginning of created things, of whom the whole family in heaven

---

[11] Ὡς ἀληθῶς and no longer simply ἀληθῶς, as in Alexandria and Rome (*Vere ...*)

and earth is named; who art alone unbegotten, without beginning, paramount, supreme, the giver (*choregos*) of all good
things, above all cause and origin, ever unchangeable and
immutable, from whom as from a source, all things came
into being. Thou art the knowledge without beginning; the
Invisible Light, the Uncreated Hearing; the Untaught Wisdom, the First in thine Essence; Alone in thy Being; and
above all number, who broughtest all things out of nothing-
ness into existence by thine Only Begotten Son, whom thou
didst before all worlds beget, without intermediary, by wisdom, and might, and goodness, the Only Begotten Son, the
Word of God, the Living Wisdom, the First-born of all creation, the Messenger of thy great counsel, the High-Priest,
the King and Lord of all rational (*νοητῆς*) and sentient nature, who is before all, by whom all things are. For thou, O
Eternal God, hast by him made all things, and dost by him
bestow upon all an apposite providence: for by whom thou
didst graciously give existence, by him also thou gavest to
fare well. O God and Father of thine Only Begotten Son,
who by him madest first Cherubim, and Seraphim, and Aeons,
and Hosts, and Virtues, and Powers, and Principalities, and
Thrones, and Angels, and Archangels, and after that madest
by him all this visible world and all things therein. Thou
didst set up the heaven like an arch, and spread it forth like
a covering, and by thy will alone didst found the earth upon
nothing. Thou didst fix the firmament, and prepare night
and day. Thou broughtest the light out of thy treasures,
and by its limitation didst restore the darkness for the repose of the creatures which move in this world. Thou didst
appoint the sun to rule the day in heaven, and the moon
to rule at night, and didst inscribe the chorus of the stars
for the praise of thy magnificence. Thou madest water for
drink, and for ablution; and the vital air, for respiration,
and for the transmission of the sound of the voice, by means
of the tongue striking the air, and for hearing, which co-oper-
ated with the air, so as by reception to perceive the speech
lighting upon it. Thou madest fire for a consolation in darkness, and for relief of necessity that we might thereby be
warmed and enlightened. Thou didst separate the great
sea from the land, and didst render the one navigable, and
madest the other passable on foot, making the former mul-

titudinous with small and great beasts, and filling the latter with creatures tame and wild, crowning it also with different plants, garlanding it with herbs, adorning it with flowers, and enriching it with seed. Thou didst constitute the abyss, setting it in a great hollow, the seas of salt waters heaped together, and didst hedge it around with bounds of finest sands; and sometimes with the winds archest its crests to the height of mountains, and sometimes smoothest it as a plain, and sometimes makest it rage with storms, and sometimes stillest it with a calm, so as to make it easily navigable for mariners on ship-board. Thou didst gird with rivers the world created by thee, through Christ, and didst water it with brooks, and irrigate it with perpetual springs; and closely boundest it around with mountains for a most sure immovable foundation of the earth. Thou didst replenish thy world and adorn it with sweet-smelling and medicinal herbs, and with many and different creatures strong and weak, for food and for work, tame and wild. Thou didst variegate it with hissing of creeping things, with songs of birds, with revolutions of years, with numbers of months and days, with successions of seasons, with courses of rainy clouds, for the production of fruits, for the support of living things, for the regulation of the winds that blow when they are commanded by thee, for the multiplication of plants and herbs.

And thou didst not only create the world, but madest in it man, the citizen of the world, displaying him as an ornament of the world. For thou saidst in thy wisdom, Let us make man in our own image and likeness, and let him have dominion over the fish of the sea, and over the birds of heaven. Therefore also thou hast made him of immortal soul and perishable body, the former out of nothing and the latter of the four elements. Thou hast given him, in his soul, reasonable discernment, discrimination between religion and irreligion, and observation of justice and injustice, and bestowedst upon his body five-fold perception and power of motion. Thou, O almighty God, by Christ didst plant a garden eastwards in Eden, adorned with all plants good for food, and didst introduce man into it, as into a magnificent habitation; and when making him gavest him a law implanted in him, so that he might naturally and of himself possess the principles of the knowledge of God (θεογνωσίας). And

when bringing him on to the paradise of delight thou didst
accord unto him power to partake of all, but forbadest the
taste of one (tree) alone, holding out the hope of yet better
things, so that, if he kept the commandment he should for
that receive immortality as a reward, But when he neglected
the commandment, and through the deceit of the serpent,
and by the counsel of his wife, tasted the forbidden fruit,
thou didst justly drive him out of Paradise, yet, in thy goodness, didst not depise him when he was utterly lost. For he
was thy creature. Subjecting the creation to him, thou hast
given him to procure himself food by his own sweat and la-
bour, thou thyself planting and increasing and fastening all
things (for him). And, causing him to fall asleep for a short
time, thou calledst him by an oath to a renewal of being,
and loosing the sentence of death didst promise life by the
resurrection. Nor was this all; for thou didst pour forth his
progeny in an innumerable multitude, and glorifying those
who clung to thee, didst punish those who revolted from thee.
Thou didst accept the sacrifice of Abel as of one who was holy,
and turnedst away the gift of Cain, the murderer of his brother, as of one accursed. Futhermore thou didst accept Seth
and Enos, and didst translate Enoch. For thou art the Creator of men, the Dispenser of life, the Provider in want, and
the Giver of Laws, and the Rewarder of those who keep them
and the Avenger of those who transgress them. Thou didst
bring the great flood upon the world on account of the multitude of the ungodly, and, in an ark, didst rescue from the deluge righteous Noe, together with eight souls, the last of those
who had gone before, to be the beginning of those who were
to come after. Thou didst kindle the fearful fire upon the five
cities of the land of Sodom, making a fertile land into a salt
lake, for the wickedness of those who dwelt therein, and didst
snatch holy Lot from the conflagration. Thou didst rescue
Abraham from ancestral impiety, didst appoint him heir
of the world, and revealedst thy Christ unto him. Thou didst
ordain Melchisedek high-priest of thy worship. Thou didst
show thy patient servant Job victor of the serpent, the be-
ginner of wickedness. Thou madest Isaac a son of promise,
and Jacob the father of twelve sons, and pouring forth his
progeny in a multitude broughtest them down into Egypt
five-and-seventy souls. Thou, O Lord, didst not forget Jo-

seph, but, as a reward of his chastity for thy sake, gavest him to rule over Egypt. Thou, O Lord, didst not forget the Hebrews when they were in bondage under the Egyptians, but on account of thy promise to their fathers didst rescue them and punish the Egyptians. And when men corrupted the natural law, and sometimes esteemed the creation fortuitous, and sometimes honoured it above measure, and made it equal unto thee, the God of all, thou sufferedst them not to wander in error, but didst raise up thy servant Moses and gavest by him a written law to confirm the law of nature. Thou shewedst the creation to be thy work, and expelling the error of polytheism didst glorify Aaron and his posterity with the priesthood. Thou punishedst the Hebrews when they sinned, and receivedst them again when they returned (to thee). Thou didst torment the Egyptians with a tenfold plague. Thou, dividing the sea, didst lead the Israelites through it, and didst chastise the Egyptians, submerging them in the water when they pursued after them. Thou sweetenedst the bitter water with the wood. Thou pouredst forth water from the precipitous rock. Thou didst shed manna from heaven, and food of quails from the air, and a pillar of fire by night for light, and a pillar of cloud by day, for a shade from the heat. Thou didst raise up Joshua (in Greek: 'Ιησοῦς) as a general, and by him overthrewest seven nations of the Canaanites. Thou didst divide Jordan. Thou didst dry up the rivers of Etham. Thou without engines or human hands didst cast down walls. Thine be the glory for all, O Master Almighty. The innumerable hosts of Angels, Archangels, Thrones, Dominations, Principalities, Powers, Virtues, Hosts, Aeons, Cherubim and six-winged Seraphim (who with twain cover their feet, and with twain their heads, and with twain fly), worship thee, saying with thousands of thousands of Archangels, and ten thousands of ten thousands of Angels, crying, without interruption of voice, unceasingly: *Holy, Holy, Holy, Lord of Sabaoth: heaven and earth are full of his glory: Blessed be He for ever. Amen.*[12]

---

[12] Brightman, *op. cit.*, pp. 14 ff. Cf. F. X. Funk, *Constitutiones apostolicae*, vol. 1, pp. 496 ff. The English translation generally followed is that of R. H. Cresswell, *The Liturgy of "The Apostolic Constitutions"* (London, 1900), pp. 54 ff.

This first part concentrates on the Father, but it states from the very first that it is through Christ that the Father created all things, and man especially, since the old covenant with Abraham was founded upon an anticipated vision of the Christ who was to come.[13] And the conclusion of the narrative of the old covenant, with the arrival in Canaan, following the Passover and the Exodus, and the establishment of the people in Palestine, emphasizes that it was the work of "Jesus," a variant form of Joshua, which in the mind of the writer is obviously very meaningful.

Louis Duchesne made the seemingly natural remark that it is surprising to see such a detailed recall of the Old Testament come to a halt at this point.[14] But it does not seem necessary to suppose with him that one part of the text had been lost. In the second part the later fortunes of Israel's history, along with the prophets' interventions, were recalled in turn. But all of this is seemingly not so much the continuance of the old covenant in the interpretation of the author of the prayer as the progressive outline, within the framework set up by it, of the new covenant which will be fulfilled in the redemptive incarnation.

The knowledge theme remains predominant, as in the Jewish *berakah* leading up to the *Qedushah*. But in this text it develops within a clearly sapiential context (as was the case with the Jewish prayers of the 7th book). As in them, Christ is introduced as the "Only Begotten Son," the "God Logos" (which is identified with the "Living Wisdom") and at the same time he is proclaimed "First Born of all creation, the Messenger of thy great counsel, the High-Priest, the King and Lord." In the expression "Messenger of the counsel" we can see Hippolytus' influence.

The creation theme, still as in the Jewish prayers, remains inseparable from that of the active providence which sustains and gives existence ($\varepsilon \tilde{v}$ $\varepsilon \tilde{i} \nu \alpha \iota$, "faring well"). Hence a great vision of all creation, described from the outset as tending towards man and being fulfilled in man's coming, created as he was in the image

---

[13] Cf. above, pp. 122-123.

[14] Cf. Louis Duchesne, *Origines du culte chrétien*, 5 th ed. (Paris, 1920), p. 61, n. 1.

of God, in a dialogue between the Father and Wisdom, and brought into a garden planted by Christ "eastwards in Eden."

This description, with its fusion of the remembrances of the first chapters of Genesis and Psalm 104, closely follows and combines the first three prayers of the hellenistic Jewish *Tefillah* which we found in the 7th book. It is still very Jewish, even though its Judaism is evidently hellenized, on account of its insistence upon the radical distinction of creator and creature, and the gratuitousness of creation. The conclusion of the narrative with the mention of the tree of good and evil furnishes the occasion for a transition from the knowledge theme to the theme of life, and more precisely, the theme of immortality which had been prepared for by the assertion of man being created as an immortal soul in a perishable body.

In this way, we also make the transition from creation to the history of sin and the first redemption in the first covenant. From the beginning of sacred history, i. e. immediately after sin, the writer of this eucharist seems to see a call to a new birth, to resurrected life. He even goes so far as to declare that death's power was already broken by this promise made at the beginning of salvation history. From this context, he selects Abel and his sacrifice as the principle of a saved mankind, in contradistinction to the descendants of Cain. Salvation is continued through Seth, Enos and Enoch who was "translated" into heaven. The history of Noah and the flood, and the fire that came down on Sodom and Gomorrah became the first effective sign of separation, both a judgment and a deliverance, between the two lines of Adam's descendants. Abraham is then mentioned, as the one who was freed from the ungodliness of his ancestors, set up as the heir of the universe, and given a primary vision of the Christ. Melchizedek and his sacrifices are connected with him, as well as Job who is declared the conqueror of the ancient serpent. In Isaac, Jacob and the twelve patriarchs, we see the promised people being constituted, and then led into Egypt by Joseph. The deliverance wrought by Moses, when this people had been reduced to slavery by the Egyptians, appears as the initial victory over the idolatry of polytheism, in the revelation of the "law to confirm the law of nature." With Moses, Aaron appears as the prin-

ciple of the levitical priesthood. The whole account of the Exodus
(even though the Passover is not expressly mentioned) is then
given, with the ten plagues and the toppling of Jericho before
"Jesus, chief of the army," the changing of the bitter waters into
sweet, the water from the rock, the manna and the quail, the
pillar of fire and the cloud. Here again, although the dependence
is not as pronounced as above, the salient points are practically
the same as in one other Jewish prayer from the 7th book, the one
which corresponds to the final petitions of the *Tefillah*. Fr. Ligier, on the other hand, has shown the astonishing similarity between this whole recounting of sacred history and those which
we find in the amplifications of the *Tefillah* and *Abodah* blessings
proper to the Day of Atonement.[15]

It will be noted that this initial evocation of creation and redemption is included in an evocation of the angelic universe. The
Angels appear, immediately after the Firstborn, the Only-Begotten
Son, the Word and Wisdom, as the first creation which was followed
by the visible world and everything in it. Symmetrically, after
the redemptive work, when Jericho had fallen and "Jesus" led
the redeemed people into its inheritance, the Angels reappear:
"Thine be the glory for all, O Master Almighty. The innumerable
hosts of Angels, Archangels, etc ... worship thee ... " In the first
enumeration of the Angels, the mention of the Aeons and the
Hosts comes after the Cherubim and the Seraphim; they are the
Angels that govern the successive and conflicting dispensations.

The second part introduces the *Sanctus*, which, as we see, has
an archaic form, in certain ways intermediary between the Egyptian version (hardly more than the Jewish version without the
blessing from Ezekiel) and the later forms. Here, we do not yet
have the blessing and the Hosannas of Psalm 118, but rather a
general blessing instead: "Blessed be He for ever." It will be
noted also that the quote from Isaiah, even though it includes the
addition "Heaven" still has "full of *his* glory," instead of "full of
thy glory" which was later to prevail.

---

[15] L. Ligier, "Anaphores orientales et prières juives," in *Proche-Orient
Chrétien*, t. XIII (1963), pp. 9 ff.

After the Sanctus, the eucharist concentrates on the Son and the fulfilment of salvation history in his Passion-Glorification.

For Holy indeed art thou, and All-Holy, the Highest and most Exalted for ever. And Holy is also thine Only-Begotten Son, our Lord and God Jesus Christ, who in all things, both in manifold creation, and in commensurate providence, ministering unto thee his God and Father, did not overlook the lost race of men, but, after the natural law, after the legal ordinance, after the prophetic warnings, after the tutelage of angels, when men had corrupted both the positive and natural law, and had cast out of their recollection the deluge and the conflagration (of Sodom), and the plagues of the Egyptians, and the slaughters in Palestine, and were on the point of universal destruction, was himself pleased, according to thy will, the Creator to become man, the Lawgiver to become subject to laws, the High-Priest to become a victim, the Shepherd a sheep; and propitiated ($\dot{\varepsilon}\xi\varepsilon\nu\mu\varepsilon\nu\dot{\iota}\sigma\alpha\tau o$) thee, his God and Father, and reconciled thee to the world, and delivered all men from the impending wrath; being born of a Virgin, and becoming flesh, of the seed of David, and of Abraham, of the tribe of Juda, according to the prophecy spoken of beforehand by himself ($\dot{\nu}\pi'$ $\alpha\dot{\nu}\tau o\tilde{\nu}$ $\pi\varrho o\varrho\varrho\eta\theta\varepsilon\dot{\iota}\sigma\alpha\varsigma$), God the Lord, the Beloved Son, the First-born of all creation. He, who fashioneth all that are born, was born of a virgin womb, the Fleshless became flesh, and he that was begotten before all worlds was born in time. Living among men holily ($\pi o\lambda\iota\tau\varepsilon\nu\sigma\dot{\alpha}\mu\varepsilon\nu o\varsigma$ $\dot{o}\sigma\dot{\iota}\omega\varsigma$), and having been brought up according to the precepts ($\dot{\varepsilon}\nu\theta\dot{\varepsilon}\sigma\mu\omega\varsigma$), driving away every disease and every sickness from men, doing signs and wonders amongst the people, and partaking of food and drink and sleep (being he who nourisheth all who have need of nourishment, and filleth every living thing with satisfaction), he revealed thy Name unto those who knew it not, put ignorance to flight, rekindled godliness, fulfilled thy will, and accomplished the work which thou gavest him to do. All which things being completed, being taken by the hands of sinful priests and high-priests, falsely so-called, and of a law-breaking people, and by the treachery of him who was diseased with iniquity, suffering many things at their hands, and enduring every indignity, according to thy permission, being handed over to Pilate the governor, he, the Judge, was judged, the Saviour was condemned, the Impassible (ἀπαθής) was nailed to the cross, the essentially immortal died, and the Life-giver was buried that he might release from suffering and deliver from death those for whom he came, and might break the chains of the devil, and rescue men from his deceit. And on the third day He rose from the dead, and after continuing forty days with his disciples was taken up into heaven, and was set at thy right hand, who art his God and his Father.[16]

We see that this eucharist of Antioch, like that of Alexandria, connects its second part to the *Sanctus* by means of a link that will be found to be the same in all the texts derived from them. But at Antioch it is no longer the idea of fulness but that of holiness which supplies it. Praised in the Father, this holiness is proclaimed in the Son also, which leads to a second recall of his association with the Father in the sustaining and preserving of every creature. The evocation of sacred history is then resumed; the gift of the natural law, the written law, the preaching of the prophets, the wonder works of God for his people, attributed to angelic interventions, are all presented as so many preludes of the incarnation. Following a line of thought which will be found again in the Cappadocian Fathers, particularly in St. Gregory of Nazianzum, it is described in a series of paradoxes: man's creator becomes man, the law-giver submits to the law, the priest makes himself a victim, the shepherd a sheep, God the Word becomes flesh, the author of all things is born of a virgin, the fleshless takes on a body, the eternal is born in time.[17] The incarnation is redemptive first of all insofar as it brings about reconciliation with the Father.

We now go on to a succinct account of Christ's earthly life: living in holiness and teaching with authority, freeing men from all infirmity, while submitting himself to the same necessities that we have, he nourishes all that lives. In all of this and through all of this Christ reveals the divine Name to those who do

---

[16] Brightman, *op. cit.*, pp. 19 ff. (Cresswell, *op. cit.*, pp. 61 ff.).

[17] Cf. the homily on the nativity of St. Gregory of Nazianzum (no. 38), P. G., t. 36, col. 312 ff.

not know it, putting ignorance to flight, rekindling godliness, and fulfilling the divine will.

This fulfilment culminates in the supreme contradiction of the ungodliness of the priests, the faithlessness of the people who betrayed him, the injustice suffered by the Judge of all things, the Saviour condemned, the impassible nailed to the cross, the immortal undergoing death. But the burial of the author of life frees from suffering and death, breaks the chains of the devil and liberates men from his wickedness (another phrase which seems to betray Hippolytus' influence). He finally rises, and after the forty days with his followers, he ascends to heaven and sits at the right hand of the Father.

The thanksgiving for redemptive history is now complete, in and through the thanksgiving for the history of the Word made flesh in order to reconcile and deliver us, the anamnesis follows, and still includes within it the institution narrative, as we have seen in the ancient Egyptian tradition represented by Serapion. The redemption's application to us through the Holy Spirit evolves from this.

> Wherefore we, having in remembrance the things which he for our sakes endured, give thanks unto thee, O God Almighty, not such as are due but such as we can, and fulfil his injunction. For he in the same night that he was betrayed, took bread in his holy and blameless hands, and looking up to thee his God and Father, brake it, and gave it to his disciples, saying: This is the mystery of the new Testament, take of it, eat; this is My Body which is broken (θρυπτόμενον) for many for the remission of sins. Likewise also he mixed the cup with wine and water, and sanctified it, and gave it to them saying: Drink ye all of it; this is My Blood which is shed for many for the remission of sins; do this in remembrance of me: for as oft as ye eat of this bread and drink of this cup, ye do show forth my death until I come.
>
> Therefore, having in remembrance his passion and death, and resurrection, and his return (ἐπανόδου) into heaven, and his future second advent, in which he shall come to judge the quick and the dead, and to give to every man according to his works, we offer unto thee, our King and our God, according to his injunction, this bread and this cup, giving

thanks unto thee through him that thou hast counted us worthy to stand before thee and to sacrifice unto thee (i.e. to perform a priestly function: ἱερατεύειν).   And we implore thee to look graciously upon these gifts lying before thee, who art the God who hast no need of aught, and to be well pleased with them to the honor of (εἰς τιμήν) thy Christ, and to send down upon this sacrifice thy Holy Spirit, the witness of the sufferings of the Lord Jesus, that he may declare (ἀποφήνῃ) this bread the Body of thy Christ, and this cup the Blood of thy Christ, that they who partake thereof may be strengthened in godliness, may receive remission of their sins, may be rescued from the devil and his deceit, may be filled with the Holy Ghost, may become worthy of thy Christ, and may obtain eternal life, thou being reconciled unto them, O Master Almighty.

Moreover we pray thee, O Lord, also for thy Holy Church from one end of the world to the other, which thou hast purchased with the precious blood of thy Christ; that thou wouldest keep it unshaken and untroubled unto the consummation of the world; and for every episcopate rightly (ὀρθοτομούσης) dividing the word of truth:

Moreover we implore thee for my unworthiness (οὐδενίας) who am now offering unto thee, and for the presbytery, for the deacons and for all the clergy, that thou wouldest instruct them all and fill them with the Holy Ghost:

Moreover we implore thee for the King, and for those in authority, and for all the army, that they may be peaceably disposed towards us, that passing all the time of our life in peace and concord we may glorify thee through Jesus Christ our Hope:

Moreover we offer unto thee also for all who have from the beginning pleased thee, the holy patriarchs, prophets, righteous men, apostles, martyrs, confessors, bishops, priests, deacons, subdeacons, readers, singers, virgins, widows, laity, and all whose names thou knowest:

Moreover we offer unto thee for this thy people, that, for the praise of thy Christ, thou wouldest make them a royal priesthood, a holy nation; for those in virginity and purity; for the widows of the Church; for those in holy matrimony; for women labouring of child; and for the babes of thy people; that thou wouldest cast none of us out:

Moreover we beseech thee for this city, and for those that dwell therein; for the sick; for those who are in bitter slavery; for those in exile; for those in prison; for those who travel by sea or by land; that thou wouldest be a Helper unto all, a Strengthener and Supporter of all:

Moreover we implore thee for those who hate us and persecute us for Thy name's sake: for those who are without and are wandering; that thou wouldest turn them unto good, and soften their wrath against us:

Moreover we implore thee for the catechumens of the Church, and for those who are afflicted by the enemy, and for our brethren who are doing penance; that thou wouldest perfect the first in the faith, and wouldest purify the second from the influence of the evil one, and wouldest receive the repentance of the last, and forgive both them and us our transgressions:

Moreover we offer unto thee for seasonable weather, and for the copious produce of the fruits; that receiving abundantly of thy good things we may ceaselessly praise thee, who givest food to all flesh;

Moreover we implore thee for those who are for reasonable cause absent; that thou wouldest preserve us all in godliness, and gather us together, steadfast, blameless, and without reproach in the kingdom of thy Christ, the God of every sentient and intelligent creature, our King:

For unto thee is (due) all glory, worship and thanksgiving, honour and adoration, to the Father, and to the Son, and to the Holy Ghost, both now, and ever and unto all perpetual and endless ages of ages. Amen.[18]

As we see, it is in the third part of the prayer, the part in which the present and future fulfilment of the mystery in us is mentioned, that the institution narrative is placed in this eucharist. As in the anaphora of Serapion, the anamnesis does not follow it; the narrative is included in the anamnesis itself. It is the "memorial" which he has commanded us to celebrate in our thanksgiving recalling his own actions and words at the Last Supper.

To the words "do this in remembrance of me" is added St. Paul's statement: "for as often as ye eat of this bread and drink of this

---

[18] Brightman, *op. cit.*, pp. 20 ff. (Cresswell, *op. cit.*, pp. 63 ff.).

cup, ye do show forth my death until I come," just as we saw in the eucharist of St. Mark. As a consequence of this the anamnesis unfolds in a commemoration as of one mystery, of the passion, death, resurrection and ascension of Christ, and of his ultimate return for the judgment. Let us also note the very special form of the words of institution which put the proclamation of the mystery on Christ's lips at the very beginning.

It is at the conclusion of this anamnesis that the sacrifical formulas make their appearance: "we offer unto thee, our King and our God, according to his injunction, this bread and this cup, giving thanks unto thee through him that thou hast counted us worthy to stand before thee and to sacrifice unto thee" (a formula that could well have come from the Greek text of Hippolytus). We pass immediately afterward to the first part of the epiclesis: "And we implore thee to look graciously upon these gifts lying before thee, who art the God who hast no need of aught and to be well pleased with them to the honour of thy Christ ..." Let us stress the moderation and at the same time the exactness with which these expressions interpret the precise sense of the memorial for a hellenistic context. It is the divine injunction of Christ which allows us to present the memorial, established by him, before God, and also to present ourselves to him in the act of thanksgiving. These gifts are then only an acknowledgement of the fact that we receive everything from him who has need of nothing, and it is upon his one gift that we base the hope that our sacrifice, and ourselves with it, may be pleasing to him.

There follows the second part of the epiclesis, in which there is the mention of the Holy Spirit. It is asked that he be sent upon the sacrifice so that he might declare (or manifest; ἀποφήνῃ) that it is the body and blood of Christ. The foundation of this invocation is a curious formula in which the Holy Spirit is called "the witness of the sufferings of the Lord Jesus." We have here a reminder of the Epistle to the Hebrews (9,14) where Christ is spoken of as offering himself through the eternal Spirit, together with an implicit citation from the first Epistle of St. Peter (5:1), where he speaks of himself as a "witness of the sufferings of Christ."

The third part of the epiclesis asks finally that all partakers in this eucharist "be strengthened in godliness, receive remission of their sins, be rescued from the devil and his deceit, filled with the Holy Ghost, become worthy of Christ, obtain eternal life, and that the Almighty Master might be reconciled to them."

Thus, we see the ancient and original invocation for the accomplishment in us of the mystery commemorated give rise to the prayer for the acceptance of the sacrifice, very skilfully connected with the expression of the sacrifice that arose out of the memorial. The link between the two original epicleses is made through the request that the Spirit, who is to accomplish the mystery in us, manifest (undoubtedly by that very fact) that the memorial is indeed the body and blood of Christ.

After this, the prayer is broken up into a litany of intercessions, involving the Church and the whole world: the universal Church, the episcopate, the presbytery and clergy, the king, those in authority or who have charge of the army that they might maintain peace and tranquility. It commemorates the patriarchs, the prophets, the righteous, the martyrs, the confessors, bishops, priests and deacons and all the faithful departed, the particular community assembled and the city in which the eucharist is being celebrated, all men, including those who hate us or who have gone astray, the catechumens, the demoniacs, the penitents, and ends with a petition for seasonable weather and fruitful harvests. These are the themes encompassed by this new *Tefillah* in which there is a constant reference in each petition to the realization of a universal praise. Note that here the prayer *against* the persecutors is not only omitted, as in Rome, but replaced by a prayer *for* them, and that the Jewish prayer for the proselytes which followed it has been transformed into a prayer for the catechumens.

If we must sum up the excellence of this prayer, we shall say that it manifests, a sense that is still very aware of the whole content of the key notions of this original eucharist, in its transcription into hellenistic context of a eucharist whose first framework was basically Jewish. Thus, in this interpretation and rearrangement, dictated by a theology and a literary esthetic that were so deeply hellenized, the substance of the Judeo-Christian eucharist was retained with hardly a loss or an alteration. This is surely quite a remarkable feat. But, in order to accomplish it, the primitive data of the eucharist were broken up and then re-

assembled with astounding ingenuity in a mosaic that is so well
pieced together as to appear as one single piece. The creation
and redemption themes are connected through the master idea of
the provident and wise God whose word is the eternal Wisdom
which is inscribed in time. Salvation history is outlined in the
old covenant and fulfilled in the new, and the anamnesis of the
saving mystery is recognized as the pe.fect sacrifice. Its acceptance is sought from the very one who brought it about, and the
Holy Spirit is asked to come upon these gifts which he has given
us, so that we, and the whole world about us, may be presented
to him in the praise of his glory. All of these ideas are ordered
with a mastery and a finesse that are indeed one of the greatest
triumphs of the hellenic clarity of mind applied to the mystery
of a Christianity that is completely biblical in its origins.

THE FINAL SYNTHESIS OF THE EUCHARIST OF ST. JAMES

This very successful result was to be perfected in another text
which undoubtedly came not too many years after. This is the
so-called liturgy of St. James. When we compare it with the liturgy we have just studied, we can think that all the secondary
elements of the latter were felicitously removed because they ran
the risk of bogging down the continuity in a series of anecdotes
and of drawing out the summary of the divine mysteries into a
mere enumeration. But also, the stylization and the fusion of the
original elements is such that more than one of them has become
unrecognizable. Irreducible factors are reduced for the sake of
the unity of a development that is faultless and without repetition at the risk of at least a partial evaporation of their content.

Yet in the economy and the balance of its composition, the liturgy of St. James nonetheless remains the most accomplished
literary monument of perhaps the whole of liturgical literature.

Even if St. James is assuredly not its author, this liturgy represents a Jerusalemite tradition, as is shown by the many allusions
to the holy places that it includes, and the role played by the constant evocation of the heavenly Jerusalem. It very quickly became widespread, undoubtedly as a result of all the pilgrims who
came to the holy city from all over in order to visit the Constan-

tinian basilicas. Not only Syria and Arabia, but also Greece, Ethiopia, Armenia, Georgia and the Slavic countries, through the manuscripts and the translations found there, attest to its extraordinary diffusion. Nevertheless it was soon to be supplanted by the two abridged formularies that are currently attributed to St. Basil and St. John Chrysostom. Their adoption by Byzantium caused its replacement throughout the whole East. It has been celebrated in Greek in recent times only as an exception, at Jerusalem and in a few other places such as the island of Zakynthos. But various Orthodox prelates have authorized and encouraged its revival in recent years. The Syrians, whether "Jacobites" or Catholics, are the only ones still using it habitually in an ancient Syriac version.[19]

Here is the eucharistic part of the liturgy, following the very valuable critical text established by Basile Mercier:

The love of God and Father, the grace of the Lord and God and Son, and the communication and the gift of the Holy Spirit be with you all.
—And with your spirit.
Lift up the minds and hearts ($\tau\grave{o}\nu$ $\nu o\tilde{v}\nu$ $\varkappa a\grave{\imath}$ $\tau\grave{a}\varsigma$ $\varkappa a\varrho\delta\acute{\iota}a\varsigma$).
—We have (lifted them up) to the Lord.
Let us give thanks to the Lord.
—That is meet and right.[20]

This dialogue, once again, presents a significant modification of the Pauline formula, for the purpose of molding it to the schema of the trinitarian theology of the fourth century. But in the present case, instead of changing the attributes of the Father and the Son (respectively love and grace), they are retained, but not

---

[19] Cf. I. M. Hanssens, *Institutiones liturgicae de ritibus orientalibus*, Tomus III, Pars altera (Rome, 1932), pp. 587 ff. To be completed by the introduction to the work of B. Mercier cited in the following note.

[20] B. Ch. Mercier, "La liturgie de saint Jacques, édition critique du texte grec avec traduction latine," in *Patrologia orientalis*, t. 26 (Paris, 1948— actually the fascicle containing this text appeared in 1946), p. 198. Let us note that the oldest Greek manuscript is from the ninth century (Vat. gr. 2282). Egeria (ca. 414-416) mentions an "Aramaic" version. A Syriac version was certainly made at Edessa in or about the sixth century. The Syriac *textus receptus* in use today is from the thirteenth century.

without modifying the order of the persons. Other slight changes
will be noted, the most important being that the "gift" of the
Spirit is placed in apposition with its "communication."

The same spirit of compromise retained "hearts" in the second
formula, and introduced the word νοῦς, as the *Apostolic Constitutions* had done, although they had replaced the former with
the latter.

Here again, it is the brief formula which won out for the invitation to the act of thanksgiving.

> How truly meet and right, equitable and availing to sal-
> vation it is, to praise you, to hymn you, to bless you, to adore
> you, to glorify you, to give you thanks! You, the creator
> of every creature, whether visible or invisible, the treasury
> of eternal good things, the source of life and immortality,
> the God and the Master of all things, who are hymned by
> the heavens and the heavens of the heavens, and all their
> powers, the sun and the moon and the whole choir of stars,
> the earth, the sea and all that is found therein, the heaven-
> ly Jerusalem, the assembly of the elect, the Church of the
> first born whose (names are) inscribed in heaven, the souls
> of the righteous and the prophets, the souls of the martyrs
> and the apostles, the Angels, the Archangels, the Thrones,
> the Dominations, the Principalities and the Authorities and
> the awesome Powers, the Cherubim with the countless eyes,
> the six winged Seraphim, who with two wings hide their
> face, with two their feet and fly with the two others, crying
> out one to the other with unceasing voices and in incessant
> theologies, the victory hymn of the majesty of your glory,
> with one great voice, singing, proclaiming, glorifying, crying
> out and saying: *Holy, holy, holy, Lord Sabaoth, heaven and
> earth are full of your glory, Hosanna in the highest. Blessed
> (is) he who has come and who comes in the name of the Lord.
> Hosanna in the highest.*[21]

This first part, which mentions the Father only, is unified by a
summary of the whole of creation, which is invited to join unanimously in the hymn of the Seraphim. All creation is, as it were,
summed up in the heavenly Jerusalem, the festal assembly (πανή-

---

[21] *Ibid.*

γυρις), the Church of the first-born whose names are written in heaven (we recognize the terms from the Epistle to the Hebrews), the spirits of the righteous and the prophets, to whom are joined the souls of the martyrs and the prophets. The *Sanctus* is found in the same completed form that the Roman liturgy has given us, and which we have commented upon in its regard (note, however, the addition "who has come" to the biblical "who comes").

The second part, as always in Syria, is connected to the first by the idea of holiness, taken from the *Sanctus*.

You are holy, King of ages and the Lord and Giver of all holiness, and holy is your Only-Begotten Son, our Lord Jesus Christ, through whom you have made all things, and holy is your all-holy Spirit who probes all things, and your own depths, O God and Father; holy are you, Almighty, who can do all things, awesome, good, merciful (εὐσπλάγχνε), you who show special compassion to your work, who made from the earth man in your image and likeness, who gave him the enjoyment of paradise and who, when he broke your commandment and fell, did not turn away from him, and, in your kindness, did not abandon him, but instructed him as a merciful Father, called him by the law, taught him by the prophets. Finally, you sent your Only-Begotten Son, our Lord Jesus Christ, into the world, so that he might renew and revivify by his coming your own image; he is the one who came down from heaven, and having taken flesh from the Holy Spirit and Mary, the holy ever-Virgin, Mother of God, and having lived among men, arranged everything for the salvation of our race. As he who is without sin was about to suffer for us sinners a voluntary and life-giving death by the cross, on the night he was betrayed, or rather when he handed himself over, for the life of the world and its salvation, he took bread in his holy, pure, spotless and immortal hands, and having raised his eyes to heaven, and presenting (ἀναδείξας) it to you, God and Father, giving thanks, he blessed it, hallowed it, broke it and gave it to his holy disciples and apostles, saying: Take, eat, this is my body, broken for you and given for the remission of sins (*People*: Amen). Likewise, after having supped, taking the cup, and having mixed into it wine and water, raising his eyes to heaven, he presented it to you, God and Father, giving thanks, blessed it, hallowed it, filled it with the Holy Spirit and gave it to his holy and blessed disciples and apostles, saying: Drink of this all of you, this is the blood of the new covenant, shed for you and for many, and given for the re- mission of sins. Do this as a memorial of me: as often as you eat this bread and drink this cup, you announce the death of the Son of man and you proclaim his resurrection until he comes (*another* Amen *of the people follows*).[22]

The initial reference to the divine holiness passes to the mercy whereby God, having created man in his image and brought him into paradise, did not desert him after his fall, but like a compas- sionate Father, called him by the law, taught him through the prophets, and finally sent his own Only-Begotten Son to restore and revivify this lost image. The narrative of the redemptive dispensation is given in one sole mold. To do this the narrative of the eucharistic institution was detached from the anamnesis, in which it must originally have been incorporated, and inserted in its place in the evocation of the Passion. The anamnesis thus simply became the conclusion of the relating of the *mirabilia Dei*. Note in this passage the twofold insistence upon the volun- tary character of the passion and the immortality of the one who hands himself over to death (even his hands, in this text, are cal- led immortal). Let us also notice that if the Pauline conclusion of the Last Supper narrative is connected with the narrative itself, it is nonetheless left in the third person.

The deacons reply to the anamnesis with the words: "We do believe and we do proclaim," and all the people (as in the eucharist of Serapion) join in and say with the priest:

We announce your death, Lord, and we proclaim your re- surrection...

Then the priest continues alone:

... we, sinners, being mindful of his life-giving sufferings, his saving cross, and his death, and his burial, and his rising from the dead on the third day and his return (ἀνόδον) to heaven and his sitting at your right hand, God and Father, and his second glorious and awesome parousia when he will

---

[22] Mercier, *op. cit.*, pp. 200ff.

come in glory to judge the living and the dead, when he will
render to each according to his works,—spare us, Lord
our God!—or rather we offer in accordance with your mercy
(εὐσπλαγχνίαν), to you, Master, this awesome and unbloody
sacrifice, beseeching you not to deal with us in accordance
with our sins and not to render to us according to our iniquities, but according to your mildness (ἐπιείκειαν) and
your unutterable love for men, abrogating and blotting out
the document that accuses us, to grant to our entreaties
your heavenly and eternal gifts which eye has not seen nor
ear heard and which have not entered into the heart of men,
(gifts) which you have prepared, O God, for those who love
you: do not reject your people on account of me and my sins,
Lord, friend to men, for your people and your Church beseech you (*the people*: Have mercy upon us. Lord, God the
Father, the Almighty); have mercy upon us, O God, O Father,
O Almighty, have mercy upon us, God our Savior, have
mercy upon us according to your great mercy, and send
upon us and upon these gifts which we present to you, your
all-holy Spirit, the Lord and Giver of Life, who shares the
throne with you, God and Father, and with your Only-Begotten Son, and who reigns with you, consubstantial and
coeternal, who spoke through the law and the prophets and
in the new covenant, the one who came down in the form of
a dove upon Our Savior Jesus Christ in the River Jordan,
and who remained with him; the one who came down upon
your holy apostles under the appearance of tongues of fire,
in the upper room of the holy and glorious Zion the day of
the holy Pentecost; send down your all-holy Spirit himself,
Master, upon us and these holy gifts which we present to
you, so that by visiting them with his holy, good and glorious presence (παρουσία) he may sanctify them and make
this bread the holy body of Christ (*the people*: Amen) and
this cup the precious blood of Christ (*another* Amen), so that
they may be for all those who partake of them for the remission of sins and for eternal life, for the sanctification of souls
and bodies, for the fruitfulness of good works, for the strengthening of your holy catholic and apostolic Church which you
have founded upon the rock of faith so that the gates of hell
may not prevail against her, delivering her from every heresy
and scandal of the workers of iniquity, preserving her until

the end of the ages. We make this offering to you, Lord, for your holy places which you have glorified by the theophany of your Christ and the visitation of your all-holy Spirit, especially for the holy and glorious Zion, the mother of all the Churches, and for all your holy, catholic and apostolic Church, throughout the whole world: grant her abundantly from this moment the gifts of your all-holy Spirit, O Master.[23]

Note the transition from the anamnesis to the epiclesis, which is made in the very touching and dramatic style of this whole prayer. The mention of the judgment elicits a fervent entreaty to the divine mercy. From it flows immediately the only explicitly sacrificial phrase of the whole text: "We offer to you ... Master, this awesome unbloody sacrifice." But it is copiously filled out by an appeal to divine grace, which is expected to destroy and wipe out the act of our condemnation (allusion to Col. 2:14) and grant us the heavenly gifts. Hence the particularly elaborate epiclesis which turns into an encomium of the Spirit, parallel to those of the Father and the Son in the first two parts. It has evidently influenced the text of the liturgy of St. Mark, in the relatively late form in which it has come down to us. Here the precise petition is not only that the Spirit manifest that the sacramental bread and wine are the body and blood of Christ, but that he *make* them the body and blood. What follows opens out into a prayer for the whole Church, which becomes concretized first in a special supplication for the holy places. As in the liturgy of the *Apostolic Constitutions*, but in an already more highly developed form, a whole Christian *Tefillah* follows, in which each petition is connected with the "memorial" by the word "remember" constantly repeated:

Remember, Lord, all our holy fathers and bishops, who dispense the word of your truth in an orthodox manner throughout all the land,
Remember, Lord, our holy father N. all his clergy and all his priests, grant him an honorable old age, preserve him for a long time in feeding your people in all godliness and holiness.

[23] Mercier, *op. cit.*, pp. 202ff.

Remember, Lord, here and everywhere, the honorable presbytery, the diaconate in Christ, and every other ministry and ecclesiastical order and our brotherhood in Christ as well as all the people who love Christ.

Remember, Lord, according to the multitude of your loving-kindness and your steadfast love, me also, lowly and sinful, your unworthy servant, and protect me in your mercy and your compassion, deliver me and free me from my persecutors, Lord, Lord of powers, and since sin has abounded in me, let your grace superabound.

Remember also, Lord, the deacons that stand around your holy altar and grant them a life without reproach, keep their deaconship spotless and obtain for them a good promotion.

Remember, Lord, this holy city, which is yours, O our God, and that city which holds the power, every city and town and all who dwell therein in the orthodox faith and godliness, their peace and their security.

Remember, Lord, our most godly and Christ-loving King, his godly and Christ-loving Queen, their whole palace and army, their assistance from on high, and their victory; take hold of the great and small buckler and rise up to help him, submit all warlike and barbarian nations, who wish for war, to him, rule over his counsels, that we may have a calm and tranquil life in all godliness and holiness.

Remember, Lord, the Christians who come and go to worship at the holy places of Christ.

Remember, Lord, the Christians at sea or on a journey, who are in foreign lands, those who are in chains and in prison, those who are captives and in exile, those who are in difficulties, in torments and bitter servitude, our fathers and our brothers, and the peaceful return of each to his home.

Remember, Lord, those who are old and powerless, the sick, the maimed and those who are afflicted by unclean spirits, their quick return to health coming from you, O God, and their salvation.

Remember, Lord, every Christian soul that is afflicted and in trial, in need of your mercy and your help, O God, and the conversion of the wayward.

Remember, Lord, those who live in virginity, godliness and asceticism, our holy fathers and brothers who struggle upon the mountains, in the caves and the holes in the earth, as well as all the orthodox communities and this one which is here, in Christ.

Remember, Lord, our fathers and brothers who work and who serve us for your name's sake.

Remember, Lord, the welfare of all, have mercy upon all, Master, be reconciled with all, give peace to the multitude of your people, dispel scandals, wipe out wars, bring a halt to the schisms of Churches, dissolve speedily the heresies that appear, break down the barrier between nations, raise up the horn of Christians, grant us your peace and your love, O God, our Savior, the hope of all the ends of the earth.

Remember, Lord, seasonable weather, peaceable showers, beneficent dews, the plenty of fruits, a favorable conclusion crowning the year with your goodness, for the eyes of all hope in you and you give them their food in due season, you open your hand and satisfy all who live in their desires.

Remember, Lord, those who have brought fruit, and who bring fruit in your holy Churches, O God, who are mindful of the poor and those who have asked us to make memory of them in prayers.

Again, remember, Lord, those who have brought offerings today to your holy altar, and the intentions for which each has made his offering or has in mind, and all those whom we mention to you ...

Remember also, Lord, our own relatives, friends, acquaintances and the brothers who are here.

All those whom we have remembered, remember, Lord, and all the orthodox whom we have not remembered, give them in exhange for earthly goods heavenly ones, for corruptible gifts, incorruptible ones, for temporal gifts, eternal ones, in accordance with the promises of your Christ, since you have authority over life and death.

Deign again to remember, Lord, those also who have been pleasing to you over the ages, generation upon generation, the holy fathers, patriarchs, prophets, apostles, martyrs, confessors, holy doctors and every righteous spirit consumed in the faith of your Christ. (Here a list of commemorations was introduced, beginning with the Virgin, the Baptist, the Apostles, and then it continues at great length. After which the celebrant goes on:)

All these, remember, God; the spirits of every flesh, of those whom we have commemorated and the orthodox whom we have not commemorated, grant them rest in the land of the living, in your Kingdom, in the delights of paradise, in the bosom of Abraham, Isaac and Jacob, our holy fathers, where there is no pain, sadness or weeping, where the light of your face, which is everywhere resplendent, shines, and for us, Lord, dispose in a Christian way of the last of our life, that it may be pleasing to you, that it may be sinless and peaceful: gather us beneath the feet of your elect, when and as you will, provided that it be without shame or sin, through your Only-Begotten Son, our Lord and God and Savior Jesus Christ, for he is the only one without sin that has ever appeared upon earth,[24] ... with whom you are blessed and glorified, together with your all-holy, good and life-giving Spirit, now and always, world without end. Amen.[25]

This form of the final intercession is the most elaborate that we found in any liturgy of the patristic age. As we have already said in regard to the Egyptian eucharist, whose later forms (particularly in the epiclesis and in those intercessions and commemorations that follow it in Syria) were certainly influenced by the West Syrian eucharist, these intercessions are the element of the eucharistic prayers which for long had remained the most malleable (as in the Jewish liturgy). But the state in which the liturgy of St. James was handed down to us, including this part, had already been reached by the middle of the fifth century, for the Syriac translations used by the Monophysite "Jacobites" of Syria attest to it in practically all its details. This great supplication, through the influence of Syria on all the pilgrims (to whom, as we saw, this prayer alludes) even more developed than that of the *Apostolic Constitutions*, seems to have left its mark everywhere on the litanies of intercession which the Roman West itself was conseqently to borrow from the East. But the Jerusalemite formula,

[24] Here, as at the end of the intercession of the liturgy of St. Mark, there is introduced a commemoration of the bishops in communion with whom the celebration is made (in the text of St. James given by M. Mercier the five patriarchs are named). It visibly interrupts the course of the prayer.

[25] Mercier, *op. cit.*, pp. 208 ff.

in this latter part as in the preceding ones, retains its own coloration, resulting from a particularly warm rhetoric, with a very biblical tone.

Yet, if we look at the eucharist of St. James as a whole, we are especially struck by the clarity of its trinitarian theology, which is expressed with much more exacting precision in its structure than could be seen in the liturgy of the 8th book of the *Apostolic Constitutions*. All the duplications and all the repetitions in thought have been definitively and categorically removed. The Father is praised for all creation, gathered together into this "Church of the first-born" which is designated as the heavenly Jerusalem. The Son is acclaimed as the one in whom and through whom the divine economy of infinite mercy has brought to fruition the plan to bring together and restore all things for the purpose of this glorification. The Spirit is invoked as the one through whom the work of the Son finds its ultimate fulfilment in us now and for eternity.

But we must look at the price paid for this synthesis. The anamnesis, which is the core of the primitive Christian eucharist became somewhat amorphous because of it and runs into the thanksgiving for the history of salvation, which originally was its introduction. The result is that the epiclesis, which at first was merely a development of the anamnesis, became detached from it, and acquired an importance and an independence which puts it on full par with the evocation of the Father as creator and the Son as redeemer. We think of the formula of St. Gregory of Nazianzum, saying that the revelation of the Father was the accomplishment of the Old Testament, that of the Son of the New, and that of the Spirit of the Church. The idea is a beautiful one, but it still remains somewhat artificial. In fact, the divine persons reveal themselves as one. The Father is revealed as Father only in the New Testament and the history of the Church. On the other hand, once the divine work is accomplished, the Spirit is revealed in the work of creation and redemption from the very beginning, and the Son was already latent in all things, in a sort of foreshadowing, even before taking flesh and transfiguring them by his presence. Consequently, however satisfying such dichotomies or trichotomies may be for a logical mind, they are dangerous for a living theology and spirituality. This is already somewhat applicable in the case of the liturgy of the *Apostolic Constitutions*. But this defect is still more apparent in the case of the liturgy of St. James, which forces the schematicism to reserve creation alone to the Father, redemption to the Son, and sanctification to the Spirit.

It remains no less true that this latter eucharist itself, despite the accomplished hellenization of its form and of the thought beneath it, is still astonishingly close to the original eucharist. Up to the expansion of the prayer of intercession in the third part, the note of doxology, which is so basic to every eucharist, is felt throughout. Nowhere else is the theme of the universal glorification of God so powerfully expressed from the very beginning, nor so consistently maintained throughout the whole development. No less remarkable, from the viewpoint of original fidelity, is the way in which everything remains centered on the joyful acclamation of the divine mercy, up to the point of the epiclesis and the intercessions. The echoes of the Jewish prayer "For abounding love" which followed the *Qedushah* seem to find a surprising resurgence in this text. This love, this mercy, culminating in the manifestation of the fatherhood of God in regard to his elect, become the key that introduces the Savior and his work into the heart of the Christian eucharist.

We must also underline a paradoxical fact, that shows admirably how the most forthright hellenization of the form and substance of a traditional text in no way means the evaporation or transmutation of its primary content. Hellenic or hellenized spirituality, centering on knowledge is too facilely opposed to Jewish spirituality which is centered on life. It is a keen observation, but one which requires great prudence in generalities of this kind, that all the ancient Christian prayers of the eucharist, following the Jewish prayers, are acts of thanksgiving for knowledge in the praise before the *Sanctus*, and that they return to the praise theme before the anamnesis, even though this second thanksgiving is dominated by life, connecting with it the themes of the knowledge of the divine law and the divine Name. On the other hand, as hellenized as it is, the eucharist of St. James from one end to the other, and right from the beginning, is an act of thanksgiving for life, in which knowledge appears only in fleeting allusions, and solely in the second part.

It is true nonetheless that it has moved away from the Jewish or Judeo-Christian models which gave it its substance much more than was the case with the eucharist of the *Apostolic Constitutions*. The pseudo-Clementine eucharist, in its first part, still retained, along with the predominance of the light and knowledge themes, an act of thanksgiving for the history of salvation in the Old Testament, connected with the thanksgiving for creation. Likewise, its second part, giving thanks for the renewed life in the accomplishment of the history of salvation leading to the redemptive incarnation, still avoided connecting the institution narrative with it. This remained incorporated in the anamnesis, and the epiclesis, as finely worked out as it had become, was still only an appendix to it. On the other hand, in the eucharist of St. James, the institution narrative was absorbed in the act of thanksgiving for the incarnation, and it is the anamnesis that is now merely an appendix at the point where the thanksgiving ends, and the starting point for an epiclesis that has become practically independent. Yet, here as in the 8th book of the *Apostolic Constitutions*, following the anamnesis with all the sacrificial formulas, which were brought together merely to be an expression of the original Jewish "memorial," restores the original unity of perspective of the eucharist: not a sacrifice *and* a memorial, but a sacrifice *as* a memorial.

The Classical Form
of the Byzantine Eucharist:
The East Syrian Survivals
of Intermediary Types

Despite its universal popularity for a time in the east, the liturgy of St. James was to be rather rapidly supplanted by related liturgies. They seem to be only reductions and reworkings, if not of this liturgy itself, at least of analogous liturgies about which the 8th book of the *Apostolic Constitutions* can give us some idea. They are liturgies attributed respectively to St. John Chrysostom and St. Basil.[1] Both were adopted by the great Church of Constantinople, and under its soon to be dominant influence, they replaced the liturgy of St. James, practically everywhere and, in Egypt, the liturgy of St. Mark as well.

The liturgy named after St. John Chrysostom seems at first to have been simply the liturgy used by him at Antioch while he was exercising his priestly and then episcopal ministry there. It is

---

[1] Cf. Hanssens, *Institutiones liturgicae*, tomus III, pars altera, pp. 569 ff.

281

possible that he brought it with him to Constantinople, from where it was to radiate out over the whole Greek-speaking world. It does not seem that he was its author, but only his reviser. This revision is visible on account of a number of formulas bearing the trace of his own personal theological concerns. It is possible that along with these additions, he also made a few abbreviations. What leads us to think so is the existence of a liturgy which is preserved today in Syriac, both by the Syrian Jacobites and Uniates and by the Maronites, under the name "Liturgy of the Twelve Apostles." This seems to come from a Greek text that is anterior to the liturgy named after St. John Chrysostom, in which the additions that bear his mark are not present, although on the other hand, we find a few, certainly very ancient, formulas which have disappeared from the text attributed to this saint.[2]

THE ANTIOCHIAN LITURGY OF THE TWELVE APOSTLES

This liturgy of the Twelve Apostles allows us to make a connection with the text of a short liturgy of Antioch, which is undeniably related to the text attributed to St. James, but which on several points is closer to the liturgy of the *Apostolic Constitutions*.[3]

Here, first, is the part leading up to the *Sanctus*:

The love of God the Father, the grace of the Only-Begotten Son and the communication of the Holy Spirit be with you all.
—And with your spirit.
Let us lift up our hearts.
—We have (lifted them up) to the Lord.
Let us give thanks to the Lord.
—It is meet and right.

It is meet and right to worship you and to glorify you, for you are the true God, together with your Only-Begotten Son and the Holy Spirit. You have brought us into being

---

[2] Cf. H. Engberding, "Die syrische Anaphora der Zwölf Apostel," in *Oriens christianus*, 1937, pp. 213 ff.

[3] In our translation we shall follow the edition of Fr. A. Raes, *Anaphorae syriacae* (Rome, 1940), vol. I, fasc. 2, pp. 212 ff. The basic text of this edition is a manuscript of the tenth century (British Museum, no. 286).

out of nothing, you have lifted us up from the fall, and you have not stopped until you have raised us up even into heaven that we might obtain the Kingdom that is to come. For all this we thank you, you, your Only-Begotten Son and the Holy Spirit. Before and about you stand the many-eyed Cherubim, and the six-winged Seraphim. They glorify and praise, together with all the other heavenly powers, with one unceasing voice, and, in unceasing hymns they proclaim and sing: *Holy, holy, holy, the Lord Sabaoth. Heaven and earth are filled with your glory. Hosanna in the highest. Blessed be he who comes and who will come in the name of the Lord our God. Hosanna in the highest.*

This part seems to be a short form of a text analogous to that of St. James, although here the central mention of the heavenly Jerusalem is replaced by that of the heavenly and eschatological Kingdom. Actually, we may wonder whether this text is an abbreviation of St. James, or whether it is not rather a short form of an analogous but earlier text, which must have taken on some local characteristics at Jerusalem. What follows, as we shall see, reinforces that impression.

Let us go on to the second part as far as the anamnesis:

You are holy and all-holy, together with your Only-Begotten Son and the Holy Spirit. You are holy and all-holy in the majesty of your glory. You have so loved the world that you gave your Only-Begotten Son that whoever believes in him may not perish but have eternal life, (your Son) who has come and who, having fulfilled the whole economy instituted for us, on the night he was betrayed took bread into his holy and spotless hands, and, having raised them to heaven, blessed it, sanctified it and broke it; then he gave it to his disciples and apostles, saying: Take, eat of this all of you, this is my body, broken and given for you and for many, for the remission of sins and life everlasting. Likewise, for the cup, having supped he mixed wine and water, gave thanks, blessed it, sanctified it and, after tasting it, gave it to his disciples and apostles, saying: Take, drink of this all of you, this is the blood of the new covenant, shed for you and for many, and distributed for the remission of sins and life everlasting. Do this as a memorial of me. As often as you eat this bread and drink this cup, you will announce my death and proclaim my resurrection until I come.

(*The people answer:*) Your death, Lord! We proclaim your resurrection and we await your return.

(*The celebrant continues:*) Being mindful, Lord, of your saving command and of the whole economy instituted for us: your cross, your resurrection from the dead on the third day, your ascension into heaven, your sitting at the right hand of the majesty of the Father, your parousia when you will come in glory to judge the living and the dead and render to each according to his works, with compassion, your Church and your flock beseech you, and through you and with you, beseech the Father, saying: have mercy on me. (*The people repeat*: Have mercy on us). And we also, Lord, who have received your graces, we give you thanks for everything and for all.

(*The people*: We praise you.)

What is most noticeable about this part is that as in the eucharist of St. James it is focused upon the recalling of the merciful love that has saved us. But here as in the later texts this recall takes the form of a quotation, in the second person, from the Gospel according to St. John (3, 16). And in this line of tradition this recall from now on absorbs the whole act of thanksgiving for the redemption. Immediately afterwards, through only one connecting phrase, we pass to the institution narrative. The anamnesis is brought about through the same amplification of Pauline origin of "Do this as a memorial of me" that we have found in St. James, although put in the first person, on the lips of Christ. The anamnesis, also as in this other liturgy, is directed toward the epiclesis through an invocation of the divine mercy. But here we see a peculiarity that seems to be very ancient. As in the eucharist of Addai and Mari, the anamnesis is addressed not to the Father, but to the Son. Perhaps more striking is the fact that no explicitly sacrificial formula has yet appeared.

Let us now proceed to the epiclesis and the prayers that follow it:

(*The deacon says:*) In silence and with fear!

(*The celebrant continues:*) We beg you, Lord almighty and God of the powers, prostrate before you, to send your Spirit upon the offerings which are presented and to manifest to us that this bread is the holy body of our Lord Jesus Christ, this cup the blood of this same Jesus Christ, our Lord, so that all who taste of it may obtain life and resurrection, the forgiveness of sins, healing of soul and body, the illumination of the Spirit and assurance before the awesome tribunal of your Christ. Let none among your people, Lord, go astray, but make us worthy to serve you in tranquility, to remain in your service all the days of our life, to enjoy heavenly, immortal and life-giving mysteries, through your grace, your mercy and compassion, now and ever and world without end. (*People*: Amen.)

We offer you, Lord almighty, this spiritual sacrifice for all men, for your catholic Church, for the Bishops who dispense the word of truth, for my unworthiness, for priests and deacons, for all believers of the country, for all the faithful people, for seasonable weather and the fruits of the earth, for our brothers in the faith who are in tribulation, for those who have brought these offerings, for those who are named in the holy Churches ... To each grant the help he needs. To our fathers and brothers who have died in the true faith, grant the divine glory on the day of judgment; enter not into contestation with them, for no living being is guiltless before you: only one was found without sin upon earth, your Only-Begotten Son, our Lord Jesus Christ, the great purifier of our race, through whom we hope to find mercy and forgiveness of sins, for us and for them.

(*The people answer:*) Forgive, blot out our sins. We are mindful above all of the holy Mother of God, Mary ever Virgin, of the holy apostles, the martyrs shining forth with victory, and of all the saints who have been pleasing to you. Through their prayer and their intercession, preserve us from evil, and let your mercy be upon us, in this world and in the world to come, that we may glorify your blessed Name, through Jesus Christ and the Holy Spirit.

(*The people conclude:*) As it was always and world without end.

Once again we find ourselves here in the presence of archaic details. The terms "offering" and "sacrifice" each appear only once, the first in the epiclesis and the second at the beginning of the intercessions. The descent of the Spirit is asked, not as in St. James so that he will make the elements the body and blood of Christ, but, as in the *Apostolic Constitutions*, that he manifest that they are so, by producing in the participants all the effects of the mystery. Instead of directly introducing the prayers that follow (and which are remarkably precise) the epiclesis has also retained its own conclusion.

FROM THE LITURGY OF THE TWELVE APOSTLES TO THE LITURGY OF ST. JOHN CHRYSOSTOM

The comparison of the text with the one which is today widespread under the name of St. John Chrysostom is most interesting. Note that the first formula of the dialogue with the exception of a few minute differences was taken literally from the Pauline text, which seems to be a first indication of a theological concern to return to the letter of the scriptural quotes, rather than an archaism. We shall see a much more striking manifestation of this in the whole eucharist of St. Basil and other analogous liturgies.

Leaving that aside, here is the form that the first part of the eucharistic prayer has taken:

It is meet and right to hymn you, to give thanks to you, to worship you in every place of your sovereignty: for you are God, *ineffable, inconceivable, invisible, incomprehensible, who are ever and for ever the same*, you and your Only-Begotten Son and your Holy Spirit; you have brought us to being out of nothing, you have lifted us up from the fall, and you have not stopped until you have raised us up even into heaven that we might obtain the Kingdom that is to come. For all this we thank you, you, your Only-Begotten Son and your Holy Spirit, *for all your benefits we know and for those we do not know, for those manifest and those hidden; we give you thanks also for this service* ($\lambda\varepsilon\iota\tauo\upsilon\varrho\gamma\iota\alpha_{\varsigma}$) *which we beseech you to accept from our hands, although thousands of Archangels attend you and tens of thousands of Angels*, the Cherubim and the six-winged, many-eyed, Seraphim, soaring, flying, proclaiming, crying out and saying: Holy, holy, holy, Lord Sabaoth; heaven and earth are filled with your glory; hosanna in the highest; blessed is he who comes in the name of the Lord; hosanna in the highest.[4]

It is clear that the preceding Syriac text translates a Greek text that is practically identical with the one we have just translated, with the exception of the series of adjectives we have italicized in the beginning and the other expansion toward the end, where we note particularly the rather curious introduction of a sacrificial formula at this juncture. We shall return to this point.

> Together with them, we also, Master of Powers and lover of men, proclaim and say: you are holy and all-holy, as well as your Only-Begotten Son and your Holy Spirit; you are holy and all-holy and filled with majesty is your glory, you who have so loved the world that you gave your Only-Begotten Son that whoever believes in him may not perish but have everlasting life, the one who has come and who, having accomplished the whole economy instituted for us, on the night he handed himself over, took bread in his holy, pure, and spotless hands, gave thanks, blessed it, broke it and gave it to his holy disciples and apostles, saying: Take, eat, this is my body for you, likewise also the cup, after having supped, saying: Drink of this all of you, this is my blood of the new covenant shed for you and for many for the remission of sins (*The people answer*: Amen).
>
> Being mindful then of this his saving command, and of everything that has happened for our sakes, the cross, the burial, the resurrection on the third day, the return to heaven, the sitting at (your) right hand, the second and glorious parousia, offering to you what is yours out of what is yours, in all and for all ...
>
> (The people answer:) ... We hymn you, we bless you, we give thanks to you, Lord, and we beseech you, our God.[5]

Note here again that with the disappearance of the transition from the first to the second person of the Trinity in the address of the prayer, there is the substitution of a sacrificial formula (close to those found at Rome and at Alexandria) for the simple invoca-

---

[4] Brightman, *op. cit.*, pp. 321 ff. The text followed is that of the *Codex Barberini*, of the beginning of the ninth century.

[5] Brightman, *op. cit.*, pp. 324 ff.

tion of the divine mercy. It is, moreover, a perfect expression of the original sense of the memorial. But what is extraordinary, and what constitutes a unique fact in liturgical history, the anamnesis no longer depends on the phrase of Christ: "Do this as a memorial of me." While this sentence in the Syrian liturgy of the Twelve Apostles as in St. James is expanded and specified through the influence of St. Paul's words (1 Cor. 11:16) already quoted in the liturgy of the *Apostolic Constitutions*, here it has completely disappeared.

Again, we offer you this spiritual (λογικήν) and unbloody worship and we call upon you, pray you, beseech you to send your Holy Spirit upon us and upon these gifts presented, and to make this bread the precious body of your Christ, changing it by your Holy Spirit (Amen), and what is in this cup the precious blood of your Christ, changing it by your Holy Spirit (Amen), so that they may be for those who partake of them, for the temperance (νῆψιν) of the soul, the remission of sins, the communication of your Holy Spirit, the fulness of the Kingdom, free access (παρρησίαν) to you, and not for judgment or condemnation.

Again, we offer you this spiritual worship for the fathers, the patriarchs, the prophets, the apostles, the preachers, the evangelists, the martyrs, the confessors, the continent who have gone to rest in the faith and every righteous man accomplished in the faith, above all the all-holy, pure, all-glorious and blessed one, our Lady, the Mother of God and ever-Virgin Mary, St. John the Fore-runner and Baptist, and the holy apostles worthy of all praise (πανευφήμων), and Saint N. whom we commemorate, and all the saints, through whose prayers please protect us, O God. Be mindful also of all those who sleep in the hope of the resurrection of eternal life, and give them the rest where the light of your countenance radiates (ἐπισκοπεῖ).

We call upon you also, Lord, to be mindful of every orthodox episcopate that dispenses the word of your truth, of the whole presbytery, of the diaconate in Christ and every sacred order.

Again, we offer you this spiritual worship for the inhabited earth, for the holy, catholic and apostolic Church, for those who spend their lives in purity and holiness, for those who are upon the mountains, in caves and the holes in the ground, for the most faithful king, for the Christ-loving queen, for their whole palace and army; grant them, Lord, a peaceable kingdom, that in this quietude we may lead a calm and tranquil life in all godliness and holiness. Be mindful, Lord, of the city in which we live and of every city and town, as well as of those who dwell therein in faith.

Above all, be mindful, Lord, of our archbishop N.

Be mindful, Lord, of those who travel by sea, who are on a voyage, who are sick or maimed or captive and of their salvation.

Be mindful, Lord, of those who bring fruit and do good in your holy Churches, and who are mindful of the poor, and send down upon us your mercies, and grant us, with one mouth and one heart, to glorify and to hymn your most precious and majestic name, of the Father and the Son and the Holy Spirit, now and always, world without end. Amen.[6]

Here the epiclesis begins with a third sacrificial formula absent from the Syriac anaphora, which seems to be taken from the anamnesis of St. James. Like the epiclesis of this latter, it asks not only that the spirit *manifest* that the bread and wine are the body and blood of Christ, but that he *make* them this body and blood. For the first time we see this supplementary specification introduced: "changing them ($\mu\varepsilon\tau\alpha\beta\acute{\alpha}\lambda\lambda\omega\nu$) by your Holy Spirit." This constitutes the first introduction in a eucharistic prayer of a technical theological formula. It is also found in the text of St. Basil that has become classic.

Again, as in St. James, the epiclesis is extended through the intercessions, without losing its continuity, until it finally ends at the doxology of the divine Name.

The additions which we have italicized at the beginning pose several problems.

The series of adjectives emphasizing the divine transcendence concords too precisely with the concerns of St. John Chrysostom in his *De incognoscibilitate Dei* for it not to have come from his pen. We must not see in it, as too many modern commentators on this tract have imagined, an influence of the pagan mysteries

---

[6] Brightman, *op. cit.*, pp. 329 ff.

or of Neo-Platonism so much as a very live reaction, begun by the Cappadocians, against the Anomean Arians, like Eunomius, who claimed that they could reduce the divine essence to an adequate concept. It is the same biblical concern that may have given rise to the invisible benefits of God, and the reintroduction of a more extensive mention of the angelic beings.

As for the sacrificial formula added before the *Sanctus*, it has no traditional antecedent in this precise position. In its substance it might come either from Hippolytus or a tradition which he himself had found.

THE LITURGY OF ST. BASIL, ITS COMPOSITION AND THE DIFFERENT STAGES OF ITS EVOLUTION

Used side by side today in the Byzantine world or in areas influenced by Byzantium, there is another anaphora, which is undoubtedly later than that of the Twelve Apostles, but certainly anterior to the reworking of it that we have just studied. It is the one attributed to St. Basil of Caesarea.

When its present text is compared to various earlier states which we can point out through an ancient Syriac version, an Armenian version, undoubtedly from the fifth century, and finally the composition still older than all of these other documents which has been preserved for us in Egypt, it poses a delicate critical problem. Dom Engberding, who treats of it, followed in particular by Baumstark, thinks that the Egyptian text must be the text of an ancient Cappadocian anaphora that Basil may later have remodeled, and which would subsequently have been further developed.[7] Fr. Hanssens questions this theory, and thinks that the attribution to St. Basil of the text that the Egyptians knew at a very early date would be incomprehensible if it were simply a question of a text serving as a basis for his own composition.[8] For our part, we should be inclined to think that this form, which is the oldest one available to us, was already the result of a very

---

[7] Cf. H. Engberding, *Das eucharistische Hochgebet der Basilius-liturgie* (Münster-in-Westf., 1931) and A. Baumstark, *Comparative Liturgy*, pp. 52 ff.

[8] I. Hanssens, *Institutiones liturgicae*, t. III, pars altera, p. 578.

personal synthesis which Basil himself may have expanded somewhat later and which after his time would have been further completed, without being substantially altered.

Whatever the case, the anaphora bearing his name was brought
at an early date into Egypt (perhaps by himself on a trip that he
made there), and must soon after, undoubtedly under a longer
form, have been transported to Constantinople, probably by a
bishop who was originally from Cappadocia and who could very
well have been a friend of Gregory of Nazianzum. It is certain
that it was established there a long time before the other anaphora
attributed to St. John Chrysostom. It was from there that it must
have spread throughout the East, before being gradually supplanted
by the latter.

It is likely that Basil's eucharist, like that of the Twelve Apostles,
was originally a condensation of a more copious text, which seems
however to have been closer to the 8th book of the *Apostolic
Constitutions* than to that of St. James. As was the case with the
text of the Twelve Apostles, this short formula in its turn underwent a process of amplification, which was to end up in the form
that is used today in the Byzantine liturgy. But, from its brief
form through its successive amplifications, it seems to have responded to a conscious plan to produce a eucharist that was as biblical
as possible in its composition. The eucharist of the 8th book of
the *Apostolic Constitutions* and even more the liturgy of St. James
had already incorporated into their texts many a biblical citation. But it seems that St. Basil was the first composer of a Christian eucharistic prayer to seek to use only literally biblical formulas in it. We could not find better confirmation of an only apparently paradoxical law suggested by Baumstark: when a liturgical text reproduces textually biblical formulas, it is a sign
not of antiquity, but of a late reworking.[9]

It is a fact that all the ancient liturgical texts, to the extent
that they are still contemporary, if not to the composition at least
to the canonization of the texts of the New Testament, manifest
no tendency to restrict themselves to their wording, nor even to
occasional citations. It is with the first great West Syrian litur-

[9] Baumstark, *op. cit.*, p. 58.

gies, admitting their relatively late date, that the first attempt was made to make use of the biblical texts word for word. But we must go to St. Basil, whose impassioned attachment to a thorough study of the Bible, inspired by Origen, is known, in order to find a eucharist which is nothing but a biblical patchwork.

Exercises of this type, which we should be tempted to see as tiresome diversions of barbaric childishness, were the delight of the *literati* of the age. After composing gospel narratives in the form of Homeric or Virgilian *centones*, once the Greek Bible came in turn to be imposed as the first literary monument of a hellenized Christianity, people set about reciprocally creating new texts by making use of the same procedure in formulas taken from the inspired writings.[10] Despite the peculiarly artificial character that such a method of composition risked giving St. Basil's eucharist, his familiarity with Scripture together with the synthetic power of his thought, since he went not merely to the wording but to the themes themselves, made his text one of the most beautiful eucharistic formularies of tradition. As with St. James, its trinitarian schema is impeccable, but the abundance of biblical material used so cleverly gives him more genuine adaptability than we might have expected. The result is a magnificent litany of all the titles and all the attributions of the divine persons in the Bible, beneath which we can see Origen's great vision, corrected by St. Athanasius and his successors, of the "economy" of salvation.

We shall give this text in its complete form, which has been in use for a long time in the Byzantine rite, but we shall put in italics the formulas added to St. Basil's text, as Dom Engberding thinks he can reconstruct it, and on the other hand in small capitals the original state that the Egyptian formulas show us.

You who are, Master, Lord, God, *almighty, adorable Father,* HOW MEET AND RIGHT IT IS in the majesty *of your holiness to praise you, to hymn you, to bless you, to worship you,* TO GIVE THANKS TO YOU, TO GLORIFY YOU, YOU WHO ALONE ARE REALLY GOD (ὄντως ὄντα θεόν), and to offer to you with a contrite heart and a humbled mind this our reasonable worship, for it is you who have given us to know your truth.

---

[10] Cf. P. de Labriolle, *Histoire de la littérature latine chrétienne*, 3rd. ed. (Paris, 1947), t. II, pp. 480-481.

And who is worthy to praise your wonders (δυναστείας), to make all your praises heard? Master of all things, Lord of heaven, of earth and OF EVERY CREATURE VISIBLE AND INVISIBLE, YOU WHO ARE SEATED UPON A THRONE OF GLORY, AND WHO PLUMB THE DEPTHS, without beginning, invisible, *incomprehensible, indescribable, immutable.* THE FATHER OF OUR LORD JESUS CHRIST, *of the great God and* Savior *of* our hope, who is the Image of your goodness, the imprint (σφραγίς) equal to its model, *who shows you in himself,* you the Father, living Word, true God before the worlds, Wisdom, Life, Sanctification, Power, true Light, through whom (παρ' οὗ), the Holy Spirit was manifested, the Spirit of Truth, the gift of sonship, the pledge of our future inheritance, the first fruits of eternal good things, the life-giving power, the source of sanctification, through which (παρ' οὗ) every rational (λογική) and spiritual creature is made capable of rendering you worship and gives you eternal glorification, *for all things are in your service.* FOR IT IS YOU WHO ARE PRAISED BY THE ANGELS, THE ARCHANGELS, THE THRONES, THE DOMINATIONS, THE PRINCIPALITIES, THE AUTHORITIES, THE POWERS, AND THE MANY-EYED CHERUBIM; THE SERAPHIM ARE AROUND YOU, EACH HAVING SIX WINGS, with two they veil their face, with two the feet, and with two they fly, they cry out to one another with mouths that do not tire, in doxologies which are never silent, *singing, proclaiming,* CRYING OUT THE VICTORY HYMN AND SAYING: HOLY, HOLY, HOLY, LORD SABAOTH, HEAVEN AND EARTH ARE FILLED WITH YOUR GLORY. HOSANNA IN THE HIGHEST. BLESSED (BE) HE WHO COMES IN THE NAME OF THE LORD. HOSANNA IN THE HIGHEST.

Together with these blessed powers, Master, lover of men, we also, sinners, cry out and we say: HOW HOLY (ἅγιος) AND ALL-HOLY ARE YOU, and there is no limit to the majesty of your holiness, *and (you are) holy* (ὅσιος) *in all your works, for* you have disposed all things for us (ἐπήγαγες ἡμῖν) in righteousness and true judgment. HAVING MADE MAN, in taking dust from the earth, and having honored him with your image, YOU HAD PLACED HIM IN THE GARDEN OF DELIGHT in promising him immortality of life and the enjoyment of the eternal good things in the observation of your commands. BUT WHEN HE DISOBEYED YOU, *you,* the true God *who created him,* AND HE WAS LED ASTRAY BY THE DECEPTION OF THE SERPENT

AND DIED in his own transgressions, you CAST HIM OUT in your justice, O God, FROM THE PARADISE IN THIS WORLD and you caused him to return to the earth from which he was taken, arranging (οἰκονομῶν) for him the salvation (which was to come) of the resurrection (παλιγγενεσίας) in your Christ himself: For YOU DID NOT REJECT FOREVER YOUR WORK, which you had made, in your goodness, *and you have not forgotten the work of your hands*, but you have visited it in manifold ways through the bosom of your mercy, you have sent him (the) prophets, you have worked wonders through your saints who were pleasing to you in all generations, YOU HAVE SPOKEN TO US THROUGH THE MOUTH OF YOUR SERVANTS THE PROPHETS, ANNOUNCING TO US BEFOREHAND THE SALVATION TO COME, you have given the law to help us, established the angels to preserve us. BUT WHEN THE FULNESS OF TIME CAME, YOU SPOKE TO US THROUGH YOUR SON HIMSELF, through whom you had also created the ages, he who is the splendor of your glory and the form of your substance, bearing all things by the word of your power, did not look upon equality with you, God and Father, as a plunder, but, being God before the ages, he was seen upon the earth, and he lived (συνανεστράφη) among men, and HAVING TAKEN FLESH FROM A HOLY VIRGIN, he emptied himself (ἐκένωσεν), taking the form of a servant, conforming himself to the body of our lowliness in order to conform us to the image of his glory. For, since by a man came sin into the world, and by sin death, it pleased your Only-Begotten Son, who is in your bosom, God and Father, born of a woman, *the holy Mother of God and ever-Virgin Mary, born under the law*, to condemn sin in his flesh, so that we who died in Adam may be brought to life in him, your Christ. Having lived as a citizen of this world (ἐμπολιτευσάμενος τῷ κόσμῳ τούτῳ), GIVING THE ORDINANCES OF SALVATION, turning us away from the waywardness of idols, he introduced us into the knowledge of you, the true God and the Father, HAVING ACQUIRED US FOR HIMSELF AS A PEOPLE WHICH IS HIS OWN, a royal priesthood, a holy nation, having purified us BY WATER and sanctified us BY THE HOLY SPIRIT, HE GAVE HIMSELF OVER IN EXCHANGE TO DEATH, IN WHICH WE HAVE BEEN HELD, SOLD BY SIN, AND HE DESCENDED INTO HELL (εἰς τὸν ἅδην) THROUGH THE CROSS, in order to fill all things with himself (or to accomplish all things by himself), *he loosed the bonds of death,*

and, HAVING RISEN ON THE THIRD DAY, and having opened
to the flesh the path of the resurrection from the dead, since
it was not possible that the dispenser of life would be dominated by corruption, he became the first fruits of those who
sleep, the first-born from among the dead, in order to have
the primacy in all things, and, ASCENDING INTO HEAVEN, HE
SITS AT THE RIGHT HAND OF YOUR MAJESTY IN THE HIGHEST,
HE WHO WILL RENDER TO EACH ONE ACCORDING TO HIS WORKS.

MOREOVER HE HAS LEFT US AS A MEMORIAL (ὑπομνήματα)
OF HIS SAVING PASSION, what we have presented to you in
accordance with his own orders. For, WHEN HE WENT OFF
TO HIS voluntary, reproachless (ἀοίδιμον) and lifegiving
DEATH, on the night he was betrayed FOR THE LIFE OF THE
WORLD, TAKING BREAD INTO HIS HOLY AND SPOTLESS HANDS,
AND HAVING PRESENTED IT TO YOU (ἀναδείξας), HE BROKE IT
AND GAVE IT TO HIS HOLY DISCIPLES AND APOSTLES, SAYING:
TAKE, EAT, THIS IS MY BODY, BROKEN FOR YOU FOR THE RE-
MISSION OF SINS. LIKEWISE, TAKING ALSO THE CUP OF THE
FRUIT OF THE VINE, HAVING MINGLED IT, HAVING GIVEN THANKS,
HE BLESSED IT, SANCTIFIED IT AND GAVE IT TO HIS HOLY DIS-
CIPLES AND APOSTLES, SAYING: DRINK OF THIS ALL OF YOU,
THIS IS MY BLOOD OF THE NEW COVENANT, SHED FOR YOU AND
FOR MANY, FOR THE REMISSION OF SINS. DO THIS AS A MEMORIAL
OF ME: FOR AS OFTEN AS YOU EAT THIS BREAD AND DRINK THIS
CUP, YOU ANNOUNCE MY DEATH AND YOU PROCLAIM MY RE-
SURRECTION. THEREFORE, MASTER, WE ALSO, MINDFUL OF
HIS SAVING SUFFERINGS, of his life-giving cross, of his burial
for three days, OF HIS RESURRECTION FROM THE DEAD, OF HIS
RETURN TO HEAVEN, OF HIS SITTING AT YOUR RIGHT HAND,
GOD AND FATHER, AND OF HIS GLORIOUS AND AWESOME SECOND
COMING, OFFERING TO YOU WHAT IS YOUR OWN FROM WHAT
IS YOUR OWN, IN ALL AND FOR ALL, ON ACCOUNT OF THIS, ALL-
HOLY MASTER, WE ALSO, SINNERS, YOUR UNWORTHY SERVANTS,
whom you have made worthy to serve (λειτουργεῖν) at your
holy altar, not on account of our justifications, for we have
done nothing good on earth, but on account of your mercies
and your compassion, that you have shed abundantly upon
us, we are bold to approach your holy altar, and, bringing
forth the symbols (προσθέντες τὰ ἀντίτυπα) of the holy body
and blood of your Christ, WE BESEECH YOU, and we call upon
you, O Holy of Holies, THROUGH THE BENEVOLENCE OF YOUR

GOODNESS, TO CAUSE YOUR HOLY SPIRIT TO COME UPON US AND UPON THESE GIFTS WHICH WE PRESENT TO YOU, THAT HE MAY, bless them, SANCTIFY THEM AND PRESENT (ἀναδεῖξαι) TO US (IN) THIS BREAD THE PRECIOUS BODY OF OUR LORD, GOD AND SAVIOR JESUS CHRIST, AND (IN) THIS CUP THE PRECIOUS BLOOD OF OUR LORD, GOD AND SAVIOR JESUS CHRIST, SHED FOR THE LIFE OF THE WORLD, *changing them by your Holy Spirit.* AND ALL OF US, WHO PARTAKE of the one bread and the (one) cup, UNITE US WITH ONE ANOTHER IN the fellowship in THE ONE SPIRIT, and CAUSE that not one of us will partake in the holy body and blood of your Christ for judgment and condemnation, but THAT WE MIGHT FIND MERCY AND GRACE WITH ALL THE SAINTS THAT HAVE BEEN PLEASING TO YOU IN THE AGES, *the ancestors, the fathers, the patriarchs, the prophets, the apostles, the heralds, the evangelists, the martyrs, the confessors, the doctors and every righteous spirit accomplished in the faith.*[11]

If we observe the variations in typography which we have used, it can be immediately seen that the later additions to the last text of St. Basil are of little importance. They are merely a few rhetorical amplifications, short explanatory formulas, or an extension of the biblical citations. We have not given here, as we did not in the case of the anaphora of John Chrysostom, the later additions to the epiclesis. But it will be noted that the clause "changing them by your Spirit," which we have reproduced, seems already to be an interpolation (undoubtedly borrowed from the preceding text), which in our text does violence to the grammar.

---

[11] See Brightman, *op. cit.*, pp. 321 ff. for the text. Cf. H. Engberding, *op. cit.*, for the separation of these different layers, as well as the Alexandrian Greek text, given by Renaudot, *op. cit.*, t. I, pp. 64 ff.

The biblical references are essentially:

Psalm 50: 19 (here we are following the Septuagint enumeration); Romans 12: 1; cf. Romans 2: 20; Psalms 25: 7; Daniel 3: 55; 1 Timothy 1: 11; Hebrews: 1: 3; John 14: 8; 1 John 1:1; John 1: 9; Romans 8: 15; Ephesians 1: 14; Psalm 118: 91; Psalm 144: 17; cf. Psalm 88: 15; Genesis 2; Genesis 3; Romans 8: 10; Genesis 3: 23; Genesis 3: 19; Hebrews 1: 1; Galatians 4: 4; Hebrews 1: 1-3; Philippians 2: 6; Baruch 3: 38; Philippians 2: 7 and 2: 31; Romans 8: 29; Romans 5: 12; John 1: 18; Romans 8: 3; John 17: 3; 1 Peter 2: 9; Romans 5: 12; John 1: 18; Romans 8: 3; John 17: 3; 1 Peter 2: 9; Romans 7: 14; Acts 2: 24; Acts 3: 15; 1 Corinthians 15: 20; Colossians 1: 18; Hebrews 1: 3; etc.

If, inversely, we look at the oldest form of the text, it strikes us by its sobriety (especially noticeable in the part preceding the *Sanctus*), but also by the biblical richness that its schema already has. The whole drama of sin and redemption is summed up in the alienation of man brought about by sin, and marked by death, and, thanks to the "exchange" to which Christ consents, in the reconstitution of mankind into a people which is his own and which finds life again through its being brought together. Baptism is thus recalled in connection with the redemptive work of the Spirit who is mentioned as the one who in the sacramental mystery communicates to us the effect of what was fulfilled in Christ himself. In its elementary form, the epiclesis again introduces the Spirit as the one who, by "presenting" us with the very body and blood of Christ under the "antitypes" of bread and wine, unites us to one another in one Spirit (the Egyptian text specified: "in one body and in one Spirit").

Such a remarkable continuity of development as this, which is already biblical and particularly Pauline, is in no way toned down by the amplifications made by St. Basil. The anthology of biblical citations that he grafts onto it merely gives increased stress to each of the divine persons. The result is a eucharist which is no less expressly trinitarian than St. James', but which escapes from the much too logical over-simplification of the latter: Father-creation, Son-redemption, Spirit-sanctification. Quite the contrary: St. Basil's chief amplification is introduced from the very first part, the thanksgiving for creation, in a way that shows how, at the beginning of all things, the Father and the Son with the Holy Spirit are inseparably united even in their distinction. Bringing together the Epistle to the Hebrews, the prologue of St. John and the great christological texts of St. Paul, the Son is praised as the living image of the Father, the Word in whom he expresses himself entirely, the lifegiving Wisdom which sanctifies and illuminates us. Through him, following the teaching of the two great complementary texts on the Spirit in Romans and Galatians, the Holy Spirit comes to us and realizes in us this sanctification whose fruit is our entering into a share in the Son's own sonship. Hence this glorification of the Father in which, from now on, we can take part as an anticipated inauguration in the Spirit of the eternal life of which Christ constitutes the promise.

After the *Sanctus*, the thanksgiving for the redemption is nurtured by a vision of the "economy" of salvation, dominated by the text of Philippians on the Son's "emptying" of himself[12] as the compensator for Adam's unbridled covetousness, and of Galatians, on the Son subjecting himself to the limitations and the constraints of sinful humanity in order to liberate us.[13] The transition is made from one to the other through the evocation, taken from the Epistle to the Romans, of Christ accepting death in order to free us from sin, just as Adam, in consenting to sin had enshrouded us in death.[14]

The amplifications before this point that bear on the evocation of the Old Testament all focus upon preparing us for the vision of faith of this opposition between sin-death, and life-redemption in the ἀγάπη where Jesus appears as the Second Adam, repairing the sin and the wrong-doing of the first. It will also be noted, in the same perspective, how in each of the two parts of the thanksgiving, St. Basil has connected the theme of "knowledge" and the Light of truth which brings us this knowledge in Christ, with the theme that was first exclusively directed toward created and restored life. This is a remarkable attestation of the fact that he did not augment the text on which he was working simply to develop it, but was concerned with restoring it to the fulness of the original eucharist. We shall see further on other evidences of the incontestable existence of this concern of his.

If we go on to the anamnesis, we notice that it has retained all of its original strength, as in the pseudo-Clementine liturgy both in its developed form and in the oldest form of our text. Contrary to the liturgy of St. James, where the institution narrative was detached from it in order to be placed in its chronological position in the thanksgiving for the redemption, here, as in the 8th book of the *Apostolic Constitutions* (and the anaphora of Serapion) the narrative is not only still bound to the anamnesis, but enclosed within it. Notice the restraint in the sacrificial expressions.

---

[12] Cf. Philippians 2: 5 ff.
[13] Cf. Galatians 4: 4.
[14] Cf. Romans 5: 12 ff.

The later developments of St. Basil only further underline the fact that we are bringing forth or "proposing" to God simply what he himself "presents" to us through Christ. We could offer nothing of ourselves to be re-presented to God, but only what Christ himself has first "presented" to him and enjoins us to re-place before him: the "memorial" of his saving passion.

This leads us to specify the meaning of the verb ἀναδεῖξαι which our text first uses in recalling the action of Christ at the Last Supper, and then again in the epiclesis (which is so closely connected with the anamnesis to the point of being merely its climax) to express what we are expecting from the coming of the Spirit. The same word used in both cases well shows the consecratory significance attached to it. Just as first celebration of the eucharist of the bread and wine as his body and blood, Christ has represented and efficaciously signified to the Father his sacrifice which was to be accomplished upon the Cross we expect that the Spirit will represent them to us as this same body and blood through which we shall be associated with the New Adam and his redemptive work. It is in this way that the ἀντίτυπα of his redemptive death, which we now "propose" to the Father, will not be symbols empty of content but the expression of the mysterious but real and efficacious presence of what they express. Moreover, the consecration of the bread and wine, in this light, is not isolated from our own consecration whereby the Spirit will make us one body in Christ. But, reciprocally, this ultimate fulfilment of the eucharist in us is based on the conviction that the power of the Spirit of Christ assures its permanent content to the memorial which he established once and for all for the Church which has faith in the word of the Savior. After this, there is hardly any need to underline how intimate the connection in this epiclesis is between the acceptance of the sacrificial memorial, the consecration of the elements and the effects of our participation: making us all the body of Christ in its fulness.

There is scarcely any other example in an elaborate liturgical text, of such a perfect fusion between the theological developments of the end of the fourth century and a vision of the eucharist that is so completely faithful to the original substance and unity of its content. Thus, far from being a simple mosaic of artificially connected biblical texts, this composition is merely an explication of the most primitive core of the eucharist by means of the connections that it controls and organizes. Far from becoming emancipated from the primary movement of the divine Word, speculation remains here so profoundly and completely rooted in it that it naturally espouses its most varied expressions. It reassembles them then not in an artificial order but in one which clearly shows their underlying connections.

The very full intercession which, in turn, is closely linked with the final words of the epiclesis is hardly less deserving of our attention. The epiclesis terminated with the evocation of all the saints, into whose fellowship the eucharist brings us. The priest then continues:

> ... especially the all-holy, spotless, pre-eminently blessed, our glorious Lady the Mother of God and ever-Virgin Mary,
>
> St. John the prophet, forerunner and baptist, the holy apostles worthy of all praise ($\pi\alpha\nu\varepsilon\nu\varphi\acute{\eta}\mu\omega\nu$), Saint ... whose memory we celebrate, and all the saints; through their prayers deign to protect ($\grave{\varepsilon}\pi\iota\sigma\varkappa\acute{\varepsilon}\psi\alpha\iota$) us, O God.
>
> Again, remember all those who have gone to sleep before (us) in the hope of the resurrection of eternal life; for the salvation, the protection, the forgiveness of sins of the servant of God ... (*Memento of the living*); for the rest, the remission of the soul of your servant ...: in a place of light, from where pain and groanings have fled, grant him rest, O our God (*Memento of the dead*), grant them rest where the light of your countenance shines; we beseech you further, Lord, to be mindful of your holy catholic and apostolic Church, from one end of the inhabited earth to the other, grant her peace, to her whom you have acquired for yourself through the precious blood of your Christ, and strengthen this holy house until the end of the ages:
>
> Remember, Lord, those who have brought you these gifts, those for whom, by whom, and in whose intention they were brought:
>
> Remember, Lord, those who bear fruit and who accomplish good works in your holy Churches by remembering the poor: grant them in exchange your heavenly riches and gifts; grant them in return for the things of the earth, heavenly things, for temporal things, eternal things, for corruptible things,

the incorruptible; remember, Lord, those who are in deserts, on mountains, in sepulchres and in the holes in the earth;

Remember, Lord, those (who live) in virginity, godliness, asceticism and who pass their lives in holiness; remember, Lord, our most venerable and most faithful kings, whom you have deemed worthy to reign upon earth; crown them with truth and benevolence; extend your shadow over their heads on the day of battle; strengthen their arm; exalt their right hand; strengthen their rule; submit to them the barbaric nations who want war; grant them a profound and immutable peace; tell their hearts good things for your Church and all your people, so that in the serenity that they will provide us we may live a peaceable and tranquil life, in all godliness and holiness;

Remember, Lord, every principality and authority, our brothers who are in the palace and all the army; preserve the good in their goodness, and make the wicked good through your goodness;

Remember, Lord, the people about us, and those who are absent for a just cause, have mercy on them and on us, according to the multitude of your mercy: fill their barns with all good things, preserve their marriages in peace and concord, bring up their children, instruct their youth, strengthen their old people, give courage to those who are failing, bring together the scattered, bring back the wayward, and unite them to your holy catholic and apostolic Church; deliver those who are afflicted by unclean spirits; sail with those who are at sea; accompany those who travel on land; take care of widows; protect orphans; free the captives; heal the sick; remember, O God, all those who are under judgment, in exile, in any tribulation or need, or in trial, and all those who have need of your great compassion, and those who love us, those who hate us and those who have asked us in our unworthiness to pray for them; and all your people, be mindful, Lord our God, and pour down on all the richness of your mercy, granting to all what they ask (of you) for their salvation. And those whom we have not remembered, out of ignorance, forgetfulness, or because of their multitude, do you remember them, O God, who know the stature and visage of each, who know each one from his mother's womb. For you, Lord, are the help of the helpless, the hope of the hopeless, the Savior of the afflicted, the port of those at sea, the physician of the sick: be all for all, you who know each one, his request, his household, and his need. Deliver, Lord, this city and every city and town from want, from famine, from earthquakes, from shipwrecks, from fire, from the sword, from foreign invasion, from civil war;

In the first place, remember, Lord, our archbishop ...: grant to your holy Churches that (he dwell) in peace, safety, honor, health, longevity, ministering faithfully the word of your truth;

remember, Lord, every bishopric of the orthodox, ministering faithfully the word of your truth;

remember me also, Lord, in my unworthiness according to the multitude of your mercies; forgive me every voluntary transgression, and do not take away on account of my sin the grace of your Holy Spirit from these gifts presented;

remember, Lord, the presbytery, the diaconate in Christ, and every sacred order, and do not confound any of us who stand about your holy altar;

look upon us in your goodness, Lord, manifest yourself to us in the richness of your mercies; grant us seasonable weather and fruitful seasons; give us showers upon the earth that they may bear fruit; bless the crown of the year with your goodness; cause schisms in the Churches to cease; put an end to the attacks of the gentiles; speedily bring to a halt the rise of heresy by the power of your Holy Spirit; receive us all into your Kingdom, consecrating us as sons of light and sons of the day; grant us your own peace and your own love, Lord, our God, for you have made us a gift of everything, and give us one mouth and one heart to glorify and to hymn your Name of incomparable majesty (πάντιμον καὶ μεγαλοπρεπές), of the Father, the Son, and the Holy Spirit, now and always, and forever and ever.[15]

Less emotional and more temperate than the intercession in the liturgy of St. James, this intercession is assuredly one of the most beautiful and most harmonious formulas of this type bequeathed to us by Christian antiquity. Once again we must point out

---

[15] For the whole end of this prayer we are following Brightman's text (after the Codex Barberini).

how very especially close it is to the most ancient wording of the
Christian prayer, with expressions that are still very near to the
Jewish prayer itself. It is not only every petition's direct connection with the memorial through the formula "Remember" that attests to this. The unfolding of the prayer itself assembles the
whole content of the Eighteen Blessings more precisely than any
other previously cited Christian formulary. And what is more,
it follows the progression of these prayers more closely than any
other text. Especially noteworthy is the fact that the commemoration of the saints, and first of all those of the Old Testament (the
Virgin, the Baptist and the apostles appearing as the end of the
Old Testament line), constitutes the basis of the whole prayer,
as in the Jewish *Tefillah*. Note in this regard that the mention
of the faithful departed continues the evocation of the saints
without interruption (a noteworthy sign of archaism). The final
return of the prayer to the celebrants of the eucharist, together
with the consecutive summary of the intentions of this celebration
is no less interesting. While in the West Syrian liturgy's systematic
reassembling of the elements of the eucharist everything that
came from the Jewish *Abodah* and *Tefillah* "blessings" generally
tended to become absorbed in the synthetic epiclesis, here we find
the original content in its original position.

These last peculiarities of the eucharist of St. Basil confirm the
impression that in re-working the West Syrian eucharist he had
the conscious intention of restoring to it many original elements
which were already tending to disappear in the pseudo-Clementine
and which the working out of the new synthesis in the liturgy of
St. James completely obliterated. It seems undeniable that in
composing his own formulary he had before him some particularly
archaic models like the author of the *Apostolic Constitutions*.
But he seems to have taken still greater care than the latter in his
respect for its original design. We may even wonder if he did not
go directly to the Jewish formularies. With such a disciple of
Origen's exegesis, recourse to the *Judaica* as well as the biblical
texts, as exceptional as this might appear in his time, would not
be unlikely. Fr. Ligier seems to have given proof of such borrowings
in the prayers proper to the Basilian anaphora for preparation for

communion.[16] In any case, it is certain that no re-formulation of
the Christian eucharist that is as late as this one, seems to be so
precisely informed about its origins or so careful in preserving
their spirit even to the letter.

SYRIAN SURVIVAL IN THE LONG FORM OF ADDAI AND MARI

These remarks on the deliberate archaisms of the eucharist of St.
Basil, and particularly of its commemorations and intercessions,
urge us to return to the East Syrian liturgical tradition, about
which we have already spoken in relation to the eucharist of Addai
and Mari. It is preserved for us today by the Nestorians, as well
as the Chaldeans in union with Rome and the Indian Church
(also Catholic) called Syro-Malabar. These three Churches still
use the eucharist named after the apostles Addai and Mari, but,
as we have seen, under a latterly developed form, which has
nonetheless preserved its oldest elements intact. The Nestorians
use two other texts in addition, attributed respectively to Nestorius and Theodore of Mopsuestia. These latter two, and especially the first one, show the unquestionable influence of the
evolved forms of West Syria. But they show more than one
peculiarity indicating the persistence and resurgence, after the
separation from Eastern Syria, of a prior Semitic tradition that
no hellenization was able to destroy. A significant detail of
this fact is the place that the epiclesis still retains: not before
but after the final intercessions. The East Syrians did adopt the
synthetic epiclesis of Antioch and Jerusalem, its combination of
the prayer for the acceptance of the sacrifice, and, consequently
the consecration of the elements, with the prayer that the celebration of the eucharistic memorial have its total effect in us. But
it seems that they could not accept the violence done to the old
prayer coming from the *Tefillah* in transferring the petition for
the acceptance of the sacrifices and the prayers of the people of
God from the end to the beginning of the supplications. Other
peculiarities which are also Semitic survived even in the liturgy
of Nestorius.

[16] See his article in *Proche-orient chrétien*, cited in note 15 of Chapter 8.

The first one concerns the introductory dialogue. In this tradition, at the beginning, there is always the formula taken from 2 Corinthians, but the biblical order of the divine persons, and their original attributions (grace to Christ, ἀγάπη to the Father) are never modified. Similarly, thereafter, it is always the "hearts" which are invited to be lifted up to God. But the third clause of the dialogue in Eastern Syria is always given in a form having no equivalent in any other tradition. For the initial "Let us give thanks ... " there is always substituted the expression "The oblation (qorban) is offered ... ." This formula is even used with the eucharist of Addai and Mari which either in its developed or original form did not include any technically sacrificial expression apart from that. It seems that here we are touching upon a very ancient testimonial of the sacrificial sense given to the "eucharist" from the time when it was still simply expressed in the terminology of the Synagogue prayers.

Another equivalency of this type, which is hardly less interesting, is the frequent use by these liturgies of the word rozo (Syriac equivalent of "mystery"). We have already seen this in the text of Addai and Mari. Its use in the text of Theodore is still more striking. The anamnesis, instead of taking up the word "memorial" at the conclusion of the eucharistic narrative, substitutes in both texts the expression "we celebrate the mystery ... , whereby salvation has come to all our race" Theodore specifies. But further on, in the part of the anamnesis that with him becomes specifically sacrificial, Theodore repeats it in a very revealing phrase:

> We offer in the presence of your glorious Trinity, with a contrite heart and humbled spirit, this living and holy sacrifice which is the mystery of the Lamb of God who takes away the sins of the world, praying and beseeching in your presence that it be pleasing (to you) Lord, adorable Godhead, and that there be accepted by your mercy this pure and holy oblation whereby you have been appeased and reconciled, for the sins of the world.[17]

[17] Renaudot, op. cit., t. II, p. 619.

The end of this text itself becomes fully meaningful when linked with what the act of thanksgiving for redemption said somewhat earlier about the cross:

... God, Only-Begotten Son, the Word, even though he was the image of God, did not look upon equality with God as extortion, but he emptied himself and took on the likeness of a slave, he came down from heaven, and put on our manhood, a mortal body and a rational, intelligent, immortal soul, from the Holy Virgin, by the power of the Holy Spirit, and thereby he perfected and fulfilled all that great and wonderful economy which had been prepared by your foreknowledge from before the creation of the world. You have yourself accomplished this, thereafter, in these latter days, through your Only-Begotten Son, Our Lord, Jesus Christ, in whom dwells corporally all the fulness of the Godhead; he is also the Head of the Church and the first-born from among the dead, and he is the fulfilment of all things which have all been fulfilled through him. He, through the eternal Spirit, offered himself to God as a spotless offering and sanctified us by the oblation of his body accomplished once and for all, and he has pacified by the blood of his cross what is in heaven and what is on earth, he who was handed over for our sins and who rose for our justification ...[18]

Then follows the institution narrative which we have already cited in discussing its original presence in the eucharist of Addai and Mari.

The closeness of these texts of thanksgiving and of the anamnesis of Theodore shows with perfect clarity that the "mystery" in this tradition, is the sacramental presence of the oblation accomplished once upon the cross, according to the expression of the epistle to the Hebrews. However, this presence in the mystery of the unique oblation is so real that the liturgical mystery celebrated may itself be called our living and holy sacrifice, a sacrifice which in turn is ultimately re-identified with the oblation of the cross. We could not wish for any clearer evidence of the fact that the sacramental mystery of the eucharist, for Theodore and his ambience, is the precise equivalent of the Jewish memorial, con-

[18] *Ibid.*, p. 618.

ceived as containing that which it evokes, and applied to the cross of the Savior.

THE EAST SYRIAN SURVIVAL OF INTERMEDIARY TYPES

We shall not cite the eucharist of Theodore at any more length, except to specify that the epiclesis here, like those of St. James and St. John Chrysostom, makes a formal petition that the Spirit "make" the bread and wine ("by the power of your name", he specifies) the body and blood of Christ. With this exception, through its abundant recourse to biblical formulas, as we can already realize from what we have given of its text, it is very close to St. Basil's eucharist. The central role that it also gives to the text of Philippians 2 would make us inclined to think that it was directly inspired by it. But the accumulation of citations (not always so well founded) and a certain redundancy of language, despite some particularly felicitous formulas, places it, we should say, slightly lower in the same class of compositions which must have included many others. That of Nestorius is another and somewhat later example, which we shall study in another chapter, and which will practically let us touch the hypertrophy and decomposition which were soon to be threatening eucharists of too didactic a theology, and a biblicism whose excess betrays its artificiality.

On the other hand, the eucharist of Addai and Mari, which we have already quoted in the entirety of its long recension, but only in order to extract from it the most archaic elements, must now again hold our attention in the state in which it is presented to us today.

In going back to this text,[19] we notice that it does not enter into the evolved schema that East Syria itelf came to accept from West Syria, if only in maintaining the epiclesis, even a synthetically developed one, as the conclusion of the Christian *Tefillah*. Like its anamnesis, its intercessions and commemorations present many analogies with those found in the text attributed to Theodore. But, on first sight, the order in which this latter series of prayers

---

[19] Cf. above, pp. 147 ff.

develops in Theodore, similar to what is found in the eucharists of the 8th book of the *Apostolic Constitutions* or St. James, seems for some incomprehensible reason to have been upset in the liturgy of Addai and Mari. However, while admitting that here as in the other parts of the developed text there may have been some clumsy reworking, Dom Botte points out that it is unthinkable that the apparently more logical order of Theodore could have been systematically destroyed to end up with this result. The mere comparison of the long text of Addai and Mari with the older kernel that it contains has already shown us the extreme conservatism that did in fact dominate its development. We saw how once the epiclesis was introduced, despite the hiatus it produced in the anamnesis, carried with it no modification of its ancient text which could have permitted a restoration of the continuity. It is very probable that the adjunction of the intercessions, as well as of the *Sanctus*, came about under analogous conditions. If we return to the continuation of the longer text, such as we have it in the liturgy that is still in use, this is how it may be summed up. The first part, the thanksgiving for creation, has substituted the formula found in the liturgy of the eucharistic meal for that which must originally have been connected with the *Sanctus* in the liturgy of the service of reading and prayers. The same is true for the thanksgiving for the redemption which follows, and which, evidently, must have originally been directly connected to the preceding. After this, IV and V constitute a genuine pre-epiclesis like the one we have seen in the rites of Rome and Egypt, but one which remains especially close to the first "blessing" of the *Tefillah*, since it is still basically a commemoration of the fathers in the faith (the martyrs were merely united with the prophets). With VI, we have the prayer for safety and peace, followed by the one for the conversion of non-believers. VII is a prayer for the hierarchy, which in the written text leads abruptly to the anamnesis, although it must have been connected to it by the intermediary of a narrative of the eucharistic institution which was very similar to the one retained in the eucharist of Theodore. There is no need to repeat here what we have already explained and just recalled with regard to the development of the epiclesis out of the anamnesis while still remaining within it.

The first remark we must make is that here as with St. Basil, we find an order which is singularly close to that of the *Tefillah*, from IV through VI. The commemoration of the saints is at the beginning, and it is associated with a first evocation of the eucharistic sacrifice, which in more evolved texts, like the Roman *Te igitur*, has taken its place. Security and peace lead to the expansion of the "knowledge" of God, and the whole terminates in a prayer for the sacred ministry which in this text, as at the end of the intercession of St. Basil, is the equivalent of the prayer for the recommendation of the sacrifices of Israel in the *Tefillah*, and which to that extent corresponds to the first epiclesis of Rome and Alexandria. After that, we can understand that if the final epiclesis, calls upon the Holy Spirit, it does not do so in order to obtain the acceptance of the sacrifice (already mentioned in IV and VI), but simply that the celebration may have its whole effect in us.

Starting with what we have called the pre-epiclesis, this plan then is almost exactly the same as the basic plan of the Roman canon. But it is somewhat more archaic, first of all because it has left the commemoration of the saints before (and not after) the intercession for the living. Further, instead of the whole thanksgiving being at the beginning, before the *Sanctus*, here, as in the Jewish prayers, it remains framed by an act of thanksgiving for creation alone which precedes it, and a thanksgiving for the redemption alone following it.

In other words the developed form of the anaphora of Addai and Mari gives evidence of the prior existence, in Syria as at Rome and in Egypt, of a eucharist in which people still limited themselves to a continuous recitation of the Christian forms of the *Qedushah* and the blessings which framed it, then the *Tefillah*, and ultimately the prayers proper to the sacred meal, with only a few elementary adjustments. Actually, the only adjustment consists here in the replacement of the "blessing" for creation in the synagogue service, which focuses on light, by the meal "blessing" focusing on life, and similarly, the blessing for the Torah by that for the covenant. After the equivalent of the *Tefillah* this only left the equivalent of the Jewish prayer for the "memorial" and its effect in those who celebrate it.

We can add that this order, insofar as it differs from that of Alexandria, certainly gives evidence of the influence in Christian Syria of the Palestinian synagogal order, in which the *Qedushah* retained its original place before the *Tefillah*. Once again, it is the same influence which even in Rome must have determined the same arrangement. We can say that we have palpable proof here of the fact that the synthetic order of the West Syrian liturgies, starting with the pseudo-Clementine liturgy, is in Syria itself where it made its appearance, the result of a remodeling. The neighboring schemas of the Roman, Alexandrian or archaic (if not original) Syrian eucharist are only local variants of an order which must have been universal from the moment that the service of readings and prayers and the eucharistic meal were joined together. The original form of Addai and Mari, evidencing a state of affairs where this connection was still unknown, brings us even further back. But, reciprocally, the hellenizing logic and rhetoric of the West Syrian order are incontestably later.

GENEALOGY AND GENESIS OF THE EPICLESIS

The conclusion of this chapter, which has permitted us to see the West Syrian eucharist attain its form which was to become classical, and at the same time to verify its genesis, by the comparison with evidence from an earlier period in East Syria, will furnish us with a recapitulatory study of the development of the epiclesis. We now have all the data, and we have seen it attain the final stage of its development with the eucharists of St. John Chrysostom and St. Basil.

If by epiclesis we understand an explicit invocation of the Holy Spirit, taking place immediately after the anamnesis, or at any event in the last part of the eucharistic prayer, its first appearance is, in practically identical terms, that which we find in the liturgy of Addai and Mari, and that of the *Apostolic Tradition*. With Addai and Mari, it seems incontestable that it does not belong to the original text. But it is probably the most ancient re-working that can be detected in it.[20] It seems indeed that the

---

[20] Cf. above, pp. 151 ff.

Spirit, and his descent upon the oblation, at this stage, are related neither to the heavenly acceptance of the sacrifice nor even less to the consecration of the bread and wine, making them the body and blood of the Savior. The Spirit is called upon at this place, simply because the petition is being made, as it was in the Jewish prayers, that the celebration of the "memorial" lead efficaciously to the building of the future Jerusalem in its definitive unity, and at the same time to the ultimate glorification of God. This unity, which for Christians will be that of the "body" of Christ attaining its fulness in the Church, and this glorification of the Father by the "whole" Christ, for them also are the work of the Spirit. His mention came quite naturally to be made at this point, sooner or later. And, when attention was called to his divinity on account of the theological controversies of the second half of the fourth century, it would be quite natural that he would not only be mentioned here but formally invoked.

If we are justified in thinking, despite the objections brought by Dom Botte against Dom Dix, that the *Testamentum Domini* allows us to go back to a prior state of the liturgy of St. Hippolytus, where there was only the mention, and not as yet the invocation of a special descent of the Spirit, we can grasp at the heart of the matter, in the two successive states of the same text, just how the transition was made from mention to invocation.[21]

Does this allow us to assert that this first and nonconsecratory form of the epiclesis already existed in Syria, in other words that it appeared in Syria before spreading elsewhere? We should be tempted to think so, although it still remains somewhat in a state of conjecture. The corroborative evidence of Rome and what seems to be the most ancient state of the Egyptian texts, incline us to think that neither at Rome nor Alexandria and its vicinity was anything like this known before the end of the fourth century. It is a supposition completely bereft of serious grounds that the ancient Roman liturgy would have known an epiclesis of this type, which would then have disappeared for some unfathomable reasons without leaving a trace.[22] In Egypt we see

[21] Cf. above, pp. 170 ff.
[22] Cf. above, pp. 216 ff.

this epiclesis of the Spirit being introduced progressively, it seems, after a period of experimentation. Either it figures in a place other than its normal and certainly original one, or else it is addressed at first not to the Spirit but to the Word, and by one of the theologians most smitten by the divinity of the Holy Spirit.[23] It seems that the other borrowings which apparently went along with it when it was ultimately accepted would only come from Syria. It is undeniably in Syria that the epiclesis of Addai and Mari was composed (and more precisely, in Syriac). Finally, once again, it would be very possible that St. Hippolytus himself was of Syrian origin. The general archaism of his trinitarian theology as well as his liturgical tastes, his penitential rigorism, his class consciousness which was almost as foreign to the questionable society of Alexandria as to the old Roman customs, are so many convergent probabilities.[24] But we cannot say anything further.

On the other hand, there is nothing peculiarly Syrian about the prayer for the acceptance of the sacrifice, which developed into a formal petition for the consecration of the elements, before it was combined with the epiclesis of the Holy Spirit, coming from the anamnesis, and which originally did not have this object. It came actually not from the "memorial" developed in the third part of the *berakah* after the meal, but from the *Abodah* prayer which was the conclusion of the Jewish *Tefillah*.[25] It is therefore in its normal place where we still find it in the Roman canon, where it first appeared in the Egyptian liturgy, and where it was to remain in the East Syrian liturgy: at the end of the intercessions and commemorations. In relation to the institution narrative, its original place is before and not after this narrative. It is only the theological synthesis worked out conjointly in West Syria along with a breaking up and a systematic reassembling of the ancient eucharistic prayers that was to lead this other pra-

---

[23] Cf. above, pp. 202 ff.

[24] Cf. above, pp. 165 ff.

[25] Cf. above, pp. 196 ff. The fact that Judaism, as we have said, already introduced the evocation of the "memorial" in the same terms, both in the *Abodah* prayer and in the third meal *berakah*, set up an equivalency between them and prepared the way for their fusion.

yer's fusion with the epiclesis of the Holy Spirit at the end of the anamnesis. From this moment on, the epiclesis made a three-fold petition: the acceptance of the sacrifice (explicitly identified with the presentation to God of the memorial of the Savior), the consecutive consecration of the bread and wine as the body and blood of Christ, and finally (which alone is original), that this descent of the Spirit, uniting us all in the body of Christ which is the Church, permit us all in this unity to glorify the Father eternally.[26]

This synthesis is unquestionably Syrian, and more precisely West Syrian. We see the central (although latest) element take on progressively greater prominence. The pseudo-Clementine anaphora is still limited to petitioning that the Spirit *manifest* ($\dot{\alpha}\pi o\varphi\dot{\eta}\nu\eta$) that the bread and wine are the body and the blood Christ in making us fully associated with him and his redemption.[27] That of St. James, which St. John Chrysostom was to follow, was more specific in asking that the Spirit *make* the bread and wine the body and blood of Christ, and it is possible that it was the same Chrysostom who added: "changing them by your Spirit," although the addition may very well be later.

The Syriac formulary of the Twelve Apostles (he worked on its original Greek text) had at this point, moreover, a word which he translated as "manifested,"[29] and which may very well have been the $\dot{\alpha}\pi o\varphi\dot{\eta}\nu\eta$ of the pseudo-Clementine liturgy. Yet it is not impossible that it was $\dot{\alpha}\nu\alpha\delta\varepsilon\tilde{\iota}\xi\alpha\iota$ which Basil was to prefer. '$A\nu\alpha\delta\varepsilon\tilde{\iota}\xi\alpha\iota$ also may be translated by "manifest." But, as we have seen, the particular use that Basil makes of it, in applying it first to the presentation of his offering by the Son to the Father, gives to this word a certainly equivalent sense to that of the English "consecrate" when we say "consecrate the bread to the body" and "the wine to the blood of Christ."[30] Everything that was later to be introduced here in the Byzantine East merely em-

---

[26] Cf. above, pp. 265-266.
[27] Cf. above, p. 263.
[28] Cf. above, p. 274 and p. 287.
[29] Cf. above, p. 284.
[30] Cf. above, p. 296.

phasizes the power of this expression, without adding anything of the sacramental realism it already in fact contained. From this point of view, the ποιεῖν of St. James and St. John Chrysostom only gives decisive clarification to the force of a thought which St. Basil, as we know, preferred to leave as long as possible, when its expression seemed novel, under the cover of formulas that were as discreet as they could be.

The Gallican and Mozarabic Eucharist

THERE IS ONE LAST STEP IN THE LITURGICAL TRADITION IN its creative period which remains for us to study: that is the Gallican liturgy[1] and the Mozarabic,[2] with which we may connect the Celtic liturgies and the fragments of non-Roman Italic liturgies that have come down to us.[3] The kinship between the Syrian East and what can be called the Extreme West is manifest in the eucharistic prayer, but it extends to many other elements, not only in their respective liturgies, but in their whole Christian outlook.

[1] On the Gallican liturgy, see W. S. Porter, *The Gallican Rite* (London, 1958), and particularly the bibliography added by F. L. Cross, pp. 57 ff. This will be completed by the chapter of Archdale A. King, in *Liturgies of the Past* (London, 1959), pp. 77 ff. and the volume of E. Kovalevsky, *Le Canon eucharistique de l'ancien rite des Gaules* (Paris, 1957).

[2] Cf. Archdale A. King's chapter in *Liturgies of the Primatial Sees* (London, 1957), and the bibliography given by A. Baumstark, *Comparative Liturgy*, pp. 212 ff.

[3] Bibliography on the Ambrosian rite in Baumstark, *op. cit.*, pp. 212-214.

315

THE GALLICAN AND MOZARABIC EUCHARIST AND
ITS KINSHIP WITH THE WEST SYRIAN TYPE

Down to our own day the arrangement of the places of worship, in Gaul as in Spain, for example, has remained basically foreign to Roman customs. Even when the Roman liturgy had spread into these areas, it did not modify it, at least up to the Renaissance (and in Spain until much later). The Western Church, like the Syrian Church, places the altar in the conch of the apse, turned to the East. A second center of the celebration is constituted by the ambo, placed toward the center of the building, and near it are the seats where the ministers take their places for the service of readings preceding the eucharistic meal, and not in some sanctuary, inaccessible to the people beyond the altar.

The same was true for the vestments and insignia worn by the ministers, such as the episcopal omophorion, the tau crozier, the very ample chasuble worn only by the priests, the dalmatic and the orarion of the deacon, and even the *paterissa* used by prelates outside the Church. They are peculiarities which subsisted for a more or less long period of time in the Extreme West even after the introduction of the Roman books, and some of them even reached faraway Rome.

All of this comes from the Syrian East, along with the taste for a ritual and a sacred art laden with symbolism, an encroaching ecclesiastical poetry, not to speak of Celtic monasticism, which were all things that Christian Rome persisted in ignoring up to well after the patristic age.

How could these traditions have gone from one end of the Mediterranean to the other? We do not know, for we know practically nothing about the origins of Western Christianity. During the Middle Ages the Romans often stated that the evangelization of the Celts was owed to them as well as that of their successive Germanic conquerors, and they, at times, are no less categorical. But the former did so in order to impose their own customs and the latter to defend theirs. There is nothing to be gained from the legends which are arguments *ad hominem*, without foundation in known historical facts. In reality, the Syrian merchants who furrowed all the seas, once they had become Christian were most probably the first bearers of their faith even to lands which were considered to be remote. At any event, it is certain that as soon as Christian communities appeared to be established, their heritage seemed to be chiefly Syrian. The liturgy of the Gauls, who had remained Celtic or variously Germanized, gives the clearest but not the sole evidence of this.

Through the Stowe missal[4] we know only scraps of the properly Celtic liturgies, in particular for the eucharist. They present a hodge-podge of uses and texts from various origins, which is very characteristic of a people who loved nothing better than to move about practically everywhere. But the primary material is still the same as we find in the Gallican or Mozarabic liturgies. Actually, these latter two do not, properly speaking, represent two liturgies but one, which as long as it was extant was characterized by an incessant proliferation of variable formularies based on a traditional schema. The Gallican or Mozarabic books are little more than different local collections of formularies of this kind. Beyond that, they differ only on relatively insignificant details. As for the plan of the great eucharistic prayer, their accord is practically complete in the variability of the formularies which are as unlimited in one place as in the other. Moreover, it is not rare that we find all or part of one and the same formulary both in the Gallican and Mozarabic books.

This liturgy, which we may call Gallicano-Hispanic, along with its Celtic or Italic relatives, was pledged to disappear practically entirely, at least at first sight, a short time after the end of the patristic period. In England, at the synod of Whitby, the old Celtic Christianity capitulated before the imperialism of the new Christians, recruited by the Roman mission of St. Augustine of Canterbury (despite the very liberal prescriptions given to him by St. Gregory the Great). In Gaul, Charlemagne's pretention at playing Roman emperor inspired him with the idea of replacing on his authority the local liturgical tradition with that of Rome, which had already won out over all of Northern Italy. In Spain, finally, the unfortunate affair of Elipand of Seville's adoptionism, taking support from the liturgical books of Visigothic Spain,

---

4 Cf. G. F. Warner, *The Stowe Missal*, 2 vol. (London, 1906 and 1915).

compromised the liturgy which we call Mozarabic in the eyes
of the Holy See. An energetic pope like Gregory VII sufficed,
with the help of the spreading of his old Cluniac confrères throughout the peninsula, to do away with it practically in one fell swoop.
At the time of the Renaissance, a cardinal and a bright light of
Christian humanism, Giménez de Cisneros, succeeded in saving
and consolidating what was left of it. But, preserved for us as
it was, more as an archeological curiosity than anything else,
the effective celebration of this liturgy was reduced to practically
nothing after the last Spanish revolution. Despite the fact that
it represents the antique worship tradition of the whole Christian
West, it only subsists today as a hasty celebration executed by
a few clerics in an obscure chapel in the Cathedral of Toledo. We
must congratulate the efforts of the Benedictines of San Domingo
de Silos for having studied and edited the ancient Mozarabic
texts, and occasionally, for having resurrected their content in
celebrations, exceptional for their rarity as much as for their
solemnity. But up till now their efforts have been able to do
little more than prolong the existence of a moribund phantom.

There is, however, another side to this sad story. When Charlemagne and his successors had obtained the Roman books, new
editions of them were made for the new Germanic empire. Those
charged with this task could not resign themselves to seeing the
demise of traditional treasures of which their masters would have
thought very little. The results were books that were Roman
in theory but in fact were stuffed with Gallican elements. Through
a curious turn of events, these books came back to Rome at a
time when she no longer shone either for her critical faculties
or her creative genius, and they were apparently received without
difficulty. The consequence is that the liturgy we still celebrate
and which we call Roman is in reality merely a Roman frame,
laden with foreign elements, and actually at least fifty percent
of its prayers and rites are Gallican. Along with a certain number
of orations, the chief element that is still quite Roman is the canon, with the exception of prefaces like that of the Trinity, not
to mention more recent ones which are generally Gallican (Mozarabic) even though they have been more or less reworked.

But, with the modern or ancient Mozarabic books,[5] a series
of Gallican books allows us all the same, at least on paper, to
evoke the ancient eucharistic prayers of our fathers. They are
the *Missale Gothicum*, the *Missale Gallicanum vetus*, the Bobbio
missal,[7] the masses published in the last century by Mone,[8] to
which must be added certain Celtic books, like the Stowe Missal.
Nor can we forget the elements that have survived in the modern
Ambrosian missal, particularly on Maundy Thursday and Easter
Even. Once again, all of these are a disconcerting abundance
of texts. In these relatively late documents that have come down
to us, not only do we find eucharists for all the Sundays and holy
days of the year, and many ferial days, with innumerable votive
masses, but interchangeable formulas for the same day or the
same mass are also manifold. It seems that we have here a treasury, exceptionally set down in writing, of liturgical improvisations within a given framework, which continued as long as this
remained a living liturgy.

Its eucharistic anaphora is made up of five distinct prayers,
only two of which remained more or less invariable. The first,
corresponding to the Roman preface, is called *illatio* in the Spanish
books (an exact translation of the Greek ἀναφορά), and in the
Gallican books *immolatio* or *contestatio*. The *Sanctus* follows
and it seems to have generally retained the Greek formulas in

---

[5] Edition of the *Missale Mixtum* of Cardinal Giménez de Cisneros in 1500,
at Toledo (reproduced in Migne, P. L., t. 85). Dom M. Férotin published in
1904 (Paris) the *Liber ordinum*, and in 1912 (Paris) the *Liber Mozarabicus
Sacramentorum* in remarkable critical editions.

[6] Published for the first time by Cardinal Tommasi, *Codices Sacramentorum nongentis anni vestustiores* (Rome, 1680). It was reproduced in
Migne, P. L., t. 72. Modern editions of the *Missale Gothicum*: H. M. Ban-
nister (London, 1917) and L. C. Mohlberg (Rome, 1961); of the *Missale Gallicanum Vetus*: L. C. Mohlberg, L. Eizenhöfer and P. Siffrin (Rome, 1958);
and of the *Missale Francorum* by the same editors (Rome, 1957).

[7] Published for the first time by J. Mabillon in his *Musaeum Italicum*
(Paris, 1687), t. I, vol. 2, pp. 287 ff. Modern edition by E. A. Lowe (London,
1917 and 1920).

[8] First edition at Frankfurt-am-M. in 1850, reproduced in Migne, P. L.
t. 138, col. 862 ff. Critical edition by Mohlberg, Eizenhöfer and Siffrin in
their *Missale Gallicanum Vetus*, pp. 74-91.

the midst of the Latin. The *Sanctus* is followed by a prayer called the *post-sanctus,* which is linked up with it by the same connective as in Syria: the use of the word "holy." As in many liturgical manuscripts of both East and West, the words of institution are not present in the properly Gallican books, except by recalling a few key words. After this part comes a final prayer called *post-pridie* in the Mozarabic books and *post-secreta* or *post-mysterium* in the Gallican ones.

The diversity that we encounter under these different headings is such that in going through these books we risk getting the first impression that every schema of a well constructed or simply consistent eucharistic prayer has been dissolved in the hazards of an unbridled improvisation. Particularly, although not exclusively, the Mozarabic books are teeming with formularies in which we become lost in a wave of words, and wonder just what they can still have to do with the eucharist. Some of them in their profuseness can rival the 8th book of the *Apostolic Constitutions.* But too often the disorder in thought is in extreme contrast here with the composition of the West Syrian authors, which, on the contrary, is perhaps too studied. The influence of St. Augustine makes itself particularly felt in many of these texts. The authors stole not only his thoughts and expressions, but even whole pages. At times, the very incongruous character of one or another of these prayers could be explained by the fact that they were erroneously placed under a heading to which they did not correspond in fact. But, more generally, we must not hesitate to acknowledge, with Walter Frere, that we are face to face here with a very real danger. The ministers are given a faculty of improvisation at a moment when a tradition is no longer lived consciously enough.[9]

Yet this is not to say that the texts that are fully in conformity with the tradition we have seen develop in the Syrian East are not legion, since many are undoubtedly most ancient although some may have been the product of a relatively late period. On the other hand, despite commentators, like Walter Frere or Eugraphe Kovalevsky, it is not certain that all the texts which de-

---

[9] W. H. Frere, *The Anaphora,* p. 106.

part from the canon we have seen develop in West Syria towards the end of the fourth century are late aberrations. There may be some, and, as we shall point out, there indeed most probably are some which give evidence of a prior state where the tradition of Syrian origin was not yet molded into the form in which it was ultimately to be enclosed at Antioch and its environs.

In any event, the dating of these prayers is extremely difficult. The Gallican manuscripts give us texts recopied in the eighth, even the seventh century, and which can even be earlier when we see no influence yet of Roman texts. The oldest Mozarabic manuscripts do not go back further than the tenth century. But, once again, neither the date of a manuscript, nor even that of a collection, suffices to decide the age of a liturgical prayer that is found there for the first time.

The influence of two brothers, St. Leander and St. Isidore who succeeded one another as bishop of Seville in the seventh century, seems discernable in the organization and expansion of the Mozarabic liturgy. But whatever they may have put on their own into the texts that have come down to us is scarcely determinable. Moreover, we must admit that the analysis of the eucharistic celebration undertaken by St. Isidore in his *De Officiis* is such that it leaves us in the dark about what he still understood of the tradition that he contributed to propagating.[10] He divided the whole mass into seven prayers, but what he tells us about the fifth and sixth (which seem to correspond to the anaphora) is neither very clear nor very convincing. The fifth, which he already calls *illatio*, brings about the "sanctification of the oblation" according to him, and the sixth, the *"conformatio sacramenti"* which is the result of the "sanctification of the Spirit." At first sight, we should be tempted to believe that the fifth is therefore only the present-day *illatio* (with the *Sanctus*), while the sixth would cover everything from the *post-sanctus* to the conclusion. Or else, in his terminology, would the *conformatio sacramenti* be only the *post-pridie*, with his *illatio* designating everything that leads up to the institution narrative? In the absence of any citation of a text whatsoever, it is impossible for

---

[10] *De ecclesiasticis officiis*, lib. I, XV; P. L., t. 83, col. 752.

us to decide. Even if the *conformatio sacramenti* is just the *post-pridie*, it is perhaps premature to conclude, as Walter Frere does unhesitatingly, that this text, according to Isidore, must be an equivalent of the fully developed Syrian epiclesis, simply because he sees there a "sanctification" of the Holy Spirit. The repeated use of the word *sanctificatio* leaves no doubt about the meaning that should be given to it. Despite these uncertainties, there is true evidence that we can find formularies which are very close in their development to the last Eastern eucharists that we have studied, both in the Gallican and Mozarabic books. Take for example the third of the Sunday masses from the *Missale Gothicum*. Its *immolatio* is composed in this way:

> It is meet and right, truly equitable and right, O ineffable, incomprehensible, and everlasting God, that we always give you thanks, we whom you do not cease to sustain (*fovere*) by your great mercy. Who, then, could worthily praise your power, you whose divinity may not be looked upon by mortal eye, and whose boundlessness may not be expressed in words? It is enough that we love you as the Father, that we venerate you as the Lord, that we receive you as the Creator, that we embrace you as the Redeemer. Grant, almighty Master, that we may come up to you along this narrow road which you have prescribed for us, whereby we may arrive at eternal blessedness; let us not be held back by any obstacle; but let the course of our progress lead to the eternity of salvation, through Christ our Lord, through whom the Angels, etc.

The *post-sanctus* with its classical connective continues:

> Truly holy, truly blessed in the highest, is our Lord Jesus Christ, the Son, the King of Israel, who led like a sheep to the slaughter and like a Lamb to the shearer, did not open his mouth. He, on the night before he suffered ...

The *post-mysterium* concludes:

> Great is this gift of mercy whereby we have been instructed to celebrate the sacrifices of our redemption, as our Lord Jesus Christ offered them upon earth, he through whom, almighty Father, we beseech you to look with favor upon these gifts placed upon your altar and cover them all with the shadow of the Holy Spirit of your Son, that we may obtain from

what we have received of your blessing, the glory of eternity, through Jesus Christ, etc.[11]

We can even point out *post-pridies* or *post-mysteriums* in the Gallican or Mozarabic books in which the verbal similarity with the epicleses developed in West Syria is still more striking. Take this prayer from a Mozarabic mass for the feast of St. Christina, which is found practically word for word in the *Missale Gothicum* for the feast of the chair of St. Peter:

> Therefore, keeping these commandments, we offer these holy gifts (*munera*) of our salvation, beseeching you, most merciful and almighty God, to deign to pour out your Holy Spirit upon these offerings (*solemnia*) that they might become for us a lawful eucharist, in your name, that of your Son and that of your Spirit, blessed in the transformation into the body and the blood of this same Jesus Christ, our Lord, (your) Only-Begotten Son, for us who eat of it unto eternal life and the kingdom without end.[12]

If such expressions were more frequent, they would be enough to make the Syrian origin of these liturgies incontestable. But those like Dom Gregory Dix who question it wish to see in the prayers of this type only evidence of a late Syrian influence. But a two-fold objection is opposed to this theory. In the first place, we hardly see any other possible trace of a late Eastern influence on the Gallican or Spanish authors. The developments of Greek theology after St. Augustine's time seem to be unknown to them. On the other hand, if Eastern patristic texts had been able to make the journey from East to West throughout the whole of the Middle Ages (although this movement was scarcely felt before the Carolingian times, and especially before the twelfth century), there is no trace of any transmission of liturgical texts at this same period. Moreover, who in Spain or Gaul, between the fifth and the ninth centuries, would have been capable of reading and translating them?

---

[11] Mohlberg edition, pp. 117 ff.

[12] Férotin edition of the *Liber sacramentorum*, col. 379; cf. the Mohlberg edition of the *Missale Gothicum*, p. 45.

It would have been necessary then for a priest or a bishop from Syria to have come to the West, and one who would have been capable of adapting the formulas he knew. But we know of no other case of this kind than that of Eusebius, bishop of Milan from 451 to 465 or 466.[13] Actually coming from Syria, Eusebius could have introduced into the Milanese liturgy certain sections, such as the characteristic development "Do this as a memorial of me," which reproduces word for word the text of the liturgy of St. James. Still, in the absence of any historical evidence, there is nothing that allows us to attribute to other hypothetical runaways everything that we find to be apparently Syrian in the Gallican and Mozarabic collections.

On the other hand, positive indications lead us to think that formulas like those we have just quoted belong to their most ancient elements. In fact, they appeared so markedly archaic at an early date that people did not dare to use them without some remodeling that betrays the prior state of the text, nor to resolve to eliminate them. It is for this reason that we find a Gallican *post-mysterium* for Christmas Eve in a manuscript fragment preserved in the library of Caius College at Cambridge, where the expression *eucharistia legitima* was evidently substituted for *verum corpus*. Actually, the clumsy corrector omitted the removal of *verus sanguis*, which could only have corresponded to it, with the result that we have this bizarre phrase: "that, through the mystery of your operation, they (the gifts) become for us a lawful eucharist and the very blood of your Son ..."[14]

In many other cases, transformations of this kind may have been made, although since they were done more dextrously they have left no trace. To admit it, it is enough to compare what St. Isidore tells us: the *conformatio sacramenti* comes about through the sanctification of the Spirit, whatever be the precise meaning he gives to these words, together with what the pseudo-Isidore will say a few centuries later. He was familiar only with the later theory of a consecration by the words of the institution narrative alone. It is understandable that once one had reached that

---

[13] Cf. Gregory Dix, *The Shape of the Liturgy*, p. 541.
[14] Caius Coll. Cambr. MS. 153.

stage, the ancient formulas may have been corrected as we have just seen, since it is most unlikely that formulas of this type could have been introduced at that time.

Inversely, we should not rush to the conclusion, with Walter Frere, that besides some twenty five prayers from the Toledo sacramentary and their hardly more numerous Gallican equivalents, containing an epiclesis in which the Holy Spirit is invoked more or less exactly in the sense of the developed Syrian exegesis, all the other formulas for this part of the eucharist are either late or reworked. Many may be, but there are many others which may be just as archaic or even more so. In the first place, the Spirit is at times simply invoked, as in the *Apostolic Tradition* or the liturgy of Addai and Mari, that he may produce in the participants the fruit of the eucharist. This is the case in the Sunday liturgy of the *Missale Gothicum* that we have quoted and in Mone's sixth mass. At other times, he is called upon simply to make the eucharist "lawful" without any other specification. Let us note in this regard that the frequency of this expression in our collections, even if it may have been introduced at a late date here and there to replace other expressions which had become troublesome for the theology that was being taught, makes unlikely the supposition that it was not part of their most ancient wording. It is, furthermore, a formula of the most archaic Christian Latin, already evidenced in St. Cyprian (in the sense of a eucharist fully conforming to the plan of its institution by Christ).[15]

But there are still other cases where the transformation of the elements is indeed asked for formally, but without being attributed to the Holy Spirit. Expressions such as "the descent of the fulness of divine majesty,"[16] or the "descent of the blessing,"[17] or the divine "power"[18] are used. But there are also cases in which the transformation is expected expressly from a descent of the

---

[15] Letter 63, par. 9; Vienna edition, t. 3 (i-ii), p. 708.
[16] Férotin, col. 475.
[17] Férotin, col. 262.
[18] Férotin, col. 177.

Word. One striking example is given by the *post-pridie* of the 3rd ferial day *post Vigesima* of the Toledo sacramentary.

> Send down your Word from heaven, Lord, through whom our sins will be taken away and our offerings sanctified.[19]

Finally, invocations of the Angels are not rare either, even if we leave aside the texts which may have undergone an influence of the Roman canon. No influence of this type seems to be discernable in the *post-pridie* for the feasts of St. Cecily on the 22nd of November or of St. Eugenia on the 16th of September.[20] A particularly curious text for the Ascension invokes the Spirit as the Angel of the sacrifice who appeared to Manoah, the father of Samson.[21]

Most of these formulas cannot be explained except as archaisms. From them we get the impression of a state of affairs that reproduces what such prayers might have been in Syria and elsewhere on the eve or at the beginning of the movement toward the systematization and rearrangement of the eucharistic liturgy that came about at Antioch toward the end of the fourth century. The final invocation that follows from the anamnesis remains basically a prayer that the mystery commemorated have its whole effect on those celebrating it. Moreover it tends to become fixed as an invocation of the Spirit, yet without the invocation of the Word, the heavenly spirits, or the simple blessing of God being able to be fully excluded. It tends also to attract the petition for the acceptance of the sacrifice offered, and to specify it in an explicit request for the transformation of the elements. But all of this remains in a state of flux and it is only rather by way of exception that we find the type of formulations which became definitive in Western Syria.

Under these conditions, it seems that we are forced to conclude that the Gallicano-Hispanic liturgy represents a transplantation in the West of the Syrian liturgy which must have acquir-

---

[19] Férotin, col. 200.

[20] Férotin, col. 28 and 427.

[21] Férotin, col. 328 (allusion to Judges 13: 23). Cf. the *post-pridie* of the second ferial of Easter, where the Angel and the Spirit appear in turn (Férotin, col. 262).

ed its autonomy at the precise moment when the latter was entering into its final phase of systematic reorganization, but before it arrived at its final stabilization. In other words, the primary layer of the liturgy of the Extreme West, as it has come down
to us particularly in the Gallican and Mozarabic books, must correspond approximately to the middle of the fourth century. Must
we stress the fact that the work of St. Hilary of Poitiers, who
represents the last phase of a Western theology fully related to
Eastern developments, is from this period precisely?

This is corroborated by the fact that there is no dearth of Gallican or Mozarabic *post-sanctus* where we can recognize some
traces, and even more than traces, of the original presence of
the consecratory epiclesis, and more especially of the epiclesis
for the acceptance of the sacrifice, *before* the words of institution.
Of course, here again, we do not include those *post-sanctus* where
a direct influence of the Roman liturgy makes itself felt, like those
of the Rogation mass or of the fifth Sunday mass of the *Missale
Gothicum*.[22] But the *post-sanctus* from the same collection for
the feast of St. Maurice betrays no influence of this type. It asks
that "Our Lord and God sanctify these species (*speciem istam*)
in order to consecrate them through the inspiration of (his) grace
and add to the human blessing, the fulness of divine favor." The
same is found in the *post-sanctus* for Easter Even:

> At your command, Lord, all things were created, in heaven
> and on earth, in the sea and all the abysses. The Patriarchs,
> the Prophets, the Apostles, the Martyrs, the Confessors and
> all the saints give you thanks. Doing likewise, we also be-
> seech you to accept with favor these spiritual offerings, these
> pure oblations. We beseech you to bless this sacrifice with
> your blessing and to pour down the dew of your Holy Spirit,
> so that it may be for all a lawful eucharist, through Christ,
> our Lord, who on the night before he suffered, etc ...[23]

We have the same thing on Easter Day:

> ... Sanctify the sacrifices which you have instituted, not
> because our merits invite you to do so, but because we sanc-

---

[22] Mohlberg, p. 86 and p. 120.
[23] Mohlberg, pp. 68-70.

tify them through your example, so that once everything has been done fittingly, death will know that it is vanquished and life that it has been revivified (*revocatam*), our Savior coming back from hell ...[24]

It is hard not to believe that prayers such as these, in this position, are evidence of a time when, even in Syria, it was still at this point that the recommendation of the sacrifice was traditionally made.

But we also find, as we must admit, particularly in the Mozarabic books which are of a later date, many prayers which are either very brief (as is the case with numerous *post-sanctus* and a certain number of *post-pridies* or *post-mysteriums*), or on the other hand, more or less prolix, in which there is no mention of the sacrifice whatsoever, nor any invocation (consecratory or not), nor even any anamnesis. It is evident that many of them are late compositions, from an age where the original themes, and even at times those which are most essential to the eucharist, had dropped from sight. But there are also some (particularly among those assigned to the most ancient feasts) where these disconcerting inadequacies are side by side with formulas that seem to be from an early period. Their irregularity must be accounted for by the omissions and the non-sequiturs to which improvisation at any time is exposed.

Among these is this *post-mysterium* for the Epiphany (which passed almost as it stands from the *Missale Gothicum* into the Gallicanized Roman missal, where it became a *"secreta"*).

Lord, we beseech you, look favorably upon these sacrifices which are placed before you, where it is no longer gold, frankincense or myrrh that is offered, but what these gifts manifested is offered, sacrificed and received ...[25]

Here, the one idea of the sacrifice has absorbed the anamnesis and reduced the epiclesis to a very general invocation. But the sacrificial theme in turn can vanish into thin air, with the whole content of the anamnesis, to say nothing of the epiclesis in prayers whose composition still does not seem to be recent. This is the

[24] Mohlberg, p. 73.
[25] Mohlberg, p. 26.

case with the second Sunday mass of the *Missale Gothicum* where the *post-sanctus* is reduced to these words:

> Truly holy, truly in the highest, the Lord our God, the Son, the King of Israel, who, on the night before he suffered ...

and the *post-secreta* is no less laconic:

> Through him, God, almighty Father, we beseech you, just as we retain the obedience of the holy mystery, may its heavenly power work in us to protect us, through Christ, our Lord....[26]

One last gap must be especially pointed out, for it became universal in the late Mozarabic use: the eucharist, instead of ending with a return to the thanksgiving in the final doxology, concluded with the last blessing of the gifts alone, which is also found at the end of the Roman canon, but which has always simply introduced the doxology itself.[27]

FROM IMPROVISATION TO IMPOSED FORMULARIES: THE PROBLEM OF THE LITURGICAL YEAR

These incongruities which seem to us to be the price paid for a liturgical improvisation left too long, and undoubtedly much too late, to the hazards of its ancient freedom, lead us to return for the time to this problem. We can do so, now that we have before our eyes such patent evidence not only of the indefinite variety but also of the almost limitless confusion to which they were to lead.

Dom Gregory Dix is one of the rare authors concerned with this problem. But the view of it that he proposes does not seem to be very satisfying. According to him, improvisation, particularly for the eucharistic prayer, remained the quasi-universal rule up to the pivotal period between the fourth and fifth centuries. At that time, practically everywhere simultaneously in both West and East, the formulas became fixed. But in the West, a new proliferation almost immediately did away

---

[26] Mohlberg, p. 116.
[27] Cf. *Missale mixtum*, P. L., t. 85, col. 554.

with this newly acquired state. In addition, this was no longer merely a return to improvisation, but the composition of new formularies, which from the outset were fixed in writing but in such a way as to be adapted to the different feasts and seasons of the liturgical year. Thus in the East, we observed two successive phases: improvisation, fixation, while in the West, three: improvisation, fixation, and a new variety, no longer produced this time by the freedom of improvisation, but by the desire to sort out the formularies in accordance with the liturgical seasons.[28]

A first objection to this is that we do not see, in the West especially, when or where this ephemeral fixation would have come about. A second is that it would be most unlikely, supposing the authorities had wanted it and obtained it, that they would almost immediately have destroyed the imposed uniformity with a new variability.

In fact, the documents give quite a different impression. Improvisation itself, much before the fifth century and even before the fourth, soon made room for written texts, in the first place for the use of the writers themselves. Then, once they were put in circulation, they were used by those who were apparently less gifted in this kind of composition. Furthermore, this use, as we have seen, went for a long time side by side with successive reworkings. When the authority, particularly as a reaction against the Arian heresy and its extensions, was concerned with supplying safe texts, most of the time it limited itself, it seems, to canonizing compositions which already tended if not to impose themselves at least to become generalized. This was due to the prestige of their authors (true or supposed), and undoubtedly even more to their intrinsic interest. But, despite many repeated prescriptions of individual prelates or councils, the acceptance of collections composed in this way and imposed in theory, as they stood, succeeded only at a very late date and only partially in winning out. The repetition of the prescriptions itself in this sense is an admission of the remodeling, the combining and the additions which for a very long time continued to be practiced. The Byzantine East, despite its Caesaro-papism, never succeeded

---

[28] Cf. Gregory Dix, *The Shape of the Liturgy*, pp. 527 ff.

on its own in imposing everywhere the two formularies, of St. John Chrysostom and St. Basil, that it claimed to canonize exclusively. It never even came to fix the text definitively. The East that had escaped Byzantium and became Nestorian or Monophysite ceased making up new formularies for itself only when Islam progressively stifled Christian culture. Where this strangulation did not happen, as in Ethiopia, or with the Maronites, the creation of new formularies continued all throughout the Middle Ages.

In the West, Rome and the Churches under her influence, very soon adopted a fixed form for the greater part of the elements of the eucharistic prayer that followed the *Sanctus*. Still, for the *Communicantes* and the *Hanc igitur*, this fixation was very late and never complete. The first part, the thanksgiving properly so-called, is not set even in our own day. Elsewhere, as long as the local rites survived, they never experienced anything of this sort. It is admittedly characteristic of the West that this multiplicity of formulas, preserved for a longer time, came down to us in a framework which more profoundly than elsewhere pressed upon it the mark of the liturgical year. But this comes first of all from the fact that the creation of new formulas continued there until after the time when the liturgical year became diversified. To the extent that, in the East as well (as is the case particularly in Ethiopia), improvisation, or at the very least the making of new compositions, was preserved concurrently with a stronger diversification of the ecclesiastical seasons, the results of the first also reflected the evolution of the second.

But even in the West, we must not rush to the conclusion that everything that will ultimately be connected with a given day was composed precisely for that purpose. What we see from the outset in the oldest collections, is a classification of interchangeable formulas which tends to be set up in view of their possible appropriateness for one day rather than another. But, in a number of cases, there remains a considerable portion that is arbitrary. This is demonstrated quite well from one collection to another where we see the same texts receiving quite different locations. It seems that it is only very progressively that the transition was made from the attribution assigned after the fact

to more or less universal formulas (with or without revising them)
to the deliberate composition of formulas with a particular objective, determined either by the liturgical year or by some votive office. We have already shown how the oldest prefaces that
have been retained in the Roman missal, such as for Easter, Christmas or Epiphany, could at first have been used generally, and
could still be interchanged today wiṭhout much difficulty. For
a stronger reason, the examples of secrets or postcommunions
which have no specific motifs that would assign them to one mass
rather than another are innumerable. In fact, all of these prayers
have been so often changed from one mass to another that it is
at times very hard to tell for what mass they were composed in
the beginning, and even whether they ever did have any definite objective.

The same phenomenon is more evident in the Gallican or Mozarabic books. Not only were there Sunday or ferial interchanging masses that never had any specific attribution, but we may
estimate that a good half of those that did were not composed
with that object in view, while a number of others can be applied specifically, but rather as a result of a fortuitous coincidence
than by preconceived design.

The *post-secreta* of the Christmas mass of the *Missale Gothicum* seems to fit into this last category.

> We believe, Lord, in your coming (*adventum*), and we re-
> call your passion. Your body was broken for the forgiveness
> of our sins, your blood shed as the price of our redemption ...[29]

It is in all likelihood the presence of the word *adventum* which
caused this prayer to be placed where it was. But it seems unlikely that it was in fact composed for Christmas. Many pieces,
even placed under the heading of a great feast day with a very
characteristic theme, do not even have such a pretext to justify
their presence here as opposed to anywhere else. It is enough
to quote the *post-mysterium* from the same collection for the Assumption of the Virgin. It obviously has nothing to do either
with this mystery or even with Mary:

[29] Mohlberg, p. 7.

Let there descend, Lord, upon these sacrifices, the Spirit Paraclete, the co-eternal cooperator of your blessing, that the oblation we present to you, from the fruit of the earth which belongs to you, through a new heavenly exchange, may return to us once it has been sanctified. May this fruit changed into your body, the cup into your blood, which we have offered for our sins become a merit for us; grant this, almighty God ...[30]

When we become aware of these facts, this question of improvisation and the authoritarian fixing of the liturgical formulas, especially the eucharistic formulas, appears in a new light. In the first place, it is not the introduction of a profusely ramified liturgical year that always preserved a certain variability of the formularies in the West. It is on the contrary the persistence of an improvisation that was more or less supervised, and more or less held in check by the authorities, that gave rise little by little to a conforming of the formulas of the eucharistic prayer to the detailed plan of this year, which in great part, actually, was artificial and *post factum*. If, on the other hand, the Byzantine East itself was able more or less successfully to impose the exclusive use of two formularies only, and Rome, one formula, but only for one part of the eucharist, it is first of all because they had come upon a few examples of such excellent compositions that the authority had only to support, and at the most press for, a spontaneous movement toward unification. In the Extreme West, as in Ethiopia or among the Syrians who had escaped from the Byzantine orbit, the continuance of improvisation to such a late date was the result of the multiplicity of passable formularies (although not one bore the authority of a great name, nor stood out because of any exceptional merit, at least in so far as there was no attempt at centralization on the part of any imperial or pontifical authority). If Rome herself, up to our own day, has allowed a multiplicity and even a continued multiplication at least of the prefaces in the eucharist, it is quite simply because there was never a text that had enough fulness or authority to be imposed. There was only a variety

[30] Mohlberg, p. 30.

of texts, which lent themselves rather to the complementarity of their alternation than to the exclusive predominance of one or other of them.

There still remains for us to shed some light upon a question that is inevitably posed by the Gallican and Mozarabic sacramentaries. Many are the masses where certain parts are lacking. We find, for example, an *immolatio-contestatio* or an *illatio*, without a *post-sanctus* or a *post-mysterium*, and even without either of these. In this case, what was the celebrant to do? Three hypotheses are possible. Either he chose at his pleasure something neutral enough from another collection, or he again improvised in order to fill out what was lacking, or else, as Mgr. Eugraphe Kovalevsky imagines, he had recourse to some hypothetical all-purpose prayer: a formulary which was able to fill up any of the gaps in the proper. The only possible foundation for this last supposition is the *Missale omnium offerentium*. But this exists only in very late manuscripts, and the *Missa Omnimoda* of the *Liber Ordinum* of Silos, which comes close to it does not seem, itself, to be prior to the eleventh century.[31] It is from this *Missale* that Giménez de Cisneros got the fixed formulas of the *Sanctus* and the words of institution (still lacking in the ancient books) in order to print them in his *Missale Mixtum* of 1500. But the formula of the Last Supper narrative begins with *In qua nocte tradebatur*, despite the fact that the prayers that follow in the Hispanic tradition are always called *post-pridie*. The hypothesis of an influence from the Eastern liturgies that could still have been felt in the eleventh century seems questionable. This exception from the old usage seems to give evidence quite simply that still at this time the freedom of improvisation in Spain was sufficiently alive for the composer of a mass to think that he was right in using the Pauline formula rather than the formula from the Synoptics, even despite local custom. If this was the case, we should be led *a fortiori* to think that the ministers of the Mozarabic rite, as long as it remained alive, were as free to improvise in all of the non-fixed parts in a given mass as they were to have recourse to the formulas of another mass.

[31] Cf. *Missale Mixtum*; P. L., t. 85, col. 530.

THE *ORATIO FIDELIUM* AND THE INTERCESSIONS
OF THE CANON

But there still remains one other general problem which the examination of the Gallican and Mozarabic liturgies allows us to clarify. It is that of the connection between the prayers accompanying the offertory which have in the Latin tradition the title *orationes* (or *oratio*) *fidelium* and the intercessions and commemorations of the anaphora. The liturgists who, in general, are ignorant of Jewish tradition, and more or less fascinated by the *Apostolic Tradition*, tend to explain the presence of such prayers in the canon as a late doublet of the *oratio fidelium*. Yet there is a general fact that ought to put them on guard against this hypothesis: that is that the unquestionable doublets, in all the liturgies of a more or less recent vintage, that we may observe between the prayers of the canon and those of the offertory, rather interpret the tendency to anticipate the themes of the eucharist from the point of the offertory, than to bring into the eucharist properly so called something that was originally to be found between the readings and this point. However, on first sight, the evolved Gallican and Mozarabic liturgies in which these invocations and intercessions are absent from the eucharist, would seem to justify the hypothesis in question. Here again, however, there are pieces which include these intercessions and commemorations, as Baumstark has already observed,[32] and which cannot be completely explained by an influence of the Roman canon. They lead us rather to suppose a more ancient stage which would have only left a few survivers behind.

The solution of this problem can only be reached through a more careful examination of the *oratio fidelium* itself. Its complete study would require a whole book, so we shall limit ourselves here to an outline of it, to the extent that it is necessary for our purpose. In the Eastern liturgies, the *oratio fidelium* was always clad in the form of an *ektenia*, that is a succession of prayers proclaimed by the deacon to which the people responded with a stereotyped formula (generally, Κύριε ἐλέησον). We

---

[32] Cf. Baumstark, *Comparative Liturgy*, p. 45, n. 6.

find the same thing in the Ambrosian masses for Lent, and it seems that it was also in this form that it was ultimately practised by our liturgies of the Extreme West.

But the Roman liturgy seems indeed to have been preserved for us in an older form. This is the *orationes sollemnes* still recited today on Good Friday. Up to the end of the Middle Ages, they were also present in the mass of Spy Wednesday, and Dom Maïeul Cappuyns has established that this indeed was the ancient form of the *oratio fidelium* in every Roman Mass.[33] After each monition (today recited by the priest, but which in the beginning must have been recited by the deacon after the priest's *oremus*), there is a moment of silent prayer on the part of all the faithful who remain on their knees. After this period of silence, the subdeacon gives the sign to arise and the celebrant concludes with a summary in the form of a collect, which must have been the essential kernel of the prayer of the congregation on the theme that had previously been indicated.

This is already enough to indicate that the *oratio fidelium* must be interpreted strictly. This is the prayer *of the faithful* in the sense that it is a prayer which the faithful are invited to make on their own in their own words. The intervention of the deacon before the prayer, or on the part of the priest after the prayer has no other aim but to give them guidance and in no way to substitute for them.

But it seems that the liturgy of the baptism of adults allows us to go back to a stage that is still earlier than that of the *oratio fidelium*. At each of the scrutinies to which the catechumens are submitted, they are invited to pray. They are then on their knees and pray in silence for a moment. The celebrant invites them subsequently to "complete" their prayer. They rise and add the *Amen* without the minister pronouncing any formula.

This leads us to suppose that in the beginning there was merely the invitation to a silent and personal prayer, without the concluding collect, and indeed possibly without any initial admonition other than the general invitation to prayer.

---

[33] D. Maïeul Cappuyns, "Les orationes sollemnes du Vendredi-Saint", in *Questions liturgiques et paroissialss*, February 1938, pp. 18 ff.

If now we were to connect all this up with the Jewish liturgy, we can only recall the ancient practice, still preserved today in the Synagogue, of preceding the recitation of the Eighteen Blessings of the *Tefillah*, solemnly sung by the celebrant, with a silent recitation on the part of each person present. But, from the Rabbis themselves we know that in the beginning each individual instead of reciting the *Tefillah* on his own account, limited himself to praying freely in silence on the well known themes which were then to be recited aloud in the prayer of the *Shaliach sibbur*.

We find then exactly what seems initially to have been the relationship between the *oratio fidelium* and the prayers of the minister, chanted in connection with the *Sanctus* and the thanksgivings connected with it. It is therefore from the minister's recitation of the great prayer (which at first was the conclusion of the service of readings, before it became the beginning of the eucharistic prayer) that the later formulations of the *oratio fidelium* derive. They are an anticipation of the sacerdotal and public prayer in a prayer which each participant made primarily on his own and in silence. Concern for giving this prayer some direction created this doublet, before the silent prayer, framed by the deacon's admonition and the priest's oration, became dwarfed beside these two additional clerical formulas.

The conclusion seems unavoidable: if the restoration of the *oratio fidelium* is most desirable, it is not enough merely to add diaconal or sacerdotal prayers to the offertory in restoring it; the personal prayer that constituted it must be recreated, and these two formulas, which in themselves are secondary, must have no other purpose than to elicit it. Under the vain illusion of restoring the eucharist to its primitive state, it would be all the more absurd were we to deprive it of a sacerdotal prayer which is in its original place in order to transport it to a position which it had only secondarily through a simple pedagogical doublet. This will remain deprived of its original meaning as long as it takes the place of the real prayer of the faithful: a personal and silent prayer, which it was only meant to inspire.

The Middle Ages:
Development and Deformation

THE CONCEPT OF "MIDDLE AGES" IS MOST NEBULOUS, FOR IT covers a succession of very varied periods. Moreover, it is as difficult to tell when this period begins as it is to specify the moment when it ended. From our point of view here, we might say that the Churches which became Nestorian or Monophysite in the Syrian, Coptic or Armenian East entered into the Middle Ages the minute that they left the Byzantine orbit spiritually as well as materially. Today, it would not be possible to say that they have yet emerged from this period. At Byzantium, on the other hand, if the Middle Ages existed, they are not really separable from patristic antiquity before the time of the fall of Constantinople, that is, at the moment that we tend to believe the Middle Ages came to an end in the West. Even at Rome we can begin the Middle Ages right after St. Gregory. But it was a long time before the greater part of the Western world entered this period itself.

THE MULTIPLICATION OF THE LATE FORMULARIES
AND THEIR DEFORMATION

We understand that we call the Middle Ages here everything that still tried to preserve the patristic tradition for better or worse, although people had already begun to misunderstand it. Consequently, this tradition continued to exist in a sort of parasitic vegetation of practices and formulas rather than through coherent developments of thought. Again, we must add that these developments did not disappear all at once. And, especially, when we are thinking of the Latin West, we must never forget that the Middle Ages were not so much followed by one "renascence" as it was crossed by successive "renascences": in the eleventh and in the twelfth and thirteenth centuries particularly, the latter being scarcely less important than the one which was to follow in the fifteenth and sixteenth centuries and seemed—in appearance only—to sweep away the Middle Ages.

Since our study here only involves the eucharistic prayer, we shall first have to speak of the latter developments—which are more deformations than developments—that the eucharist in this restricted but original sense was to experience. Then we shall come to the problem of the "silence of the canon," a silence into which the eucharistic prayer, most significantly, fell almost everywhere from the beginning of this period. Lastly we shall treat all the new creations that were proposed to fill up this silence. They were first aimed at the faithful or the simple clerics who followed the priest's mass instead of still taking part in the mass with him. But very shortly since the priest himself began, through force of circumstances, by being a simple cleric, and before that a more or less devout layman, he was no longer able to enter into the silence of the canon, supposedly reserved for him, without bringing along a very curious grab-bag of a substitutive eucharistic piety. At this moment, despite sporadic efforts at revival, or simple reaction, the eucharistic prayer survived only as a venerable mummy, respectfully embalmed and shrouded with protective strips. Some "reformers" who were only slightly more impatient than their predecessors were then able to come onto the scene. They thought that all they had to do was to throw out this old dried-up relic in order to rediscover the original eucharist. But after this, nothing more was left.

After successively adopting the liturgies of St. Basil and St. John Chrysostom, the Byzantine Church, as we said, held invariably to these two texts, eliminating little by little all those that had competed with them. If the following generations were to develop considerably the secondary parts of the eucharistic liturgy, they made no more modifications in the eucharistic prayer except a few variants of minor importance.[1] The only exception on this point is an overloading of the epiclesis, particularly among the Slavs, which doubled it through the introduction of a prayer addressed directly to the Holy Spirit and taken into the eucharist from the divine office.[2]

The Armenians have been practically as conservative concerning the eucharistic prayer, despite the richness of their own compositions in general, and their liberal borrowings from other traditions, from the old Byzantine tradition to the most evolved medieval forms of the Roman liturgy. After using St. James, St. Basil and St. John Chrysostom, they finally settled upon one eucharistic prayer which they attribute to Athanasius of Alexandria, but which seems to be a properly Armenian reworking of St. Basil or St. James and difficult to date. Yet they also used in the past versions in their own language of more or less late Syrian or Egyptian liturgies, like those named after St. Ignatius or St. Gregory of Nazianzum on the one hand, and St. Cyril on the other, as well as a mysterious liturgy of St. Isaac (would this be the Nestorian bishop, Isaac of Niniveh?), and another more or less autochthonous liturgy attributed to their great missionary, Gregory the Illuminator.[3]

This progressive reduction of the variety of the eucharistic prayers down to one or a few relatively ancient models did not come about in the other Churches separated from Byzantium, with the one exception, to a certain extent, of the Church of the Nestorians. Not only is the very archaic liturgy of Addai and Mari, which they have preserved encased in a development which itself is very old, unquestionably from a rather early period (with the exception of a few interpolations), but so also are the two

---

[1] Cf. the text of the *Codex Barberini* given by Brightman and the modern text that follows it, in his edition. On this subject, see P. N. Trempelas, *The Three Liturgies after the Greek Manuscripts* (in Greek) (Athens, 1935).

[2] Cf. F. Mercier, *La prière des Églises de rite byzantin*, vol. I (Amay-sur-Meuse, 1937).

[3] Cf. I. Hanssens, *Institutiones liturgicae*, t. III, pars altera, pp. 584 ff.

other liturgical prayers which they use, attributed respectively to Nestorius and Theodore of Mopsuestia.[4]

The Jacobites of Syria, on the contrary, while retaining the anaphora of St. James, have added to it numerous eucharistic prayers, a great number of which have also been kept in use by the Maronites. Brightman, at the end of the last century, pointed to 43 known formularies, of which only 19 were published in the original Syriac, the others being available through the Latin translations of Renaudot or Assemani. He pointed out that there were 21 other known anaphoras that were never published. It is enough to glance at the more recent findings of Fr. Hanssens to observe the extent that these numbers have grown in half a century, and now discoveries have not yet ceased.[5]

The same is true with the Copts of Egypt. The ancient Church of Egypt, besides the liturgy of St. Mark which was more or less influenced in its evolved forms by the Syrian liturgies, used an archaic form of the liturgy of St. Basil, and an anaphora attributed to St. Gregory of Nazianzum, and which in any case is a Syrian anaphora brought to the desert of Skete by monks of this nationality. The Coptic documents have versions of these three anaphoras (generally attributing that of St. Mark to St. Cyril), which permit us frequently to go back to a state of the Greek texts that is older than the one that is directly available to us. But they include a multitude of other later eucharistic prayers, like the series of anaphoras recently brought out by Dom Emmanuel Lanne.[6]

The Ethiopians, while borrowing the basic part from the Copts and many other anaphoras from the Syrians and even the Armenians did not fail to add compositions of their own making. Such are the anaphora of Our Lord or that of Our Lady as well as texts attributed to the "318 Orthodox" (the Fathers of the Council of Nicaea), to St. Athanasius, to St. Epiphanius, etc. Here we also find, under the name of the Anaphora of the Apostles, a combination of the eucharist of Hippolytus with a

---

[4] *Ibid.*, pp. 622 ff.

[5] *Ibid.*, pp. 596 ff.

[6] *Ibid.*, pp. 635 ff. Cf. D. Emmanuel Lanne, "Le grand Euchologe du monastère blanc," in *Patrologia orientalis*, t. 28, fasc. 2, 1958.

framework and complementary elements taken from St. Mark-St. Cyril.[7]

The Roman canon, once it was imposed everywhere, hardly ever varies in the West except in the preface. These prefaces were very varied in patristic times, enriched from Gallican or Mozarabic sources and continued to proliferate throughout the whole of the Middle Ages.

We could not dream of examining in detail this enormous body of literature, of which only one part has been published. We shall then be content with a few probings. They will soon show us that originality now mostly consists only in more or less felicitous variations on themes we have already encountered, when it is not merely negative. In fact, what dominates this enormous production is a general tendency to conceal, if not to disintegrate the original and basic themes of the eucharist under parasitical vegetation. A tradition which attempts to protract itself, admits that it no longer has any control over itself except very imperfectly. When it is not fixed, it tends only to dissolve.

THE EUCHARIST OF NESTORIUS: SCHOLASTIC THEOLOGY AND BIBLICAL OVERLAY

The eucharist that the Nestorians attribute to Nestorius was for some time looked upon by Baumstark as the old liturgy of Constantinople of which the liturgy of St. John Chrysostom would be only an abbreviation. Schermann saw the unlikelihood of this hypothesis and Dom Engberding demonstrated it so clearly that Baumstark, with a good grace that is uncommon with critics, frankly acknowledged his mistake.[8] Quite the contrary is true. It is the formulary attributed to St. John Chrysostom, or perhaps to his old Antiochean forebear, which must have undergone copious scriptural and theological injections before it arrived at the formulary named after Nestorius. We must even admit that there is among these additions at least one section which only with difficulty seems attributable to a fifth-century editor.

---

[7] *Ibid.*, pp. 638 ff.
[8] Cf. Baumstark, *Comparative Liturgy*, pp. 55-56.

Here, first of all, is the whole part of the prayer that goes up to the words of institution inclusively:

Lord, mighty one, you who are, eternal, God the almighty Father who are always what you are, it is meet, fit and right that we praise you, that we confess you, that we adore you, that we exalt you always and ever. You are indeed the true, incomprehensible, infinite, inexplicable, invisible, simple, imperceptible to the senses, immortal, sublime God, above the thought and the intelligence of all creatures, you who are in every place, and understood nowhere, you and your Only-Begotten Son, and your Holy Spirit. Do you, Lord, give us the ability to speak that we might open our mouths in your presence, and offer to you, with a contrite heart and a humbled mind, the spiritual fruits of our lips, (our) reasonable worship: you are indeed our God and the Father of our Lord and Savior Jesus Christ, our hope, the one in whom all the treasures of Wisdom and knowledge are hidden, and through whom we have received the knowledge of the Holy Spirit, the Spirit of truth who proceeds from you, O Father, and is of the hidden nature of your divinity. It is through him that all rational natures, visible or invisible, are fortified, sanctified and perfected. And to you, to your Only-Begotten Son and to your Holy Spirit, they offer always perpetual praise, for all are your work. For it is you who have brought us forth and ordered us out of nothing to existence. We have sinned and we have fallen, but while we were perishing in our decline, you renewed us, lifted us up and redeemed us, you had no rest until you have visited us all in your great solicitude, in order to raise us up to heaven and to give us, by your mercy, your Kingdom which is to come. And for all these benefits in our regard, we give you thanks in truth, O God the Father, and to your Only-Begotten Son and your living and Holy Spirit as well, and we worship you for all these benefits you have accorded us, both those that we know and those we do not know, those that are manifest and those that are secret. We give you thanks also for this ministry, beseeching you to receive it from our hands: indeed, what would suffice to tell the miracles of your power and to make all your praises heard?

If even all creatures were but one mouth and one tongue, they would not suffice, Lord, to speak of your majesty. For, before your Trinity, Lord, there stand a thousand thousands and ten thousand myriads of Angels: all flying together unceasingly and for ever, with one shrill voice that is never silent, praise and exult you, crying out to one another, saying and answering:

Holy, holy, holy, Lord, Strong One, of whom heaven and earth are full!

And together with these heavenly powers, we also, good Lord and merciful God, cry out and say: you are truly holy, truly worthy of being glorified, exalted, O Sublime One, you who have made your worshippers on earth worthy of being likened to those who glorify you in heaven. Holy also is your Only-Begotten Son, our Lord Jesus Christ, together with the Holy Spirit, (this Son) who coexists with you from all eternity, partaking in the same nature, and the author of all creatures. We bless, Lord, God the Word, the hidden Son, who proceeds from your bosom, who, although he was like you, and the image of your substance, did not look upon equality with you as plunder, but emptied himself and took on the likeness of a slave, a perfect man with a rational, intelligent and immortal soul, and a mortal human body, which he conjoined to himself and united to himself in glory, power and honor, although he was passible by nature, he who was formed by the power of the Holy Spirit for the salvation of all, made from a woman, made under the law, to redeem those who were under the law and to give life to all those who died in Adam; he destroyed sin in his flesh and destroyed the law of the commandments with his commandments; he opened the eyes of our blinded minds and made straight for us the path of salvation, and he enlightened us with the light of divine knowledge. To those who received him, he gave the power of being made children of God; he purified us and he made atonement for us through the baptism with holy water, and he sanctified us by his grace in the gift of the Holy Spirit. Those who were buried with him in baptism, he resurrected, he raised them up, he transported them to heaven with him in accordance with his promise. And as he had loved his own in this world, he loved them even to the end, and offering himself in our stead for the punishment due to the sin of our race, for the life of all he gave himself for all over to the death which ruled over us and to whose

power we were subject, having been sold to it because of
our sins, and by his precious blood he redeemed and saved
us, he descended into hell and untied the bonds of the death
which was devouring us. But, since it was right that the
prince of our salvation be not held in hell by death, he rose
from the dead on the third day and became the first fruits
of those who sleep, in such a way that he was the first in
all things; he ascended into heaven, sat at the right hand of
your majesty, O God. And he left us a memorial of our salvation, this mystery which we have offered in your presence.
For, when the time had come for him to be handed over for
the life of the world, after having supped, on the Passover
of the law of Moses, he took bread into his holy, spotless
and immaculate hands, he blessed it, broke it, ate, and gave
some to his disciples and said: Take, eat of it all of you, this
is my body which is broken for you for the remission of sins.
Likewise, he mixed wine and water in the cup, blessed it,
drank of it, and gave it to his disciples and said: Drink of
this all of you, this is my blood of the new covenant which
is shed for a great number for the remission of sins, and do
this as a memorial of me until I come. Indeed, as often as
you eat of this bread and drink of this cup, you proclaim
my death until I come. Thus, whoever with a genuine faith
comes forth to partake of it, let them be for him, Lord, for
the remission of sins, the great expectation of the resurrection from the dead, and the new life in the Kingdom of heav-
en.[9]

This prayer, undoubtedly, has very attractive aspects, like beginning the second part of the thanksgiving with the glorification
of God for the very fact that he has allowed us to join in the glorification that the heavenly spirits give him. However, we can
also find here a primary root of the subjective elements which
were to lead to those apologies whereby the priest, before performing his function of proclaiming the *mirabilia Dei*, would inter-
mingle supplications and thanksgivings for the awesome privilege
given him of standing at the altar. But, over all, if the whole of

---

[9] See in the Anglican edition of Urmia, 1890, *Liturgia sanctorum Apostolorum* etc., pp. 40 ff. for the Syriac text. Latin translation in Renaudot,
t. II, pp. 627 ff.

this text, as is obvious, reminds us of the other great example of a theological and biblical anaphora, which we owe to St. Basil, and from which it makes many borrowings, it certainly does not benefit by the comparison. It may be said of the eucharist of Nestorius that it has the effect of a Basilian anaphora which lost out on two accounts. It is no less doctrinal and no less scriptural, yet it still does not succeed in fusing the biblical references into an organic whole, nor in marrying to its own theology the great continuous line of the history of salvation. The quotations from the holy books are merely a rattling off of references, as in a mediocre scholastic tract. It could not be otherwise, once theology itself was no longer the development of a contemplation of the divine Word, but a simple pile-up of scholarly digressions.

We shall find the same weaknesses, and even more developed if possible, in the anamnesis. Like other more or less late prayers which we have already encountered, it turns in order to the confession of faith. But, what is more, it cannot always resist every temptation, either to pile up quotations or to lose itself in some equally idle digression. The following intercession, which is equally prolix, is well formed.

And we also, Lord God, mighty Father, commemorate this command and the salvation which it has accomplished for us. Before all things, we believe you and we confess you, God, the true Father, and the eternal Son, Only-Begotten, of (your) divinity, who proceeds from you, conjoint with you by his consubstantiality, his admirable economy which has come about through our humanity and which has been dispensed for our salvation; the cross and the passion, the death. the burial, the resurrection on the third day, the ascension into heaven, the sitting at the right hand and the second coming to us in glory of our Lord Jesus Christ, whereupon he is to judge the living and the dead, and to render to each according to his works. We confess also the Holy Spirit, who is of the glorious substance of your divinity, who, with you and your Only-Begotten (Son) is adored and glorified; and we offer you this living, holy, acceptable, glorious and unbloody sacrifice, for all creatures; and for the holy, apostolic and catholic Church, from one end of the earth to the other, that you may preserve her in your tranquility and in shelter from every scandal, and that there may be in her no spot or blemish or wrinkle or anything of that sort, indeed, you have said, through your Only-Begotten Son, our Lord Jesus Christ, that the gates of hell would not prevail against her. And for all Bishops in every place and region who announce the orthodox word of the true faith. And for all Priests, who perform their sacrifice in your presence, in the righteousness and holiness of truth. And for all Deacons, who preserve the mystery of your faith in a pure conscience. And for every condition of your devout and holy people everywhere. And for all those who knowingly or in ignorance have sinned and offended you. And for your unworthy and guilty servant whom you have made worthy by your grace to offer this oblation before you. And for all those who celebrate your holy Church by works of righteousness in a praiseworthy manner. And for all those who dispense alms to the poor. And for all faithful Kings and the stability of their rule. And for all the princes and authorities of this world; we beg and beseech you, Lord, strengthen them in your fear, impress your truth upon them, and submit all barbarian nations to them. We call upon your Godhead, Lord, that you might repel wars to the ends of the earth and that you weaken those nations who wish war, so that we might dwell in tranquility and serenity, in all temperance and fear of the Lord. And for the fruits of the earth, and a healthful climate, that you may bless the crown of the year with your grace. And for this place and those that dwell therein, that you may have mercy upon them, that you may bless them, that you may keep and protect them by your clemency. And for all those who travel, on sea or on land. And for all those who are in chains, in anguish, persecutions, oppressions and trials on account of your name. And for all those in exile, in tribulations and in prisons, sent to far off islands and to unending suffering, or subject to a bitter slavery. And for all our captive brethren; we beseech you, Lord, to come to the aid also of those who are afflicted with miseries and painful infirmities. Finally, we call upon your mercy, Lord, by your grace, for all our enemies, and those who hate us, and for all those who think evil against us; not for judgment or vengeance, Lord, mighty God, but for lovingkindnesses and salvation, and the forgiveness of sins, for you will that all men live and be converted to the recognition of truth. It is you, indeed, who have commanded us, through your beloved Son, our Lord Jesus Christ, to pray to you for our enemies and for those who hate us, and for those who dominate us violently and unjustly ...

... Lord, powerful God, we beseech you, in blessing and worshipping you in your presence: convert the wayward, enlighten those who are in darkness, strengthen the weak, raise up those who have fallen, sustain those who are upright, and everything that can be fitting and useful, procure for all through your lovingkindnesses. Again we beg and beseech you, Lord, to be mindful in this oblation of the Fathers, the Patriarchs, the Prophets, the Apostles, the Martyrs, the Confessors, the Doctors, the Bishops, the Priests, the Deacons and all those who partake in our ministry and who have left this world, and all our brothers in Christ who have left this world in the true faith, whose names are known to you: absolving and forgiving them all their sins, all in which they have offended you, as men subject to error and to passions, through the prayer and intercession of those who have been pleasing to you. Look upon us and have mercy upon all, your servants and handmaids, who stand before your altar. Make us worthy of having a part in the inheritance of the saints in light, and give us, in the abundance of charity and the purity of thought, to live before you, in this world wherein we are pilgrims, in the possession of an exact knowledge of the true faith in you, and communicating in your awesome and holy mysteries, that we may not be confounded and condemned when we stand before the terrible throne of your majesty. And as in this world you have made us worthy of the ministry of your awesome and holy mysteries, so grant us in the world to come to partake, with uncovered face, of all the good things which neither pass away nor perish. When you consummate what we attain here in figures and enigmas, may we possess openly the holy of holies in heaven.[10]

We have omitted a prolix apologia of the celebrant, which for the length of a page interrupts the prayer for the Church. It

---

[10] Renaudot, *op. cit.*, pp. 630 ff.

seems difficult to attribute it to the original text, despite its tendency to digress. The epiclesis which comes at the end of the prayer, in accordance with the order proper to the East Syrian liturgies, here as in the long form of the eucharist of Addai and Mari is introduced by a return to the theme of the anamnesis, which on the other hand is found complete in the liturgy of Theodore at the beginning of the intercessions.

Wherefore we, Lord, your useless, weak and infirm servants, who were far from you but whom, through the multitude of your kindnesses you have made worthy to stand and to accomplish in your presence this awesome, glorious and excellent ministry, we beseech your adorable Godhead which restores all creatures: Lord, let the grace of your Spirit come, let it dwell in and repose upon this oblation which we have offered in your presence, let it sanctify and make this bread and this cup the body and the blood of our Lord Jesus Christ, transforming them yourself and sanctifying them through the operation of your Holy Spirit, so that the reception of these holy mysteries may be for us who partake of them (a source of) eternal life and of resurrection from the dead, atonement of body and soul, illumination of knowledge, confidence before you and the eternal salvation about which you have spoken to us through Jesus Christ our Lord, so that all of us together may be joined unanimously, by one and the same bond of charity and peace, and that we may become one body and one Spirit, just as we have been called in one hope of our vocation. Let no one eat or drink of them unto the condemnation of his body and soul, and let no sickness or infirmity come to him on account of his sins, because he would have eaten this bread and drunk this cup unworthily. May he rather be strengthened and confirmed for all that is pleasing to you, so that we may be worthy to communicate with a good conscience in the body and blood of your Christ. When we stand before you, at that awesome and glorious tribunal, in the presence of the throne of your majesty, may we obtain mercy and grace, enjoy the future good things which do not pass away, with all those who, over the centuries, have been pleasing to you, by the grace and the mercies of your Only-Begotten Son, with whom, Lord, be glory, honor, power, and exaltation unto you, and to your

living, holy and sanctifying Spirit, now and always and forever and ever.[11]

Here again, as we see, the successful passages are unhappily
smothered by the exhausting dissertations which have more the
feeling of coming from a professorial chair than an altar. Yet we
should not neglect to point out, in the epiclesis which closes the
intercessions, as well as at their beginning after the anamnesis, the
profound doctrinal perspective that places the Church, its fulfilment,
first in holiness and then in unity, at the beginning and at the
end of the supplication included in the eucharist.

Again we decided to quote this text in its entirety despite its
intolerable longwindedness, or rather because of it. Here we can
see actually how the eucharist, at the end of the patristic period,
tended to expand into what first was merely a pedantic rhetoric,
but ultimately soon turned into pious ramblings.

THE ARMENIAN EUCHARIST: FIDELITY TO TRADITION IN NEW DEVELOPMENTS

However, we can still find in this body of late literature some more
successful examples of a new expression of the perennial themes.
The best is perhaps that of the Armenian eucharist in the form
that was to prevail and which is attributed by the books (without
a shade of probability) to St. Athanasius of Alexandria. We have
already said that the Armenian liturgy is both one of the most
eclectic in its sources as well as one of the most creative in original
ritual pieces or details. But it possesses further the rare privilege
of synthesizing all of this into organic wholes which maintain a
sumptuous but always orderly beauty with the most oriental
opulence. Devotion can be at its fullest without the sense of the
sacred ever being disturbed. It would be most easy for this super-
Byzantine liturgy to become theatrical and melodramatic but an
unfailing esthetic and religious sense preserves it from ever being
so. These features are nowhere more in evidence than in this last
of the ancient eucharistic prayers that we shall quote integrally.

---

[11] Renaudot, *op. cit.*, pp. 633 ff.

It is generally looked upon as a reworking of the Basilian anaphora, but, despite analogies with this text, it seems to us that it rather follows the development of St. James. The interventions on the part of the faithful (today replaced by the choir) and of the deacon which gradually invaded all the Eastern liturgies constantly interrupt the celebrant's prayer to paraphrase it. This commentary now has reached the point of hiding its object. But it is interesting to see in this liturgy the rare example of an evolution which despite this managed to come to a halt just at the point where the balance between tradition and novelty was threatening to break down.[12]

The priest himself says:
  May the grace and the love and the divine power of the Father and of the Son and of the Holy Spirit be with you and with all.
Choir: And with your spirit.
  It is now the *deacon* instead of the priest who continues: The doors! The doors! With wisdom and attentiveness! Lift up your minds in the fear of God.
Choir: We have lifted them up to you, Almighty One.
Deacon: Give thanks to the Lord with all your heart.
Choir: It is meet and right and availing to salvation (to give thanks to him), for in all places this Christ of God is sacrificed. The Seraphim quake, the Cherubim tremble, and all the heavenly powers cry out and say:

During this last response, the priest now says in a low voice the whole beginning of the eucharist:

  It is truly meet and right to glorify you with all our might in worshipping you always, Almighty Father, you who have broken the bond of the curse by your ineffable Word, the creator together with you, who has formed his Church from the peoples who believe in you, and who was pleased to dwell among us, through the lowliness of our nature, in accordance with the dispensation that was fulfilled in the Virgin, and

---

12 We are following the text given in the *Ordo divinae Missae Armenorum*, published at Rome in 1644. There are Latin and French translations in P. Lebrun, in the third volume of his *Explication ... des prières et cérémonies de la Messe*, pp. 156 ff., of the reedition of 1843.

who thus made a heaven of earth, through a new work, a most divine creation. He whose spendor the heavenly armies, stricken with fear by the brilliant and inaccessible light of the Godhead, cannot bear, he has become man for our salvation and has allowed us to join our voices to the heavenly choirs,

Then he continues aloud:

and to be bold with one voice, together with the Seraphim and the Cherubim, and to proclaim with assurance, and to cry out and say: Holy, holy, holy, Lord God of the Powers.

Then the choir sings:

Holy, holy, holy, Lord God of the Powers. The heavens are full of your glory: blessing in the highest. Blessed are you, who has come and who will come in the name of the Lord. Hosanna in the highest.

For the moment let us leave this striking example aside, the first which we have encountered, of a late development where the choir reduced to silence a basic element of the eucharistic prayer pronounced by the celebrant. It seems that here we find the primary, if not the sole origin of this "silence of the canon" which was soon to become universal. We shall return to it. For the moment, let us rather observe the introduction of the theme of the Church from the very first words of the priestly eucharist after the mention of the creation and the fall. It develops splendidly into the idea of the union of the earth with the angelic worship which is also present in Nestorius' text. But here we see no tendency toward warping the eucharist into some sort of subjectivism. On the contrary, it is the most objective view of the mystery which is given to us, earth becoming heaven and mankind becoming one with the heavenly choirs.

A curious consequence of this view seems to be reflected in the formula of the *Sanctus*. While the ancient *Qedushah* spoke only of the earth being filled with God's glory to which the first Christian *Sanctus's* (inspired, as we said, by the *targumim*) added heaven, in the Armenian *Sanctus* only heaven remains. The blessing which is followed and not preceded by the Hosanna expresses the apocalyptic view of the one who "has come and who will come."

The priest continues, again in a low voice, while the choir sings the *Sanctus*:

Holy, holy, holy, you are truly holy: who could claim to express in words the tender outpourings of your immense kindness towards us? O you, who from the beginning, raising fallen man in so many ways, have comforted him through the prophets, by the gift of the law, by a priesthood in which the victims offered are figurative, but who, when the time was fulfilled, wiping out entirely the bond of our debts, gave us your Only-Begotten Son, to pay for us, to be our ransom, to be the victim, the anointed one, the lamb, the heavenly bread, the high-priest and the sacrifice which, while it is always dispensed to us, cannot be consumed, for having become truly man, and having taken flesh through a union without misunderstanding of the godly and holy Virgin Mary, he passed during the time of his flesh through all the sufferings of human life without sin, and to save the world and for our salvation, handed himself over voluntarily to the cross.

Taking bread into his holy, divine, immortal, spotless and creative hands, he blessed it, gave thanks, broke it and gave it to his chosen and holy disciples, while they were at table with him, saying:

The deacon interrupts: Bless, Lord!

The priest continues aloud:

Take, eat of it all of you: This is my body which is dispensed for us for the expiation of sins.

The deacon: Amen. Bless, Lord!

The priest, again in a low voice:

Likewise, taking the cup, he blessed it, gave thanks, drank from it, and gave it to his chosen and holy disciples, while they were at table with him, saying (*now aloud*): Take, drink of this all of you, this is my blood of the new covenant, which is shed for you and for many for the expiation and forgiveness of sins.

The deacon adds a double Amen, and the choir sings:

Heavenly Father, you who have handed over to death your Son, laden down with our debts, we beseech you, by the shedding of his blood, to have mercy upon your true flock.

Note the analogy with the anaphora of St. Basil in that a litany of biblical expressions defining the redemptive role of Christ is focused on a capital Pauline text (no longer Philippians 2, but Colossians 1): the bond against us on account of our trespasses which is nailed to the cross. But now everything is unified in a vision of the specifically priestly redemption, although there is constantly superimposed upon the sacrificial images the image of the cancelled debt. At the same time, the whole prayer breathes a very special atmosphere of warm devotion (close to St. James), and also of penance. This is a beautiful example of what ancient monastic asceticism summed up in the word compunction ($\varkappa\alpha\tau\acute\alpha$-$\nu\nu\xi\iota\varsigma$). It is a marked characteristic of the whole of Armenian tradition. The broadest expression of it is found in the beautiful book of prayers of Gregory of Narek, which was to remain down to our own day the favorite popular manual of devotion among the Armenians.

Here now is the anamnesis, continued in a low voice during the singing of the choir. It is only here, as in the liturgy of St. James, that the thanksgiving for the great deeds of redemption is completed. As with Nestorius, it is highly developed, but without ever lapsing as his does, into a scholarly commentary.

Your Only-Begotten Son, our benefactor, has commanded us to do this always as a memorial of you, and going down into the land of the dead, in accordance with the flesh he took from us, and bursting the gates of hell in his power he made known to us that you are the one true God, the God of the living and the dead.

Wherefore we, Lord, following this command, presenting here this saving sacrament of the body and the blood of your Only-Begotten Son, we make the memorial of his sufferings for our salvation, of his life-giving crucifixion, of his burial for three days, his blessed resurrection, his divine ascension, and his sitting at your right hand, O Father; we confess his awesome and glorious second coming.

The deacon: Bless, Lord!

The priest continues aloud (the Armenian rubric adds: "shedding tears"):

We offer you what is your own from what is your own, for all and for all things.

The choir continues immediately:

You are blessed in all things, Lord: we bless you, we praise you, we give you thanks, we beseech you, Lord, our God.

During this chant, the priest inserts a sacerdotal apologia analogous to what is found with Nestorius, although shorter, and incorporated within the rest of the prayer:

It is right, Lord, Lord our God, that we praise you, and that we continually give you thanks, you, who, overlooking our unworthiness, have made us ministers of this awesome and ineffable sacrament, not because of our merits, for we are too poor and bereft of every good thing, but always having recourse to your great mercy, we dare to exercize the ministry of the body and the blood of your Only-Begotten Son, our Lord and Savior Jesus Christ, to whom be glory, principality, and honor, now and always, world without end. *The choir continues*:

Son of God, who have immolated yourself to the Father for our reconciliation and who are distributed among us as the bread of life, by the shedding of your blood, we beseech you, have mercy upon us, the flock which you have redeemed. *Meanwhile, the priest goes on to the epiclesis, still in a low voice*:

O beneficent God, we worship you, we beseech you and beg you; send down upon us and these offered gifts your co-existent and co-eternal Holy Spirit, in order through him to make this blessed bread the body of our Lord and Savior Jesus Christ (*the deacon says*: Amen) and this blessed cup the blood of our Lord and Savior Jesus Christ (*another* Amen *of the deacon*), that through him from this blessed bread and wine you may make the true body in his own flesh and the true blood of our Lord and Savior Jesus Christ, changing them by your Holy Spirit, that he may be for all those who approach them not for their condemnation but for the propitiation and remission of sins (*final* Amen *of the deacon*).

Then follows the intercession which is constantly interlined with admonitions on the part of the deacon and the singing of the choir (which we shall omit):

Through him, grant us charity, steadfastness and a desirable peace to the whole world, to the holy Church, and to all orthodox bishops, to priests, deacons, to the kings of the whole world, to princes, to peoples, to travelers, to those at sea, the captives, the condemned, the afflicted and to those struggling against the barbarians. Through him, grant seasonable weather, the fruits of the earth, and speedy healing to those who suffer various ills.

Through him, grant rest to all those who sleep in Christ, to the holy fathers, the pontiffs, the apostles, prophets, martyrs, bishops, priests, deacons and to all the clergy of your holy Church, as well as to all the laity, men and women, who have departed from us in the faith (*he continues aloud*): with whom we beseech you to visit us, beneficent God.

That memory in this sacrifice be made of the Mother of God, the holy Virgin Mary, John the Baptist and Stephen the Protomaryr and all the saints, we beseech you ...

Again in a low voice he continues:

Remember, Lord, in your mercy, to bless your holy, catholic and apostolic Church which you have redeemed by the precious blood of your Only-Begotten Son and delivered by the holy Cross; grant her a lasting peace; Remember, Lord, in your mercy, to bless all the orthodox bishops who dispense to us in sound doctrine the word of truth (*aloud*) and especially our arch-prelate the true patriarch of the Armenians N.; preserve him for us for a long time in sound doctrine.

He continues in a low voice:

Remember, Lord, in your mercy, to bless this people here present, and those who offer this sacrifice and grant them what is needful and useful.

Remember, Lord, and have mercy upon those who offer you vows and bear fruit in your holy Church and who are mindful of the poor with compassion, and return to them a hundredfold, according to your bounty and generosity, here and in the world to come.

Remember, Lord, in your mercy to be propitious to the souls of the departed, and to the one for whom we have offered this sacrifice ... Give them rest, and light, and number them among your saints in your heavenly Kingdom, and make them worthy of your mercy.

Remember, Lord, and have mercy upon the soul of your servant ... according to your lovingkindness: (*if he is alive*) deliver his body and soul from every snare.

Remember, Lord, all those who have been recommended to our prayers, living and dead; direct our prayers and theirs according to your saving good pleasure, and grant to all their reward, but not passing and perishable goods: purifying our thoughts, make us temples worthy of receiving the body and the blood of our Lord and Savior Jesus Christ (*aloud*) to whom, with you, the almighty Father as well as the lifegiving and liberating Spirit, be glory, principality and honor, now and always, world without end. (*Choir*): Amen.

Note the explicit connection, from the beginning of the anamnesis, between the presence of Christ himself upon the altar, as the eternal propitiatory victim, and the intercessions.

This eucharistic prayer can be considered unique because of the balance it was able to preserve in the pure design of the ancient eucharist, while still introducing a devotion to the humanity of the Savior and a penitential piety, both of which are medieval. These sentiments which became prevalent in the Latin West in no way obscure the glorious vision of the accomplished redemption in this venerable text.

LATE SYRIAN ANAPHORAS AND THE ETHIOPIAN ANAPHORAS

In this regard, we could bring up the eucharist so dear to the monks of Skete, which they attributed to St. Gregory of Nazianzum, if it did not show this absolutely unwonted characteristic of being entirely addressed to the Son. However, Baumstark was inclined to take their attribution seriously, for this eucharist undeniably evokes the formulas of prayers to Christ which abound in the sermons and poems of Gregory. For our part, we would be of the opinion that it must have been composed by a reader of his work, molded by his christocentric piety and filled with the memory of his expressions.

But if we go, for example, to the Maronite anaphoras, even the most traditionally developed one, called *Charar*, or the anaphora of St. Peter, which made use of elements from Addai and Mari, we are put off by the exuberant amplification of all the formulas, the superabundance of the apologias that interrupt at every moment, and a whole tone of melodramatic pleading which transports us decidedly into another world than that of the traditional eucharist.[13]

What can be said of the Ethiopian anaphoras, in which all continuity of thought is destroyed by a succession of exclamations and digressions that are practically limitless![14]

The anaphora of our Lord, after a few words addressed to the Father, turns to the Son:

> We give Thee thanks, Holy God, the End of our souls, the Giver of our Life, the incorruptible Treasure, the Father of the Only-Begotten, Thy Son our Saviour who proclaimed Thy will, for Thou didst will that we should be saved through Thee. Our hearts give thanks to Thee, O Lord, to Thee, the Might of the Father, and the Grace of the Gentiles, the Knowledge of truth, the Wisdom of the erring, the Physician of the soul, the Greatness of the humble, our Friend. Thou art the Staff of the righteous, the Hope of the persecuted, the Haven of those that are tempest-tossed, the Light of the perfect, the Son of the Living God. Make to shine on us, from Thy grace which is 'unsearchable' firmness and strength, trust and wisdom, power of faith that bendeth not, and hope that changeth not. Grant knowledge of the Spirit to our humility that we Thy servants, O Lord, may ever be purified in righteousness, and that all Thy people may glorify Thee ...

From this point there is a return to the Father until after the words over the bread. Then, abruptly, the prayer is again addressed to the Son, which results in the words over the cup being reported only in an indirect style. The anamnesis itself continues to call upon the Son, but the epiclesis invokes the Father. Then, as in certain East Syrian prayers, the oblation is presented to the whole Trinity, before the end of the prayer returns to the Father. From one end to the other, the same looseness that we observed

---

[13] The liturgy of St. Gregory of Nazianzum will be found in t. I of Renaudot, pp. 99 ff.

[14] We shall quote the Liturgy of Our Lord and that of our Lady from J. M. Harden, *The Anaphoras of the Ethiopic Liturgy* (London, 1928) pp. 60 ff. and pp. 66 ff. The first is evidently inspired by the *Testamentum Domini*.

in the beginning of the prayer is simply reinforced by these continual interchanges.

Still more extravagant is the eucharist of Our Lady, in which the greatest part of the prayer is addressed not to a divine person but to the Virgin. Beyond that, the disorder of thought (?) is complete with digressions so far from the subject that the author himself even says, with a naïveté that makes him more likable than his curious composition: "but let us return to what I was saying!"

Here are a few samples of this singular piece of work, which undoubtedly ought to satisfy us:

> Let us arise in the fear of God to magnify and praise Her who is full of praise, saying, O full of grace, O river of joy, far greater the majesty of aspect in Thee than the majesty of the cherubim with many eyes and the seraphim with six wings ...

Whereupon the prayer returns to the Son to declare his virginal conception ineffable, and we then pass to the *Sanctus*, conceived as a praise of the incarnate Son:

Then we return to the Virgin:

> O Virgin. O fruitful one, who art eaten, and gushing fountain who art drunk ... O the bread that comes from Thee! ... O the cup that is derived from Thee! ... And now we shall offer our praise to Thy Son ...

Again, we return to the Son, and then finally to the Father in a thanksgiving for the redemptive incarnation which ends with the institution narrative ...

We must say that all of this has neither head nor tail, and the whole eucharist is dissolved, as it were, in a sentimental farrago in which the only thing floating on the surface is disjointed debris.

We would be wasting time to pile up examples of this kind. It is clear that in the East as in the Gallican or Mozarabic West, eucharistic improvisation, without ever completely ceasing to experience partial successes, became very soon lost in a disorderly abundance and drowned in pious verbiage.

PREFACE, *COMMUNICANTES* AND *HANC IGITUR* IN THE
SACRAMENTARIES

In the West, the adoption of the Roman canon, which gradually
became universal between the ninth and the eleventh centuries as
a result of Charlemagne's decisions practically to abolish the Mozarabic rite (like what happened in the Byzantine East with the
liturgies of St. Basil and St. John Chrysostom), acted as a dike
against the dissolution of the eucharistic prayer. But it did not
protect it so completely, since the Roman canon itself permitted
a certain persistence either of improvisation or variability in its
"preface." And, as we have seen, as the whole basic element of
thanksgiving for the creation and the redemption very shortly
became concentrated in this preface, it is this fundamental element
itself that remained subject to the hazards of inspiration.

We can calculate the inevitable risks of this flexibility (and its
possible fecundity as well) that had been preserved even in the
oldest Latin sacramentaries.

Without at this point being able to tackle all the historical
problems to which these collections give rise, we must at least
recall what seems sufficiently well established today in regard
to their origin and their formation.[15] What is called the Leonine
sacramentary is certainly not the sacramentary of St. Leo, as was
imagined for some time, when it was discovered in the eighteenth
century in the Verona library. This mutilated collection (what we
have left of it begins at the month of April) seems to be a fragment
from an eclectic copy of *libelli* which were used by the popes at
the beginning of the seventh century. This was made for the use of
an unknown bishop. Bourque, Capelle and Chavasse thought they
could see in it the presence of a fascicle going back to Gelasius I
(492-496) and another one to Vigilius (the end of the first half of the
sixth century). Nevertheless, a number of pieces, if they cannot
with all certainty be attributed to St. Leo himself, may at least
reflect an evident influence of his thought and style. This is the

---

[15] See for example A. G. Martimort, *L'Église en prière*, 3rd ed. (Paris,
1961), pp. 288 ff.

case, among others, of a certain number of masses from the fascicle that must have been compiled by Gelasius.[16]

The so-called old Gelasian sacramentary, which we know from a Vatican manuscript that must have been copied in the area of Paris at the beginning of the eighth century, is still less Gelasius' sacramentary than the Leonine is St. Leo's.[17] Chavasse has established that its principal stock is made up of a presbyteral sacramentary, i. e. one used not by the pope but by the priests of the Roman *tituli*, at the end of the seventh century.[18]

What is called the Gelasian sacramentary of the eighth century is a synthesis between this old Gelasian, a recension of the earlier Gregorian sacramentary of half a century before, and Gallican sources. This compilation must have been worked out in Burgundy, probably at the Abbey of Flavigny. It became the source of many other sacramentaries recopied in Frankish country up to the eleventh century.[19]

The so-called Gregorian sacramentary seems indeed to have as its basis a collection composed by St. Gregory the Great for his own personal use. But the oldest example of it is the manuscript preserved at Cambrai which is called the Hadrianum and seems to be the one sent to Charlemagne at his request. It reflects contemporary papal usage.[20]

---

[16] Cod. Bibl. Caplt. Veron. LXXXV (80). First edition by F. Bianchini, *Codex Sacramentorum vetus Romanae Ecclesiae* (Rome, 1735). Another edition of the Ballerini brothers at Venice in 1754 which Migne reproduced in P. L., t. 65, col. 21 ff. Modern editions by C. L. Feltoe, *Sacramentarium Leonianum* (Cambridge, 1896) and L. C. Mohlberg *Sacramentarium Veronense* (Rome, 1956).

[17] Cod. Vat. Regin. 316. Published for the first time by Tommasi in his *Codices etc.*, in 1680. Another edition by Muratori, reproduced by Migne in P. L., t. 74, col. 1055 ff. A modern edition by H. A. Wilson, *The Gelasian Sacramentary* (Oxford, 1894).

[18] A. Chavasse, *Le Sacramentaire gélasien* (Tournai, 1958).

[19] Cf. E. Bourque, "Étude sur les sacramentaires romains," t. II, *Les textes remaniés, Le gélasien du VIIIe siècle* (Québec, 1952) and A. Chavasse, "Le Sacramentaire gélasien du viiie siècle," in *Ephemerides Liturgicae*, vol. 73 (1959), pp. 249 ff.

[20] Edited by H. Lietzmann, in *Das Sacramentarium Gregorianum* (Münster-in-W., 1921). The manuscript is at Cambrai.

A manuscript preserved at Padua, but which must have been copied in Belgium in the ninth century, represents an adaptation to Roman presbyteral usage of the same basic collection, which was undoubtedly made after 650.[21]

Further, we must not forget that all the Gallican books that have come down to us, except Mone's masses, certainly include a good number of Roman pieces. In all these collections, which have preserved for us the oldest fund of Roman pieces available, we see that they are already intermingled with later pieces. In the edition that was made for the use of the Frankish Gauls on the basis of the Hadrianum, a copious supplement was added, containing the Easter Vigil, with undeniably Gallican elements, such as the blessing of the candle, and propers for ordinary Sundays (absent from the papal sacramentary). In this last part, a good number of prayers were brought together from other collections of Roman origin, of the Gelasian or Paduan type.[22] It is this expanded Gregorian which was the basis of the medieval sacramentaries, with the Gelasian of the eighth century whose influence persisted.

Among the oldest of these various collections, the Leonine (despite its mutilated state) is distinguished for the number of its prefaces (267). Like the Gallican books, almost all of these books present interchangeable pieces, leaving a wide choice to the celebrant. It is for this reason that the Leonine has 8 masses for Christmas, 28 for Sts. Peter and Paul, etc.

The old Gelasian is already considerably less rich, since it gives only 54 prefaces. But the different recensions of the newer Gelasian increase this number to about 200. The Hadrianum, on the other hand, has only 14 prefaces, but the Paduan has 46.

The supplement added in Frankish Gaul to the Hadrianum introduced a miscellany of prefaces of either Roman or Gallican origin.

---

[21] Biblioteca Capitolare, MS. D. 47. Edited by L. C. Mohlberg, *Die älteste erreichbare Gestalt des Liber sacramentorum* (Münster-in-W., 1927).

[22] This supplement is generally attributed to Alcuin. Recent research seems to show that it is owed rather to St. Benedict of Aniane.

Towards the end of the tenth century, the canonist Burchard of Worms attempted to reduce the authorized prefaces to 9, by producing a decretal attributed to Pelagius II (who died in 590), but which he most probably made up completely himself. These were the prefaces of Christmas, Epiphany, Lent, the Cross, Easter, Ascension, Pentecost, Trinity and the Apostles (not to mention the common preface), which are still in the Roman missal today. All come from the Hadrianum, except the Cross (which only made its appearance in the ninth century), the Trinity (which already figured in the old Gelasian, but must have come from the Mozarabic books) and Lent (common to the Paduan and the newer Gelasian). The preface of the Virgin, as we still use it today, made its appearance only in the ninth century, but it came from the elaboration of a formula from the newer Gelasian.[23]

Still, throughout the Middle Ages, the pseudo-decretal of Pelagius had scarcely any effect. The sacramentary of Saint Amand (ninth century) contains 283 prefaces, that of Chartres (tenth) 220, and Moissac (eleventh) 342. The same was true in Italy. The Missal of Pius V came down just to the prefaces of Burchard and that of the Virgin. But, through the local propers, a number of more or less ancient prefaces were to find their way again into the Roman liturgy, not to speak of modern compositions resulting from the veneration of St. Joseph, the Sacred Heart or Christ the King. For its part, the Ambrosian missal still includes today a distinct preface for each mass.[24]

We must admit, furthermore, that Burchard's reaction, and later that of the Tridentine reformers, are very understandable. For, even at a very early date, we find in the Roman or Romano-Frankish books (as well as in the Gallican or Mozarabic books about which we have already spoken) formulas which have little (or nothing) to do with the traditional eucharist. Undoubtedly Jungmann was right in showing in the "confession" of the εὐχαριστία the response to the εὐαγγέλιον previously proclaimed. It might therefore have seemed normal to give to each mass an

[23] A. Jungmann, *The Mass of the Roman Rite*, vol. 2 (New York, 1955), pp. 117-118.

[24] *Ibid.*, pp. 118 ff.

echo in the preface of the particular theme underlined in the Gospel of the day within the great harmony of the Christian mystery. But even in many of the most successful compositions from this viewpoint, we note an inevitable tendency to retain only a secondary aspect of the mystery. And, only too often, the result was that the eucharist turned into a moralizing didacticism. And what should we say of those prefaces which evidently were composed much less to correspond to the Gospel than to reiterate, for the Almighty, a theme from the homily of which the author was particularly fond, even though we might wonder through what aberration he could have reduced the matter of his eucharist? Popes like Gelasius and Vigilius had already fallen into this bad habit. And eucharistic prefaces finally appeared which were nothing more than diatribes against one or another adversary!

Later, it was not polemics so much as a more or less fanciful hagiography that distorted the eucharist. Or else, in the Sunday prefaces, a simple moralism was substituted for the evocation of the mystery.

Prefaces of martyrs, however, particularly in the old part of the Leonine sacramentary, often lent themselves to a satisfactory evocation of the redemptive mystery, like this following text:

> ... Through Jesus Christ, our Lord, who, in order to triumph more fully over the enemy of the human race, beyond this singular glory (which he acquired for himself) in trampling him under foot in an ineffably divine manner, again subjected him to the martyrs, so that this same victory passed into the members, (a victory) which the Head had first won ...[26]

A similar and even better example is found more than once in the Sunday prefaces of the late Gelasian sacramentary. Here is a preface from the last Sunday in Advent:

> It is meet and right, equitable and availing to salvation, to give thanks to you always and everywhere, Lord, holy

---

[25] Cf. Gelasius I, *Lettre contre les Lupercales et XVIII messes du sacramentaire léonien*, ed. Pomarès (*Sources chrétiennes*, n° 65), Paris, 1959, and A. Chavasse, "Messes du Pape Vigile dans le Sacramentaire léonien," in *Ephemerides liturgicae*, vol. 64, 1950, pp. 161 ff.

[26] Feltoe edition, p. 18; Mohlberg, p. 20.

Father, almighty and eternal God, sanctifier and creator of the human race, you, who, through your Son reigning with you in the eternal light, at the beginning, gave life to man taken from the slime of the earth in the image of your glory, and who, when he sinned by yielding to temptation, willed to restore to him the eternal succor of the grace of the Spirit by sending us Jesus Christ our Lord, through whom ...[27]

But we must acknowledge that Burchard's choice was not a bad one and that the prefaces he retained, if they are looked at side by side, undoubtedly give the best global expression ever brought together in the West of the eucharistic mystery. What, on the other hand, can be regretted is that nothing better has been found than the so-called common preface to replace the old Sunday prefaces. Certainly this formula is older, since we see it together with the Roman canon from the earliest examples. But it is only the most common schema of the ancient prefaces, having a specific application, which was simply cut off from this latter. The result is that neither the creation nor the redemption are explicated as a motif of the eucharist—an assuredly disastrous lacuna! The Mozarabic preface of the Trinity which is substituted for it on the Sundays where green vestments are worn presents the same deficiency, for which its litany of abstract formulas could in no way compensate.

Moreover, we must not forget that the preface is not the only element that has remained variable in the Roman canon. The *Communicantes* and the *Hanc igitur* were also variable for a long time, and the variants of the *Communicantes* had the valuable good fortune of maintaining, at least on the great feasts, an explicit recall of the redemptive mystery within the canon. But far from profiting from the possibilities that it was bequeathed, the Middle Ages simply witnessed the withering away of the richness of the old sacramentaries. Of the six *Communicantes* that are found in the oldest of these collections, we have lost the one for Whitsun Eve, as well as two different formulas, for the Ascension and Whit-

---

[27] In the L. C. Mohlberg edition, *Das fränkische Sacramentarium gelasianum*, 2nd ed. (Münster-im-W., 1939), nº 1454.

sunday respectively, which are also found in the Leonine sacramentary.[28]

The still greater variety of the *Hanc igiturs* seems to have been
reduced from the time of St. Gregory, not without some going
back to the traditional basic source attested to by the Hadrianum
at Rome, before the Romano-Frankish supplement. For this last
prayer, the Middle Ages knew a new proliferation of formulas,
specifying the particular intentions of the offering. It can be
followed through the Frankish, Irish or Italian sacramentaries
or missals. But again, when we are not faced merely with considerations that are totally foreign to the subject, we are reduced
to hollow wordiness.[29]

THE SILENT CANON AND THE ACCOMPANYING
FALSE DEVELOPMENTS

But while the development of the eucharistic prayer petered out,
the liturgical evolution caused other factors to appear which tended
to bury what was most traditional in what had survived in this
eucharist. The first of these factors is what we call the "silence
of the canon," or, to use an older formula "the silence of the mysteries."

We must admit that this question itself is the most obscure
mystery of perhaps the whole of the history of the liturgy. Yet we
hardly get this impression when we read most of the studies on the
subject that have been piled up since the seventeenth century.
Whatever position the authors take—whether they believe this
practice to be original and essential, or condemn it as late and
unfortunate—one would think, in reading them, that the matter
is clear and can be plainly settled by a few irreproachable texts.
But when we go to the sources without any preconceived ideas,
it is hard to share this optimism. Yet we do not deny that we can
reach certain firm conclusions from examining them. But, as
will be seen, they are neither so easily accessible, nor of a nature

---

[28] Cf. A. Jungmann, *The Mass of the Roman Rite*, vol. 2, p. 176 ff.
[29] *Ibid.*, pp. 179 ff.

as to dispel all the obscurities of one of the most complex problems of the history of the liturgy.

A point of departure seems certain: the great *berakoth* of the Jewish liturgies were certainly recited aloud by the celebrant, or more precisely chanted to a melodic type similar to our *tonus praefationis*.[30] It is likely, therefore, that the practice was the same with the first Christians. Certain indications allow us to be of this opinion. But we must acknowledge that they are mostly negative. If the bond of continuity that we have established between the Jewish *berakoth* and the Christian eucharist did not exist, these indications of themselves could establish only a limited probability.

Actually, we do not have any clear statement on the question in the patristic period. The arguments which people seem to think furnish proof for the fact of the recitation aloud of the eucharist in antiquity, are generally merely inferences drawn from the importance attached by the Fathers to the people's final *Amen*.[31] But at least for twelve centuries in the West, and for still more in certain regions at least of the East, the people gave this *Amen* in response to a few words uttered aloud by the priest in concluding, and they never seemed to have been concerned about hearing or even knowing exactly what he might have said previously and inaudibly for their sake. The supposition that they must previously have been more exacting, in order to be tenable, needs confirmation from the Jewish prayers.

What is certain after that is the fact that from the eighth century onward in the Roman liturgy, and from the beginning of the sixth century in certain Eastern liturgies, either express rubrics or formal commentaries certify that the priest recited the greater part of the canon or anaphora in 'a low voice.' In the West this applied to everything following the *Sanctus*, up to the *Per omnia saecula saeculorum* (with the sole exception of the words *Nobis quoque peccatoribus*). In the East, what corresponds to our preface (without its final words), and everything that follows the *Sanctus* is also silent with the sole exception generally of the words

---

[30] See Eric Werner, *The Sacred Bridge*.
[31] In this regard the 1st *Apology* of St. Justin, par. 65, is always cited.

of Christ in the institution narrative, and two or three sentences from the anamnesis, the epiclesis and the intercessions, along with the final doxology.

We have some solid indications for believing that this state of affairs, which had become practically universal, must not have existed very long before it is presented to us in the documents. But the documents themselves do not permit us to date the change precisely nor even less to discern exactly what the reasons for it were.

The 17th homily of the Nestorian Narsai, that can be dated from the first years of the sixth century, gives us very clear evidence that the practice then was the rule, in his Church, for all practical purposes and no one evidently questioned it.[32] We find evidence of this in the Byzantine Church, at least such decided evidence, only two centuries later. But an intermediary document might allow us, to shed light on the way in which it came about. Again, we must acknowledge that its interpretation, first textual and then historical, is quite sticky.

We are talking of the *novella* no. 137 of Justinian. We have the authentic Greek text, but no corresponding Latin text. It dates from the 26th of March 565.

But in fact, up until recently, it was not mentioned in this debate except in a later Latin text, in which its content is amalgamated with the *novella* no. 123, of the 1st of May 546. What is more serious is that people have limited themselves to quoting only a few lines of it. Read in this way, outside of their original context, as we find them in the eighteenth century with Le Brun or Robbe, and then with all those who were content with quoting them through these latter people, there is no doubt that they give the impression that the emperor wished to establish something new, but that this "novelty" is not the recitation of the prayers in a low voice, but their recitation aloud. It seems that for pedagogical reasons, the emperor, supported only by an overly emphasized quote from St. Paul, wanted to introduce a practice that was in contradiction with what had become established.

---

[32] *The Liturgical Homilies of Narsai*, ed. R. H. Connolly (Cambridge, 1909), pp. 12 ff.

Bishop was the first to show that the impression is reversed when we take the trouble to read the particular *novella* in its original text, and entirely. But this still does not mean that all obscurities disappear at once.[33]

The emperor began by asserting that he wanted to assure respect for those canons that had been violated by clerics, monks and even certain bishops, in response to some complaints that he had received. All of this, he explained, was due to the negligence that resulted in the abandoning of the regular holding of synods. Hence the wide freedom in ordaining men who did not even know the prayers of the anaphora or of baptism. No longer should men be ordained who had not first put down in writing "the profession that they must say aloud, like the divine anaphora in the service of the Holy Communion, the prayers in holy baptism, and the other prayers." After this came the detailed prescriptions for the annual holding of synods. Finally, we have the formal declaration: "Moreover, we order all bishops and priests to say the prayers used in the divine anaphora and holy baptism, not inaudibly, but in a voice that can be heard by the faithful, so that the mind of those listening may be aroused to a greater compunction ... " This is followed by the Pauline citations and the conclusion: "It is fitting, therefore, that the prayers made to the Lord Jesus Christ, our God, as well as to the Father and the Spirit, in the holy anaphora and elsewhere, be said $\mu\epsilon\tau\dot{\alpha}$ $\varphi\omega\nu\tilde{\eta}\varsigma$: those who refuse must answer before the tribunal of God and, when we meet up with such a case, we shall not let it go unpunished."

The first of these two paragraphs admits of more than one ambiguity. Does Justinian wish to say that the candidate for ordination must put down in writing a confession of faith that he must recite aloud before being ordained, just as he must write the ritual prayers out, in the same examination? Or does he mean that he must write down his own confession of faith, before uttering it, in order to be ordained, just as he must (in the exercise of his ministry) utter aloud the ritual prayers? Or, finally, does he want simply that the candidate put down in writing the whole

[33] See E. Bishop, "Silent Recitals in the Mass of the Faithful," Appendix V of the volume cited in the preceding note, pp. 121 ff.

of these texts (confession of faith and prayer) that he will later have to say aloud? Grammatically, all three interpretations are equally possible. But the parallelism with the final paragraph leads us to think that it is the second, more probably, or perhaps the third, which is meant.

This whole conclusion of the *novella* leaves no doubt on this point: the emperor sees in the practice of the recitation of the prayers in a low voice only intolerable negligence, and he does indeed intend to extirpate it. But his insistence betrays the fact that the practice must already have been rather general. It must even have been general enough for the emperor, as was his wont, not to dream of invoking an immemorial contrary custom, but rather to have recourse to imperfectly convincing exegetical considerations and respectable pedagogical motives, although they do not teach us anything themselves about the *statu quo ante*. The only firm indication that he established, or wished to establish, a tradition in the process of being lost, is the reference at the beginning of the *novella* to the violation of the canons. But, if it is evident that the ignorance of too facilely ordained priests is involved under this heading, it is not so clear that the fact of saying the prayers in a low voice, in itself, is directly involved. This can be concluded with certainty only if we are already certain that the final prescription aims at re-establishing a prior tradition ... Unfortunately, this is precisely what is not clearly stated. We therefore find ourselves in a vicious circle. All that we can retrieve from this text is that it seems rather in favor of the antiquity of the recitation aloud than of the contrary. But we could not state that it proves it.

Whatever may have been its immediate effect—of which we have no knowledge—from the end of the eighth century at least (as is evidenced by the *Codex Barberini* from circa 800), the major part of the Byzantine "eucharist," despite the imperial threats and commands, was said μυστικῶς (secretly) according to the rubrics themselves which we have been given.[34]

Yet if we look at the loud parts on the one hand, and those where the celebrant prays silently on the other, it becomes diffi-

---

[34] Cf. the text given by Brightman, *op. cit.*, pp. 32 ff.

cult to avoid the impression that this distinction only came about gradually, and that its origin is simply to be found in the slovenliness of the celebrants. More precisely, the thesis already upheld by Dom Claude de Vert in the eighteenth century and embraced by Fr. Hanssens, seems to be most natural.[35] It seems that today we have come to this practically universal state simply because a development of the collective chants induced the ministers to continue the prayer in a low voice whenever the choir sang, only to resume aloud those words which gave rise to a new choral intervention. This would therefore be a pure and simple negligence: an impatience (a very clerical one, we must admit) to be more quickly done with the progressively overloaded offices, which would have given rise to the "silence of the mysteries."

To be absolutely precise, it is likely that a process of reciprocal causality came about at a rather early date, even though we can not say exactly when. The choral chants, as they developed, gave the first pretext for a hasty reading by the celebrant half aloud. But this, in turn, fostered an extension of the choir's chants, to the extent that there only remained a few brief *ekphoneses* on the celebrant's part, punctuating a series of chants. To this must be added a growth in the "admonitions" of the deacon, which filled out, when necessary, all the gaps that might have remained between the chants of the choir and those of the priest.

Certain observations seem to bring a practically decisive confirmation to this explanation. The most interesting one concerns the beginning of the anaphora. As said before, while in the Roman rite the preface has always been sung (or at least recited aloud), in the Byzantine rite, what corresponds to it has become silent. But in the latter, we observe that the response: "it is meet and right" has grown into: "it is meet and right to worship the Father, the Son and the Holy Spirit, consubstantial and indivisible Trinity." In this case, it is understandable that the Byzantine priests in contrast to their Roman colleagues were led to recite in a low voice this first part of their eucharist. It is interesting to note that the Barberini manuscript, which does not yet include the addition to the response, also does not include the rubric (which will

---

[35] I. Hanssens, *Institutiones liturgicae,* tomus III, pars altera, p. 484.

be found later) to recite the first part of the eucharist *μυστικῶς*. Still, that this was to have begun at that time is proved by the rest of the text which no longer introduces the prescription to recite aloud the words immediately preceding the *Sanctus* ...

In the West we are, if that is possible, even less clearly informed as to the distinct date of the evolution. Many contemporary authors, assert with Jungmann that it can be situated between the *Ordo Romanus I* and the *Ordo Romanus II*. Actually, the texts are not so clear. The *Ordo Romanus II*[36] certainly presupposes a canon recited in a low voice (at least relatively so). But neither does the *Ordo Romanus I* permit us to conclude with certainty that at its time, at any rate, the canon was said from beginning to end out loud, nor do the later *Ordines* allow us to believe that the *Ordo Romanus II* was the first to put an end to this practice.

Undoubtedly this latter text is categorical about the silence which must follow the *Sanctus*: *Surgit solus pontifex et tacite intrat in canonem*. In other words, while everyone was involved in the singing of the *Sanctus*, "the pontiff alone arose and entered in silence upon the canon." That it must be understood as a recitation in a low voice is unquestionably confirmed by the prescription, occurring further on, that he must say the words *Nobis quoque peccatoribus* "*aperta clamans voce*," so that the subdeacons will rise and begin the fraction.

But since the *Ordo Romanus I*, was evidently written by someone who could not have known *Ordo II*, we must not rush to the conclusion that everything that it does not mention and that is found in its successor was necessarily unknown to it. After the *Sanctus* which was sung by everyone, the text says simply: *Quem dum expleverint, surgit pontifex solus (et intrat) in canonem*. Likewise at the *Nobis quoque* the author is content to say that the subdeacons arose at that time for the fraction. With our recitation, which at this point had become so silent that even the ministers nearby at the altar did not hear what the priest said, it could seem reasonable to conclude that *Ordo I* implicitly excludes the silence supposed by *Ordo II*. But when we realize, as what follows will show, that the "silence of the canon" in the Middle Ages, did not

---

[36] Cf. A. Jungmann, *The Mass of the Roman Rite*, vol. 2, pp. 101 ff.

precisely signify at all such a silence where the ministers would not hear anything at all, but one which they alone could hear, the comparison of the two texts does not seem quite as conclusive. All that can be said is that the composer of *Ordo I* thought it useless to prescribe a recitation in a low voice. That he was unfamiliar with such a practice is nothing more than a probable inference.

Inversely, the *Ordo III* seems to give evidence that a recitation aloud may have subsisted after the *Ordo II*. Envisioning the case of a concelebration, it prescribes that the concelebrants who are standing to the left and the right of the bishop "say the canon at the same time as he ... in such a way that the bishop's voice is dominant." Yet, once we remember the relative character of the medieval silence in the canon, to which we shall return, we must admit that this text can simply mean that they should speak in a voice that is still lower than the bishop's and not that he should speak in a voice still louder than theirs!

However, it is the *Ordo XV*, attributed to John the Archcantor, which is a Frankish reworking of the Roman ordo from the middle of the eighth century, which permits us to see the silence of the canon become established elsewhere than in Rome, and at the same time to become clear. After the *Sanctus* it directs the celebrant: *Et incipit canere dissimili voce et melodia, ita ut a circumstantibus altari tantum audiatur.* This chant, in a tone of voice and a melody that are different from those of the *Sanctus*, and even from the foregoing preface, evidently implies only a mitigated "silence." That in the thirteenth century it still could be heard in this manner is evidenced by canon 36 of the Synod of Salisbury in 1217, which prescribes: *ut verba canonis in missa rotunde et distincte dicantur.*

Nevertheless, at the end of the eighth century, when we read the *Expositiones Missae*, like those that begin with *Quotiens contra se, Introitus missae quare*, that of Remigius of Auxerre and others, it becomes certain that in the Frankish lands as at Rome, from the *Sanctus* on, the faithful could no longer hear what the priest was saying.

As for what may have been done in the Gallican rite or in the old Mozarabic rite, we know absolutely nothing. The supposition that is sometimes formulated, that the *post-mysteriums* or *post-secretas*, because of their titles, would have been said aloud, but after the words of institution said in a low voice, is only an unverifiable inference.

What stands, on the other hand, is that the *Expositiones Missae* explain that the canon was said in a low voice because of the sacred mystery that was being accomplished, and because of the reverence it must inspire in us. The same thing was found already with Narsai in the sixth century, and asserted just as decisively. People then wanted to conclude that the "silence of the canon" or the "silence of the mysteries" resulted from a deliberate intention to remove the eucharistic prayer from any possibility of profanation, and that this was a typical example of an influence of the pagan mysteries of hellenistic antiquity upon the Christian liturgy. But to say this is to jump too quickly to a conclusion, and to involve a whole series of blockings which are not sufficiently justified.

In the first place, the most ancient authors with whom the themes of respectful fear and the awesome and sacred mystery make their appearance in relation to the eucharist, do not betray the slightest inkling of any conformity between this "mystery" viewpoint and a recitation of the prayers in a low voice. In general, they seem even to be totally unaware of this custom. This is still the case with St. John Chrysostom, in his homilies on the divine ineffability or in his treatise *On the Priesthood,* and even with the Pseudo-Dionysius, and again with his commentators like St. Maximus in the seventh century. Furthermore we do not see how people who still might be familiar with something of the hellenistic mysteries could have associated the two. If these mysteries were so called, it was so precisely for the opposite reason since the initiates were able to see and hear in them what the non-initiates were not supposed to know. If they did not see and hear without hindrance, it would have been superfluous to command them so severely to reveal nothing of what they had seen and heard. The explanation of the "silence of the canon" by arguments of this kind betrays its false and *post-factum* character. People were thereby enabled later to justify a state of affairs the real reasons of which had been forgotten, and which could not have been arrived at in this manner.

We can observe in Narsai himself that the expressions of respectful fear before the ineffability of the mystery envelop the secret pronouncing of the words, rather than pretending to explain it.

This explanation was able therefore to consolidate the evolutionary process but it did not determine it. Furthermore, the extension of the choral responses in the East contradicts this explanation. For in their own fashion they bring out the significance of what is being accomplished at the same moment through the words of the priest. For an even stronger reason the same thing must be said of the more and more prolix explanations of the deacon which came little by little (particularly in the Armenian rite) to fill the rare gaps in which the singers were not heard between the priest's "*ekphoneses.*"

It is therefore back to this gradual extension of choral or diaconal elements that we must go, it seems, in order to arrive at the source of our problem. Once again, the progressively growing silence of the priestly prayer probably originated here, just as this silence, in turn, fostered their development. But why were these new chants of the choir and admonitions of the deacon introduced?

In the beginning, there were no choral interventions other than the introductory responses, the *Sanctus* and the final *Amen.* The deacon, for his part, was limited (at the most) to short admonitions which at the outset focused on the attitude to be observed rather than constituting explanations of the rites: "Let us be attentive" or, in Egypt, at the resumption of the thanksgiving after the intercessions: "Toward the East," etc.

At this time, it is clear that the chants or responses—which were so simple—were made by the whole assembly. But already in our oldest Greek manuscripts of the liturgy of St. James, the deacons at the first words of the institution narrative exclaimed: "For the forgiveness of sins and everlasting life." The faithful then answered: "Amen," not only at the end of the whole eucharist as before, but even after the words over the bread, and then after the prayers for the cup. Immediately after the first development of the words: "Do this as a memorial of me," the deacons again exclaimed: "We believe and confess," and the people followed with: "We announce your death, Lord, and we proclaim your resurrection."

Before the epiclesis, when the priest said: "Your people and your Church beseech you," the people replied: "Have mercy upon us, Lord God, almighty Father," and they inserted two of their *Amens* in the conclusion of the epiclesis. After other diaconal interventions inviting the people to prayer during the great final intercession, the people exclaimed: "Take away, forgive, pardon, O God, our voluntary and involuntary offenses, those that are known and those unknown."

Most of these responses must be ancient, for they are found also in the Syriac manuscripts and there are even some which find their equivalent in Serapion.

Likewise, the liturgy of St. John Chrysostom, even in the form given to us by the *Codex Barberini,* contains the four *Amens* of the words of institution and the epiclesis, along with the response "We hymn you" after the *ekphonesis* terminating the anamnesis.

We may think that these interventions of the faithful were introduced to revivify their wavering attention during a prolonged eucharist. Does St. Basil not already allude to the fact that even among monks many minds wandered during the eucharistic prayer?

But the development and the growing complexity of these interventions, supposedly on the part of the people, soon caused them to be given to a choir of chanters. This choir, after first leading and supporting the people, came to be more or less totally substituted for them. The chants which had become more and more ornate in their melodies, soon became singable only by specialists. At the same time their length reduced the formulas of the priest pronounced aloud to a few *ekphoneses* which are all that remain of these in the East. The diaconal admonitions, as we saw particularly in the Armenian liturgy, tended for their part to swell to the point of filling out all the remaining intervals. Then, we find ourselves with a eucharistic commentary that has followed this step by step. But, with the purpose of facilitating the people's understanding of it, it substituted a repetition of the thought which was only an approximate parallelism. This is precisely the same phenomenon that came about recently in our own day when the "commentators" repeated in the vernacular an old Latin prayer which tended to become independent of the celebrant. At this stage, it may be said that a eucharistic prayer that has become exclusively sacerdotal is only a survival of the ancient eucharistic prayer, which has now been deprived of direct contact with the faithful. A didactic liturgy was grafted upon it for their use, which, in fact, no longer allowed them to participate in the action since they merely listened passively. In this way it covered the true liturgy, in which they had no part, with a false excrescence whose spirit had become more and more foreign to it. Narsai could still say that the priest was everyone's voice. It is a voice which undoubtedly speaks in the people's name. Yet, it no longer expressed their common prayer but a prayer in which their own tended simply to become parallel.

In the West it was still worse. The diaconal admonitions were never introduced there. And the chants of the choir grew without any direct connection with the prayer of the priest. Under the pretext of praying for the priest who prays for us, in the eleventh and twelfth centuries the choir came in many churches to sing throughout the whole of the canon psalms and orations that no longer had any relationship to it. The *Missa Illyrica*, for example, prescribed the recitation of psalms 19, 24, 50, 89, and 90, followed by verses and prayers for the intention of the priest and the faithful.[37] In the religious orders, the lay brothers were taught during this time to recite a series of Paters. It may be said that the priest had become so enshrouded in the silence of the canon that in the eyes of the faithful he appeared to vanish within it. For their part, they also prayed, but without any concern for any concordance between their prayer and his.

People were to go even further afield from the traditional eucharist. When the priest celebrated it, since he himself was first formed in following it in this extrinsic manner, he soon thought that he could no longer do so devoutly without including all kinds of personal prayers. Evidently, these better responded to his own devotion than the official text which he was content to perform functionally. These are the "apologias" and the related prayers. After becoming multiplied as a prelude to the whole of the mass, the reading of the Gospel and the eucharistic prayer itself, they came to pervade the latter like some foreign growth. Nothing of the old liturgy was left intact, and it came to be considered merely as a support for a private devotion which was inspired from other sources.

---

[37] Jungmann, *op. cit.*, pp. 137 ff.

The same phenomenon appeared in the East at a rather early date, but it never knew a similar growth. The liturgy of Theodore of Mopsuestia, under the form in which it has come down to us, already possesses an "apologia" of this type, that is obviously an addition between the *Sanctus* and the prayer destined to follow it. Even earlier, we can perceive the first root of this practice in the intercessory formulas of the great Syrian eucharistic prayers in which there was a proliferation of the invocations for the ministers themselves who offered the sacrifice. Something of this is already found in the oldest Greek or Syriac manuscripts of the liturgy of St. James, and even in the evolved form of the liturgy of Addai and Mari. We have pointed out the intrusion of a formula of this type, which was particularly developed, in the liturgy of Nestorius, between the anamnesis and the intercessions. It is worth quoting both for its individualism and its penitential character, which are harbingers of the most characteristic traits of Medieval devotion both in the East and the West.

Lord God, the merciful, the compassionate, and the clement, here am I beginning to speak before you, I who am only dust, sinful, powerless and poor, guilty before you from my mother's womb, in exile from the moment I left her bosom, a transgressor since that time. Have mercy upon me, Lord, according to your lovingkindness, and snatch me from the ocean of my faults through your clemency; bring me out of the abyss of my sins through your goodness; heal the ulcer of my vices and the wounds of my trespasses, you, the comforter and healer. Grant me to open my mouth in your presence, and make me worthy to move my lips before you. Grant me to render you propitious towards my offenses, so that I may obtain the forgiveness of sins, and the pardon of faults, the wiping away of my own blemishes and of the sins of those who are like me and my companions: may I ask of you what is suitable to your Godhead, and what should be asked of you; for you are rich and your treasure is never exhausted; divers petitions are ever made to you, and an abundance of numberless gifts is distributed by you in answer. In your goodness and longsuffering, be not angry with me, for I do not have such assurance in your presence that I can say things with a good conscience before your majesty; yet accept from me this audacity, for your great name has been invoked upon me. Receive this sacrifice from my powerless hands for your people and the sheep of your pasture, wherefore I give thanks to your name, and offer worship to your majesty, O Lord of all.[38]

Formulas of this type, in the West, came to be introduced everywhere. The famous *Missa Illyrica* is the best known example. But it is far from being unique! It received its name from the reformer Flacius Illyricus who published it in 1557, thinking that he had a liturgy of the eighth century without any mention either of the eucharistic presence or sacrifice. In fact, it dates from the eleventh century.[39] It is a group of 35 devotional formulas which the priest is invited to say during all the chants of the mass, and in connection with each of the rites he is performing up to after the *Sanctus* and during the communion. It is a fact that it no longer reflects anything of the spirit of the ancient eucharist, but an interpretation of the eucharistic ritual popularized by the *Expositiones Missae*, especially after Amalar's time.[40] Still, the first outlines of these explanations are found in Theodore of Mopsuestia and Narsai. All the rites receive a symbolic interpretation, dominated by a dramatic notion of the ritual that is obviously completely imaginary. The rites and formulas, according to it, would be only a theatrical imitation of all the gestures and words of Jesus during his passion. Spread on this canvas, the new prayers express only a pathos of personal unworthiness, mingled with pity before the sufferings of the Savior.

At this stage, even if the traditional eucharist is still present, it may be said that a eucharistic spirituality, and even a theology of the eucharist, both without any serious roots in tradition, have buried it and almost completely stifled it with their parasitical excrescences.

---

[38] Renaudot, t. 2, p. 632.
[39] Cf. Jungmann, *op. cit.*, vol. 1, pp. 79 ff.
[40] Cf. Jungmann, *op. cit.*, vol. 1, pp. 87 ff.

Modern Times:
Decomposition and Reformation

BEGINNING WITH THE TWELFTH CENTURY, THE OFFICES RE-
cited by the choir in the West during the eucharistic prayer, although practically independent from its content, were in the
process of disappearing. They were progressively replaced by another development, which is not without its analogy with that of
the choir chants in the East, although its virtue is even more uncertain. It is not that entirely new chants or responses were added,
but that people began to amplify the *Sanctus* and *Benedictus*
(and all the other chants of the ordinary) with what were called
tropes. Their origin seems to be Germanic, but they were soon
seen to proliferate throughout all of "Gothic" Europe, with the
one exception of Italy. Concurrently with the melodic and soon
to be polyphonic developments of the old chants, interpolative
words came to be introduced into the flowery vocalizations which
had begun by indefinitely extending the individual syllables.
Either in Latin or the vernacular, they started out as a paraphrase of the basic text. But from paraphrase a transition to

380

free amplification was soon to be made, and this became less and less connected with the original text.[1]

THE EUCHARIST BURIED UNDER UNTRADITIONAL
FORMULARIES AND INTERPRETATIONS

These tropes are a reflection of the religious feeling of the times: adoration of the humanity of the Savior present in the eucharist, an effective recall of his passion, an expression of the feeling of unworthiness on the part of those who approach the august mystery are their better themes. But all sorts of ideas soon came to be added. At the end of the Middle Ages, in the compositions with multiple parts, it was not uncommon to hear one of the voices sing the words of a popular song which had been taken over for use in the liturgy, intermingled with the Latin phrases of the *Sanctus*.

For the priest himself, the apologies and the acts of affective devotion to the Savior as present and sacrificed still continued to inflate the recitation of the canon.[2]

Beginning with the thirteenth century a new factor presented itself, which was to weigh heavily on the evolution of the eucharist. This was the new elevation of the species which was introduced immediately after the institution narrative, and the raising up of the host for all to see which was its reason. Attended by motets composed precisely for this action, in order to adore the presence of the Savior, this ceremony was to draw the whole popular devotion in the mass to itself. It was the result of a theology that was developed to counteract Berengarius and his denial of a real presence of the true body of Christ: as a reaction, the entire mass tended to center around the production of this presence, which was seen as the result of the repetition of Christ's words over the bread and wine.[3]

At the same time, as communions became rarer, so-called private masses came into being. They were offered for the most varied

---

[1] Cf. A. Jungmann, *The Mass of the Roman Rite*, Vol. I, pp. 106 ff., 123.
[2] Cf. A. Jungmann, *op. cit.*, p. 108 ff.
[3] *Ibid.*, pp. 119 ff.

intentions, which were often mingled with a superstition undeniably more magical than religious. At the very least, there resulted a tendency to look upon the mass as a sort of recommencement of Calvary, which was destined to obtain for us each time everything that we might especially be wishing for. The later assertion of the Augsburg Confession (which stated that people had come to believe that the Cross had atoned for original sin alone, and that each mass was destined to atone for actual sins) is perhaps an exaggeratedly systematized description. Yet is is hard to deny that it does express a tendency that was at least in the air and which was not even the worst of the deformations that were to be found at the time.[4]

Without going so far as these extreme cases, we must admit that the best commentaries on the mass produced for the use of priests during the Middle Ages, such as that of Innocent III,[5] or later with Gabriel Biel,[6] in which Luther's eucharistic piety was formed, one could find merely traces of the original sense of the eucharist as a thanksgiving for the *mirabilia Dei*, or of the anamnesis as the sacramental presence of the redemptive mystery. The "thanksgiving" was reduced to an expression of gratitude for the gift of God received in communion, or expected from the celebration. The sacramental actuality of the sacrifice gave way to the consideration of the "fruits" that were expected from it and which no one tired enumerating. But, most often, they had very little in common with the ancient view of the whole Church being fulfilled in its common participation in the one redemptive sacrifice, so magnificently expressed by St. Augustine.

In the piety of the best of these commentaries, the mass appears as a "representation" of the sacrifice, not in the sacramental sense such as the word might have with Tertullian, for example, but in the sense of a devotional play. Through its figured recall of Calvary, it was to excite feelings of compassion and com-

---

[4] *Ibid.*, pp. 109 ff.

[5] *De sanctissimo altaris mysterio*, P. L., t. 217.

[6] *Gabrielis Biel Canonis Misse exposito*, inspired by his teacher Egeling Becker. It knew a widespread popularity from its publication under Biel's name in 1488. It was re-edited by Heiko A. Oberman and William J. Courtenay (Wiesbaden, 1965).

punction which the immediate and tangible presence of Calvary could awaken in pious souls. Spirituality, like theology, retained only the words of institution among the formulas of the canon since they seemed to resurrect this spectacle for the soul meditating upon them at the moment where they renewed the real presence of the body broken and blood shed for our sins.

Fr. Francis Clark, S.J. has recently attempted to prove erroneous those Protestant or Anglican (... and even Catholic) historians who pointed out these deformations. To do this he gleaned a few fine formulas in which something of the ancient tradition had survived down to the end of the Middle Ages.[7] It goes without saying that this tradition could not become completely defunct in the Church, but the whole question is to what extent these formulas were really characteristic of the average piety either of the clergy or the simple faithful. One of Fr. Clark's confrères, Fr. Stephenson, had no difficulty in establishing that we are quite wide of the mark.[8] He went so far as to maintain that the "repraesentatio" of the Cross in the eucharist for St. Thomas himself must be understood in the purely imaginative sense in which we understand the word "representation" today. Without being fully convinced by this counter-proof, we must acknowledge that a few formulas of the saintly doctor do reflect something of such a notion. The least that can be said is that it was already one of the most widespread ideas in the context in which he found himself.

In any case, we may say that the best theologians and divines at the beginning of the sixteenth century were convinced that all of this required an energetic "reformation" along with many other things in the practice and even the theory of the Church. In addition, through returning to the sources it so praised, the best of Christian humanism was capable of rediscovering what was essential; it recovered the original and restored its genuine interpretation which had been forgotten or warped through so much overlay and so many aberrant commentaries. The misfortune of the Protestant Reformation, on this point as on many

[7] Francis Clark, *Eucharistic Sacrifice and the Reformation* (London, 1960).
[8] See *Theological Studies*, vol. 22, 1961, pp. 588 ff.

others, was that a more enthusiastic than enlightened impetuosity often rejected the best with the worst, instead of returning to the most authentic sources. The result was that instead of retaining what was original and essential, it was the most secondary and the most recent that remained.

The story of the *Missa Illyrica*, which we have mentioned, is such a perfect illustration of this failure that it seems hardly believable.[9] At the height of the controversies on the eucharist between Protestants and Catholics, Flacius Illyricus came upon an eleventh century manuscript giving a series of priestly devotions containing a prayer for each rite or formula of the traditional mass. But no clear expression of the real presence was to be found, even though it had become obsessive in the following centuries as a reaction against Ratramnus and Berengarius. Nor was there any mention of the eucharistic sacrifice as the Fathers had conceived of it. Eveything boiled down to a childish explanation of the ritual, interpreted as an itemized evocation of every detail of the Passion. Onto this canvas there was added a series of prayers of penance and emotional meditations on the sufferings of the Savior. Flacius Illyricus thought he had brought to light a primitive liturgy that was unharmed by medieval corruptions, and he published his discovery as a justification of the Protestant theses and practices regarding the eucharist. In reality, as he soon had to acknowledge, all he had disinterred was a compilation of late formulas aimed at riddling the traditional liturgy with their fanciful additions. But he had unwittingly demonstrated that those liturgies and theologies which boasted about being the most "reformed," instead of returning to the original eucharist, actually retained only those developments of the medieval eucharist which had no foundation in Christian antiquity.

LUTHER'S *FORMULA MISSAE* AND *DEUTSCHE MESSE*,
THE LAST PRODUCT OF MEDIEVAL DEVIATION

These findings are all the more striking since Luther might have seemed relatively well equipped for getting back to the original

[9] Cf. above, p. 379.

subsoil through the morass of medieval excrescences. In the first place, as Gustaf Aulén so well showed in his beautiful book *Christus Victor*, Luther certainly did very soon rediscover something of the patristic idea of the Cross as God's victory in Christ, overturning all the powers of enmity between man and God and restoring man to a filial relationship with the heavenly Father.[10]

On the other hand, Yngve Brilioth has no less justly underlined the spiritual riches, which are equally as patristic, in the sermon *Von dem hochwürdigen Sakrament des heiligen wahren Leichnams Christi und von den Brüderschaften* (1519). This is a renewed expression of the Augustinian notion that in the eucharist Christ is present with his whole mystical body in order to incorporate us in it and to make us live from then on a life which is but the unfolding in us of his saving mystery. Nor is Brilioth wrong in underlining that Luther retained his attachment to the forms of the traditional eucharist, not out of a simple conservatism but on account of an indelible impression of man's encounter with the divine mystery that the devout use of these forms had left with him.[11]

Yet, after 1523, when under the pressure of those about him he wished to translate all of this into liturgical innovations, it became not only warped but even devitalized. If we try to find out why, it soon becomes evident that his polemical preoccupations, however weighty they may have been, were much less the cause than the inertia of medieval notions and practices from which he was no more capable of freeing himself than the other Protestants who came after him. Undoubtedly, from this point on, he was obsessed by a fixed idea: to rid the concept of the sacrifice of the mass of every idea that tended to make it a sacrifice different from that of the Cross and one which man could offer for novel ends. But to do this he saw no other possibility than to get rid of any notion of a presence of Christ's sacrifice in the mass, and therefore to remove from the canon of the mass every-

---

[10] Cf. G. Aulén, *Christus Victor* (New York, 1960), the whole chapter on Luther.

[11] Cf. Y. Brilioth, *Eucharistic Faith and Practice, Evangelical and Catholic* (London, 1930), pp. 94 ff.

thing which expressed such a notion. Yet in doing so he merely stretched the logic of the medieval Latin idea that only the words of institution, isolated from their traditional context, were essential for the eucharistic consecration. And without further resistance, he yielded to the devotion which as a consequence of this centered on the showing forth of the consecrated host and its adoration.

Doubtless other factors did tend to compensate to a certain extent for these two defects inherited from the Middle Ages and pushed to their ultimate extreme. Luther's reaction against the abusive multiplication of private masses, together with the reintegration of the communion of both the faithful and the priest as being an essential aspect of the celebration had a positive effect. But this was soon weakened by the fact that Luther, still following the medieval pattern, looked upon the communion as the foremost opportunity for acts of penance grafted upon the worship of the *Christus passus*. The sole "thanksgiving" he retained was the medieval thanksgiving for the assurance of forgiveness that was renewed in this way.

His idea that the mass is above all Christ's "testament," giving us his body and blood as a perpetual witness to the forgiveness of our sins, with the richness that his idea of the redemption gave to this expression, might have allowed him to link up with the primitive idea of the eucharistic "memorial."[12]

Actually, the polemical way in which he flatly opposed it to the idea of a presence of Christ's sacrifice prevented him from drawing the most positive consequences from it. He was well aware that the eucharist must involve us in a pure "sacrifice of thanksgiving" for the gift received from the Savior. But, for him, and even more narrowly for his followers, this gift tended to be reduced to the subjective awareness of forgiveness. In this way, we come face to face with the greatest paradox of the Protestant eucharist: in order to prevent the mass from appearing to be a new sacrifice, distinct from Christ's, which the priests could perform at will, no other sacrifice was admitted than the subjective self-offering made by the believer in his grateful commitment

---

[12] Cf. Brilioth, *op. cit.*, p. 98.

to God's service elicited by his renewed sense of forgiveness. Among strict Lutherans, for whom this is possible only on the basis of an effective communion in the dead and risen Christ, this was to be a possible starting point of a return—at least in embryo—to the patristic views on our participation in the unique saving sacrifice. But, as Eric Mascall rightly observed, with the other Protestants who more or less decidedly reject the real presence, there can no longer be any other sacrifice in the eucharist than the very Pelagian sacrifice that man, and man alone, offers to God in gratitude for his benefits.[13] How could it be otherwise, since they have excluded every notion of a participation in the unique and completely divine sacrifice in rejecting the sacramental communication of its reality?

The *Formula Missae* brought out by Luther in 1523 is a kind of monument to his basic failure, even though the best of the Lutheran liturgies down to our own day have been taken from it. With the exception of the restoration of general communion, it in no way represents a return to the original eucharist. On the contrary, it is the final result of certain of the most aberrant tendencies that threatened the whole practice and theory of the eucharist in the Middle Ages. Yet we must not neglect to acknowledge its undeniable literary merit, although this simply resulted from having adapted, more ably and more daringly than anything that had been attempted previously, the old eucharist to the eucharistic piety and theology of the Middle Ages in what was most foreign there to the original tradition. To do this, it was necessary, as Luther did, to throw out all the elements whose meaning had tended to be lost even before Luther, and refashion the others in a sense which was no longer theirs.

Luther kept the common preface, but only up to the *Per Christum Dominum nostrum*. At this point, through a clever discovery, he immediately introduced the *Qui pridie pateretur* and the rest of the institution narrative. Only then do we have the *Sanctus*. During the *Benedictus*, the priest raised the host and cup together. At this moment, the eucharist properly so-called, in the primary sense of the term, is accomplished. We pass immediately to the

---

[13] Cf. E. Mascall, *Corpus Christi* (London, 1965), 2nd ed., pp. 106 ff.

Pater, then to the *Pax Domini*, and the communion is distributed during the *Agnus Dei*, after the priest has said aloud, but in the plural, the second of the preparatory prayers from the modern Roman missal: *Domine Jesu Christe, Fili Dei vivi, qui ex voluntate Patris*, etc.

The singing of the communion antiphon follows the communion proper (as was already the medieval practice), instead of accompanying it. The celebration ends with an invariable postcommunion, composed from the two medieval devotional prayers *Quod ore sumpsimus* and *Corpus tuum* (the plural was also introduced into this latter prayer).[14]

This service is certainly of a very skilful and fully harmonious composition. But it is in no way a reformation of medieval practice, if we mean by that a return to the eucharist of the Fathers and the New Testament. It is rather an ultimate deformation of that type which reduced everything to the adoration of the real presence, consecrated solely by the words of institution, before a communion in which forgiveness for sins absorbs all the other aspects of the believer's union with the crucified Savior. On the other hand, the "thanksgiving" is nothing more than an anticipated thanks for the evidence that we are about to receive of this forgiveness.

Two years later, Luther produced another liturgy, which was no longer in Latin like the *Formula Missae*, but in German: the *Deutsche Messe*. It went even further in getting rid of the most primitive elements of the mass. It may be considered as the first of these innumerable Protestant liturgies of the eucharist which strictly speaking no longer contain anything "eucharistic." The preface disappeared, and it was not another prayer that replaced it but an exhortation addressed to the faithful which led up to the *Verba Christi*. These are no less expressly called "conse-

---

[14] Luther D. Reed, *The Lutheran Liturgy*, 2nd ed. (Philadelphia, 1960), pp. 71 ff. and Brilioth, *op. cit.*, pp. 114 ff. What Luther said in the *Formula Missae* about the retaining of the elevation, especially where the faithful were instructed in its meaning, signified that it was no longer to be connected with the sacrifice but with the adoration alone. We might say that he reduced the mass to a "Benediction of the Blessed Sacrament" a century before the Catholics themselves had invented this ceremony!

cratory" (*dermunge*). The communion is distributed immediately, in principle with the host after the words over the bread and with the cup after those over the wine, while the *Sanctus* and *Agnus Dei* are sung in German paraphrases. But Luther still underlines the fittingness of the elevation immediately before the *Sanctus* as in the *Formula Missae*. This time, we may say that the irresistible logic of the medieval inheritance finally triumphed over everything which still resisted ejection in the authentically traditional eucharist.[15]

Yet we should not forget that in Luther's mind this "German Mass," according to its preface, was merely a transitional last resort, destined for the instruction of less enlightened peoples. Throughout his own explanations, we can see the confusion resulting in the effective loss of elements of tradition whose value he continued to acknowledge, even though he no longer knew what place to give them in his teaching. He plainly admits that he is not in favor of an exclusive use of the vernacular in the liturgy, with the exception of the bible readings and the chorales which were more or less direct paraphrases of traditional hymns. He feared that a completely German liturgy would become a source of religious provincialism and a severance from the tradition of the universal Church. More profoundly, he wanted the traditional forms of the eucharist to be retained as much as possible. His express wish therefore was that the type of the *Formula Missae* would for this reason remain the customary usage for schools and universities in particular.

In fact, the *Deutsche Messe* of 1525 served as a model only for the liturgies of the Rhineland where Lutheranism was soon influenced by another form of Protestantism, much more radical in its break with tradition: that of the "Reformed" Churches, influenced either by Zwingli or Calvin. These were the *ordines* of Würtemberg (composed by Brenz), of Strasbourg (by Bucer), of Baden, Worms, Rhein-Pfalz, etc.

As in the Zwinglian or Calvinist liturgies, the eucharistic prayer simply disappeared. But contrary to what happened with these latter liturgies, the words of institution continued to be looked

---

[15] Cf. Reed, *op. cit.*, pp. 74 ff. and Brilioth, *op. cit.*, pp. 120 ff.

upon as effecting the real presence of the body and blood of Christ in the elements of bread and wine, even though these words were no longer part of a prayer but were included in an exhortation addressed to the faithful.

In most of the other Lutheran Churches, people generally held to translations and adaptations of the *Formula Missae*, which often brought it closer to the traditional order. For example, the immediate connection between the preface and the *Sanctus* was reestablished, or the various proper prefaces were retained.

But frequently too, the influence of the *Deutsche Messe* made itself felt. For example, the Lord's Prayer, as in the *Deutsche Messe*, was said not after but before the consecration. This is what we find in the liturgy composed in 1528 by Bugenhagen for Brunswick, and which was used practically in the same state in Hamburg and Lübeck, and then in Denmark. The same thing is found in the liturgy of Saxony, composed by Jonas in 1539, for feastdays (there the *Deutsche Messe* was still retained for ordinary Sundays). Inversely the Brandenburg-Nuremberg liturgy of 1553 knew only the schema of the *Deutsche Messe*, although it returned the Lord's Prayer to its traditional place and retained a goodly number of Latin prayers and chants.

In the Electorate of Brandenburg, on the other hand, the liturgy composed under the influence of the Elector Joachim II, by Stratner, Buchholzer and Matthias von Jagow went much further than the *Formula Missae*. The Latin prefaces followed by the *Sanctus* were preserved, and during the singing of the latter, the celebrant said four prayers in a low voice and in German: for the Emperor, the authorities, the clergy, the unity of the Church, for the forgiveness of sins, after which he recited or sang in German the words of consecration, followed by the elevation and a Latin motet or a German song. There followed the Lord's Prayer and the *Agnus Dei*. Then there was inserted an exhortation inspired by the *Deutsche Messe* (taken word for word from the Nuremberg *ordo*) before the communion. Again in 1571, David Chytraeus composed a liturgy of analogous inspiration for the Lutherans of Austria. The same tendencies appeared at Riga (1530), and at Pfalz-Neuburg (1543). But, generally speaking, it is the model of the *Formula Missae* which more or less completely predominated in Lutheran Germany.[16]

It is interesting and even amusing to see Luther's reaction to these divergent tendencies. When questioned with some anxiety by Bucholzer, Joachim's chaplain, about his master's liturgical conservatism, he made no objection. The comic nature of his answer gives a characteristic picture of an irony which did not spare the scruples of the most "advanced" reformers any more than it did the ritualism of the Elector. "If your lord, the Margrave and Elector, allows the Gospel of Jesus Christ to be preached openly, clearly and purely, and the two sacraments of baptism and the flesh and blood of Christ to be administered and given in accordance with his institution ... then, in the name of God, go in procession, wear a cross of silver or gold, a chasuble and alb of velvet, silk or linen! And if a chasuble or an alb are not enough for your lord Elector, then put on three one on top of the other like Aaron! ... For such things, if they are not mingled with abuse, take nothing more away from the Gospel than they add to it ... And if the pope were willing to allow us freedom in this regard, and if the Gospel were preached, he could certainly order me to wear my breeches about my neck. I should do as he pleased!"[17]

THE UN-EUCHARISTIC EUCHARIST OF THE REFORMERS: ZWINGLI, OECOLAMPADIUS, FAREL AND CALVIN

This rather likeable mixture of traditional spirit and freedom was not at all to the taste of the other reformers, and especially those who called themselves "reformed," who were as much opposed to the Lutherans as to the Catholics, like Zwingli and Calvin. For them there could be no question of reforming the mass, but only of abolishing it.

What they put in its place, under the name of "Holy Supper," while claiming to return to the original eucharist, retained only the institution narrative, immersed in more and more wordy

[16] On all of this see Reed, *op. cit.*, pp. 88 ff.
[17] Endels, *Martin Luthers Briefwechsel*, vol. XII, pp. 316 ff.

and less and less religious exhortations. Moreover, the prayers that could be added to it were constantly developing in accordance with the very medieval impetus of the apologies and the affective meditations on the passion. Thus, this break with tradition, in the name of "Gospel alone" ended up in fact by retaining only the most anemic elements of a tradition that came after the ninth century. Rarely have we seen a reform end up with a practice that was such a total contradiction of its theoretical principle.

Zwingli in Zurich, like Oecolampadius at Basel, radically denied not only the sacrificial character of the mass but any idea of a real presence in the eucharist. For Zwingli in particular "to eat the flesh and drink the blood of the Son of man" meant exclusively to be nourished by the faith of the word of the gospel. The eucharist is merely a community meal in which the faithful proclaim their common faith in gratitude to God, by imitating and recalling the last meal taken by Christ with his followers. But there is no question of the sacrament in itself, however it is understood, uniting them to Christ. He remains in heaven and it is explicitly asserted that he is not more present or present in a different way in the celebration of the Holy Supper than in any other gathering where people listen together to his word.[18]

In a first phase, however, Zwingli in Zurich, like Oecolampadius in Basel, was careful not to introduce a service that would be so obviously different from the mass as the reformed Holy Supper was to become. His *De canone missae epicheiresis* of 1523 agrees to keep the mass practically as it was up to the *Sanctus* inclusively. But then for the Roman canon he substituted four Latin prayers leading up to the institution account, completed by the sentence from St. Paul on the "proclamation" of the death of Christ in the eucharist. Then came the communion, introduced by Christ's call: "Come to me all you who labor and are heavy laden and I shall give you rest," and followed by the *Nunc Dimittis*. The first of these four prayers (which follows the Our Father) is a commemoration of the history of salvation in a thanksgiving that is not without its reminder of the ancient anaphoras. But

[18] Cf. Brilioth, *op. cit.*, pp. 153 ff.

the second, in beseeching God to feed us with the heavenly bread, specifies that this bread is the word of Christ alone. The third, despite this, speaks not only of Christ's giving himself as food to our souls under the forms of bread and wine, but again of our partaking of his body and his blood. If it is read without reference to the foregoing one, we might think that it had kept the traditional sense of the eucharist:

> ... He gave himself to us as food, so that just as he vanquished the world, we, nourished by him, might hope to vanquish it in turn ... Grant us, therefore, merciful Father, through Christ, your Son, our Lord, through whom you give life to all and renew and sustain all things, that we may manifest him in our life, so that the likeness we have lost in Adam may be recovered. And so that this may come about, grant effectively to all of us who partake of the body and blood of your Son to have but one mind and one purpose and to be ourselves one in him who is one with you.

Finally, the last prayer is a petition that the communicants through the light of grace might partake worthily in the banquet of the Son, "in which he is himself both our host and our food," and this leads directly to the institution narrative. We must acknowledge the paradoxical fact that this eucharistic prayer more than any ancient Lutheran formula, comes close to the traditional formularies. Read by a devout but uncritical reader it could certainly arouse a eucharistic devotion of good quality, despite the vague character of its allusions to the sacrifice, even that of the cross. But read with care, it betrays a quasi-Renanesque art for expressing merely rationalizing platitudes under the guise of traditional formulas and with an unctuous tone that is most proper for leading people astray.

The same year we have in Basel an analogous attempt with *Das Testament Jesu Christi* of Oecolampadius, although the prayers here make use more clearly of the sacrificial themes, but exclusively in order to apply them to the offering of one's self in faith on the part of the Christian.[19]

---

[19] Cf. Brilioth, *op. cit.*, pp. 159 ff.

Zwingli, less than any one else, was not to take his first liturgical composition seriously, since he had conceived it merely
as a transition destined to prepare people's minds for what he
hoped would be his end result. After April 1525, feeling more
sure of himself in the city, he published his *Action oder Bruch
des Nachtmahls*. A characteristic trait of developed Zwinglianism is that all singing was banned. The deacon here and not
the celebrant read an exhortation. After this the Lord's Prayer
was recited. Then the celebrant read the one institution narrative, and the bread and wine were distributed to the seated
congregation.

The service began felicitously, before the meal proper, with a
prayer asking for the grace to perform fittingly "the praise and the
thanksgiving which your Son, our Lord and Savior Jesus Christ
has commanded us, his faithful, to do in memory of his death."
But this praise and thanksgiving are realized concretely only in
the recitation of the *Gloria in excelsis*, inserted between the reading of 1 Corinthians 11: 20-29 and John 6: 47-63, before the meal,
and that of psalm 113 (according to the Hebrew numbering) afterwards. There is no longer the least trace of a properly eucharistic
prayer.[20]

This eucharistic liturgy without a eucharist, on the other hand,
is foreseen for only yearly celebrations (Christmas, Easter, Whitsunday and once during the autumn). It is looked upon entirely
as a feast of the Christian community in which the community
expresses its solidarity in this unfrequent meal. It is indeed a
socio-religious act, but one which tends to be merely social. It
has been justly pointed out that as a consequence there persisted
the disconcerting fact in Zurich that the communion service brought
out a much larger congregation than the regular attendance at
Sunday worship.

Partly under the influence in Strasbourg of what Lutheran
elements Bucer had preserved, Calvin made an effort to restore
to this "Supper" a religious and sacramental content. Without teaching the real presence in the elements themselves, as
the Lutherans continued to do, he maintained that eating of this

[20] Cf. Brilioth, *op. cit.*, pp. 160 ff.

meal was not simply a sign of our common faith in the word of
the Gospel, but a sign given by God of a real communion in the
body and blood of his Son crucified for us. Yet, like Zwingli,
he maintained that the body of Christ existed now only in heav-
en and could not come down again. But he asserted no less ener-
getically that the signs given by God raise us up to heaven, provided that we receive them with faith, and incorporate us into
the glorified Christ so that the Church becomes, mystically but
really, his very body.[21]

Yet he did not make any really substantial changes in the Zwinglian Supper which had come to Geneva in a much more lengthy
if still unimproved form through Guillaume Farel.

After a first exhortation, Farel's service included a formula
of confession of sins, the Lord's Prayer, the Apostles' Creed, a
second exhortation leading to the institution narrative, a third
exhortation, the distribution of communion, and finally a fourth
and last exhortation before the blessing and the dismissal. Here
the most obsessive didacticism took the place, not only of the
eucharistic prayer, but of every prayer, with the exception of
the confession of sins.[22]

After a prayer for the Church, and the reading of the institution
narrative (according to St. Paul), Calvin's service introduced
an excommunication with regard to a whole series of sinners re-
garded as particularly scandalous, which was borrowed from the
Strasbourg ritual composed by Bucer. Then came a very long
exhortation in which Calvin tried to explain completely his doctrine of the Supper (we have given a summation of it above, precisely according to this text). The distribution of communion
followed immediately, accompanied either by the singing of a
psalm or biblical verses recited by the minister. A prayer of "thanksgiving," in the narrow sense of gratitude for the gifts received

---

[21] Cf. Brilioth, *op. cit.*, pp. 175 ff., and especially J. Cadier, "La doctrine
calviniste de la Sainte-Cène" in *Études théologiques et religieuses* (Montpel-
lier, 1951).

[22] Cf. Brilioth, *op. cit.*, pp. 172 ff. The *Manière et fasson*, attributed to
Farel, was printed at Serrières (near Neuchâtel) in 1533.

and commitment to a renewed fidelity, ends the service with the *Nunc Dimittis* and the blessing.[23]

Calvin wanted this Supper to be celebrated each Sunday after the service of readings and prayers. Despite his doctrinal attempt to infuse it with a content totally missing in the Zwinglian Supper, it is understood that this service, which was almost as heavily didactic as Farel's, never ca.ne to be celebrated much more often than Zwingli's. Calvin's theoretical sacramental realism changed nothing of the anemic reality of the ritual meal to which he applied it: people were still left with a non-eucharistic "eucharist."

SURVIVALS AND FIRST ATTEMPTS AT RESTORATION AMONG THE LUTHERANS; THE SWEDISH LITURGY FROM OLAUS PETRI TO JOHN III

On the other hand, throughout the whole of the seventeenth and well into the eighteenth century, the Lutheran mass remained the living hearth of the piety of Lutherans: a piety which the theological renewal of the great tradition coming from Johann Gerhard nourished with a genuine mysticism of Christ-in-us, taken particularly from the Greek fathers. Whatever its defects may have been, and they were, once again, medieval defects pushed to their extreme, this Lutheran mass preserved for the faithful all that they had found best about the mass of the Middle Ages. The absence of elements from the canon such as the anamnesis, as shocking as that may be, passed practically unnoticed. For a long time, these elements had not only not been understood but were not even known to the laity, since no account of them had been given in the teaching that they had for centuries been receiving on the eucharist. On the other hand, following a rather lengthy service of readings and chants in which nothing had been changed from the pre-Reformation mass, the preface, the words of consecration uttered aloud, kneeling at the sound of the bell for the adoration of the holy presence, which was heralded by the *Sanctus* and

---

[23] Cf. Bard Thompson, *Liturgies of the Western Church* (Cleveland and New York, 1961), pp. 185 ff. The first edition of the Calvinist liturgy at Geneva in 1542 (*La forme de prières*, etc.).

Benedictus, not only retained but popularized whatever properly eucharistic elements remained in the liturgy of the Middle
Ages thanks to the vernacular and the catechetical instruction. Re-
lieved of the pervading burden of the tropes and adventitious
devotions, enriched by the tender and virile piety of the chorales,
this liturgy on the other hand preserved the best aspects of the
affective devotion to the dying Savior for us in a petition for the
forgiveness expected from his saving grace and it recentered it
around frequent communion which was restored to its normal
place in the eucharistic celebration. Along with the ceremonial,
liturgical chant, sacred vestments, the crucifix and statues, incense
and candles, the mass of devout Lutherans still found in their worship the whole atmosphere of adoration which the best Christians
of the Middle Ages found in the holy presence and the evocation of
the saving cross. But, unwittingly, leaving aside the certainly capital fact that they were no longer content merely to assist at mass
but that they took communion, they had certainly progressed rather than regressed along the fateful path that had never ceased to
lead their forebears astray from the tradition of the ancient and
primitive Church. However rich their eucharistic piety often was,
it was still attached merely to a stunted concept of the eucharist.[24]

In Germany at least, this situation hardly survived the difficulties wrought by the Thirty Years War, and began to decom-
pose under official influence in the states where union with Prussia required conformity to the most devitalized "reformed" practices. But this abolishment itself was to give rise as a reaction
to a conscious rebirth of old Lutheranism which in our own day
has become at times very close to the Catholicism of the first
centuries.

This rebirth only came about three centuries after the Reformation. Yet it was at least outlined beginning with the end of
the sixteenth century in some particular instances which merit our
attention. It is the first of these liturgical renascences in Protestantism, and it was to mark the Church of Sweden permanently.[25]

---

[24] Cf. Reed, *op. cit.*, pp. 105 ff. and Brilioth, *op. cit.*, pp. 126 ff.

[25] Cf. Brilioth, *op. cit.*, pp. 228 ff. See also Lebrun, *op. cit.*, t. 4, in the re-
edition of 1843, pp. 100 ff.

Protestantism had been introduced into Sweden, as in many other places, for reasons that were chiefly political. But it remained extremely moderate in its transformation of the traditional forms of church life, and particularly church worship. Its chief promotor was the preacher Olaus Petri who was formed at Wittenberg. He is the author of the first Swedish mass, published in 1531.

It is very close to the *Formula Missae* of Luther in the sense that it connects immediately the words of institution with the *Per Christum* of the preface, while the *Sanctus* and the *Benedictus* announce the elevation. But it differs from it on a capital point in that it reintroduces something of the traditional anaphora, not in a form of intercessory prayers more or less directly inspired by those of the canon, as in the Brandenburg liturgy of 1540, but through an amplification of the preface itself.

This amplification combines unexpectedly, but most fortuitously, the medieval and Protestant emphasis on the forgiveness of the sins of the participants with an evocation of the history of salvation. Brilioth, doubtless correctly, thinks that this amplification must have been inspired by the Easter preface. But we may not absolutely exclude the supposition that this is a first instance of a perceptible influence on a Protestant liturgy if not of the Eastern liturgies, then at least of the Greek Fathers. Here is the text:

> Verily it is meet and right and blessed that we should in all places give thanks and praise to thee, holy lord, almighty father, everlasting God for all thy benefits, and especially for that one that thou didst unto us, when we all by reason of sins were in so bad a case that nought but damnation and eternal death awaited us, and no creature in heaven or earth could help us, then thou didst send forth thine only-begotten Son Jesus Christ, who was of the same divine nature as thyself, didst suffer him to become a man for our sake, didst lay our sins upon him, and didst suffer him to undergo death instead of our all dying eternally, and as he hath overcome death and risen again into life, and now dieth nevermore, so likewise shall all they who put their trust therein overcome sins and death and through him attain to everlasting life, and for our admonition that we should bear in mind and

never forget such his benefit, in the night that he was betrayed, etc ...

After the *Sanctus-Benedictus* we come to the communion through the Lord's Prayer, the *Pax Domini* and the *Agnus Dei*. Right before the distribution there is introduced an exhortation taken from the Nuremberg liturgy, as is the singing of the *Nunc Dimittis* accompanying the communion itself.[26]

On the other hand, the subjective and penitential aspect is still present in the formula of collective confession that precedes the whole service, before the Introit, one of the first examples of such compositions in a Protestant liturgy. Yet, it is absent from the fixed postcommunion which ends the service, and which is quite traditional in spirit with its remarkable eschatological reference.

This Swedish mass was not destined, it seems, to replace the High Mass, but rather to furnish what we should call a low mass with communion. Forty years later, Archbishop Laurentius Petri, Olaus' brother, adapted his brother's formulary for the High Mass itself. But he retained the possibility of keeping and singing (still in Latin) the proper prefaces, along with all the traditional Latin chants. In this case he prescribed that they immediately follow from the *Sanctus* before the words of consecration. This specification was accompanied by a detailed ordinance which has allowed the Church of Sweden to retain down to our own day the whole complex of ceremonial and liturgical decor which had been part of Catholic tradition. But this ordinance, in its doctrinal teachings, is still more interesting. For the first time in Protestantism Archbishop Laurentius, relying on Olaus' own formulas, attempted to develop a positive doctrine of the eucharistic sacrifice, which is very close to the teachings of the Fathers.

---

[26] The Swedish text and English translation in Yelverton, *The Mass in Sweden* (Henry Bradshaw Society, n. 57, London, 1919), pp. 37-38, commentary in Reed, *op. cit.*, pp. 113 ff. It will be noted that the final formula "Wherefore with the Angels and Archangels, etc." was reintroduced by John III before the *Sanctus*.

Not only did he admit the "sacrifice of praise and thanksgiving" in terms which show well that he means much more by it than the reformers did (who saw in it merely a metaphorical expression of our gratitude for the gifts received); not only did he connect this sacrifice which consists in the offering of ourselves with the will of God, but he added a capital phrase which is practically unparalleled in the other Lutheran authors of the time:

But, if you wish also to call the mass a sacrifice because it signifies or represents the sacrifice made by Christ on the cross, and not as if you were appropriating to yourself or to the priests who are said to offer it Christ's own function, then it can be accepted.

He goes so far as to add in a formula that is both very medieval and very Lutheran that the mass is indeed a sacrifice "because the priest and the people place it between their sins and God's wrath as a pledge of peace."[27]

Here we have the seed, as it were, of a joint recuperation of the liturgical and theological traditions. This movement was to continue under the episcopate of his son-in-law and successor, Archbishop Laurentius Petri Gothus, under the aegis of King John III, aided by his secretary Petrus Fecht, a former pupil of the humanist and chief collaborator of Luther, Melanchthon.

This "return to the sources" bore its fruits in a revised liturgy which King John made obligatory for some years and which certainly represents the boldest traditional reaction that could yet be seen in a Lutheran country.[28] It was not simply a return to the Roman canon, but an attempt (more ingenious, perhaps, than successful) to restore many discarded elements to the schema of Olaus Petri's mass, without modifying its structure inherited from the *Formula Missae* of Luther. Further, to this we must add an effort, which this time cannot be doubted, to derive inspiration from Eastern liturgies. One sentence from the new formulary, taken word for word from the liturgy of St. John Chrys-

---

[27] Cf. Brilioth, *op. cit.*, pp. 249 ff.

[28] Lebrun reproduced the entire Latin text of this liturgy in t. 4 of his work, pp. 115 ff.: *Liturgia suecanae Ecclesiae, catholicae et orthodoxae conformis*, Stockholmiae, 1576. Cf. also Yelverton, *op. cit.*, pp. 78 ff.

ostom, is enough to attest to it. What is more, the King himself justified his liturgical reform in advance, before the whole
body of clergy in Stockholm in 1574, by voicing the need to return to the ancient models of the liturgies of St. James, St. Basil,
St. Chrysostom, St. Ambrose and St. Gregory. A reading of the
new text in fact easily convinces us that if the Eastern liturgies
which Olaus Petri had already claimed as supporting his composition could have been advanced with confidence by him, it
was certainly no longer the case here.

Similarly, in the liturgy of Laurentius Petri (the father-in
law of Laurentius Petri Gothus), a connection was made between
the ancient proper prefaces like Olaus' preface, or the common
preface (given as an interchangeable formula for Sundays and
ferial days) and the words of consecration through the intermediary of the formula: "And he, that we might never forget his
benefits, in the night he was betrayed, etc ..." After the traditional conclusion of the ancient prefaces the *Sanctus* is then
sung or recited. But, while it is sung during the High Mass, or
once it has been recited in a low mass, the priest adds an anamnesis and an epiclesis for which no Lutheran liturgy, even the
most conservative, had an equivalent before that time. They
paraphrase in a most interesting way the *Unde et memores*, the
Supra quae and the *Supplices* of the Roman canon:

> Therefore we also remember, o Lord God, this blessed com-
> mand and the same thy son our Lord Jesus Christ's holy
> passion and death, his resurrection and ascension. And this
> thy son thou hast in thy boundless mercy sent and given
> unto us, that he might be an offering for our sins, and by
> his one offering on the cross pay the price of our redemption,
> fulfil thy justice and make perfect such an offering as might
> serve for the welfare of all the elect unto the end of the world.
> The same thy Son, the same offering, which is a pure, holy
> and undefiled offering, set before us for our reconciliation,
> our shield, defense, and covering against thy wrath, against
> the terror of sins and of death, we take and receive with faith
> and offer before thy glorious majesty with our humble sup-
> plications. For these thy great benefits we give thee fervent
> thanks with heart and mouth, yet not as our bounden duty
> is but according to our power.

And we humbly beseech thee through the same thy son, whom thou in thy Godly and secret counsel hast set before us as our only mediator, that thou wilt vouchsafe to look upon us and our prayers with mercy and pitying eye, suffer them to come to thy heavenly altar before thy Divine majesty and be pleasing unto thee, that all we who are partakers at this altar of the blessed and holy food and drink, the holy bread of eternal life and the Cup of eternal salvation, which is the holy body and precious blood of thy Son, may also be fulfilled with all heavenly benediction and grace.[29]

This is followed by a *Nobis quoque* where the saints' names although not their general mention have been removed, which leads to the conclusion of the Roman canon: *Per quem haec omnia,* etc ... The end of the service corresponds to that of the liturgy of the previous Archbishop, except that several alternative post-communions have been proposed.

It is equally interesting to note what the anamnesis retains from the Roman *Unde et memores* and what it adds to it. It begins by connecting the memorial to Christ's precept (*mandatum*). At first sight this appears to be traditional, but what is not traditional is that the memorial in fact becomes here a subjective commemoration of the Last Supper, before indirectly recalling the passion and the whole work of salvation. From the outset we find ourselves in the context of the medieval and Protestant view of things. But everything that follows is an attempt to force it, in so far as that is possible, to rejoin the ancient notion. The second amplification, emphasizing the divine mercy and exalting the uniqueness of the sacrifice of the cross, has not only the Epistle to the Hebrews to recommend it but also similar formularies from the patristic era like the Armenian liturgy. Still, there is no doubt that these formulas are there in order to satisfy a Protestant theology in which the uniqueness of the redemptive sacrifice is confounded with the impossibility not only of repeating it but of perpetuating its sacramental presence. The explanation given of this sacrifice, as if it were reduced to the Anselmian notion of penal satisfaction, is quite typical not only of Luther himself but of Lutheran

---

[29] Lebrun, *op. cit.*, pp. 142-143; cf. Yelverton, *op. cit.*, pp. 106 ff.

scholasticism which took over this explanation precisely in order to set the whole redemption within the strict framework of the past. The subsequent use, then, of expressions like *hostiam puram, hostiam sanctam, hostiam immaculatam* applies them solely to the cross, and no longer to the sacrament of the sacrifice.

But the context prepares for a reintroduction of everything which seems to have been excluded, in an exceptionally skilful way. The turn-about was effected through an accumulation of expressions taken directly from Luther which, however, as Aulén has shown so well, connect his thought very closely with the thought of the Greek Fathers. The crucified Christ is called *propitiationem, scutum et umbraculum nostrum contra iram tuam, contra terrorem peccati et mortis.* The presentation of the dead Christ to the Father, in order to protect us from his wrath, is an expression familiar to Luther to describe the way in which he conceives our justification by faith. The idea that we find liberation here from the terrors of sin and death is no less his, but it is taken directly from the biblical text most often quoted by the Fathers (the Greeks in particular) to express the effect of the redemption (Hebrews 11:14-15). It is in this context that the prayer, in terms that are still quite Lutheran, manages to reintegrate the idea of an objective presence of the Cross in the mass and a consecutive offering of the one sacrifice which we can here make our own: *eumdem Filium tuum, ejusdem mortem et oblationem ... nobis propositum fide amplectimur, tuaeque praeclarae majestati humillimis nostris precibus offerimus.* In one sense, there is nothing more Lutheran than this "grasp" of the one oblation of Christ by the believers in the prayer of faith. But that Christ and his offering of himself, inseparably, are considered as *nobis propositum* in the eucharistic celebration, and that it is said that "we offer him" by this very prayer which "grasps" him in faith, comes down to introducing into the very heart of the most unquestionably Lutheran notion of salvation that traditional notion of the mass which Luther, in fact, was never successful in integrating into it. Indeed, how could he have been, since for him the eucharistic sacrifice always had meant either a sacrifice other than that of the cross (which he obviously had to reject) or else merely an expression of our gratitude for the forgiveness granted to our faith? Here on the contrary, the eucharist becomes again the sacramental encounter in which our faith can effectively grasp the Cross, since the dead and risen Christ is objectively "proposed" to it, with the result that we become associated with his one offering in the prayer which grasps this heavenly gift. We may say that everything positive in the Lutheran notion of salvation has been retained, but the whole is reintegrated into the ancient notion of the eucharist to which Luther at times came very close, although he never quite succeeded in clearly untangling it from its later caricatures.

As ingenious as this composition was in successfully making use of all those formulas (which were the cause in the first place of the idea of sacrifice being expelled from the eucharist) in order that it might reintroduce the notion of sacrifice, it still remains very artificial. Indeed, for it not to be factitious, the reintegration that it hoped for would have required the initial abandonment of the false notion that the "memorial" was merely a subjective commemoration of Jesus' last meal with his followers. As long as the Protestants were unsuccessful in ridding themselves of this strictly psychological and anecdotal notion, a most unfortunately uncritical inheritance from the Middle Ages, all their attempts at escaping the alternative: one sacrifice of the cross or a multiplication of sacrifices added to the cross, would appear to be a wish to reconcile the irreconcilable.

The epiclesis reflects a process exactly like that of the anamnesis. It fuses into one the *Supra quae* and the *Supplices*, in a way that might have been suggested by the *De Sacramentis* (let us recall that John III expressly cited St. Ambrose among the sources of the ancient eucharist to whom a return should be made). But it omits the mention of the ancient sacrifices and the Angel, and substitutes in their place an evocation (once again inspired by the Epistle to the Hebrews) of Christ interceding for us in the heavenly sanctuary. The conclusion repeats that of the *Supplices*, although at this point it inserts two formulas which had disappeared from the *Unde et memores* (*panem sanctum vitae aeternae et calicem salutis perpetuae*). But it is obvious that they did not wish here to extend the idea, outlined in the preceding prayer, of the one sacrifice becoming our own in the eucharist, with the result that they limited themselves to asking for the acceptance upon the heavenly altar not of this sacrifice but only of our prayers. Yet, since these prayers themselves somewhat earlier had acquired a sacrificial meaning, it is not impossible to transfer to this epiclesis the ancient content of the Roman formulas that inspired it.

There is nothing to be said about the *Nobis quoque*, but it is worthy of note that they did not dare to introduce either the *Memento* of the dead or any formal prayer for the departed, for fear of colliding with the suspicion that every prayer for the dead in the mass implied a repetition of the one sacrifice and not merely its sacramental actualization.

But we must mention the strangest peculiarity of this whole liturgy, which is not only that they reintroduced a properly consecratory epiclesis before the institution narrative and, in imitation of the Eastern liturgies, addressed it to the Holy Spirit, but also that they placed it before the beginning of the eucharist proper. The reason for this curious innovation is quite simple: as long as they wished to keep intact the schema of the *Formula Missae* adopted by Olaus Petri, they were unable to find any other place for it. The offertory, then, concludes with a series of three prayers: the first is a sort of fixed "secreta," the second a recoup of the *Te igitur* in which, once again, the mention of the sacrifice is replaced by the mention of our prayers, and the third, the text that follows:

> O Lord, God, who willest that thy Son's holy and most worthy Supper should be unto us a pledge and assurance of thy mercy: awaken our heart, that we who celebrate the same his Supper may have a salutary remembrance of thy benefits, and humbly give thee true and bounden thanks, glory, honour, and praise for evermore. Help us thy servants and thy people that we may herewith remember the holy, pure, stainless and blessed offering of thy son, which he made upon the cross for us, and worthily celebrate the mystery of the new testament and eternal covenant. Bless and sanctify with the power of thy holy Spirit that which is prepared and set apart for this holy use, bread and wine, that rightly used it may be unto us the body and blood of thy Son, the food of eternal life, which we may desire and seek with greatest longing. Through the same ...[30]

---

[30] Lebrun, *op. cit.*, p. 137; cf. Yelverton, *op. cit.*, pp. 101 ff. It is likely

Here, more than ever, they attempted the impossible: after the most intensely subjective formulation of the "memorial," the eucharist is nonetheless designated by the expression *"mysterium peragere,"* enhanced by its parallel with the " *"hostia ... in ara crucis peracta."* The conclusion, too, is a consecratory epiclesis which is as clear as it can be, although there is a repetition of these expressions *"sacro usui destinatae"* and *"in vero usu"* which are familiar to Protestant ears. But, for the Lutheran scholasticism influenced by Melanchthon and concerned with coming as close as possible to the Calvinists, these words signified that the eucharistic presence is reduced to the celebration, and even to the act of consuming the species. It seems evident that nothing of this sort is any longer meant by these words, but merely, at the most that the mass is availing for the salvation of those participating only insofar as they come to it with the proper dispositions. In other words, in this prayer (more perhaps than in any of the others) we can see the twofold ambiguity of the whole of this liturgy: all the Lutheran formulas have assuredly become susceptible of a perfectly Catholic sense, but all the Catholic formulas, for their part, are presented in such a disjointed way that they can appear to have only a Lutheran sense. Actually, the King's sincere intention does seem to have been to return to the ancient tradition, but without thereby losing any of the positive elements of Lutheranism. However, we must admit, the procedure followed seems to pretend to adapt the Catholic formulas to Lutheran doctrine, in order to camouflage a Catholic doctrine beneath Lutheran formulas. The undeniable wish of the King to return Sweden to Catholic unity at a time when men were in no way prepared for it, and the secret maneuverings of too crafty negotiators flurrying about his court, soon persuaded practically everyone that such was the true nature of this text. As Archbishop Laurentius Petri Gothus had foreseen, at the very moment when he had endorsed it, the "red book" of John III could not truly satisfy either the

---

that the *Veni Sanctificator*, which had already been introduced into the offertory of the medieval Roman mass, would have encouraged the insertion of this true epiclesis at this point. Hence, once again we have the accentuation of a medieval deviation by the Reformation, *viz.* the offertory tending here to become an anticipated doublet of the canon.

Protestants or the Catholics. Once the King was dead, in fact, his liturgy furnished an excellent pretext for the small party of radical "reformed" theologians supported by the Regent, Duke Charles, to attempt to swing the Swedish pendulum to their side. But their efforts were not destined to be any more successful than his, and Sweden soon returned to the liturgy of Olaus Petri in the form that Laurentius Petri had worked out in 1571. It was to retain it practically intact down to our own day.[31]

CRANMER AND THE ANGLICAN EUCHARIST

A very different example of a Protestant liturgy susceptible of a Catholic interpretation was offered in the middle of the century by the first Anglican eucharistic liturgy. But in this instance, the intention was not to reintroduce a Catholic sense into Lutheran formulas, but rather the possible introduction of a Zwinglian sense into the Catholic formulas (something which, as we have seen, Zwingli had already tried in his first and completely provisional liturgy). We mean naturally the text composed by Cranmer and published in 1549 in his first *Prayer Book*.

This book itself proceeds from a still-born liturgy: the one that had been patronized by the Archbishop of Cologne, Hermann von Wied, and which was composed by Bucer in collaboration with Melanchthon. It reflected something from most of the Lutheran *ordines* that were already published, especially the two divergent *ordines* of Brandenburg, while making an effort, like the Swedish liturgies, to come closer also to the ancient liturgies. The energetic opposition of the chapter, upheld by the university, prevented this composition, published in 1543, from ever having any local use. Charles V forbade its use and Hermann, excommunicated by Paul III in 1546, died deprived of his see in 1552. Although it was never used at Cologne, the book to which he gave his name did have some success among the Lutherans of Hesse and the Saar and in a few places in Alsace.[32]

---

[31] Cf. Brilioth, *op. cit.*, pp. 254 ff.

[32] Cf. Reed, *op. cit.*, pp. 102 ff., Brilioth, *op. cit.*, p. 202. It will be noted that an English translation of the Cologne *Ordo* appeared in 1548. See the

For his liturgy of the English mass, Cranmer took from it only the formula of general confession of sins at the beginning and the biblical verses (the "comfortable words") which accompanied the absolution that followed. But he took no inspiration from its eucharistic preface in which there seemed to have been a combination of Gallican and Eastern influences and which was followed by the institution narrative immediately after the *Sanctus*. Actually, if Cranmer's personal literary taste caused him to retain as many as possible of the traditional formulas to which Henry VIII remained strongly attached (just as he was to the Catholic doctrines on the sacraments), he was not and never had been more Lutheran than his master. Nonetheless, he had abandoned the medieval doctrines on the eucharist, although he took great care not to let Henry see this, and immediately adopted a radical Zwinglianism. He was to try, with the same prudence shown by Zwingli in Zurich, first to insinuate it beneath a phraseology which was still Catholic in appearance at the end of Henry's reign, and then with the Protestantism of the government of Edward VI to express it plainly.

Dom Gregory Dix has established irrefutably that the interpretation long given by catholicizing Anglicans of the difference between his eucharist of 1549 and the one he produced in 1552 is untenable. Far from being still Catholic or, at the most, "Lutheranized," the first eucharist is only Catholic in appearance and simply disguises under a veil of ambiguities the same doctrine which is so frankly stated in the second, a doctrine which is not only "reformed" but properly Zwinglian. But, like Zwingli's first liturgy and still more skilfully, Cranmer's first liturgy retains all that could be kept of the ancient formulas in making them susceptible of a completely different understanding. The same prudence guided him, not only for the sake of the King, but because of the sentiments of the mass of the people and a great part of the English clergy, which had remained basically Catholic. We must just add that his refined humanism caused him to bring to

introduction of *The First and Second Prayer Books of Edward VI*, in the *Everyman's Library* edition (new ed., London, 1952) with a bibliographical and historical note by E. C. Ratcliff), p. viii.

his task the taste of an antiquarian and an artist, without which the astounding and lasting success of this ambiguous composition would be incomprehensible.[33]

Here is this text, which is basic for the whole history of the Anglican liturgy:

It is very mete, righte, and our boūden dutie that wee shoulde at all tymes and in all places, geue thankes to thee, O Lorde, holy father, almightie euerlastyng God ...

Therefore with Angels and Archangels, and with all the holy companye of heauen: we laude and magnify thy glorious name, euermore praisyng thee, and saying: Holy, holy, holy, Lorde God of Hostes; heauen & earth are full of thy glory: Osanna in the highest. Blessed is he that commeth in the name of the Lorde: Glory to thee O lorde in the highest.

Almightie and euerliuyng God, whiche by thy holy Apostle haste taught us to make prayers and supplicacions, and to geue thankes for al menne: We humbly beseche thee moste mercyfully to receiue these our praiers, which we offre unto thy diuine Maiestie, beseching thee to inspire cōtinually the uniuersal churche, with the spirite of trueth, unitie and concorde: And graunt that al they that do cōfesse thy holy name, maye agree in the trueth of thy holye worde, and liue in unitie and godly loue. Speciallye we beseche thee to saue and defende thy seruaunt, Edwarde our Kyng, that under hym we maye be Godly and quietly gouerned. And graunt unto his whole coūsaile, and to all that be put in aucthoritie under hym, that they maye truely and indifferently minister iustice, to the punishemente of wickednesse and vice, and to the maintenaunce of Goddes true religion and vertue. Geue grace (O heauenly father) to all Bishoppes, Pastors, and Curates, that thei maie bothe by their life and doctrine, set furthe thy true and liuely worde, and rightely and duely administer thy holy Sacramentes. And to al thy people geue thy heauenly grace, that with meke heart and due reuerence, they may heare and receiue thy holy worde, truely seruying thee in holyness and righteousnes, all the dayes of their life:

[33] See Gregory Dix, *The Shape of the Liturgy*, pp. 648 ff. and Stella Broom, *The Languages of the Book of Common Prayer* (London, 1965).

And we most hūbly beseche thee of thy goodnes (O Lorde)
to coumfort and succour all them, whyche in thys transystory
life be in trouble, sorowe, nede, syckenes, or any other aduer-
sitie. And especially we commend unto thy mercifull goodnes, this congregacion which is here assembled in thy name,
to celebrate the commemoracion of the most glorious death
of thy sonne; And here we do geue unto thee moste high
praise, and hartie thankes for the wonderfull grace and vertue declared in all thy sainctes, from the begynning of the
worlde: And chiefly in the glorious and most blessed virgin
Mary, mother of thy sonne Jesu Christe our Lorde and God,
and in the holy Patriarches, Prophetes, Apostles and Martyrs, whose examples (O Lorde) and stedfastnes in thy fayth,
and kepyng thy holy commaundementes: graunt us to folowe.
We commend unto thy mercye (O Lorde) all other thy seruauntes, which are departed hence from us, with the signe
of faith, and nowe do reste in the slepe of peace: Graūt unto
them, we beseche thee, thy mercy, and euerlasting peace,
and that at the day of the generall resurreccion, we and all
they which bee of the misticall body of thy sonne, may altogether be set on his right hand, and heare that his most ioy-
full voyce: Come unto me, O ye that be blessed of my father,
and possesse the kingdom, whiche is prepared for you, from
the begynning of the worlde: Graunt this, O father, for Jesus
Christes sake, our onely mediatour and aduocate.

O God heauenly father, which of thy tender mercie, diddest
geue thine only sonne Jesu Christ, to suffre death upon the
crosse for our redempcion, who made there (by his one obla-
cion once offered) a full, perfect, and sufficient sacrifyce, obla-
cion, and satysfacyon, for the sinnes of the whole worlde, and
did institute, and in his holy Gospell commaund us, to celebrate a perpetuall memory, of that his precious death, un-
tyll his comming again: Heare us (o merciful father) we besech thee: and with thy holy spirite & worde, vouchsafe to
blesse and sanctifie these thy gyftes, and creatures of bread
and wyne, that they maie be unto us the bodye and bloude
of thy moste derely beloued sonne Jesus Christe. Who in
the same nyght that he was betrayed: tooke breade, and when
he had blessed, and geuen thankes: he brake it, and gaue it
to his disciples, saiyng: Take, eate, this is my bodye, which
is geuen for you, do this in remembraunce of me. Likewyse,

after supper he toke the cuppe, and when he had geuen thankes, he gaue it to them, saiyng: drynk ye all of this, for this my bloude of the newe Testament, whyche is shed for you and for many, for remission of synnes: do this as oft as you shall drinke it in remembraunce of me.

At this point, a rubric prescribes that the priest, as he takes the bread and then the cup into his hands, remain turned towards the altar, without any elevation or showing of the Sacrament to the people. The prayer continues:

Wherefore, O Lorde and heauenly father, accordyng to the Instytucyon of thy derely beloued sonne, our sauiour Jesus Christ, we thy humble seruauntes do celebrate, and make here before thy diuine Maiestie, with these thy holy giftes, the memoryall whyche thy sonne hath wylled us to make, hauing in remembraunce his blessed passion, mightie resurreceyon, and gloryous ascension, renderyng unto thee most hartie thankes, for the innumerable benefites procured unto us by thesame, entierely desiryng thy fatherly goodnes, mercifully to accepte this our Sacrifice of praise and thankes geuing: most humbly beseching thee to graunt, that by the merites an death of thy sōne Jesus Christ, and through faith in his bloud, we and al thy whole church, may obteigne remission of our sinnes, and all other benefites of hys passyon. And here wee offre and present unto the (O Lorde) oure selfe, oure soules, and bodies, to be a reasonable, holy, and liuely sacrifice unto thee: humbly besechyng thee, that whosoeuer shalbee partakers of thys holy Communion, maye worthely receiue the moste precious body and bloude of thy sonne Jesu Christe; and bee fulfilled with thy grace and heauenly benediccion, and made one bodye with thy sonne Jesu Christe, that he maye dwell in them, and they in hym. And although we be unworthy (through our manyfolde synnes) to offre unto thee any Sacrifice: Yet we besech thee to accepte thys our bounden duetie and seruice, and commaunde those our prayers and supplicacions, by the Ministery of thy holy Angels, to be brought up into thy holy Tabernacle before the syght of thy dyuine maiestie: not waiyng our merites, but pardonyng our offences, through Christe our Lorde, by whome, and with whome, in the unitie of the holy Ghost: all honour and glory, be unto thee, O father almightie, world without ende. Amen.[34]

This English eucharist seems to have been very badly received by the laity, who as a whole were in no way anxious to abandon the Latin liturgy with which they had always been familiar. But it is incontestable that the mass of the clergy which had come in contact with humanism, even though it was still so attached to Catholic doctrines, saw no objection to using these Anglicized formulas rather than the canon of the Roman mass. Somewhat later Bishop Gardiner relied on two passages from this text to uphold against Cranmer himself the permanent legitimacy within the Anglican Church of the teaching which had always been that of the Catholic Church. In the first place, he cited these words from Cranmer's canon, immediately before the institution narrative: "Hear us, O merciful Father, we beseech thee: and with thy Holy Spirit and word, vouchsafe to bless and *sanctify* these thy gifts, and creatures of bread and wine, that *they may be unto us the body and blood* of thy most dearly beloved Son Jesus Christ." With these he connected the words that followed in the same narrative: "most humbly beseeching thee, that *whosoever shall be partakers of this holy Communion, may worthily receive the most precious body and blood of thy Son ...* " To which he again added this formula from the preparatory prayer for communion: "Grant us therefore ... so to eat the flesh of thy dear Son Jesus Christ, and to drink his blood *in these holy mysteries,* that we may evermore dwell in him ... ." But Cranmer replied drily that to interpret these texts as the Bishop of Winchester did was "a plain untruth."

Indeed, we must pay close attention to the sense that Cranmer, in Zwingli's wake, gives constantly to the evangelical formulas concerning the eating of Christ's body (or flesh) and his blood becoming our drink. His *Defence* repeats tirelessly that the only

---

[34] Bard Thompson, *op. cit.,* pp. 255 ff. From the *Everyman's Library* edition mentioned above (pp. 221 ff.), it will be noted that Cranmer retained the proper prefaces of Christmas, Easter, Ascension Day, Whitsunday, and Trinity, but in a paraphrased text (which is at times reduced as in the case of Trinity, and at times expanded as for Whitsunday).

possible sense of these expressions is "to believe in our hearts, that His Flesh was rent and torn for us upon the cross and His Blood shed for our redemption." As he says again, this eating is in no way specific to the Eucharist; we eat and drink Christ and feed on him as long as we are members of his body (obviously the mystical body), with the result that he may be eaten and drunk in the Old Testament just as well as today. Under these conditions the Supper was instituted "that every man eating and drinking thereof should remember that Christ died for him, and so should exercize his faith, and comfort himself by the remembrance of Christ's benefits." Not only does he expressly reject every idea of a sanctification of the elements other than the material fact of their being set aside for the celebration, but even Calvin's idea of of a spiritual but real eating of the body and blood of Christ present in heaven is quite foreign to him. For him, "to eat the flesh and drink the blood" is only a metaphor for believing (in the presence of the bread and wine, but without this presence as well) in the benefits of the cross which the word of the Gospel alone allows us to know. One could not be clearer than he on this point.

The same is true, for stronger reasons, in regard to the sacrificial expressions that he may use in his eucharistic prayer. The "sacrifice of praise and thanksgiving" (still according to this *Defence*) is set off against the propitiatory sacrifice whereby Christ has reconciled us with God. It is "another kind of sacrifice ... which doth not reconcile us to God, but is made of them that be reconciled by Christ, to testify our duties unto God, and to shew ourselves thankful unto Him; and therefore they be called sacrifices of laud, praise and thanksgiving. The first kind of sacrifice Christ offered to God for us; the second kind we ourselves offer to God by Christ. And by the first kind of sacrifice Christ offered us also unto His Father; and by the second we offer ourselves and all that we have, unto Him and His Father. *And this sacrifice generally is our whole obedience unto God, in keeping His laws and commandments.*"

Not only, then, are the propitiatory sacrifice offered by Christ alone and our sacrifice of pure gratitude and obedience completely distinct, but we cannot say that Cranmer even left the way open for some sort of presence of the Savior's sacrifice in the eucharist, so that it might become the source of our obedient act of thanksgiving. For him, there is no presence in the eucharist of any sacrifice other than this latter. "In this eating, drinking and using of the Lord's supper, we make not of Christ a new sacrifice propitiatory for remission of sin. But, the humble confession of all penitent hearts, their "knowledging" of Christ's benefits, their thanksgiving for the same, their faith and consolation in Christ, their humble submission and obedience to God's will and commandments, is a sacrifice of laud and praise, accepted and allowed of God no less than the sacrifice of the priest." In other words, according to him, there is no other sacrifice (and his liturgy does not speak differently) than the faithful's feelings of gratitude and their disposition to obey God in all things.[35].

Evidently, the fact that no other alternative than either a recommencement of the Cross or a purely subjective "sacrifice" occurred to him and to so many other Protestants, shows the extent that the notion of sacrificial and sacramental memorial had decomposed in the religious mentality of the end of the Middle Ages. But in these circumstances what happens to this "sacrifice" whose sole presence they are still willing to acknowledge in the eucharist? Cut off in this way from any actual relationship to Christ's sacrifice, on the basis of a sacramental presence, this sacrifice of our praise, our gratitude and our obedience becomes, as Eric Mascall points out, a completely Pelagian sacrifice: man does offer it after Christ and as a response to his sacrifice, but it is no longer solely by virtue of his own.

Once we have understood this transposition of all the traditional notions, we can admire the skill (which is much more refined than that of Zwingli himself in his first eucharist) with which Cranmer in his liturgy succeeded in retaining even in its details the schema of the ancient Roman eucharist. In adapting it not only to his ideas but to the language and rhetoric of his age, he produced a

---

[35] On all of this, see Gregory Dix, *op. cit.*, pp. 648-658, which we have merely summarized. The more recent work of A. Kavanagh, *The Concept of Eucharistic Memorial in the Canon revised by Thomas Cranmer, Archbishop of Canterbury* (St. Meinrad, Indiana, 1949) shows the purely subjective character of the "Memorial" in Cranmer's understanding.

work which, literarily, is not without analogy with the remodeling of the ancient eucharists that we have seen come about in fourth century Syria. In this reworking, however, he was not as daring as men were then. He limited himself to regrouping into one series the different intercessions and commemorations which seemed to be scattered throughout the Roman canon. Instead of bringing them together as a conclusion, he assembled them as a block in the first section, arranging them around the *Te igitur*, the *Memento of the living*, and then the *Communicantes* and the *Hanc igitur*. But he allowed to remain in their original places what we have called the pre-epiclesis of the *Te igitur*, the consecratory epiclesis of the *Quam oblationem*, immediately preceding the institution narrative, and the second epiclesis, arising from the anamnesis in the *Supra quae* and the *Supplices*, and beseeching that the eucharist have its full effect in those who celebrate it.

If we pay close attention to the interpretations given by Cranmer himself to the formulas he uses, all of these prayers and the anamnesis itself seem to be deprived of their original content. But, since they retain practically all of the ancient expressions, with the minimum of retouching that was necessary in order to be able to bend them to the devitalized sense in which he understood them, a person who is without the key to his perpetually metaphorical language, can be easily taken in. One might think that one were simply re-reading the old canon in a more obviously coherent order and in a casing of devout humanist rhetoric. It is true that those terms that were hardest to allegorize in this way, like oblation and sacrifice, surreptitiously disappeared from those places where they could only have one meaning which he no longer was willing to give them. But they are found elsewhere, where they are used either of the Cross of Christ alone or of the Christians' offering of themselves, and one must be very alert to observe that the eucharistic celebration is never expressly envisioned as an objective connection between the two. If one were vaguely suspicious about the sleight-of-hand that had taken place, the fact that all the secondary details of the old prayers have remained in their original places, from the initial call to God's fatherly clemency to the references to the heavenly altar and the Angel of the sacrifice, concluding with the opposition between the inadequacy of our own merits and the limitless generosity of divine grace, would be enough to reassure us of the author's good intentions. If a formula that is too unequivocal happens to be paraphrased, this is always done under the cover of a biblical allusion chosen with such infallible dexterity, and the whole is expressed in such a melodious and consistently unctuous literary setting that even after the very pointed declarations of the *Defence*, it is hard to be persuaded that so much skill and so much devotion is in the long run merely the skill of speaking piously in order to say nothing.

It is more easily and readily forgotten that Cranmer, when he is not concerned with emptying the properly sacrificial or sacramental formulas of their content, shows himself to be a liturgist of equal stature with the greatest of antiquity. The most felicitous characteristic of his skill is the delicacy with which from the beginning to the end of the prayer he was able to keep the basic act of thanksgiving constantly uppermost with a word or an expression. He does this so well that it is everywhere present and runs through this lengthy prayer like a golden thread binding it together. The same must be said for the theme of the Church and her unity: from one end of the eucharist to the other, beginning with the first part of the intercessions as their connecting link, it is constantly recalled through a succession of impeccable strokes of the bow before it finally emerges in a magnificent crescendo. The recall of the "grace and heavenly benediction" of the Roman canon is specified here in the unforgettable final invocation, that we become one body with Christ and that he abide in us and we in him.

Particularly successful also is the "retractatio" of the *Quam oblationem* through which Cranmer introduces the combined mention of the Spirit and the Word to "bless and sanctify" the eucharistic elements. Was his wish, through this addition, to reconcile the tenor of this prayer which remains typically Roman not only with the Syrian epiclesis but with the old Alexandrian epicleses like Serapion's? It seems that he was not sufficiently familiar with the Eastern liturgies to have such a synthesis in mind, and therefore that it was merely the result of his instinctive good taste. Dom Gregory Dix is probably right in supposing that at this point he was only inserting an explanation of the eucharistic consecration that had come from Paschasius Radbertus,[36] but which the whole of the Middle Ages had reproduced attributing it to St. Augustine. This eucharistic liturgy of Cranmer's is an incontestable masterpiece. The rhythmical perfection of his language and style succeeded in making it so attractive that those who made use of it in good faith as a fully Catholic liturgy always found their disillusionment with it most painful. But, once one has become advised of the perpetual ambiguities that allow it to clothe the most rigid denial of their whole content in the most traditional expressions, we have to admit that it is an equivocal masterpiece. It is only right to acknowledge that Cranmer had too uneasy a conscience about his work to want it to be perpetuated. Hardly three years had gone by before the progress of Protestant ideas in England permitted him to speak openly, at least in the upper classes. Instead of his eucharist of 1552, that of the second Prayer Book, being merely an unhappy decomposition of a first and still Catholic liturgy, succumbing to the pressure of the continental reformers (as conservative Anglicans have long tried to persuade themselves), it is a fully thought-out work in which he was finally able to say openly what he had been merely able to insinuate in the preceding book. If he did take many elements from his first text, this proves but one thing: the extent to which that text had already been impregnated with ideas that had long been his. It sufficed to get rid of the artificially imposed framework of the Roman canon for the paraphrase that he had made of it to be reorganized in accordance with his own logic and to allow its real meaning to become finally uncovered.

In the 1552 liturgy all the intercessions and also the mentions of sacrifice that were still connected with the anamnesis were removed from the eucharistic prayer which was quite natural since any propitiatory or impetratory character was denied it. The intercessions simply took the place of the old *oratio fidelium* after the sermon. Meanwhile, the mentions of the "sacrifice," returned to their proper place, reveal its true nature: they figure now only in the prayer of "thanksgiving" (in the non-liturgical sense of the

---

[36] *De corpore et sanguine Domini*, 12; P. L., t. 120, col. 1310 C.

term), that follows the communion. Cranmer himself was so aware that his "sacrifice of thanksgiving," in the sense that he understood the term, had no necessary connection with the communion, that he retained these formulas only in an *ad libitum* prayer. The postcommunion of 1549 (which made no mention of sacrifice) could be substituted for it at will. He further modified it also so that it no longer read: "we give thee thanks ... that thou hast nourished us in these holy mysteries with the body and the blood of our Saviour ... " but only: "we give thee thanks that thou consentest to nourish us, who have received these holy mysteries, with the body and the blood of our Saviour ... " In other words, it is no longer in the communion that we are nourished with Christ's body and blood (in the very special sense in which he understands this expression), but only in the remembrance of his passion, reawakened at the very most through the celebration of the Supper.

On the other hand, in this reworking, not only was everything that remained of the ancient epicleses removed, but also the anamnesis as in the Lutheran liturgies. Consequently, with the exception of an apology inserted after the eucharistic preface and the *Sanctus*, all we have is the institution narrative. Merely a few connective words were kept to introduce it. But, detached as they are from their former context, it is now clear that the purpose of these words is not only to exclude any notion of the sacramental presence of the sacrifice which the Lutherans were the first to reject, but to exclude as well the idea of the real presence of the body and blood of Christ that they still retained:

> Almighty God oure heauenly father, whiche of thy tender mercye dyddest geue thine onely sonne Jesus Christ, to suffre death upon the crosse for our redempcion, who made there (by hys one oblacion *of hymselfe* once offered) a full, perfecte and sufficiente sacrifice, oblacion, and satysfaccion for the synnes of the whole world: and dyd institute, and in hys holye Gospell commaunde us, to continue a perpetuall memorye of that his precious death, untyll hys comynge again. Heare us O mercyfull father wee beeseche thee: *and graunte that wee receyuing these thy creatures of bread and wyne, accordynge to thy sonne our Sauioure Jesu Christes holy institucion, in remembraunce of his death and passion,* may

be partakers of his most blessed body & bloud: who in the same night that he was betrayed, etc ...[37]

It is enough to compare this text with the preceding one, and particularly the italicized passages which were modified, in order to convince ourselves about the intention which governed both these changes and the keeping of the introductory formula in its polished state: its purpose was to exclude the very idea of any sort of a real presence of the body and blood of Christ in the sacrament along with any idea of a sacramental presence of the sacrifice.[38]

After the various re-establishments of Anglicanism, first after the Catholic interlude of Mary Tudor, under Elizabeth and then after Cromwell, no one dared to return to the 1549 text. It was only the expurgated prayer of 1552 that was retained, but in 1662 it was given the name "Prayer of Consecration." For his part, Cranmer was careful not to give it this title, since he knew better than anyone, that it was unsuitable if one understood it in its obvious sense. Did not he himself say that there could be no other consecration of the bread and wine in the eucharist than the separation that sets them aside at the offertory for liturgical use, and that this involved no other change?

THE FIRST REDISCOVERY OF TRADITION BY THE ENGLISH CALVINISTS

Yet even under Elizabeth, and even more under the Stuarts, Anglican theologians were generally unsatisfied with Cranmer's eucharistic theology which was so contrary to the whole of tradition. The Thirty-Nine Articles reintroduced a doctrine of the real presence which was neither completely Catholic nor properly Lutheran, but which could be called, according to Jardine Grisbrooke's formula a "dynamic virtualism."[39] But this was less due to Catholic influences than to the influence of the Pu-

---

[37] Bard Thompson, *op. cit.*, p. 280.
[38] Cf. Gregory Dix, *op. cit.*, p. 650.
[39] Cf. W. Jardine Grisbrooke, *Anglican Liturgies of the XVIIth and XVIIIth Centuries* (London, 1958), p. xv.

ritans. The English and Scottish Puritans, we too often forget, emphasized to the utmost Calvin's expressions concerning the real presence as an effect of their Calvinism which was fired with a devotion to Christ which was very medieval in its warmth and color.[40]

On the other hand, if the great Anglican theologians of the seventeenth century, the Caroline divines, beginning with Archbishop Laud, made the first steps in the direction of a rediscovery of the sense of the eucharistic sacrifice in the Fathers and the ancient liturgies, they still remained attached to a symbolic view of Christ's presence in the sacrament. We cannot say that they escaped completely from a rationalizing interpretation of the Alexandrian and Augustinian symbolism, which the Calvinists for their part had overcome. When an attempt was made in 1637, under Charles I, to introduce a revised Prayer Book in Scotland, it was not so much because of what was Catholic in it that it was rejected by the Scottish Calvinists, but rather because it was the work of English prelates whom they abhorred. But if in 1661, even in England, the Puritans still refused Cranmer's eucharist, their explicit motive was that they did not find in it as frank an assertion of the real presence as in what they had themselves, under Scottish influence, in their own *Book of Common Order*. They maintained that "the manner of consecrating the elements is not explicit or distinct enough."[41]

The *Form of Prayers* of John Knox, the great Scottish reformer, which was published in 1556, already contained a eucharistic prayer which has no equivalent in the French Calvinist liturgies:

O Father of mercye and God of all consolation, seinge all creatures do knowledge and confesse thee, as gouerner, and lorde, it becommeth vs the workemanship of thyne own handes, at all tymes to reuerence and magnifie thy godli maiestie, first for that thou haste created vs to thyne own Image and similitude: but chieflye that thou haste deliuered vs, from that euerlasting death and damnation into the which Satā drewe mankinde by the meane of synne: from the bondage

---

[40] *Ibid.*, pp. 1 ff.
[41] *Ibid.*, p. 6.

wherof (neither man nor angell was able to make vs free) but thou (ò Lord) riche in mercie and infinite in goodnes, haste prouided our redemption to stand in thy onely and wellbeloued sone: whom of verie loue thou didest giue to be made man, lyke vnto vs in all thynges, (synne except) that in his bodye he myght receiue the ponishmentes of our transgression, by his death to make satisfaction to thy iustice, and by his resurrection to destroye hym that was auctor of death, and so to reduce and bring agayne life to the world, frome which the whole ofspringe of Adame moste iustly was exiled. O Lord we acknowledge that no creature ys able to comprehende the length and breadthe, the depenes and height, of that thy most excellent loue which moued thee to shewe mercie, where none was deserued: to promise and giue life, where death had gotten victorie: to recue vs into thy grace, when we could do nothyng but rebell against thy iustice. O Lord the blynde dulnes of our corrupt nature will not suffer vs sufficiently to waye these thy moste ample benefites: yet neuertheles at the commaundement of Iesus Christ our Lorde, we present our selues to this his table (which he hath left to be vsed in remembrance of his death vntvll hys coming agayne) to declare and witnes before the world, that by him alone we have receued libertie, and life: that by hym alone, thou doest acknowledge vs thy chyldren and heires: that by hym alone, we have entrance to the throne of thy grace: that by hym alone we are possessed in our spirituall kingedome, to eate and drinke at his table: with whome we haue our conuersation presently in heauen, and by whome, our bodies shalbe reysed vp agayne frome the dust, and shalbe placed with him in that endles ioye, which thou (ò father of mercye) hast prepared for thyne elect, before the foundation of the worlde was layde. And these moste inestimable benefites, we acknowledge and cōfesse to have receaued of thy free mercie and grace, by thy onely beloued sonne Iesus Christ, for the which therfore we thy congregation moued by thy holy sprite render thee all thankes, prayse, and glorie for euer and euer.[42]

It will be noted that the institution narrative is not present in this prayer. Indeed, the Calvinists believed that it had to be

[42] Bard Thompson, *op. cit.*, p. 303.

addressed to the believers themselves as with every evangelical sentence. In addition, even in liturgies which like these reintroduced a "eucharist" that seems to be a direct echo of those of Christian antiquity, the narrative is placed before the eucharistic prayer in an exhortation to the faithful.

Nevertheless, the so-called Savoy liturgy, which Baxter in 1661 opposed to Cranmer's *Prayer Book*, allows the replacing of this narrative after the eucharistic prayer, and connects the two with a real epiclesis; its notion and content had already been strongly defended by the Scottish Calvinist theologians, like Row, in the first half of the century.

Here is Baxter's formulary:

> Almighty God, thou art the Creator and the Lord of all things. Thou art the Sovereign Majesty whom we have offended. Thou art our most loving and merciful Father, who hast given thy Son to reconcile us to thyself: who hath ratified the new testament and covenant of grace with his most precious blood; and hath instituted this holy Sacrament to be celebrated in remembrance of him till his coming. Sanctify these thy creatures of bread and wine, which, according to thy institution and command, we set apart to this holy use, that they may be sacramentally the body and blood of the Son, Jesus Christ. Amen.

Then (*or immediately before this Prayer*) *let the Minister read the words of institution, saying*:

> Hear what the apostle Paul saith: (there follows the institution narrative of the eucharist after the first Epistle to the Corinthians).

Then let the Minister say:

> This bread and wine, being set apart, and consecrated to this holy use by God's appointment, are now no common bread and wine, but sacramentally the body and blood of Christ.

Then let him thus pray:

> Most merciful Saviour, as thou hast loved us to the death and suffered for our sins, the just for the unjust, and hast instituted this holy Sacrament to be used in remembrance of thee till thy coming; we beseech thee, by thine intercession

with the Father, through the sacrifice of thy body and blood, give us the pardon of our sins, and thy quickening Spirit, without which the flesh will profit us nothing. Reconcile us to the Father: nourish us as thy members to everlasting life. *Amen.*

Then let the Minister take the Bread, and break it in the sight of the people, saying:

The body of Christ was broken for us, and offered once for all to sanctify us: behold the sacrificed Lamb of God, that taketh away the sins of the world.

In like manner let him take the Cup, and pour out the Wine in the sight of the congregation, saying:

We were redeemed with the precious blood of Christ, as of a Lamb without blemish and without spot.

After having addressed the Father and the Son in turn he concludes his prayer by addressing himself to the Spirit:

Most Holy Spirit, proceeding from the Father and the Son: by whom Christ was conceived; by whom the prophets and apostles were inspired, and the ministers of Christ are qualified and called: that dwellest and workest in all the members of Christ, whom thou sanctifiest to the image and for the service of their Head, and comfortest them that they may shew forth his praise: illuminate us, that by faith we may see him that is here represented to us. Soften our hearts, and humble us for our sins. Sanctify and quicken us, that we may relish the spiritual food, and feed on it to our nourishment and growth in grace. Shed abroad the love of God upon our hearts, and draw them out in love to him. Fill us with thankfulness and holy joy, and with love to one another. Comfort us by witnessing that we are the children of God. Confirm us for new obedience. Be the earnest of our inheritance, and seal us up to everlasting life. *Amen.*[43]

Then they proceed to the distribution of communion.

It is incontestable that these prayers of Knox and Baxter, even though they lack Cranmer's inimitable style, are from the point of view of both their doctrine and their spirit much closer to the

---

[43] Bard Thompson, *op. cit.*, pp. 399-400.

ancient eucharistic prayers than any Protestant or Anglican text
that we have encountered up to now.

THE RESTORATION OF THE ANGLICAN EUCHARIST
IN SCOTLAND AND WITH THE NON-JURORS

If the *Prayer Book* composed for Scotland in 1637 tended to be
closer to the tradition of the ancient Church on the basis of Cranmer's formulas, despite the storms that it was to cause among
the Scottish Calvinists, certainly did not suggest to them a formula of the eucharist that was more Catholic than their own.[44]

The finishing touches on this book were due chiefly to a Scottish Bishop, Wedderburn. Like the majority of his colleagues,
he professed a eucharistic theology that was close to Laud's. That
is to say that with a notion of the presence that was both more
attached to the elements themselves than the Calvinists' but
less realistic (what Jardine Grisbrooke calls "dynamic virtualism"),
they combined a notion of sacrifice that was appreciably more
traditional. Laud expressed it by saying:

> For, at and in the Eucharist, we offer up to God three sac-
> rifices; One by the priest only; that is the commemorative sac-
> rifice of Christ's death, represented in bread broken and wine
> poured out. Another by the priest and the people jointly; and
> that is, the sacrifice of praise and thanksgiving for all the ben-
> efits and graces we receive by the precious death of Christ.
> The third, by every particular man for himself only; and that is
> the sacrifice of every man's body and soul, to serve Him in both
> all the rest of his life, for this blessing thus bestowed on him.[45]

The whole question rests obviously on the extent that this
"commemoration" and "representation" of the one sacrifice is
objective and not a purely figurative representation, giving rise
to a merely subjective commemoration. It seems that the authors of this 1637 liturgy, like Laud himself, would have tended
to uphold the first sense, although they remained subject to the

---

[44] Jardine Grisbrooke, *op. cit.*, pp. 1 ff.
[45] *A Relation of a Conference between William Laud ... and Mr. Fisher
the Jesuit*, in Laud, *Works*, vol. 2, pp. 339 ff.

fear of introducing anything that would suppose a renewed actuality of the Cross. Their text, in any case, even though it retained unchanged the greater part of Cranmer's formulas could,
at least as much as the first version, lend itself to a fully traditional understanding.

After the unchanged preface and *Sanctus* of Cranmer, the prayer continues in these words:

> Almighty God, our heavenly Father, which of thy tender
> mercy didst give thy only Son Jesus Christ to suffer death
> upon the cross for our redemption; who made there (by his
> one oblation of himself once offered) a full, perfect, and suf-
> ficient sacrifice, oblation, and satisfaction for the sins of
> the whole world, and did institute, and in his holy gospel
> command us to continue, a perpetual memory of that his
> precious death and sacrifice, until his coming again: Hear
> us, O merciful Father, we most humbly beseech thee, and
> of thy Almighty goodness vouchsafe so to bless and sanctify
> with thy word and Holy Spirit these thy gifts and creatures
> of bread and wine, that they may be unto us the body and
> blood of thy most dearly beloved Son; so that we, receiving
> them according to thy Son our Saviour Jesus Christ's holy
> institution, in remembrance of his death and passion, may
> be partakers of the same his most precious body and blood:
> Who, in the night, etc.[46]

What follows reproduces word for word the 1549 text, except
that the words: "and commaunde these our prayers and supplicacions, by the Ministery of thy holy Angels, to be brought up
into thy holy Tabernacle before the syght of thy dyuine maiestie"
are omitted, and the central sentence was mitigated by the substitution of the words: "And we entirely desire" for Cranmer's
participle: "entierely desiryng."

Apart from that, the first obvious difference is the abbreviation wrought by the disjunction of the eucharist and the prayers
for the Church (the whole of the intercessions taken from the
Roman canon), which are now relegated to the offertory. On
the other hand, the first epiclesis was modified: not only is the

---

[46] Text in Jardine Grisbrooke, *op. cit.*, pp. 177 ff.

Word mentioned before the Holy Spirit (out of a concern for logic), but the text was burdened by a very heavy prolepsis from the anamnesis, destined, it would seem, both to accentuate the realism of the consecration and to specify that the presence is requested only in view of the communion and for the effective commemoration of the Savior.

This reworked text is of great historical importance. If the English *Prayer Book* officially knows even today only Cranmer's second formulary, it is this modified return in 1637 to his first formulary which since then in Anglicanism has remained the basis of all the attempts to return to a more traditional eucharistic prayer.

The Non-Jurors, those heirs of the Caroline theologians who after the fall of the Stuarts were excluded from the Established Church for having refused to swear allegiance to William of Orange and Queen Mary, pushed the tendency to recuperate the ancient tradition still further. They produced or inspired a whole series of liturgies that were emended in this direction. They are all characterized by the same effort to be inspired by forms of the West Syrian eucharist, either the liturgy of the 8th book of the *Apostolic Constitutions* or that of St. James. The first is that of 1718. According to the explanations given by its chief author, Thomas Brett, it went back to Cranmer's 1549 text for the anamnesis as well as for the consecratory epiclesis and the intercessions (including the commemoration of the dead), but it dislodged the two latter elements in order to place them after the anamnesis. In their place, the first part of the eucharist after the *Sanctus*, completely abandoning Cranmer and the Roman canon, reproduced the corresponding part of the text of St. James.[47]

Moreover, in 1734, one of the most archaizing Non-Jurors, Thomas Deacon, produced a liturgy that was still more radical in its return to what was considered to be an apostolic model, since for the canon it followed the liturgy of the 8th book of the *Apostolic Constitutions* practically word for word.[48]

---

[47] See Jardine Grisbrooke, *op. cit.*, pp. 275 ff. for the text and pp. 71 ff. for a commentary.

[48] *Ibid.*, pp. 299 ff. and 113 ff.

But a Scottish Bishop (of the small disestablished Episcopal Church which had managed to survive beside the official Presbyterian Church of Scotland), Thomas Ratterary, who was himself very much influenced by the Non-Jurors, thought that he had found the most ancient form of the liturgy of Jerusalem, through a comparison between the liturgy of St. James and that of the *Apostolic Constitutions.* It is this liturgy of St. James, which had been pruned not without perspicacity, that he proposed as the ideal eucharist.[49] Published in 1744 after his death, Ratteray's liturgy was to influence a new reworking of Cranmer's liturgy in the Episcopal Church of Scotland. It is this latter, published in 1764, that has furnished the starting point for most of the modern revisions of the Anglican eucharist, from that of the Protestant Episcopal Church of the United States to the project of revision of the English *Prayer Book* which the British parliament twice rejected in 1927 and 1928.[50]

In this Scottish text of 1764, the connecting link of the second part of the eucharistic prayer was reinserted, following the ancient usage. But it is attached not to the word *Holy*, but to the word *Glory*, with which Cranmer had translated the second *Hosannah*:

All glory be to thee, Almighty God, our heavenly Father, for that thou of thy tender mercy didst give thy only Son Jesus Christ to suffer death upon the cross for our redemption ...

Immediately following there is another modification. Cranmer, in order to remove from the eucharist any oblation of Christ's own sacrifice, had written: "who made *there* by his *one* oblation once offered ..." The new text substituted *own* for *one* and leaves out *there*. We read then: "who by his own oblation of himself once offered ..." With one stroke the narrowly Protestant character of the formula was attenuated, and the idea so dear to the Non-Jurors that the oblation that made the Cross a sacrifice took place at the Supper was given expression.

[49] *Ibid.*, pp. 319 ff. and 136 ff.
[50] *Ibid.*, pp. 335 ff. and 150 ff.

Cranmer's epiclesis, with its mention of the word and the Spirit is retained as it was, except that the word is mentioned first, as in 1637, although this epiclesis is transferred to after the anamnesis. The great prayer for the state of the Church is returned to the canon, but it is now placed after what corresponded there to the second epiclesis, developing the idea of the sacrifice of praise and the offering of ourselves to God, which is also preserved (except for two adverbs) as it was in 1637. It is obvious that all these displacements have no other purpose than to reproduce the West Syrian order, popularized by the Non-Jurors' liturgies and especially by Ratteray's.

It may be said that the revisions of the Anglican liturgies down to our own day were all dominated by this Scottish liturgy of 1764.

The Americans took over the text practically as it was except for once again returning the prayer for the Church to the offertory.

In 1927, Walter Frere and the other revisers of the English *Prayer Book* put *one* back in the place of *own*, replaced *Testament* with *Covenant* in the institution narrative, modified the word order here and there, particularly in the anamnesis, and returned the intercessions to the offertory as well. Apart from that, they refrained from eliminating the Word from the epiclesis, in order to make it what they judged (wrongly) to be a purer original epiclesis.[51]

When one has read Frere's sarcasm in regard to the Roman canon, which according to him has been carved up and disfigured, to the point that the ancient Roman eucharistic prayer (he is referring, of course to Hippolytus!) has become unrecognizable,[52] we must admit that we have difficulty restraining our own sarcasm in the face of the product of his efforts. Wishing to provide the Anglican Church with an ideal eucharist, he found nothing better than to propose to it a neo- or pseudo-Syrian eucharist, constructed with previously selected elements and then put together again in quite a different order, taken from the Roman canon as passed

[51] Cf. Bernard Wigan, *The Liturgy in English*, 2nd ed. (London, 1964), pp. 68 ff.

[52] Cf. W. Frere, *The Anaphora*, pp. 135 ff.

through Cranmer's Zwinglian rolling-press ... Any commentary would be a needless cruelty.

As unsatisfactory as these Cranmeresque mosaics may be—notions from which the Anglicans have still to free themselves—and as illusory as the idea may be that the West Syrian eucharist represents *the* type of the original eucharist or in any case the only ideal type, we must acknowledge that the evolution of their liturgies has reached the point, through these tortuous paths, of rejoining and reconstituting for better or worse a eucharist which is certainly intentionally traditional.   Such texts, when we overlook their genealogy, are certainly capable of expressing the eucharistic mystery for those who have rediscovered what it means.   But we must certainly applaud the courageous efforts of those contemporary Anglican liturgists, faithful to the best of the Non-Jurors' inspiration, to break once and for all with Cranmer's yoke and compose directly a eucharistic prayer taken from the best sources. It is quite true that it is not easy to escape from the charm of the hallowed prose of this great humanist who was a disappointing theologian and too able a politician. But we may hope that they may succeed, perhaps by retaining many felicitous phrases that have come from his pen and hallowed by a long use which has restored to them what he had wished to eliminate, in producing an Anglicized eucharist which will be really Catholic without thereby being any less evangelical.

THE RETURN TO TRADITION WITH THE FRENCH REFORMERS: FROM OSTERWALD TO TAIZÉ

This evolutionary process, which despite its weaknesses is so very appealing and brought Anglicanism back to the traditional path, has also come about, although more slowly and painfully, in most of the major Protestant Churches.

We have already pointed out the very interesting instance of the English-speaking Calvinists. Under the influence of the *Prayer Book*, but also by virtue of their knowledge of patristic antiquity, they were the first of the "Reformed" to reintroduce something of a proper eucharist into the liturgy of the Supper. Under the same Anglican influence, the first analogous example that we

meet in a continental reformed liturgy is that of the Church of
Neuchâtel at the beginning of the eighteenth century.

In 1713, Osterwald succeeded in replacing Farel's *Manière et Fasson* (doubtless, as we have seen, the poorest of the liturgies of the
Supper) with a text of his own composition. He reintroduced the
preface, the *Sanctus* and a "consecration" which includes the institution narrative in a rather frail (to be frank) outline of the canon,
in which supplications and acts of thanksgiving are closely united.
The fact is all the more singular since Osterwald was purely Zwinglian and since it was hardly possible to find in his liturgy anything which recalls Calvin's sacramental realism. But something
of the ancient eucharistic prayer, as a glorification in the thanksgiving for the *mirabilia Dei*, reappears here for the first time in
the Reformed liturgy of the continent.[53]

Osterwald kept the exhortations and the penitential prayers,
while still appreciably restricting their quantity. He still had the
institution narrative figure as a formula of evangelical proclamation, but then repeated it further on in the prayer itself. The minister, still in the pulpit, made the transition from exhortation to
the prayer after a *Sursum corda* and a *Gratias agamus* without
responses. He then pronounced a preface (most of the *Prayer
Book* prefaces were taken over practically as they stood), and
said the *Sanctus* (without the *Benedictus*) himself. He continued
with a prayer that introduced, like Cranmer's first liturgy, a universal intercession into the eucharist. At this point, the flow was
interrupted by a penitential exhortation. After the Lord's Prayer
there was a brief confession of sins and a rather vague absolution.
When that was over, the minister came, as the text says, to the
"consecration which takes place at the table." This is the prayer:

> O almighty God, and our heavenly Father, who by your
> great mercy delivered your Son to the death of the Cross
> for our redemption; who offered himself in sacrifice for the
> sins of the whole world, and commanded that the perpetual
> commemoration of his death be made in his Church until

---

[53] Published at Basel in 1713, this liturgy was reproduced and commented
upon by Lebrun in t. 4 of his *Explication ... de la Messe* (pp. 167 ff. of the
reedition of 1843). Cf. Brilioth, *op. cit.*, pp. 179 ff.

he comes on the last day: receive our prayers and our praise,
O merciful God, which we present to you through Jesus Christ,
who on the night he was betrayed, took bread and having
given thanks to you, eternal Father, broke it and said: Take,
eat, this is my body which is broken for you; do this in memory of me. Likewise after having supped, he took the cup
and gave thanks and gave it saying: Drink of this all of you,
for this is my blood, the blood of the new covenant, which
is shed for many (*plusieurs*) for the forgiveness of sins; do
this, as often as you drink of this, in memory of me.

The communion followed immediately.

At the beginning of the nineteenth century we also see in the
German Reformed Churches at least the germ of a eucharistic prayer being introduced. Actually, at the start, this was hardly more
than a diplomatic compromise, to try to make the Lutherans feel
at home in the Prussian "evangelical" union, into which they were
forced by the Hohenzollerns in 1817 to enter with the Reformed
Churches. It is for this reason that Frederick William III introduced the preface followed by the *Sanctus* into his *Agende*. But
the absence of any real restoration of the eucharist in this practically completely decorative liturgical reform is evident from the
fact that the preface and the *Sanctus* were said whether or not
there was a celebration of the Holy Supper! It is piquant to see
German Protestantism, evidently quite unwittingly, restore these
prayers practically to the place they held in the worship of the
synagogue: a simple act of thanksgiving for the Word to which
the congregation had listened, without any essential reference either
to the cross or to our union with the crucified Savior.[54]

One further step was made towards the end of the nineteenth
century with the French liturgy of Eugène Bersier, composed by
him for his Reformed parish of the Étoile in Paris. Bersier had been
influenced for a time by Irving, a famous Scottish Presbyterian
preacher. This Scot had undertaken the foundation of a rather
bizarre Church in which apocalyptic speculations, glossolalia and
other quaint practices were combined with a liturgical restoration
of a disheveled romanticism. Bersier was not the only serious-

---

[54] Cf. Brilioth, *op. cit.*, pp. 146 ff.

minded Protestant to find in this context an unexpected initiation into liturgical tradition. For his part, he drew from it the inspiration for a eucharistic liturgy which is not a copy but an equivalent of Cranmer's, i.e. a paraphrased and slightly accommodated translation of the Roman canon. His redundant and limp prose is unfortunately very far removed from Cranmer's singing language. But it was still the first sign-post, as it were, for French speaking Protestantism, pointing towards a rediscovery which remains slow and painful.[55]

Bersier's example was to encourage Pastor Schaffner, in his Lutheran parish of the Ascension in the Rue Dulong in Paris, to bring back French Lutheranism (which up to that time had been very un-Lutheran in its liturgy) to the traditions of seventeenth century German Lutheranism which Löhe in Germany had just resurrected. But in the French-speaking Reformed Churches, we had to wait until after World War I to see Bersier's example bear fruit.

A group of pastors from Lausanne and the surrounding area, under the leadership of Pastor Pasquier, founded at that time a movement called *Église et Liturgie*, out of which came some of the most interesting ecumenical initiatives in Protestantism, like the monastery of Taizé. The eucharist composed by the brothers of Taizé, which greatly influenced many attempts at a restoration of the eucharist in the Reformed world, was the final product of this movement. We shall quote their eucharistic liturgy, for which the book of Max Thurian bearing this title is both an explanation and a justification.

After the preface and the Sanctus, the eucharistic prayer begins with the "invocation of the Holy Spirit upon the holy Supper:"

Our Father, God of the hosts of heaven,
fill with your glory this our sacrifice of praise.
Bless, perfect and accept this offering
as the figure of the one and only sacrifice of our Lord.

---

[55] Brilioth, *op. cit.*, pp. 181 ff., showers this liturgy of Bersier with praise, without seeming to suspect that it follows the Roman canon step by step, a work which he denounces for its incoherence on p. 76 of the same book. Bersier's liturgy was published in Paris in 1874.

Send your Holy Spirit upon us and our eucharist:
consecrate this bread to be the body of Christ
and this cup to be the blood of Christ;
that the Creator Spirit
may fulfill the word of your well-beloved Son.

After which the "institution of the Lord's Supper by Christ"
repeats the Pauline narrative. To "Do this as the memorial of
me" is immediately added the following verse from St. Paul:

Whenever we eat this bread
and drink this cup,
we proclaim the Lord's death till he come.

There then follows the anamnesis, which is called the "memorial
of the mysteries of Christ":

Wherefore, O Lord, we make before you
the memorial of the incarnation and the passion of your Son,
his resurrection from his sojourn with the dead,
his ascension into glory in the heavens,
his perpetual intercession for us;
we await and pray for his return.
All things come from you,
and our only offering is to recall your gifts
and marvelous works.
Moreover we present to you, O Lord of glory,
as our thanksgiving and intercession
the signs of the eternal sacrifice of Christ,
unique and perfect, living and holy,
the bread of life which comes down from heaven,
and the cup of the feast in your kingdom.
In your love and mercy
accept our praise and our prayers in Christ,
as you were pleased to accept
the gifts of your servant Abel the righteous,
the sacrifices of our father Abraham,
and of Melchizedek, your high priest.

Then comes the "invocation of the Spirit for communion:"

Grant us the power of the Holy Spirit,
that we may discern the body and the blood of Christ.
May his communion transform our lives,

take away our sins,
fill our hearts with the Holy Spirit,
give us the fulness of the Kingdom of heaven
and confidence before you,
and deliver us from all condemnation,
through Christ our Savior.

Finally the "conclusion in praise to the Lord":

By whom, O Lord,
you create, sanctify, vivify, bless
and give us all your benefits.
By whom, and with whom, and in whom,
be unto you, O Father Almighty,
in union with the Holy Spirit,
all honor and glory,
forever and ever. *Amen.*[56]

It is difficult, I must admit, for a Catholic theologian who has spent many years in unraveling the skein of the history and the ups and downs of the eucharistic prayer in Catholicism, Eastern Orthodoxy and Protestantism to read this prayer without being deeply moved. We may make a few criticisms of it, and particularly regret that it yielded to the unfortunate simplification (which, however, was already present in the old Gallican and Hispanic tradition) of relegating the intercessions to the offertory. But apart from that, it seems that it has succeeded admirably in safeguarding the essential content of the Roman canon, while expressing in terms that are very well adapted both to making its meaning come alive for people of today and to dispelling the prejudices of the Protestants towards its expressions.

The first paragraph is obviously constructed on the *Quam oblationem*. But on the one hand it is very felicitously linked up with the *Sanctus* by a phrase in which the eucharistic theme is summed up in an evocation of the divine glory, a central theme of the hymn of the Seraphim. Indeed, the glory of God in the biblical sense, as Dr. Ramsey in his great book on the glory of God and the transfiguration of Christ has so well shown, is both the manifestation and the essential communication of God's life to his creatures

---

[56] Text in Max Thurian, *The Eucharistic Liturgy of Taizé* (London, 1959).

who have achieved their plenitude in the redemptive incarnation. The eucharist which allows us to participate in the mystery of the incarnation constitutes the supreme realization of this glory in the Church and in the world.

On the other hand, the way in which the Word and the Spirit are introduced into this consecratory epiclesis excellently explicate the complementary aspects of Eastern and Western Catholic tradition. It is the Spirit, communicated by the redemptive mystery, who accomplishes the effect of the creative and salvific Word, proclaimed by and in Christ. And it is in the prayer in which the Church grasps through faith the "memorial" of the Savior, that this mystery of the Spirit is fulfilled, precisely as the fulfilment of the mystery of the Word.

For its part, the anamnesis, developed by the evocation of Christ ascended into heaven and interceding for us in the heavenly sanctuary which he has entered as our precursor, until the Parousia, expresses the realization of our eucharist, inseparably praise and supplication, in the presentation to God of the "memorial" which comes from him through his Son.

The second epiclesis, then, asking that the celebration of the mystery have its full effect in us, explicates in turn the sense of the *Supra quae*. The conjunction of earthly worship with heavenly worship is brought about by the descent of the Spirit in us, filling us with this grace and this blessing of which the *Christus passus et glorificatus* is the unique source. From this flows the blessing of all creation, and the inseparable glorification by this sanctified creation, of the triune God.

We should certainly not have any illusions about the number of persons in the Reformed Churches who can now accept this eucharist and assimilate all of its meaning, even in a form that is so well within their grasp. Nevertheless, the fact that so many at Taizé or elsewhere have been already able to join in its celebration without hardship or scandal is an encouraging sign. And it is a further source of encouragement that the revisions of the official Reformed liturgies, whether French or not, which have already been made, all more or less timidly reflect something of this text.

THE EUCHARIST OF THE CHURCH OF SOUTH INDIA

We now proceed to another example of a modern Protestant eucharistic prayer, which is rather different in its origins, but no less worthy of note. It is the eucharist that was worked out by the united Church of South India. We know that this Church recently brought together the missionary Churches of the Anglicans, Methodists, Presbyterians and Congregationalists. Its constitution gave rise to very heated arguments particularly within the Anglican Communion. Side by side with real tendencies toward an ecumenism in depth, we must admit that we do find in it much of that diplomatic ecumenism, created out of simple compromises, which characterized so many fallacious "unions" in the past like the celebrated "union of Prussia" which we have mentioned several times. We might consequently be tempted to say that what is traditional in this liturgy is little more than a superficial concession to Anglican traditionalism, but without any doctrinal import. As a matter of fact, such a view, it seems, would be profoundly unjust and gravely erroneous.

In Scottish Presbyterianism, particularly, and even in modern Congregationalism, not to speak of Methodism where the nostalgia for Anglican forms was never extinguished, the rediscovery of the traditional eucharist, which started with the old *Book of Common Order*, has certainly made great progress in recent years. The coalescence of these different Christian groups in South India was therefore able to effect a genuine recovery of the tradition which the new liturgy seems to be enriching day by day.

> It is verily meet, right, and our bounden duty, that we should at all times and in all places, give thanks unto thee, O Lord, Holy Father, almighty and everlasting God; Through Jesus Christ thy Son our Lord, through whom thou didst create the heavens and the earth and all that in them is, and didst make man in thine own image, and when he had fallen into sin didst redeem him to be the firstfruits of a new creation. Therefore with angels and archangels and with all the company of heaven, we laud and magnify thy glorious name; evermore praising thee, and saying, Holy, Holy, Holy, Lord God of hosts, heaven and earth are full of thy glory.

Glory be to thee, O Lord most high. Blessed be he that hath come and is to come in the name of the Lord, Hosanna in the highest.

The "Presbyter" continues alone:

Truly holy, truly blessed art thou, O heavenly Father, who of thy tender love towards mankind didst give thine only Son Jesus Christ to take our nature upon him and to suffer death upon the cross for our redemption; who made there, by his one oblation of himself once offered, a full, perfect, and sufficient sacrifice, oblation and satisfaction, for the sins of the whole world; and did institute, and in his holy gospel command us to continue, a perpetual memory of that his precious death, until his coming again: Who, in the same night that he was betrayed, took bread, and when he had given thanks, he brake it, and gave it to his disciples, saying, Take eat, this is my body which is given for you: do this in remembrance of me. Likewise after supper he took the cup, and, when he had given thanks, he gave it to them, saying, Drink ye all of this; for this is my blood of the new covenant, which is shed for you and for many for the remission of sins: do this, as oft as ye shall drink it, in remembrance of me.

The people answer:

Amen. Thy death, O Lord, we commemorate, thy resurrection we confess, and thy second coming we await. Glory be to thee, O Christ.

The "Presbyter" continues:

Wherefore, O Father, having in remembrance the precious death and passion, and glorious resurrection and ascension, of thy Son our Lord, we thy servants do this in remembrance of him, as he hath commanded, until his coming again, giving thanks to thee for the perfect redemption which thou has wrought for us in him.

The people:

We give thanks to thee, we praise thee, we glorify thee, O Lord our God.

The Presbyter:

And we most humbly beseech thee, O merciful Father, to sanctify with thy Holy Spirit us and these thine own gifts of bread and wine, that the bread which we break may be the communion of the body of Christ, and the cup which we bless the communion of the blood of Christ. Grant that, being joined together in him, we may all attain to the unity of the faith, and may grow up in all things unto him who is the Head, even Christ, our Lord, by whom and with whom, in the unity of the Holy Spirit, all honour and glory be unto thee, O Father almighty, world without end. *Amen*.[57]

Here again we have the doubtful transfer of all the intercessions to the offertory. On the other hand Cranmer's formulas in the introduction of the institution narrative and in the anamnesis are easily recognizable. But they have been both mitigated by some redundancy and inserted into a context of formulas taken from the ancient eucharists, which tends to give them a greater clarity and a surer content. All the Protestant objections to the traditional sense of the eucharist are placated by the assertion of the uniqueness of the sacrifice of the cross. But, although they are very discreet, the formulas of the anamnesis and the epiclesis lend themselves to expressing belief in our effective union with the sacrifice of the cross through the eucharist and our real communion in the body and blood of Christ, making us one body in him. Everything obviously depends upon the ecclesiological and theological context in which they are placed. If it develops in the line of Bishop Newbigin's book on the Church, *The Household of Christ*, this eucharist may be considered very moderate (which is no mean virtue) in the way it satisfies the traditional point of view.

The epiclesis, which is completely in the spirit of the West Syrian epicleses, is particularly successful in the way in which it joins the sanctification of the gifts and those who receive them, in the Church as the body of Christ for the purpose of her fulfilment.

In a Church such as this, made up of Orientals, the connecting of the whole prayer to this tradition seems very natural. The same

---

[57] *The Book of Common Worship of the Church of South India* (London, 1963), pp. 15 ff.

things must be said of the few parts given to the people, where
they assert their adhesion to the eucharist of the minister.

THE NEW EUCHARISTIC LITURGY OF THE AMERICAN
LUTHERAN CHURCH

We shall conclude our review of the eucharist in Protestantism
with an examination of the new Lutheran liturgy that was composed for the use of eight groups of American Churches which
have joined to form the new United Lutheran Church of the United
States.

This reunion is an ecumenical gesture which is quite different
from the union of the Churches of South India. Here we do not
have a reunion of very different Churches, that in their origins
were even opposed to one another, but a tightening of the bonds
that had never been completely broken among Churches issuing
from the same particular tradition; they have succeeded in becoming reunited through a common return to their origin. And this
is no less a return to the sources of what was most positive in the
first form of Protestantism. These American Churches owe much
to the movement of revival within Lutheranism that sprang up in
nineteenth century Germany out of the enlightened resistance to
the attempts at reunion, such as the union of Prussia, which were
basically political and doctrinally laxist. One name symbolizes
this whole movement, that of the Bavarian pastor Wilhelm Löhe
of Neuendettelsau. With him and his circle a revival came about
similar to what had begun in the seventeenth century with Johann
Arndt, Johann Gerhard and Paul Gerhardt. This was a renewed
awareness among the Lutherans, resulting from persecution by the
Reformed Churches, of the fact that they were practically the only
ones among the Protestants to retain something of the Catholic
tradition. It awakened in them a sense of rejuvenation. The book
on the Church, brought out by Wilhelm Löhe in 1845, *Drei Bücher
von der Kirche*, is the theological monument of this renascence.
It materialized in a resurrection of the religious life: first the
foundation of deaconesses, who in Löhe's mind were to be in the
Lutheran Church what the consecrated virgins had been in the
primitive Church, and second, in a restoration of the liturgy and

spirituality. The Lutheran Churches of North America, where a
good number of German Lutherans emigrated, chased from their
own country by the intolerance of the Reformed Church, were
perhaps even more active than the German Churches in developing
these seeds of life and thought. Also, it is not astonishing that
it was in this country that a great Lutheran Church became the
first to produce a liturgy that was not content merely with a rediscovery of all that the original Reformation had preserved of
tradition, but which courageously went back to the patristic sources in order to regain its basic atmosphere. The eucharistic liturgy
adopted in 1958 by the United Lutheran Church of America is the
first to make a decided break from the *Formula Missae*, and to
rediscover the schema and the content of the ancient anaphoras,
without any of the circuitous subtleties of John III's Swedish
liturgy.

After the preface and the *Sanctus*, we have this prayer:

Holy art thou, Almighty and merciful God. Holy art thou,
and great is the Majesty of thy glory.

Thou didst so love the world as to give thine only begotten
Son, that whosoever believeth in him might not perish, but
have everlasting life; who, having come into the world to fulfill for us thy holy will and to accomplish all things for our salvation. In the night in which he was betrayed, took bread;
and when he had given thanks, he brake it and gave it to his
disciples, saying: Take eat, this is my Body, which is given for
you; this do in remembrance of me.

After the same manner, he took the cup, when he had supped,
and when he had given thanks, he gave it to them, saying,
Drink ye all of it; this cup is the New Testament in my Blood,
which is shed for you, and for many, for the remission of sins;
this do as oft as ye drink it, in remembrance of me.

Remembering, therefore, his salutary precept, his life-giving
Passion and Death, his glorious Resurrection and Ascension
and the promise of his coming again, we give thanks to thee,
O Lord God Almighty, not as we ought, but as we are able;
and we beseech thee mercifully to accept our praise and thanksgiving, and with thy Word and Holy Spirit to bless us, thy
servants, and these thine own gifts of bread and wine, so that
we and all who partake thereof may be filled with heavenly

benediction and grace, and, receiving the remission of sins, be sanctified in soul and body, and have our portion with all thy saints.

And unto thee, O God, Father, Son, and Holy Spirit, be all honor and glory in thy holy Church, world without end. Amen.[58]

Doctor Luther D. Reed, who is the chief author of this text explained its construction and content in his work *The Lutheran Liturgy*. Once again, we have a liturgy that deliberately returns to the West Syrian pattern, although the intercessions are absent. The first sentence is a combination of St. James and St. John Chrysostom, which connects, through the citing of John 3:16, with the central theme of the Jewish *berakah*: "With an abounding love you have loved us." The transition from the evocation of the redemptive incarnation to the institution narrative is made with a formula of St. Basil's on the perfect accomplishment in the cross of the divine will, inspired by John 19:28. The anamnesis returns to the terms of St. James, inspired by an adaptation found in the 1940 edition of the Scottish Presbyterian *Book of Common Order*. The revived expression of the act of thanksgiving with which it concludes goes back to the *Apostolic Constitutions*. The epiclesis, with its mention of the Word and the Spirit, is a return to Cranmer's first *Prayer Book* (with the Scottish emendation, putting the Word in the first place). The whole conclusion combines the *Supplices te rogamus* with St. James (the sanctification of soul and body) and St. Basil (our share with the saints).

It would be hard to be more ecumenical! But all of these elements, chosen with great discernment, have been molded into a composition that is as moderate as it is natural. In its brief simplicity this prayer has a concise fulness that we are not accustomed to seeing except in Christian antiquity. Here, as in the liturgy of the Church of South India, its eschatological orientation gives it a very primitive sound. Once again, this liturgy must be judged Catholic and orthodox to the extent that the traditional formulas it uses, with hardly an echo of the polemics of the Reformation,

[58] Text in Luther D. Reed, *op. cit.*, pp. 356-357.

are in fact taken in their full and primary sense by the Church that uses them.

Such texts show the profundity of the rediscoveries that are going on or have already been made in the most live sections within the Reformation Churches. If the Christian communities that use these formulas are to take their original place one day within Catholic unity, we see no reason that would prevent them from continuing their use. Such texts, which are the result of so much honest and courageous research, are such a striking evidence of the work of the Spirit among these Christians in good faith, that it would seem deplorable should they actually become fully part of the one Church, if they would not bring these texts with them.

The Catholic Eucharist Renewed

THROUGHOUT THIS WHOLE PERIOD IN WHICH THE CHURCHES OF
the Reformation were engaged in the slow task of rediscovery, what
happened with the eucharist in the Catholic Church?

Here, obviously, with the eucharistic canon and its retinue of
prefaces, the ancient eucharist still subsisted. However, even
though it was not necessary to retrieve it, a pressing need still
existed to divest it from much incongruous veneer, and to return
it to an intelligent manner of being observed.

On the first point, the work of the Council of Trent and of St.
Pius V, despite its relative timidity, did effect the most necessary
reforms. The modern Roman missal, without excluding completely the apologies and the other medieval devotional prayers,
restricted them to the preparation of the celebrant and his ministers,
to the offertory and the communion. Furthermore, it generally
retained only the best of these. As for the tropes, they disappeared completely, only to return, unfortunately, in our own day
in a still less felicitous form with too many inadmissible paraphrases
of the chants of the ordinary and trivial commentaries.

As far as the understanding of the eucharistic prayer went,
if we read the commentaries on the sacrifice of the mass like those

of Lessius, Lugo and many others, we might get the impression that instead of excluding the erroneous medieval notions, Counter-Reformation theology was used to defend and to systematize some of the most indefensible ones. Without overlooking the very positive contributions made by men like Tallhofer, De la Taille, Lepin, Vonier and Masure, we may have to admit that they caricaturized to some extent the theories that they wished rightly to discard. The eucharistic consecration of the broken bread and the cup implies an immediate reference to Christ's passion which these more modern theories, as attractive as they are, did not always take sufficiently into account. It might be that our successors will not be any more gentle in this regard, with the systems that hold sway today than we are toward their predecessors.

But above all, we must not forget that the Counter-Reformation is but one part of the Catholic Reformation that issued from what was most solid in the Christian humanism of the fifteenth and sixteenth centuries. In the domain of the liturgy, the work of the great scholars at the end of the Renaissance and in the seventeenth century is still far from being as appreciated today as it ought to be. Cardinal Bona's *De Sacrificio Missae* is the first revival of the traditional sense of the eucharist based on a primary access to the ancient sacramentaries. Their publication by Cardinal Tommasi and then the publication of the *Ordines Romani* rediscovered by Dom Mabillon, made a decisive step in the rediscovery of the ancient eucharist and its meaning. The publication of the Eastern liturgies by Renaudot and the Assemani's was no less important. If we should wish to understand the doctrinal riches that those works restored to eucharistic theology and spirituality at the end of the eighteenth century, it is enough to read Fr. Lebrun's *Explication ... des prières de la Messe*. The least that can be said is that modern works certainly do not make a reading of this book superfluous.

The missals for the faithful with their magnificent translations and their often excellent commentaries from the second half of the seventeenth century made this available to a wide public. Despite a few too hasty decisions and some errors (of which we are still not yet completely free), the reform of the liturgical books and practices, particularly but not exclusively in France, was the product of the same research. It may be said without exaggeration that not one of the essential reforms decided upon by the second Vatican Council was not anticipated by them.

It is undeniable that for the first time in the Western Church since the high Middle Ages, what may be called the first liturgical movement at this time came to produce a sufficient understanding of the eucharist on the part of the priests and the faithful, and a living practice from which we may still derive much inspiration. The best index of this fact is found perhaps in the new prefaces which were composed at that time, and which have been maintained particularly in France. Composed by people who were fully familiarized with the treasures of the old sacramentaries and the medieval missals, they took from them and retained what was most durable in prayers that were often worthy of competing with the most beautiful formularies of Christian antiquity.

The preface for the Dedication of a Church, with its praise of God for having built a Church as Temple, Body and Spouse of Christ is possibly the masterpiece of these modern liturgists. The preface for All Hallows, whose Pauline Augustinianism so enraged poor Dom Guéranger, is hardly less beautiful or less substantial, with its evocation of the cloud of the martyrs, washed and glorified in the blood of Christ.

When we compare these magnificent eucharists with the unhappy products recently introduced into the Roman missal, we fall from heaven to earth. A few fine Pauline expressions redeem the Sacred Heart preface, but they are incapable of saving the Christian-Democrat triumphalism of the preface for the feast of Christ the King. What can be said of the poverty of the one assigned to St. Joseph! Here we have the lowest depth to which the Roman liturgy has ever descended. Nevertheless, what was produced under Benedict XV for Requiem masses is a striking exception. It gives evidence of the survival of the capacity for eucharistic expression that is worthy of the greatest days of the ancient Church. The tact with which a Mozarabic *illatio* was reshaped and revised has made of it, through an anonymous stroke of genius, the equivalent of these finest examples from antiquity where we think we can see the hand of St. Leo.

But the most precious legacy of this Catholic Reformation of the seventeenth and eighteenth centuries is still the immeasurable effort of research, analysis and interpretation of liturgical tradition that it inaugurated. Our whole study could have done no better than digest the results produced by this renewed effort after an eclipse of more than a century. This is a thought which ought to inspire in us a great sense of gratitude toward those who have gone before us, as well as considerable humility.

THE TWENTIETH CENTURY

The liturgical renewal in the twentieth century, inaugurated by the prophetic work of Dom Lambert Beauduin in Belgium, carried on in Germany and Austria by Dom Odo Casel at Maria Laach and Pius Parsch at Klosterneuburg, resumed and developed after the second World War by the *Centre de Pastorale liturgique*, founded in Paris by the Dominican Fathers Roguet and Duplayé, is the modern heir of its precursors. Pius XII's encyclical *Mediator Dei* and above all the pastoral Constitution on the Liturgy of Vatican II were to make it the common property of the whole Church. Under the impetus of the *Consilium ad exsequendam constitutionem de Sacra liturgia* a remolding of the whole Western liturgy promises to be the result. The work on the celebration of the Mass has just been completed and we can now begin to appreciate its import.

In a first stage, the restoration of the first part of the eucharistic celebration as a proclamation and a hearing of the Divine Word in the Church brought about the necessary conditions for a properly eucharistic restoration, since the eucharist cannot be understood except as the response to this Word which it alone can elicit.

Along the way the *Consilium* naturally came across those pseudo-critical interpretations of the Roman canon which tended either to cast it aside altogether or to refashion it fancifully. We have demonstrated the vanity of such ideas, and the *Consilium* rightly refused to involve itself in such a disastrous deadlock.. On the other hand, it devoted itself to restoring to the initial act of thanksgiving in the Prefaces, all its fulness and substantial richness. It therefore resolved to discard the common preface which, as we have said, is merely a framework emptied of its essential content: the theme of thanksgiving. For it, the *Consilium* has substituted either other proper prefaces added to those already in use or a variety of common prefaces, all of which contain an explicit glorification of the work of creation and the history of salvation. These prefaces have brought back into use, with at times some modifications or adaptations, everything that is most substantial in the treasury of the old sacramentaries. And possibly the new compositions which have been added will not appear unworthy beside their ancient neighbors, such as this preface for the ferial days of the year which is all woven from Pauline expressions:

> It is truly right and just, proper and helpful toward salvation, that we always and everywhere give thanks to you, O Lord, holy Father, almighty and eternal God, through Christ our Lord, in whom it has pleased you to establish all things; you have willed to favor all of us with the fulness of him who, being divine, emptied himself and by the blood of his Cross reconciled the universe; for this reason he was exalted above all things and became for all those who obey him the principle of eternal salvation. Through him, etc. ...[1]

If we add to this necessary reform the new (or ancient!) *Communicantes* and *Hanc Igiturs* which will re-establish in the Roman canon, along with the fulness of the commemoration of the *magnalia Dei*, a newly diversified expression of the Church presenting to the Father the unique sacrifice of the eternal Son, there is reason to hope that we shall again grasp all of the imperishable beauty of this jewel of the eucharistic tradition of the West that is the Roman canon. Moreover, along side this restoration of the Roman canon, we must rejoice in the intention to enrich the modern Latin liturgy with complementary examples from the riches of Catholic tradition. At the same time, the goal has been to revive among the faithful the plenary sense of the eucharist, by proposing to them formularies that are as explicit and as directly accessible as possible both in their structure and their language. For a long time there was hesitation about setting out upon such a path.

---

[1] Cf. Colossians 1:16 ff.; John 1:16; Philippians 2:6-7; Colossians 1:20; Philippians 2:9; Hebrews 5:9.

But in recent years, the haphazard multiplication of formulas, not only in Holland but elsewhere as well, made it imperative to restore to the official liturgical texts basic elements of tradition in all their variety, and at the same time to present them to the faithful in an easily assimilable form. Beyond this immediate pastoral necessity, more far-reaching considerations militated in favor of such an initiative. What we continue to call the "Roman liturgy" has in effect practically become since the time of Gregory VII the liturgy of almost the whole Latin Church. In modern times, the missionary spread of Catholicism has implanted it throughout the whole world. Surely, as we have said, this did not come about without its having in turn absorbed all sorts of elements from the ancient Gallican liturgies. But the canon, with the exception of a few prefaces, has indeed remained one of the rare elements that are exclusively Roman. It was highly desirable then, first of all, to reintroduce into it the best of the traditional treasure of the Celtic, Hispanic and Gallican eucharists. And it was equally as desirable that this liturgy, which in fact had become universalized in its use, open wide its doors both to what we still have of the forms of the eucharist of the first centuries and to the most fruitful developments of Eastern tradition. Yet, it seemed necessary, so as not to confuse the faithful, to retain in these renewed eucharists certain of the most salient elements of the Roman canon's structure, particularly the distinction (which, as we saw, was original) between a properly consecratory epiclesis, corresponding to the *Abodah* prayer of the synagogue, retained before the institution narrative and the communion epiclesis at the conclusion of the anamnesis. In addition to this reservation, it was thought more pedagogical in these new prayers to group all the intercessions and commemorations in the last part of the prayer as the Eastern tradition does.

On this schema, three formularies have then been established. The first uses word for word the greatest part of the eucharist of the *Apostolic Tradition*. The second adopts the development and certain of the most felicitous formulas of the Mozarabic and Gallican tradition. The third is directly inspired from the great Eastern formularies, particularly the *Apostolic Constitutions*, *St. James* and *St. Basil*.

Into the first of these eucharists have been introduced the *Sanctus* and the intercessions and commemorations, even though the latter retain a very short form. Actually, from the moment that the type of formulary preserved by St. Hippolytus was to be used in a eucharistic meal immediately following the service of readings, it was necessary that the eucharistic prayers which come, as we have seen, from the service of readings and which always accompanied it with both Christians and Jews, be incorporated into it.

The great act of thanksgiving for creation and redemption has thus quite naturally become a preface of particular fulness:

> It is truly right and just, proper and helpful toward salvation that we always and everywhere give thanks to you, holy Father, through the Son of your love, Jesus Christ, your Word through whom you have made all things (and) whom you have sent to us as Savior and Redeemer, made flesh of the Holy Spirit and born of the Virgin. Fulfilling your will in order to acquire for you a holy people, he extended his hands in his passion in order to destroy death and show forth the resurrection. Therefore, together with the angels and all the saints, we proclaim your glory and say: *Holy, Holy, Holy* ...

It is enough to go back to St. Hippolytus' text to see that in this preface there has been brought together everything that it contained in regard to an evocation of the work of creation and redemption, while simply discarding a few archaic expressions that might for some reason astonish the congregation.[2]

After this, the *Sanctus-Benedictus* leads up to the consecratory epiclesis through a *Vere Sanctus* in the Gallican tradition. Its substance was taken from the *Post-Sanctus* of the *Missale Gothicum* for the Easter Vigil.[3] This text was chosen for the simplicity of its formula which harmonizes spontaneously with those of Hippolytus. The institution narrative retains the introduction of the *Apostolic Tradition*, but for this prayer and for the following ones the *Verba Christi* are in the form of the Roman canon with the ad-

---

[2] This is true for the expression *puer*, applied to Christ, and his designation as *inseparable* Word.

[3] *Post-Sanctus* 271; Mohlberg ed., p. 69.

dition of the mention of the body "which will be given for you," and the omission of *mysterium fidei*. This latter expression is of uncertain origin and meaning and it complicates the task of the translators to the point of requiring hardly tolerable repetitions in most modern languages.

> Truly holy are you, O Lord, source of all holiness;
> We beseech you, therefore, to sanctify these gifts by the dew of your Spirit, that they may become the body and blood of our Lord Jesus Christ, who, as he was about to undergo his voluntary passion, took bread, and giving thanks to you, broke it and gave it to his disciples, saying:
> Take and eat: this is my body which will be given for you. Likewise, having supped, and taking the cup, again giving thanks to you, he gave it to his disciples saying: Take and drink this all of you, for this is the cup of my blood, the blood of the new and eternal covenant, which will be shed for you and for many for the forgiveness of sins. Do this as a memorial of me.

At this point an acclamation on the part of the people has been introduced, as in many Eastern liturgies, in the same terms, inspired by the Pauline narrative, as those found in the anaphora of *St. James*. As we saw, from there it passed into the Ambrosian canon.

> We announce your death, O Lord, and we proclaim your resurrection until your return!

Then follows the anamnesis which leads directly into the second epiclesis. Again, it preserves the terms which seem best attested in the text of St. Hippolytus and which are at the same time powerfully expressive in the most simple language of the work of the Spirit in the Church, the fruit of the eucharistic celebration of the holy sacrifice.

> Being mindful, therefore, of his death and resurrection, we offer you the bread of life and the cup of salvation, giving thanks to you that it pleased you to make us worthy to present ourselves before you and to serve you. And we beg and beseech you to gather us together in unity through the Holy Spirit, by making us participate in the body and blood of Christ.

The intercession for the whole Church follows naturally, and is based and upon the final allusion to the Church in the text of Hippolytus.

Remember, Lord, your Church, spread throughout the whole world, in order to perfect it in charity, with our Pope N. and our bishop N ...

After a short silent prayer for all the living, there is the commemoration of the dead:

Remember also our brothers who have already gone to sleep in the hope of the resurrection, and all the departed, and admit them into the light of your countenance ...

After a second pause, the evocation of the saints is directly connected to these intercessions and brings us back to the eschatological perspective of the final doxology:

We beseech you, have mercy upon us all, that with the blessed Mother of God, Mary, the blessed apostles and all the saints who have pleased you throughout the centuries, we may have part in eternal life and may glorify you through your Son Jesus Christ.
Through him, honor and glory are yours, with the Holy Spirit, now and forever and ever. *Amen.*

The clarity and the biblical simplicity of the wording in this prayer make it a genuine eucharistic catechesis, appropriate for every day celebrations as well as for masses directed toward children and neophytes.

Once again, the second of the new eucharistic prayers borrows the schema for its prayers and its most characteristic expressions as well from the best Gallican and Hispanic tradition. It is suited particularly, like the Roman canon, for all Sunday and festive celebrations. The first part is made up of one of the variable prefaces which will be as easily adaptable to it as they were to the old Roman eucharist.

The *Sanctus* is followed by a *Post-Sanctus* in two closely connected parts. The first begins with a Mozarabic formula (for the Feast of the Circumcision) which associates all of creation with the praise

of the angelic spirits and the Church.[4] From here the prayer goes
on to a mention of the Spirit working in creation in order to gather together the Church of Christ, so that history's term may be
the establishment of this people of God which will offer him the
same unique and pure oblation from one end of the world to the
other. These perspectives go back to the most consistent patristic
tradition, which is itself engrafted upon the Jewish tradition,
through St. Justin particularly. Their cosmic and universalist
breadth give to the Church and at the same time to the Eucharist
all the dimensions of the great Pauline *berakoth* with which the
captivity epistles open.

> Truly holy are you, Lord, and it is right that all creation
> praise you, for through your Son, our Lord Jesus Christ,
> and the operation of the Holy Spirit, you vivify and sanctify
> all things, and you do not cease to gather to yourself a people
> which offers you from the rising of the sun until its going down
> a pure offering.

In these last words, you will recognize the allusion to Malachi
1: 11, which is familiar to the Eastern and especially the Egyptian
liturgies. It offers a natural transition to the consecratory epiclesis which follows it immediately:

> Therefore we beg and beseech you, Lord, to deign to sanc-
> tify by the same Spirit these gifts which we have brought to
> you for you to consecrate, so that they may become the body
> and blood of your Son, our Lord Jesus Christ, whose command
> we fulfil by celebrating these mysteries.

This last sentence itself is reminiscent of the formulas of *Addai
and Mari* as well as of the liturgy of Theodore of Mopsuestia.
It leads us to the institution narrative. We find the words of Christ
in the same form as in the preceding liturgy, but with significant
variations in the narrative formulas.

> And he, on the night he was betrayed, in order to accomplish
> in truth the figures of the ancient sacrifices, took bread, and
> giving thanks to you, blessed it, broke it and gave it to his disci-
> ples, saying:

---

[4] Cf. *Missale Mixtum*; P.L., t. 85, col. 222A.

Take and eat: this is my body which will be given for you.
Likewise, having supped, taking the cup, and giving thanks to
you, he blessed it and gave it to his disciples, saying: Take
and drink this all of you, for this is the cup of my blood, the
blood of the new and eternal covenant, which will be shed
for you and for many for the forgiveness of sins. Do this as a
memorial of me.

Note the introduction here of the words "blessed it," making
explicit the consecratory sense included in the act of thanksgiving.
Further, the Pauline formula : "on the night he was betrayed"
is used. It is generally retained by the Eastern eucharists as well
as by the ancient Mozarabic and Gallican liturgy. The mention
of the unique sacrifice in which the preparations of the figurative
sacrifices find their fulfilment, expresses the connection between
the old and new covenants in terms that echo the great vision of
the history of salvation developed in the *Post-Sanctus*.

There is the same acclamation of the people as in the previous
prayer, responding to the consecration. Then comes the anamnesis
which, as in many Eastern liturgies, introduces an explicit link
between the celebration of the eucharistic memorial and the expectation of the parousia.

Being mindful therefore, Lord, of the saving passion of
your Son, as well as his wonderful resurrection and ascension
into heaven, and beseeching his second coming, we offer you
in thanksgiving this living and holy sacrifice.

The second epiclesis takes on here a particular development,
which stresses the uniqueness of the sacrifice of the cross. The
very beautiful formula, taken from the Mozarabic *Postpridie* of
the fourth ferial day after Easter,[5] expresses with unusual success
the essence of the eucharistic sacrifice, as the presentation by the
Church to the Father of the very sacrifice of the cross, in the sacramental pledge which he himself gave us. This is precisely the
substance of the "memorial" as Jeremiah interprets it and the
ecumenical value of this formula is obvious. We may say that it
does away with the most basic objections and misunderstandings
held by the Protestants against the traditional doctrine.

[5] Cf. *Missale Mixtum*; P.L., t. 85, col. 502A.

> O Lord, look upon the offering of your Church: recognize the Victim through whose immolation you were willing to be propitiated, and grant to those who are nourished by the body and blood of your Son that, filled with the Holy Spirit, they may be one body and one spirit in Christ. May he make us an eternal offering to your glory.

The bringing together in this text of the acceptance of our offering joined to that of Christ, and of which he himself remains the unique offerer in us as in himself, along with our incorporation in his body and our participation in the Spirit, stresses even more the ecumenical character of this whole prayer. In a singular fulness of expression of the whole of both Eastern and Western Catholic tradition, its formula fuses the terms of *St. Basil* in its Egyptian form with those of one of the most beautiful *Secrets* of the Roman tradition.

The prayer goes on without interruption to a commemoration of the saints, in such a way that we return to the great Augustinian evocation of the whole Church offered to the Father with and in Christ:

> ... Thus may we have part in the inheritance of your elect, in the first place with the blessed Virgin and Mother of God, Mary, with your blessed apostles and glorious martyrs, with Saint(s) *N.* (*the patron of the place or the saint of the day*) and with all your saints, whose perpetual intercession comes to our aid, and attaches us to you.

As in the liturgy of *St. Basil* the intercessions here merely extend this commemoration of the saints, which is itself directly associated as in the Jewish tradition with the "memorial" of the *mirabilia Dei*. Note the universal cosmic opening which corresponds to what characterized the *Post-Sanctus*.

> May this Host of our reconciliation, we beseech you, O Lord, be profitable for the peace and salvation of the whole world. Deign to strengthen in faith and charity your Church on pilgrimage on earth, with your servant, our Pope *N.* and our Bishop *N.*, the whole episcopate and all the people whom you have acquired for yourself. Hearken to the wishes of this whole family which you have permitted to present itself before you. Merciful Father, in your mercy, bring back to your-

self all your sons who are everywhere scattered ... In your goodness, admit into your kingdom our departed brothers and all those who have left this world, seeking the countenance of your Christ, where we all hope to be filled with your glory, through Christ our Lord through whom you grant to the world all good things.

Two pauses, at the middle and at the end of this paragraph, allow the detailed mention of the living and the dead for whom we wish especially to intercede.

The same concluding doxology as in the Roman Canon ends this prayer:

Through him, in him, with him, in the unity of the Holy Spirit, all glory and honor is yours, Almighty Father, forever and ever. *Amen.*

The third and last of these eucharists is the most ample. Like the first, it has its own preface, or rather the complete schema of the Christian eucharist in its most clear and most synthetic form. It makes explicit everything that it implies, but always in the manner of the liturgy of *St. Basil,* by keeping to as moderate and scriptural a language as possible. It ought to open to all the faithful of today the way toward deepening their awareness of all the traditional riches of the Christian eucharist, placed within their grasp in a language which they can perfectly understand.

It is truly right to give you thanks, it is truly just to glorify you, holy Father, for you alone are the living and true God, who are before all ages and who dwell eternally, living in inaccessible light.[6] But you are also good and the source of life. You have also made all things to fill your creatures with your blessings, and to make the multitude rejoice in the splendor of your light (*tui luminis claritati*). Therefore in your presence stand the unnumbered troops of angels serving you and contemplating the glory of your face night and day, unceasingly glorifying you. With them we too, and by our wish every creature under heaven, proclaim your name in exultation and sing: *Holy. Holy, Holy, etc.*

[6] Cf. 1 Timothy, 6:16.

Note in this text the glorification of God in his transcendent
eternity and in the economy of creation in which the unfathomable
goodness of the thrice-holy God is reflected. Note also the two
themes, traditional since Judaism, of light and life: the inaccessible
light of the divine glory which belongs only to God, but which
is also but one with the life that he willed to give the world. Its
most perfect realization is in his conscious creatures for whom
life will be to see God in his own light and to reflect his glory in
their praise of his goodness.

The second part of the act of thanksgiving after the *Sanctus*
then evokes the history of salvation which despite the original
fall, in which the creation of man and his universe seem to have
been engulfed, has made a reality, in the redemptive mystery of the
incarnate Son, of the primordial design in a manner which surpasses
all expectation.

> Holy Father, we proclaim you because you are great and
> have done all your works in wisdom and love. You had created
> man in your image and you had given him care over the
> whole universe that he might dominate over all creation in
> serving you, his creator. And when he lost your friendship
> through his disobedience, you did not abandon him to the
> power of death but you came to the aid of all men that they
> might seek you and come to you. At different times you of-
> fered them your covenant and you instructed them through
> the prophets in the hope of salvation.

> And, Holy Father, you so loved the world that in the ful-
> ness of time you sent us your only-begotten Son as a Savior.
> Made man by the Holy Spirit of the Virgin Mary, he came
> among us, like us in all things save sin, he announced the
> Good News to the poor, redemption to the captives, and joy
> to those who weep (*maestis cordi*).

> To fulfil your plan he gave himself over to death, and risen
> from the dead, he destroyed death and renewed life. And
> that we might no longer live for ourselves but for him who
> died for us and rose, from your side, Father, he sent the Holy
> Spirit so that he might accomplish in this world the work that
> he had done, and achieve its sanctification.

As we can see, this second part emphasizes the unfaltering
continuity of the divine plan which despite the fall assures man's

predestination to dominate over all visible creation in the Son
of God made man. The universal call to salvation, the drawing
of all sinful men towards a rediscovery of God who calls them with
his grace, introducing the successive covenants and the prophetic teachings, paving the way for the fulness of time when the redemptive incarnation was to come about. As in the liturgy of St.
John Chrysostom it is the use of the Johannine text on God's immeasurable love for the world which lights the way for the coming
of the only-begotten Son in the flesh, who is made like to us in
all things save sin, according to the words of the Epistle to the
Hebrews, and whose earthly life is described in terms of the prophecy of Isaiah which Christ applied to himself in the synagogue at
Nazareth. The mention of the accomplishment of the divine plan,
in equally Johannine terms, leads us to the evocation of the saving
passion, described as the victory over death in a succession of
biblical and patristic expressions that radiate with joy. The sending of the Spirit by the risen Christ, ascended to the Father, in
accordance with a last formula taken from the discourses after the
Last Supper, closes the narrative of the redemptive work in showing
in the Spirit the one who accomplishes Jesus' own work in us, by
"sanctifying" us just as he "sanctified" himself for us.

This final recall of Pentecost makes the immediate transition to
the consecratory epiclesis.

> We therefore beseech you, O Lord, that this same Holy
> Spirit will deign to sanctify these gifts that they may become
> the body and blood of our Lord Jesus Christ, and that we may
> celebrate this great mystery which he has left us as an ever-
> lasting covenant.

After the mention of the successive covenants, the invocation
of the Spirit makes his descent upon the eucharistic gifts the consecration in them of the everlasting covenant, in our celebration
of the mystery of salvation through the "memorial" which Christ
himself has left to us. Once again we come back to the ancient
expressions of the East Syrian liturgy, in the perspectives of the
new and eternal covenant outlined by Jeremiah and Ezekiel.
The recalling of Christ's commandment introduces the institution
narrative which brings together the Johannine themes of the great
discourse:

> Since the hour had come when he was to be glorified by you, Holy Father, and while he did love his own in this world, he loved them to the last, and, while they were at table for the evening meal, he took bread, blessed it and broke it, and gave it to his disciples, saying: Take and eat: this is my body which will be given for you. Likewise, taking the cup filled with the fruit of the vine, giving thanks, he gave it to his disciples, saying: Take and drink of this all of you, for this is the cup of my blood, the blood which will be shed for you and for many for the remission of sins. Do this as a memorial of me.

Again, observe in this narrative the parallelism between "bless" in the first instance and "give thanks" in the second, as well as the mention of the "fruit of the vine" which is frequent in the Eastern liturgies. It is an allusion to the text of St. Luke of which, we have given the full meaning.

After the people's acclamation there comes the anamnesis which like the initial act of thanksgiving, is expressed in a form that is as complete as possible:

> It is also for this reason that we, as we now celebrate the memorial of our redemption, recall the death of Christ and his descent into hell: we acclaim his resurrection and his ascension to your right hand, and in the expectation of his coming in glory, we offer you his body and his blood as the sacrifice pleasing to you and the salvation of the whole world.

Along with the emphasis on the uniqueness of the sacrifice, we find here once again the explicit connecting of the re-presentation to the Father of the "memorial" of the saving passion with the expectant supplication for the return in glory. The second epiclesis will underline still more strongly the uniqueness of the saving Host together with the fact that the Church as "offerer" merely presents to the Father what he himself has given her.

> O Lord, look upon the Host which you have given to your Church, and grant to those who partake of the one bread and cup that they may be gathered into one body by the Holy Spirit, so that they may be made in Christ a living Host to the praise of your glory.

The acceptance of the eucharistic sacrifice is coupled by this prayer to our own acceptance by the Father, as a living sacrifice (according to St. Paul's words) in the very body of his Son and by the power of his Spirit.

A new acclamation of the people hails the conclusion of this prayer:

> We praise you, we bless you, we glorify you. Be gracious to us, O Lord, and have mercy on us all.

The second epiclesis is now extended into the intercessions and then the commemorations which follow them here and lead us back to the eschatological orientation of the final doxology.

> And now, O Lord, be mindful of all those for whom we have made this offering to you: in the first place, your servant, our Pope N., our bishop N., and the whole episcopate, but also be mindful of all those who make this offering, those who are here present, your whole people, and all who seek you with a sincere heart ...

Here can be introduced a detailed memento of the living, which is followed by the memento of the dead:

> Remember also those who have died in the peace of your Christ and all the departed whose faith you alone know. ...

After another pause for a second memento by name, we proceed to the commemoration of the saints and the doxology:

> To all of us, your sons, Merciful Father, grant that we may obtain the eternal inheritance, with the blessed Virgin Mother of God, Mary, with the apostles and the saints in your kingdom, where with every creature freed from the corruption of sin and death, we may glorify you through Christ our Lord, through whom you grant to the world all good things. Through him, in him, with him, in the unity of the Holy Spirit, all glory and honor is yours, almighty Father, forever and ever. *Amen.*

One final characteristic of this third eucharist ought to be underlined: its conformity with the trinitarian plan which is such a marked characteristic of the West Syrian eucharist. Still, there is great care to avoid any artificial schematization in the distinction of the three basic parts corresponding to the three persons of the Trinity. From beginning to end the person of the Father is not only the one to whom the prayer is addressed, but he is also the principal of all the divine missions and the explicit term to which they return. The sanctifying work of the Spirit, similarly is always here in correlation with the redemptive work of the Son. However, we might perhaps have wished that from the first part the Son would have appeared as the First-Born and the principal of all creation, and the Spirit as the breath of divine life that pervades the whole work of the creative Word. But it seemed more in conformity with the progression of biblical revelation to introduce the Son explicitly only at the end of the preparatory covenants, and the Spirit only at the completion of his saving work.

If in conclusion we juxtapose and compare these three prayers, we will be struck by the consistency with which they give to the Holy Spirit, both in regard to the consecration and the communion, the same broad place that the Eastern liturgies progressively gave him. This is a new ecumenical factor in the proposing of these texts to the Latin Church, after their so biblical and patristic expressions of sacrifice. Undoubtedly this will contribute toward a rapprochement with the East as well as toward the reunion of the Christian West. It must be added more specifically that these texts bear witness to the fact that if the consecration of the eucharist finds its source in the words of the Savior, as is attested in the East by St. Cyril of Jerusalem or St. John Chrysostom, it becomes effective in each celebration within the prayer of the Church in which she uses these words herself in order to invoke their accomplishment from the Father through the sole power of his Spirit. Thus we may hope that they will contribute towards a reconciliation of those viewpoints (more complementary than opposed) which have too long divided the theologies of East and West.

The most radical, and at first sight most unusual novelty in the structure of the new texts is that they follow up to a certain point the remodeling of the most ancient eucharistic schemas worked out by the West Syrian liturgy, while retaining the ancient and more primitive distinction between the two epicleses as in both the Egyptian and Roman traditions. This is a point which may possibly be not merely of pedagogical interest, in order to permit Christians familiar with this latter tradition to come to know the complementary riches of the Eastern tradition. This particular construction which is not without certain antecedents still attested today by transitional forms of the ancient Extreme-Western liturgy, can be rightly interpreted in its canonization by the Roman Church as a recognition of the underlying harmony in the two traditions which up to now have seemed separate. At the same time the maintaining of the Roman canon, restored to its full meaning through the re-insertion of a more explicit act of thanksgiving through the renewed prefaces and also the *Communicantes* and *Hanc Igiturs*, will attest to the continuity of the most fertile developments of Catholic tradition with its original sources.

It is worthwhile to note here that at the very moment that this reform of the eucharistic liturgy is being accomplished in the Catholic Church, the different branches of the Anglican Communion, many Lutheran Churches, and even many of the Protestant Churches that had lost almost all of the ancient tradition, are undertaking revisions of their own eucharists. The convergence with the Catholic renewal is striking. One of the best examples is that of the new eucharistic prayer which has just been put into use *ad experimentum* in the Episcopal Church in the United States. Faced with this fact, it is surely not simply a superficial enthusiasm that has been expressed in the remark of several Anglican or Protestant observers that the new Catholic eucharists could very well come to be used in many Churches at present separated from Rome.

Oscar Cullmann has observed more than once that the Bible, whose study in the sixteenth century had separated Catholics and Protestants, is on the contrary today what brings them closest together. The same return to the source in a critical way, but also in faith, may soon produce an even more unexpected rapprochement in regard to the eucharist. Nothing gives greater promise of a possible reintegration within the unity of the Church willed by Christ of Christian communities which today are still separated.

Conclusion

What we have had to say ought to fall into place of itself. Yet, in concluding, it may be worthwhile to collect and sum up our thoughts. In these pages we have not striven to construct a new theology of the eucharist. We have limited ourselves to a succint retracing of the theological development that we have managed to follow in the eucharistic prayer itself, and to suggesting a few consequences of this development.

A primary conclusion which imposes itself before any other is that the schema of the paramount liturgical service, the mass as we call it in the West (with its two separate parts that in the beginning were quite distinct: the service of readings and the eucharistic meal), is in no way merely a fortuitous conjunction of two barely related elements. Quite the contrary. The eucharist can be understood only as a follow-up to and a consequence of the hearing of the Word of God. Properly, it is the response in word and deed, elicited in man through a divine word which is creative and salvific.

The Word uncovers for us a divine Design: to make from fallen mankind a people after God's heart. At the same time it reveals the divine Name to us. For this Design is to imprint this Name on man's whole being. In the New Testament, the sacred Name is ultimately revealed as the Name of the Father, and the definitive People of God will be a filial people.

The Word, moreover, as it speaks, makes a reality of what it says. For God himself comes to us in it; in it he descends into our history and fills that history with his presence. The Gospel is the definitive proclamation of the creative and salvific Word, in the coming of the Word made flesh, who is the proper and only-begotten Son of God. In this way we are made sons in the Son.

From Old Testament times, consequently, the Word has elicited a response, which acknowledges it in faith and which therefore welcomes its coming in surrendering unreservedly to it. This response was formulated in the *berakah*. The *berakah* is the contemplative praise of the *mirabilia Dei*. In the *berakah*, Israel opens itself to the accomplishment in itself of God's Design and is consecrated by the imposition of the Name of God on its whole life.

The synagogal *berakoth* of the service of readings, before the recitation of the *Shemah*, glorify the creator of light, visible and invisible, which has given us the knowledge of his Law whereby we are marked with his personal seal.

The Eighteen Blessings of the *Tefillah*, after this, petition for the perfect accomplishment in Israel of this Design, for the purpose of the perfect glorification of the fully revealed divine Name.

All the *berakoth* which accompany the pious Israelite in every moment of his existence extend this consecration to his whole life in the world, and by that fact to the world itself. Israel is thus set up as the priest of all creation. By the divine Word and the prayer which welcomes it, all things with man are restored, to their original purity and transparency, and the universe becomes a choir of divine glorification throughout the life of consecrated man.

The meal *berakoth*, particularly, glorify God as the creator of life, the one who unceasingly nourishes and sustains it and in the fruits of the promised land turns it into a paradise where all things in their renewal tell of the glory of God. The supplication which develops calls for the final gathering in of the elect, in the eschatological banquet where all the redeemed will celebrate for ever this eternally triumphant glory.

Therefore, the community meal in the messianic expectation definitively expresses the meaning of all the sacrifices of Israel. It tends itself to become the pre-eminent sacrifice, i.e. the offering of the whole of human life and of the entire world with it to the acknowledged will of God.

As the comparative history of religions shows, is not every sacrifice originally a sacred banquet in which man acknowledges that his life comes forth from God and reaches its fulfilment only in an unceasingly renewed exchange with him? This was the primary meaning of the Passover, as a banquet consecrating the first fruits of the harvest. But the Jewish Passover took on a renewed meaning when it became the memorial of the deliverance whereby God had snatched his people from the slavery of ignorance and death in order to bring them to the promised land in which they would know him as they have been known by him, and live in his presence.

The memorial that this meal constituted attested to the permanent reality of the divine wonderworks for Israel as a pledge given by God of his saving and ever faithful presence. In representing it to him in their *berakah*, the Jews who were also faithful to his precept were confidently able to remind him of his promises and to ask efficaciously for their fulfilment: that there would come the Messiah who would perfect the divine work and establish the divine Rule in the reconstructed Jerusalem where God would be praised unendingly by the People of God who have achieved perfection.

This is what was fulfilled on the night of the Last Supper when Jesus, who was to hand himself over to the Cross as the supreme fulfilment of Passover, pronounced the *berakoth* over the bread and the cup as a consecration of his body broken and his blood shed, in order to reconcile in his own body the "dispersed children of God," and to renew them in the eternal covenant of his love.

At the same time he made of this meal from then on the memorial of the mystery of the Cross. In giving thanks with him and through him for his body broken and his blood shed which are given to us as the substance of the Kingdom, we represent 'to God this mystery which has now been accomplished in our Head, so that it may have its ultimate accomplishment in his whole body. That is to say that we give our consent to the completion in our flesh of the sufferings of Jesus for his body which is the Church, in the steadfast hope of his Parousia in which we shall all participate together in his resurrection. Thus we inaugurate the eternal glorification of God the creator and savior who on the last day will make the Church the *panegyria*, the festal assembly, in which all of mankind will join in the heavenly worship and be brought before the Throne following the Lamb which was slain, but which now lives and reigns forever.

The whole substance of this Christian sacrifice is in the one saving act of the Cross, which was done once and for all at the peak of human history by the Son of God made man. But the Cross took on meaning only through the offering of himself to which Christ consented at the Last Supper and which he proclaimed by making the *berakah* over the bread and wine the "eucharist" of his body broken and his blood shed "for the forgiveness of sins." And the Cross is effectively redemptive for mankind only insofar as men associate themselves with it through the eucharistic eating of his flesh and his blood. The life-giving Spirit will become their own spirit only insofar as they will adhere by faith to the Word who proposes that flesh and blood to them, i.e. insofar as they make the very "eucharist" of the Son their own.

Indeed, in the Supper and the Cross, the Word of God which efficaciously signifies his love for us is realized in fulness, and, at the same time, the perfect *berakah*, the perfect "eucharist" of Christ gives it the response it sought and elicited. All we can do is receive in turn this unique Word of salvation by making this unique response our own.

But this is possible for us only through the Messiah's almighty will to give us in the eucharist which we repeat after him, according to the pattern he has set for us, the memorial of his mystery. The reality of this memorial is perpetually attested to by the bread we break as the communion in his body and the cup of blessing we bless as the communion in his blood.

In the eucharistic celebration of this memorial, the bread and the wine of our community meal, of the *agape* banquet, become sacrificial to the extent that they become for our faith what they represent, through the power of the divine Word and Spirit. And insofar as we ourselves, in this faith, are thus associated with the unique salvific oblation, we become one sole offering with Christ. Thus we can offer our own bodies, with his and in his, as a living and true sacrifice, giving to the Father, through the grace of the Son and in the communication of his Spirit, the "reasonable" worship which he expects from us.

All this is but the fulfilment in us of the Word of salvation who was made flesh for us in Christ and who spoke the last word, as it were, of the paternal heart at the Last Supper, sealed in fact upon the Cross; we never cease to proclaim him as often as we celebrate the eucharist until the Parousia. And this Word is accomplished in our association by faith with the Savior's priestly prayer on his way to the Cross, a prayer in which following him we glorify the Father as our creator and savior, in this same Son through whom we were created and in whom we were redeemed.

Just as this prayer on Christ's lips became an act in the effective acceptance of the Cross, so it becomes an act in our communion in the broken body and the shed blood. In this way the Spirit of the Son wells up in us. The Father pours him out into our hearts that from now on we might live and die in his love, the love that the Son has revealed perfectly to us in inviting us to walk in his footsteps. To repeat this eucharistic prayer without communicating in the sacrifice it expresses and consecrates would make no more sense than communicating without making our own, by means of the same prayer, the sentiments that were in Christ when he handed himself over to the Cross. Indeed, they are voiced in his supreme act of thanksgiving and his supreme supplication of the Father for the coming of his Kingdom.

An act of thanksgiving for the *mirabilia Dei* reaching their total fulfilment, a supplication for the full flowering of the Church which will be their result at the time of the Parousia, the memorial of the Cross, a communion with the sacrifice in the communion with the host which is but one with the priest: through all these aspects the unity of the eucharist is evidently infrangible. In this view, the unsolved problems which we have mentioned in the first pages of this book find their only acceptable solution.

East and West have long been on opposite sides of the question as to whether the eucharist was consecrated by the recitation of the words of institution over the bread and the cup or by the in-

vocation, the epiclesis, calling down upon these elements the descent of the Spirit. Surely the answer must be that the whole reality of the eucharist proceeds from the one divine Word, uttered in
the Son, who gives us his flesh to eat and his blood to drink, But
this reality is given to the Church as the reality promised to her
"eucharist," in the prayer whereby she adheres in faith to the
salvific Word. And the final object of this prayer is surely that
the Spirit of Christ bring alive Christ's Word in us.

In other words, the consecrator of all of these eucharists is always Christ alone, the Word made flesh, insofar as he is ever the
dispenser of the Spirit because he handed himself over to death
and then rose from the dead by the power of this same Spirit. But
in the indivisible totality of the eucharist, this Word, evoked by
the Church, and her own prayer calling for the fulfilment of the
Word through the power of the Spirit come together for the mysterious fulfilment of the divine promises.

Protestantism, then, set itself apart from traditional Catholicism
at a moment when Catholicism gave only a stammering expression
of the eucharistic tradition; the Protestants maintained that the
Cross was not to be begun again and that only its memorial was
to be celebrated among us. This is true. But this memorial itself,
in the fulness of its biblical sense, implies both a continued mysterious presence of the unique sacrifice that was offered once, and
our sacramental association with it. The result is that we become
offerers with and in the one priest, and offerings with and in the
one victim. Thus, only the Savior's Cross can become the source
of this "reasonable" worship in which we offer our own bodies, our
whole being, as a living and true sacrifice, to the Father's will,
acknowledged, accepted and glorified.

Finally and above all, the eucharistic presence of Christ in the
elements and of his sacrifice in the repeated celebrations both
become intelligible.

As Dom Casel and his school understood, the eucharistic mystery is inseparable from the mystery of the presence of the Redeemer himself *and of his redemptive act.* But the explanation
for this must be sought not in a forced and disappointing analogy
with the pagan mysteries, but in the quite biblical and Jewish
notion of the memorial.

The memorial is a symbolic pledge, given by the divine Word who accomplishes the *mirabilia Dei* in history, a pledge of their continued presence, which is always active in us and for us. It is through faith that we grasp it. In the Old Covenant, the Passover was present in every one of its repeated liturgical celebrations, because God's coming down upon it and his intervention in it, through his freeing the People from ignorance and death, were perpetuated there for the purpose of the People's fulfilment.

At the Last Supper at which the Cross was decided upon and where it received its salvific meaning through the free and sovereign act with which Christ accepted it, foreseeing and proclaiming the paternal Design and its fulfilment, the Passover of the Old Covenant found its own fulfilment. From this point on, the whole People of God, all of redeemed mankind who were to be part of it, is "recapitulated" according to the word used in the epistle to the Ephesians, in the body of Christ, that is, in the total reality of his humanity fully achieved in this supreme offering to the will of the Father. From now on, redeemed mankind, the definitive People of God, has substance only in this humanity of Christ, which is voluntary death delivered to the Spirit's power of resurrection. The bread and the cup, the objects of the eucharist, become therefore the memorial, inseparably both of the Savior and of the act of salvation.

This is to say that when we, in keeping with his command and by the power of his Word accepted by the faith of the Church, redo his eucharist over the bread and the cup, we there acknowledge by faith the efficacious pledges of his body and blood. Handed over for us to the Cross, they are given to us effectively *here and now*. In the eucharist, we therefore become one Body with him through the power of his Spirit. At the same time, the salvific act, immortalized in the glorified body, together with the perfect human response which is inseparable from it, becomes our own. It becomes, through the Spirit, the principle of our renewed life as a life of sons in the Son. This is present, objectively, in the eucharistic celebration, which merely actualizes in us the unique offering consecrated at the Supper, just as in the sacramental elements, the body and the blood are objectively presented to us so that we will from now on be but one with the One. But this is present in this way only in order that it might become *ours* through faith, a faith in which all our being surrenders to the Father's will revealed in his Word, just as in the Word made flesh this will became a reality in our world.

The Protestants, following Calvin in particular, were not wrong in seeing in the eucharist only a dialogue between the divine Word and the faith of the new man in Christ. But this dialogue has the whole reality of the creative and saving Word which upon the Cross became the dominant fact of history. Therefore, if for the senses the bread and the wine remain merely bread and wine, faith, which recognizes their significance attested to by the Word, grasps there the realities that this Word, in the Spirit, communicates to it. And in this way faith surrenders our own selves, with the same reality of the Spirit taking possession of us, to conform our being to the being of Christ and our life to his Cross. We receive the body of Christ and we are made this body. We proclaim Christ's saving death and we bear that death within us, crucified with him in order that we might rise again with him.

This comes down to saying that the objective realities of the sacramental mystery are given to us in such a real way only in order to be the object of a no less real adhesion in faith. This is why they are given to us in the sacramental elements in conjunction with the eucharistic prayer: that prayer which in exulting praise acknowledges the saving and recreative act; it surrenders to it in the invocation of its accomplishment in us. And his invocation is assured of being heard, since it is founded upon the pledge, the objective memorial, which God in Christ has given us only that we might represent it to him with this full assurance of faith.

We are led thereby from meditation upon the eucharistic mystery to its concrete realization in the eucharistic celebration.

This mystery is the "mystery of faith." It can only be celebrated in faith. Its celebration is properly the paramount act of faith of the whole Church. Presented with the total and unique object of her faith, the "mystery," the Church in the mass grasps it or rather surrenders to it.

The food of faith is the Word of God. It was therefore quite a natural process of evolution that led the Church to celebrate the eucharistic meal at the conclusion of the service of biblical readings, from the moment, or very nearly, that Christians no longer attended the synagogue. It would not only be an uncalled for archaism but an absurd step backward to wish to separate the two again. The meaning of the homily, at the end of the service of readings which culminates in the Gospel, ought to make the transition from the Word proclaimed to the Word becoming fulfiled in us through the sacrament of the sacrifice. According to St. John, Jesus himself celebrated his eucharist, which was to generate all other eucharists, only by accompanying it with his supreme teachings, at the precise moment when all that he had foretold about himself was to be consummated in the unique act of the Cross.

But again, in order that the eucharistic mystery be celebrated as the "mystery of faith," it is necessary that this be done in as effective as possible an act of faith by the Church in all her members. Hence the importance of a eucharistic prayer in which this living faith which receives the mystery is expressed fully, directly and comprehensibly. We have seen how Jewish tradition progressively shaped the mold in which this prayer was to be cast, just as the Word of the Old Testament prepared the way for the Word of the Gospel. We have also seen the evolution of the great formulas of the eucharist of the Church, which have now become classic. We can say that they express the eucharist perfectly, in all its relief, only when taken all together, just as the four Gospels express the "Gospel."

The idea which is sometimes suggested of returning to archaic forms, like that of the eucharist of Hippolytus or of Addai and Mari in its original form, without the *Sanctus* or the intercessions and commemorations, is one more untenable retrogressive archaism. These first forms of the eucharist, however venerable they may be, take on their full meaning, like the meal *berakoth* from which they came, only when they are added to the other great berakoth which immediately followed the readings from Holy Scripture. When the primitive Church still was only using this rudimentary eucharist, as we saw, its celebration as a matter of fact, always presupposed the prior recitation of these other *berakoth* with the *Sanctus*, intercessions and commemorations in the then distinct service of readings.

From the instant that the two services were brought together, a synthetic and total eucharist came into being through the joining of these different elementary "eucharists." And, we must add, as the Jews already understood, the liturgical *berakoth* in their totality take on their full sense only if they extend into the whole life of the pious Jew or the faithful Christian through a constantly renewed attitude of eucharistic prayer and sacrifice. Indeed, it is our whole life and all things with us that are to be consecrated through the eucharist to the glory of God, in Christ, by the power of the Spirit.

The ideal eucharist does not have one form in tradition, but rather complementary forms which illuminate one another. The Syrian model is more systematic than the Roman and Alexandrian ones. It illustrates the profound unity of the eucharistic prayer. But it somewhat blurs the primary elements which it superposes and fuses at the risk of destroying the original profile. On the other hand, at Rome and Alexandria, this relief remains intact.

The complete eucharist is always a confession of God as creator and redeemer, through Christ, and more especially a glorification of God enlightening us with his knowledge, vivifying us with his own life, in the supreme gift of his own Spirit. At the same time, and inseparably, this eucharist is a supplication that the mystery being celebrated have its complete fulfilment in us, in the perfect Church and all her members. It concludes with the representation to God of the memorial of this sacred mystery, together with the invocation that he consecrate our union with the sacrifice of his Son and bring it to its eschatological perfection through the power of the Spirit. Thus in concert, as one in *the* One, we shall eternally glorify the Father together with the angelic powers. This supreme invocation gathers all of our supplications for the growth of the Church as the body of Christ and for the salvation of the world, and crowns the supplication that summed them all up: that the Father, in the memorial of his Son, accept all the prayers and all the sacrifices that his People present to him, by making them one prayer and one sacrifice, Christ's own eucharist and his own Cross.

This prayer is a typically sacerdotal prayer, i. e. one that can be made only in the name of the Head of the Church by one who represents him among us, either a bishop or a priest. But it is made for us all and is to bring all the members of the Church, following her Head, into the immediate presence of the Father, in the heavenly sanctuary. This normally supposes that the faithful associate themselves with it as perfectly as possible. And it is therefore most desirable that the prayer be pronounced by the celebrant in a manner that can be heard by all, like their common participation, expressed by the initial responses, the singing of the *Sanctus* and *Benedictus* and, at the very least, the final *Amen*.

To detach the prayers for the Church from this eucharist under the pretext of returning them to the offertory—as we have explained—would be to mutilate it. If the act of thanksgiving for the mystery is its basic theme, the supplication for its full accomplishment in the Church is no less essential. Once again, does not St. John show us Jesus at the Last Supper addressing to his Father his priestly prayer that all his followers might be one in him?

In this way, refreshed for the faithful through an explanation nourished on the tradition that produced it, the Roman canon, despite the fantastic theories whose worthlessness we think we have shown, remains one of the richest and purest formulations of this prayer.

The only point where its present form had to be filled out was the preface, and particularly the common preface, where the basic themes of the thanksgiving are not explicated. It was certainly fitting to reintroduce into it a recall of the creation by the Son and the redemption accomplished in his incarnation and his cross, and of the divine knowledge and the divine life, communicated by the Spirit. Any other project which would tend to modify the economy and the composition of the Roman canon would give rise to aberrations that are as contrary to critical history as they are to traditional theology.

The author of these lines, along with other liturgists, of whom Dom Bernard Botte is in the first rank, once suggested that in addition to the Roman canon, the Western Church might make widespread use either of formularies taken from the best in Gallican tradition, or also at least some of the most typical from Eastern tradition, such as the eucharist of St. Basil, preferably in its most ancient form preserved by the Church of Alexandria.

On the first point, the second of the new Roman eucharistic formularies fully answers our expectation. The second proposition was upheld most vigorously by the Secretariat for Christian Unity. There is no doubt that there could be no more decisive step towards a rapprochement with the Eastern Church, taken by the Latin Church. But, furthermore, when used not only for more or less exceptional ecumenical celebration, but also, as in the Byzantine Church, for the ferial days of Lent, the Basilian liturgy would constitute an ideal preparation for the Easter celebrations.

Nevertheless, without rejecting this possibility for the future, it seemed good to the Roman authorities to wait before putting it into practice, for the Latin rite Catholics to become familiar with the new formularies about which we have spoken in our last chapter, and which are assuredly best adapted to widening and deepening their living understanding of all of Catholic tradition on the eucharist.

This renovation will naturally be greatly facilitated by the widely granted faculty of celebrating these eucharists, like the restored Roman canon, in the people's language. Nevertheless the greatest care has been brought to the composition of the new eucharists in a Latin that is faithful to the expressions and the style of the best Roman tradition, with respect for the flow in language which will allow them to be sung like the Roman canon. The better these formularies, and the Roman canon with them, are known and understood, the easier it will be, when occasion demands, as at the time of international Catholic meetings, for especially well-formed Catholics to use all these texts in their original tongue. Formulas which successive generations have said over and over again before us, or which will remain common to all Catholics of the West are of too great a price for us to lose this advantage. Let us not forget that the eucharist does not only unite those who are materially about the altar, but in addition those of every time and every place.

As much as a dead conservatism would be opposed to vitality, so a frenzy for the up-to-date and too narrow an emphasis on localization would be contrary to the catholicity to which the liturgy should lead us. Between the advantages of the vernacular and those of a traditional language charged with imperishable values through long use, there is no choice. Both should complement one another harmoniously.

But above all, what is important whether in the vernacular or in Latin for an active aware and fruitful celebration of the whole liturgy, and especially of the eucharist, is the understanding that the best reforms of the texts will be useless if they are applied practically as merely a change in rubrics. It is a renewal in depth that these changes themselves ought to elicit: a vital rediscovery of the meaning of the eucharist, its constitutive prayers, its basic themes and their living unity. Without this, even the best texts, either through their faithfulness to tradition or the skill of their adaptation to the intelligence of our contemporaries, will still remain fruitless and barren. The eucharistic renewal will amount to nought unless it is a renewal in the Spirit and in Truth.

University of Notre Dame, Indiana
St. Patrick's Day, 1966
Brown University, Providence, R. I,
Feast of the Epiphany, 1968

BIBLICAL INDEX

INDEX OF RABBINICAL TEXTS

INDEX OF THE SYNAGOGUE LITURGY

INDEX OF ANCIENT CHRISTIAN WRITERS[1]

1 In principle, up to the eighteenth century inclusive, but the authors
that came after the Renaissance, who used the historico-critical methods
that made their appearance at that time, are found in the index of modern
authors.

INDEX OF CHRISTIAN LITURGIES

INDEX OF MODERN AUTHORS